Below-the-line Promo

The Marketing Series is one of the most comprehensive collections of books in marketing and sales available from the UK today.

Published by Butterworth-Heinemann on behalf of the Chartered Institute of Marketing, the series is divided into three distinct groups: *Student* (fulfilling the needs of those taking the Institute's certificate and diploma qualifications); *Professional Development* (for those on formal or self-study vocational training programmes); and *Practitioner* (presented in a more informal, motivating and highly practical manner for the busy marketer).

Formed in 1911, the Chartered Institute of Marketing is now the largest professional marketing management body in Europe with over 22,000 members and 25,000 students located worldwide. Its primary objectives are focused on the development of awareness and understanding of marketing throughout UK industry and commerce and in the raising of standards of professionalism in the education, training and practice of this key business discipline.

Books in the series

Below-the-line Promotion

John Wilmshurst

Published on behalf of the Chartered Institute of Marketing

Butterworth-Heinemann Ltd
Linacre House, Jordan Hill, Oxford OX2 8DP

⟨R A member of the Reed Elsevier group

OXFORD   LONDON   BOSTON
MUNICH   NEW DELHI   SINGAPORE   SYDNEY
TOKYO   TORONTO   WELLINGTON

First published 1993

British Library Cataloguing in Publication Data
Wilmshurst, John
  Below-the-line Promotion. – (CIM
  Professional Development Series)
  I. Title   II. Series
  659.1

ISBN 0 7506 0548 0

Printed in England by Clays Ltd, St Ives plc

Contents

Preface

Below-the-line Promotion supplements two of my other books – *The Fundamentals and Practice of Marketing* and *The Fundamentals of Advertising*. There does not appear to be another text on the broad category of promotional methods usually referred to as 'below the line'.

The book fills that gap for anyone working in marketing, sales, public relations or business generally, who needs an overview. There are plenty of books covering individual aspects such as direct mail but this one puts it all together. Students of the CIM and CAM diplomas and similar courses of study will also find it valuable.

As always, many thanks are due, especially in this case to Adrian (Mac) Mackay, who did much of the research and drafting. Without his support the book would never have been written. Wendy Thompson spent countless hours at the word processor and deciphered acres of difficult handwriting.

Also necessary is the usual assurance that views expressed are mine, as is the responsibility for any errors.

John Wilmshurst

Introduction

This book has one main purpose – to provide a *comprehensive* guide to a wide range of below-the-line promotional activities. Thus it deals not only with sales promotion, but also the other main below-the-line activities.

Definitions are a problem in this field, as many terms are used in a variety of different ways. Thus some people equate 'below-the-line' with sales promotion. To others, including the author, 'below-the-line' includes virtually all forms of promotion except paid-for advertising.

Wherever it seems likely to be helpful, the book contains definitions of the more important terms where they are used for the first time.

Many of the below-the-line promotional techniques individually have a significant literature. However, there has been nothing which deals with the whole field, in spite of the fact that skilled practitioners are well aware that it makes no sense to deal with sales literature, exhibitions and special offers, for example, quite separately. They would in practice normally be part of an overall promotional campaign.

The first seven chapters (Part One) of the book therefore deal with the proper management of a below-the-line promotional campaign, and should be studied for general guidance whatever the particular form(s) of publicity the reader is interested in. They can be ignored or skimmed through quickly by people who are very experienced, e.g. in planning advertising but want deeper insight into particular techniques. This is provided by the later chapters (Part Two) which give more specific guidance on a range of the more important techniques available.

Part One

Part One

1 Above and below-the-line

1.1 Introduction

This book will help sales and marketing people, whatever their field of business (manufacturing, retailing, service industries, etc.) to carry out effective promotion. Even more important, it will help them to know what results they are getting and be sure that their promotion is cost-effective. The book will thus be particularly valuable to people who have targets to meet.

Much of the book refers to companies that have a definite tangible product to sell, such as a can of baked beans, a fork-lift truck, or a tape-recorder. However, there are many companies whose 'product' is less tangible, like an insurance policy, consultancy advice or health care. Such intangibles are often referred to as services. Even though these companies do not sell a physical product, their intangible 'product' can be promoted in very much the same way. Throughout this book, where the terms 'manufacturer' and 'product' have been referred to, 'supplier' and 'service' can be substituted. But we also give specific examples of the promotion of intangible products or 'services' whenever appropriate. Retailers, distributors, brokers and dealers (the 'middlemen' or 'resellers') can also use the same methods of promotion very effectively.

It was once customary for advertising agencies to invoice their clients by first listing all advertising booked on their behalf in the main media (press, cinema, posters, radio and TV). On these activities the agency drew a commission from the media owners, which paid for its services. (Increasingly these days, agencies are paid by an agreed fee, rather than by commission.)

At this point a line was drawn on the invoice so that commission could be recorded. Then the other expenditure 'below-the-line' followed – point of sale material, sales literature and so on. On these the agency did not draw a commission from suppliers and so usually charged a service fee for this part of the work. From this purely administrative convenience have derived the two terms:

- *Above-the-line*: all main (commissionable) advertising media.

●　　*Below-the-line*: other (non-commissionable) publicity activities.

Who first used the terms is uncertain – Procter & Gamble is one company to which the honour is sometimes given.

We shall see later in this chapter how the importance of below-the-line activities has grown, particularly over the past decade or two.

Above- and below-the-line are convenient terms because they have been widely used and understood over many years in the advertising business. They provide a useful shorthand that often overcomes the necessity to reel off a long list of media and methods.

To limit any possible confusion it is probably safer to refer to above-the-line *advertising* and below-the-line *promotion*. That still leaves us with the potential problem that one of the most important sets of below-the-line techniques is called sales promotion (see Chapter 8).

To help explore the distinction further, let us consider the manufacturers (or suppliers – especially if the 'product' is an intangible service) and their relationship with the consumers or users. On the left is the manufacturer, on the right the consumer:

Manufacturer (————————————) Consumer

The line between them is a continuum or line of communication; and, like all lines of communication, the shortest, most direct route with the clearest and most relevant message will be the most effective. If the manufacturer produces an advertisement of some kind, that advertisement is in fact a communication between the manufacturer and one *single* consumer. Even though advertising generally communicates with a 'mass audience', it does so *one* at a time. (If you view your audience as a grey mass, your advertising is likely to be viewed in the same way.)

So along this line from left to right the manufacturer speaks to the consumer; and this can be achieved by advertising. But this is not, by any means, the only method of communication available. For example, the package says something about the product. So does the price. So does the type of store that stocks it. So does the type of person whom your customer sees consuming it. So may the behaviour of the manufacturing company – how its other products perform, how it treats its workers, how it treats its immediate environment. Public relations, the transmission of the company's non-advertising communication to its publics (see Chapter 13), is clearly important in this respect. Finally, and probably most importantly, the loudest message of all is that delivered by the product itself . . . *PERFORMANCE*.

Along the line right to left, in the opposite direction, the consumer speaks to the manufacturer – often through research. Market research is the message from the consumer telling the manufacturer if a product is bought, how often, where, in what quantities and when. Attitude research delivers a somewhat less direct message, telling the manufacturer what the consumer thinks and feels about the product, why it is not bought, and, with luck, why it is.

There are many aspects to communications and all are parts of the marketing mix – the *product*, its *price*, where it is sold (*place*) and the means by which customers find out about the product and are persuaded to use it (*promotion*). One ingredient in the mix – promotion – no matter how 'right', how well planned and executed, cannot make up serious shortfalls in the rest of the mix.

If we return to the communication line between a manufacturer and its customer, we can regard 'advertising' as messages close to manufacturer, but distant from the consumer at the point of purchase, while sales 'promotion' (an important aspect of below-the-line promotion (see Chapter 8) comprises messages closer to the consumer when the decision to buy is being made.

This is summarized neatly by Hugh Davidson in *Offensive Marketing*, referring to one specific aspect of below-the-line publicity:

The role of (sales) promotion is to encourage purchase by temporarily improving the value of a brand. It is part of the overall marketing mix, and ties in with advertising, product performance, and pricing. In general, the purpose of advertising is to improve attitudes towards a brand, while the objective of promotions is to translate favourable attitudes into actual purchase. Advertising cannot close a sale because its impact is too far from the point of purchase, but (sales) promotion can and does.

Remember, the foregoing is only a generality. There are many instances where advertising *can* close a sale, e.g. 'direct response' advertising, where a telephone number is given for placing orders or an order form is clipped from the magazine carrying the advertisement.

'Promotion' unfortunately has a range of meanings. It can be used (see above) to describe the marketing communications aspect of the marketing mix or, more narrowly, as in sales promotion. In its very broad sense it includes the *personal* methods of communications, such as face-to-face or telephone selling, as well as the impersonal ones, such as advertising. When we use a range of different types of promotion – direct mail, exhibitions and personal selling – we describe it as the promotional mix.

1.2   Types of below-the-line promotion

If we take a look at Figure 1.1, we can see an overview of the promotional mix from above-the-line 'advertising' to below-the-line promotion.

There is a large grey area around 'the line'. Is direct marketing advertising? After all, all you are doing is putting your advertising message down a communications route that you probably do not own, (e.g. the Royal Mail, British Telecom). But since direct marketing uses vehicles of communication in much the same way as sales promotion, it is considered in this context (the subject is covered in more detail in Chapter 9). Equally, house magazines may be used to carry advertising messages, as well as editorial articles and features but have been included in below-the-line promotion because they do form a useful promotional vehicle and because they are media owned by the users as distinct from advertising in, say, a consumer magazine owned by someone else.

Many of the activities that fall below-the-line are concerned with translating attitudes into sales and, because these activities have such an immediate effect on sales, 'sales promotion' has been used as an all-embracing term by many. This term is best used more narrowly, however, and is defined in the specific section on sales promotion (Chapter 8).

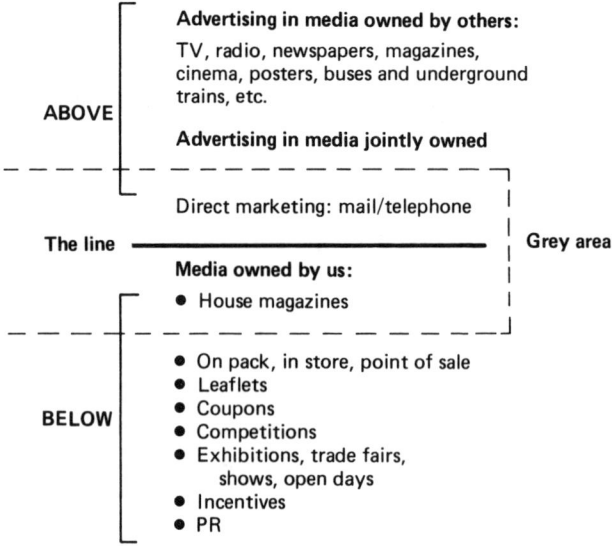

Figure 1.1   *An overview of promotion*

1.3 What about price-cuts as promotion?

It is possible to split below-the-line activities into price- and non-price-related promotions, i.e.

Price-related	*Non-price-related*
Consumer *price* promotions	In-store display
Trade advertising allowances	Merchandising
Dealer promotions	Competitions
Free goods	Self-liquidating premiums
National accounts discounting	Public relations
Over-riders	
Trade bonuses	

Note that since price is such an important issue, a whole chapter in this book (Chapter 2) has been dedicated to a detailed treatment of the subject. If one were to look at companies whose marketing budgets ranged from 5 per cent of turnover to 40 per cent, one would find some advertisers spending the bulk of their budget on advertising, and others on below-the-line activities, of which price dealing would often form a large part. The 'average' brand (if one could be imagined) would have a marketing budget that was 20 per cent[1] of its national turnover, and of this approximately half would be spent on consumer advertising, and the bulk of the remainder being on some form of price dealing.

This situation is far from desirable, because the pricing of a product is so critical that the price decision should be separated from the question of the size of the advertising budget or expenditure on other forms of promotion. So, in order to take sensible decisions about price and advertising expenditure, it is clearly desirable to estimate how sensitive your customers are to changes in price and the level of advertising support. By looking closely at these issues one would find price elasticities varying widely; however, it is likely that many products would be underpriced, especially consumer goods. Sales volume is often bought at the expense of profit.

The first thing you need to do then is to make absolutely sure that prices are right. Once you have done that, you will have been able to maximize your gross profit margins, and you will be in a better position to decide how much you need to spend on promotion as a whole to meet your turnover targets. Only advertising and non-price-related promotions should really be funded from your promotional budget.

Remember, your promotional budget should ideally be used to support your brands. Price promotions generally support the retailer or dealer. Of course retailer or dealer support will be essential in some cases, but only provided brand support is ultimately achieved.

So where does this leave the marketeer trying to allocate funds? The allocation of expenditure to the assorted media and techniques open to you varies a good deal between consumer and industrial promotion. This difference was well illustrated in the IPA Forum 19, Institute of Practitioners in Advertising, London in Figure 1.2

How does your business compare? Remember, Figure 1.2 serves to illustrate the general differences between two types of business: industrial (or 'business to business') and consumer orientated.

1.4 A decade of growth

Below-the-line expenditure has been increasing rapidly, especially the sales promotion (including price promotions) element.

In 1985 Mintel published its first report on the sales promotion industry. While reviewing the sales promotion industry is not as straightforward as dealing with finite markets, e.g. motor cars or baked beans, because sales promotion is far more diverse and much more complicated, at least the report serves as a starting point in reviewing the size of the market.

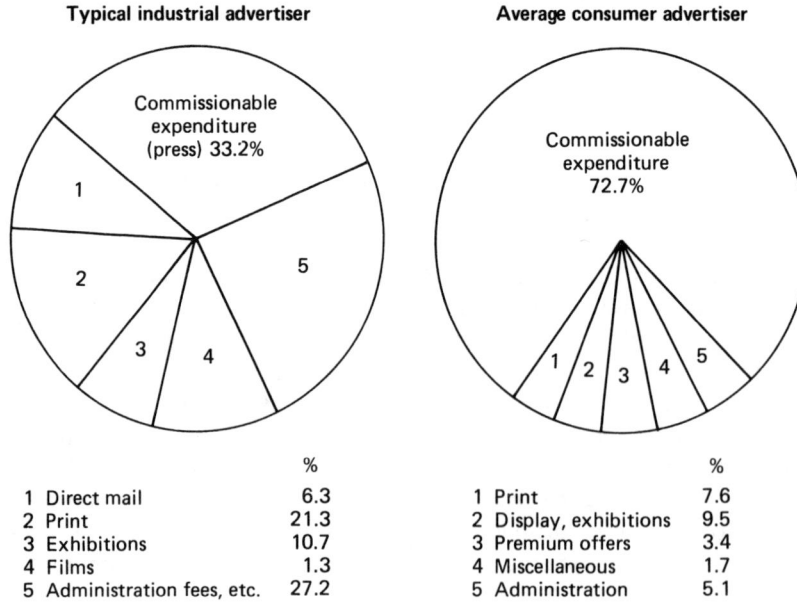

Typical industrial advertiser	%
1 Direct mail	6.3
2 Print	21.3
3 Exhibitions	10.7
4 Films	1.3
5 Administration fees, etc.	27.2

Average consumer advertiser	%
1 Print	7.6
2 Display, exhibitions	9.5
3 Premium offers	3.4
4 Miscellaneous	1.7
5 Administration	5.1

Figure 1.2 *Comparison of the allocation of publicity resources of industrial to consumer business, 1980*

Defining what constitutes the industry and its size is a little like trying to estimate the size of the black economy: it gets very fuzzy round the edges. Mintel, however, estimates it at anything between £1bn and £5bn in the UK, but a large proportion of the higher figure is accounted for by manufacturer's price dealing directed at the major multiples. In fact, price dealing is often the largest expenditure within the total budget of many brands. Without price dealing, the consumer sector of the industry is put at around £2bn. While rather a 'guesstimate', it is apparently at the right level when compared to the 1984 advertising expenditure of around £4bn.

Mintel concentrates on these elements of the industry, which are primarily connected with what it terms 'consumer pull', rather than 'trade push'. In looking at growth in the industry over the period, Mintel provides figures for the broader £5bn sector, describing the eight-fold increase in expenditure over 10 years as 'impressive'. Indeed, impressive it is, but when compared to advertising expenditure (which was omitted from the report) as shown in Table 1.1, a similar impressive level of growth is seen.

Table 1.1 *Increase in sales promotion and advertising, UK*

Year	Sales promotion £m % increase	Total advertising £m % increase
1974	650	900
1975	900	967
1976	1225	1188
1977	1850	1499
1978	2150	1834
1979	2350	2131
1980	2600	2555
1981	3000	2818
1982	3500	3126
1983	4000	3579
1984	5000	4000(est)
% increase 1974–84	769%	444%

Source: Mintel and the Advertising Association.

It is of no surprise to anyone that the Institute of Sales Promotion in 1983 estimated that the total UK expenditure below-the-line now exceeded the money spent on media advertising. Around the same time published data on the year-to-year growth of advertising and sales promotions in the USA confirmed considerable advancement. See Figure 1.3.

The *Marketing Pocket Book* (1992) published by the Advertising Association refers to a survey conducted jointly by the AA and the Institute of Sales Promotion in 1988. It concluded that: '. . . the size of

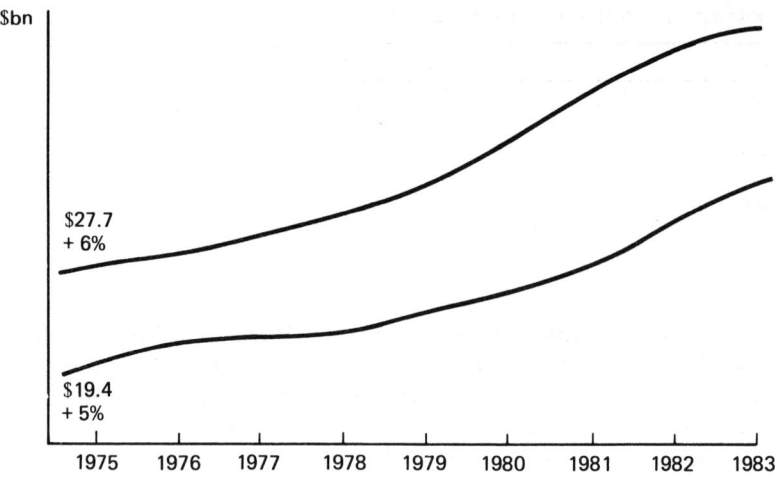

Figure 1.3 *Year-to-year growth of advertising and sales promotion ($billions)*

the sales promotion business is highly dependent on the definition of sales promotion used, especially with regard to trade and consumer price discounting. Using a restricted definition suggests that expenditure on sales promotion in 1987 was of the order of £1500 million with some £1000 million of this being non-price related items.' At the time of going to press more up-to-date figures were not available.

One can see why both in the UK and the USA there has been increasing concern among advertising managers and advertising agencies, and increasing delight among sales-promotion managers and sales-promotion agencies, over the shift of funds from media advertising to sales-promotion activities. This trend has produced a boom in the growth of specialist sales-promotion agencies.

Before exploring that area of the industry, let us first take a brief look at some detail of sales promotion in the 5 years to 1988. According to MS Survey's annual report on sales-promotion activity in the UK (published in March 1988), 1988 showed a downturn in the level of *new*, grocery-type promotions for the first time for 5 years (down 7 per cent on 1987). However, the reality was that, compared with longer-term trends, 1987 was something of a peak year (up 6 per cent on 1986), and if this distortion is removed, 1988 can be viewed as continuing a steady, longer-term 3 per cent annual growth rate. See Table 1.2.

It is interesting to speculate how much, if any, of the drop in 1988 was a reflection of the downturn in commercial outlook following Black Monday. Despite the apparent reversal in 1988, it is interesting, and significant that *new* promotions i.e. those appearing in the market

Table 1.2 *Yearly sales-promotion trends*

Year	No. new promotions
1984	3629
1985	3678
1986	3840
1987	4455
1988	4128

place for the first time, show a continuing increase in their proportion of total promotional activity evident in the market place at any one time. This demonstrates the continuing trend towards more shorter-term promotional activity and continues to raise the question of the role of promotion as a strategic rather than a tactical weapon.

1.5 Below-the-line promotional decisions

Once we have separated out price-cutting techniques, decided how much these are going to cost us and agreed where they are going to be funded from (as suggested earlier), we find that below-the-line promotion techniques are not fundamentally different from above-the-line but merely alternative ways of achieving promotional objectives. In just the same way one must be clear:

- Who the target audiences are.
- What needs to be communicated to them.
- For what reason and with what purpose.

So, let us look at the criteria for successful below-the-line activities:

1 First and foremost, they need to be part of a totally integrated marketing campaign, part of the right mix.
2 While below-the-line activities may have a short-term impact, they should contribute to specific long-term objectives.
3 Senior management should strictly monitor performance against targets.
4 Last but not least, wherever possible, cost-effectiveness studies should compare these media with above-the-line alternatives.

1.6 What's below-the-line can support what's above-the-line

Equally, what goes on above-the-line can 'hold up' below-the-line activities. While it seems obvious that the promotional mix from above-the-line advertising through to below-the-line promotion should be coordinated, it is surprising how this is sometimes overlooked. There would be no point in advertising Stella Artois lager as an up-market expensive lager and then offering 5p. off the MRP (Manufacturers Recommended Price) of a can (fortunately, Stella Artois don't!).

An excellent example of how above-the-line advertising was used in harmony with below-the-line publicity occurred in the 1988 Institute of Sales Promotion competition. A special award was presented by British Telecom for the most imaginative use of the telephone. The judges found a clear winner in The Antiquary Challenge; this promotion also took the overall ISP Award, where the striking and memorable posters supported the sales promotion.

The deluxe whisky sector peculiar to Scotland is led by Johnnie Walker Black Label, with 60 per cent market share. Antiquary is at number two with 10 per cent share. Black Label has distribution throughout the UK, whereas Antiquary has a strong business base in Scotland – a base in need of support but with a limited budget to do the job.

The objectives, clearly stated at the outset, were to sustain traditional trade sales and stocking levels for the Christmas/New Year period, to stimulate extra interest in the brand, and to increase awareness of the product. Mainly Adshel posters were used, in Glasgow, Edinburgh and Aberdeen, and these posters invited consumers to estimate the value of certain antiques featured with the product.

By telephoning the local number, consumers could not only hear a description of the antique to help with their valuation, but could also transmit their entries over the phone. The first prize was the object's auction value as determined by Christie's.

Since the total budget available was only £60,000 (1983 prices), including media support, an ephemeral and pedestrian campaign in the trade and consumer press might have been the predictable agency response. What was required was a far more cost-effective and visible push for the brand. The integration of a promotional incentive with brand value-building resulted in advertising that demanded a response from the consumer.

The recorded message acted as a complete 'leaflet', clearly setting out the prize, mechanic, rules and instructions – as well as advertising the product. The term 'mechanic' is used to describe the physical component parts of a promotion which provide the means by which people become involved in the promotion. Examples include scratch cards, coupons, proofs of purchase etc. Further, the competitor could make an entry via the same telephone call. If the budget could have been stretched a little further, each caller could have been sent a confirmation of entry by direct mail along with, say a coupon, as a further incentive to purchase.

So one can see that this totally integrated campaign, using techniques drawn from above- and below-the-line, worked successfully to achieve its objectives.

1.7 Summary

1 Above-the-line advertising and below-the-line promotion are alternative ways of communicating with customers. Advertising is a less direct method, and tends to be used to improve or strengthen attitudes to and feelings about companies and their products in the long term. Below-the-line promotion, especially sales promotions, can be a very direct way of encouraging purchase by temporarily improving the value of a brand and generating extra sales quickly.

2 It is important to distinguish between below-the-line activities that call for price cuts and those that do not. Ideally the price of a product should be set independently of promotional considerations.

3 The distribution of expenditure across the various above- and below-the-line techniques varies widely from one type of market to another.

4 The growth of below-the-line publicity has been very dramatic (from £650m in 1974 to £5,000m in 1984, and continuing at around 3 per cent per annum. In July 1992 *Marketing Week* recorded that: '. . . agency new business has slumped in the first half of the year. . . . According to Rav's New Business Monitor, the value of new business fell from £970m to £620m – a decline of 36 per cent – in the first six months of 1992, compared with the same period in the previous year. Sales promotion seems to be highly vulnerable – like other forms of promotional expenditure – to the pressure to cut costs which develop during a severe recession.'

5 Below-the-line promotional expenditure must be planned and controlled in exactly the same manner as above-the-line advertising.

Reference

1 ADMAP, December 1980 - Andrew Roberts, Director of Op. Research, D'Arcy, MacManus and Masius, at ADMAP Conference, 1981.

2 Are price-reductions true below-the-line promotion costs?

2.1 Why not just cut the price?

As we saw in the last chapter, below-the-line promotion can be split into price- and non-price-related activities. We argued that price reductions, however well disguised, could not be considered as true marketing costs. Whatever accounting system your company adopts, price reductions are direct costs to the business and, as we shall see later, a pound off the list price reduces the gross profit accordingly and you will need to work harder, i.e. sell more, to earn the same amount as before the price cut.

A while ago airlines were vying for business on international routes, notably the North Atlantic. Fierce competition led to unprecedented cuts in air fares. At the centre of the debate was Sir Freddie Laker. Hailed by some as the 'entrepreneur of our time', he was accused by his competitors of 'reckless pricing' and 'providing a catalyst for the industry's problems'. Before the collapse, Laker boasted that he could offer lower fares than his much larger competitors because he had lower costs. Unfortunately he was caught out by his inability to service debts and could not withstand the hostile environment in the same way as the large state-owned/national airways. Sadly he left many suppliers unpaid and forced redundancies at a time when there was already high unemployment. Richard Branson's Virgin Airways, however, offers competitive but not suicidal pricing, and a level of service that adds value to your air ticket.

The heady years that led to the boom in sales promotion were a period when sales were all. Similarly, there was a significant investment in the capacity to meet that volume. However, this became a vicious circle: more-sales-needs-more-capacity-needs-more-sales. Eventually one ends up with having to buy sales volume at the expense of profit; and that can become a very slippery slope. Some promotions, such as price reductions, do not reinforce the belief that a brand is worth paying for and draw particular attention to price as a choice determinant.

Continuous, indiscriminate and badly executed price-cutting is clearly dangerous. (Beware the sales manager whose first question is 'What discount can I give?') However, to ignore the role of 'normal' price and tactical short-term price reduction as key weapons in the marketeer's armoury is equally dangerous at a time when more and more purchasing decisions are being made at the point of sale.

At this juncture we need to stress a couple of important points. The first concerns brand value. In 1989 a strong move developed towards companies assessing the value of their brand names and adding that value to their balance sheets. So valuable are some brands that price reductions devalue the brand's image, so as to cheapen its character. Having done so, it will be virtually impossible to get the price back up to its former (profitable) level without a major relaunch or repositioning, probably requiring significant above-the-line expenditure to alter it.

On top of this a lower price can lower customers' whole valuation of the product. A cheap Rolls-Royce is not an option.

This is why the concept of 'adding value' to a brand by using the appropriate promotion is the most fruitful method in the long run. More of this later.

The second point worth highlighting is that of strategic (long-term) versus tactical (short-term) pricing. In tactical pricing, for example, one might offer money off the recommended retail price to encourage new buyers or persuade 'lapsed' buyers (those who had switched away from your brand) to return to it. Strategic pricing may take the form of deliberately undercutting the competition if one wanted to establish a reputation for 'low prices', or promoting the fact that your store offered the best prices in town. Boots the Chemist, among others, runs a promotion saying that 'If you can buy the same item anywhere else for less, we'll refund the difference.' Boots' promotion is a direct response to other chemist multiples, which give the impression that they are more like 'supermarket chemists' and offer lower prices. When one walks into some chemist multiples, the store layout is deliberately intended to give the impression of low prices. Boots, while maintaining its 'upmarket' store image, needed to respond to keep its share of the market.

Price can be used strategically in the opposite way – to build an image. Stella Artois was quoted earlier as an example of a premium priced lager. With advertising like 'Time, gentlemen, please: haven't you got mansions to go to?' ordering Stella Artois says something about its consumer. Rather like wearing a (real) Rolex watch!

One frequently quoted anecdote concerns the market trader selling fruit and vegetables. At one end of his stall he had apples at 30p a pound, and at the other identical apples selling at 45p a pound. Why?

Well, those apples at 45p were for those people who wanted to *buy* apples at 45p a pound. Remember, some prices are quite elastic and many consumer goods are underpriced.

To hark back to 1977, when price competition was particularly fierce, many foods and certain household goods were on so-called 'permanent discount'. At this time Tesco launched 'Operation Checkout', followed by Sainsbury's 'Discount '78'; and there were a series of other catchy campaign slogans such as Asda's 'Pocket the Difference', Woolworth's 'Crackdown' and the Co-op's 'Price Right'. Tesco's campaign boosted its market share in packaged groceries from about 8 per cent to 12 per cent within a few months. By mid-1982 Tesco's share was 13.5 per cent, compared with Sainsbury's 15.5 per cent and Asda's 8.0 per cent.

The Sunday Times, in reporting the movements of quoted retail sector shares since the start of the 'Price War', noted that Marks & Spencer, which had applied a contrary policy of *increasing food prices* (or 'upgrading', as Sir Marcus Sieff preferred to term the policy) had achieved an *increase* in food volume of more than 10 per cent during the year of the bitterest price conflict, boosting its market share.

Tesco relaunched its scheme as 'Checkout '82' in an attempt to win back share, but the conditions in the market were somewhat different to 1977 and there was some doubt whether the volumetric gain would compensate for reduced margins. Before exploring the volume versus profit issue a little further, let us first consider why companies cut the price.

2.2 So why do companies cut the price?

2.2.1 *A corporate response*

When a price war breaks out in a given sector of the market, it is invariably the company's marketing manager who is at the centre of activity. In a typical case upward pressure is generated from sales managers and representatives close to the market, rapidly followed by downward pressure from the board to clarify the situation and propose short-term action. As the news spreads, horizontal pressure from colleagues in production, finance, R & D, etc. intensifies as they begin to assess the implications.

In the heat of the moment the marketing manager may simply slash the price to remain 'competitive'. However, it is far better to assess the rationality of the situation. Why did a competitor cut the price? Is it the market leader, a new entrant, or an existing supplier with the aspiration of increasing market share? Is there a pattern to the price-cut? Is it related to a specific product, product range or across the full range of products? This is the stage when clear thinking is required, fuelled by sound information.

Is the price reduction temporary (tactical) or a long-term (strategic) measure? Is someone trying to off-load old stock or fill spare capacity at marginal prices (tactical), or present a new image (as supermarkets did strategically in the late 1970s). Maybe price reductions are predictable as products reach a certain stage of product or technology life-cycles, or because of economies of scale.

What contingency policies does your company have in the event of hostilities?

These fundamental questions tend to be treated lightly by the less experienced marketing executives. The stock answer is 'We are dealing with imperfect markets and imperfect information', and they discuss the economists' classical models as too simplistic and not applicable to them. While this may be true for many markets, this does not make many well-thought-out economic models invalid: you must develop some logical approach rather than merely rely on intuition. Hacking a percentage off the price to remain competitive without thinking things through properly is a classic example of 'marketing myopia'.

2.2.2   Psychological factors

Price-cutting is as much a function of the personal characteristics of executives as it is of events in the market. When salesmen give more discount away than they really need to in order to win a sale, they are either insecure or over-generous with someone else's money!

Aggression and risk-taking are high on the list of entrepreneurial traits sought by certain employers. Such executives frequently resort to the price weapon because they genuinely believe that by positive action and good timing they can steal a march on competitors. There are many examples of alert executives, in possession of sound information and making good use of a unique set of circumstances, forcing weaker, lethargic competitors to withdraw from the market.

It is interesting to speculate what would happen if a sales representative asks for a 10 per cent price reduction, and a 10 per cent reduction in his running costs and expenses is agreed at the same time!

There is also of course, the other side of the coin: the customer's perception of price cutting. Price carries an image of quality: remember those apples at 45p. a pound. As with any group of customers, there are always some people who want to pay a good price for a good product or service, just like at M & S; maybe that group of customers is where your secure future lies rather than your trying to be all things to all people.

2.2.3 Prices, costs and volumes

Executives often use a price reduction as a way of buying extra volume. That extra volume is required to 'keep the factory running efficiently', or to win more market share, or even just to get retailers to stock the product in the first place.

Companies setting prices based on costs do so because they wish to set minimum acceptable prices to ensure a reasonable margin, e.g. cost-plus pricing. Demand-oriented pricing, however, relies heavily on good market research and an understanding of the sensitivity of demand at different price levels and in various segments of the market. Some might argue that prices originate in the market place, and costs are specific to companies. However, profitability is such an important issue that price and costs are inseparable. The ideal pricing policy is based on profit, is cost-conscious, market-oriented and in line with the other aims of the business.

2.2.4 Price attrition: or not putting your prices up

This is characterized by long periods during which the total price package is gradually worn down and the true state of affairs is only apparent when one competitor calls in the receiver! Some marketing managers are not consciously aware that they are eroding hard-won profit margins and make no attempt to access the costs/benefits of their actions. Looked at another way, price attrition can negate improvements in production efficiency and savings made by shrewd purchasing and reasonable pay settlements by employees. Here are some common causes of price attrition.

Price holding
This means forgoing or delaying the recovery of increased costs.

Extending the credit period
Once an extension is offered, it is difficult to reduce, unless the supplier holds a powerful position in the supply chain. It may also be expensive. For example, a customer buying £100,000 worth of goods a year on 30 days credit could have £8220, i.e. 30/365 × 100,000, outstanding. Extending this period by just 10 days to 40 days, would increase the

amount outstanding to £10,960. Remember that in mid-1989 the banks were charging 14% interest on overdraft facilities.

Holding stocks on behalf of a customer
For multi-product companies, stockholding ties up a large proportion of working capital. Large customers often try to push the responsibility and cost of product back on their supplier. Again, someone has to pay for it.

Discounts
These fall into three main types:

(a) Trade discounts, depending on the re-seller's role.
(b) Quantity discounts, where volume is exchanged for price.
(c) Prompt payment discounts, offered as inducements to limit credit periods.

Whatever is negotiated with the buyer, the sales manager must keep a sharp eye on the sums – income versus percentage discounts – and monitor the behaviour of buyers prone to changing their order pattern and delaying payment to the last possible moment.

The lesson to be learnt from these examples is that price is seldom a single figure offered or negotiated on the day of sale. Price should be considered as a package, and must be carefully monitored during periods of high inflation and interest rates if cash-flow problems are to be avoided.

2.3 Balance the price:volume equation

Business is about exchange: the exchange of a product or service that the customer wants for something that you want, usually money. It is acknowledged that trade with some countries may consist of the exchange of goods when foreign currency is scarce; however, money is the ultimate goal! (Now this is a statement that that renowned marketing planning guru, Malcolm H.B. MacDonald would call a BGO (A Blinding Glimpse of the Obvious!). Why is it then that so many people give away money as discounts but don't get at least an *equivalent* back in return? This is probably because they haven't done their sums first: 10 per cent off the price exchanged for 10 per cent more volume is not a fair exchange, it is daylight robbery!
   If you have got a calculator handy, you can prove it for yourself.

Suppose we take a market trader selling shirts. He can buy shirts at £10.50 each and usually sells them at £15.00 each; making £4.50 on each shirt. Now, on market days when trade is brisk, he can sell fifty shirts a day. So at £4.50 profit per unit our trader makes £225 gross profit on the day (50 × £4.50).

Non-market days, Mondays and Tuesdays, are quiet days, and suppose our humble trader feels that if he offered 10 per cent off his usual price of £15.00 he could sell a higher volume of shirts than he otherwise might. After all, if he sells more shirts on the day, surely it will make setting up the stall more worthwhile. But how many extra shirts will he have to sell to make the same gross profit? Perhaps 10 per cent more?

No. Let's do the sums. Remember, he made £225 gross profit on selling fifty shirts at full price. So, if he sells fifty shirts at £13.50 (10 per cent discount), he will make £3.00 gross profit per shirt or a total of £150. The shortfall of £75 will be made up on the sale of 25 more shirts (75/3 = 25). Hence, by cutting the price by just 10 per cent our trader must sell 50 per cent *more shirts* (seventy-five) than he would have had to do before cutting the price. Table 2.1 demonstrated the sales increase needed to earn the same gross profit as before the price-cut. So, in our example above, the trader's gross profit was 30 per cent (£4.50 on £15); so by cutting his price by 10 per cent, a sales increase of 50 per cent was necessary to achieve the same gross profit.

Ask yourself some fundamental questions about your company. What is the current gross profit in per cent of turnover terms. Do you cut prices, if so by what percentage? Do you have any mechanisms to ensure that you exchange that price-cut for an appropriate volume or are you willing to sacrifice gross profit on your own volition?

Let us return to our humble trader. What are his options to increase his turnover on quiet days? Well, let us speculate as to why he decided to cut the price in the first place. He may have been bored perhaps, and wanted to talk to more customers so that he kept busy. The most likely reason, however, probably had something to do with his profit on poor days. Maybe his fixed costs, i.e. the cost of his stall rental, the van to shift his shirts around in, the cost of his stock, etc., were such that unless he made £225 on the quiet days, there was little point in getting up on those days. After all, there is no point going to all that effort selling shirts if one is not making a reasonable return. So, how can he help himself?

Well, he could actually put the price *up* on quiet days. Work it out for yourself, since you have probably still got your calculator nearby. A small 5 per cent increase in price to £15.75 means that he can sell 14 per cent less of his usual volume turnover to clear £225 on the day (forty-three shirts).

Table 2.1 Sales increase needed to earn same gross profit as before price-cut*

Expected price cut (%)	Current gross profit									
	5%	10%	15%	20%	25%	30%	35%	40%	45%	50%
1	25.0%	11.1%	7.1%	5.3%	4.2%	3.4%	2.9%	2.6%	2.3%	2.0%
2	66.6	25.0	15.4	11.1	8.7	7.1	6.1	5.3	4.7	4.2
3	150.0	42.8	25.0	17.6	13.6	11.1	9.4	8.1	7.1	6.4
4	400.0	66.6	36.4	25.0	19.0	15.4	12.9	11.1	9.8	8.7
5	–	100.0	50.0	33.3	25.0	20.0	16.7	14.3	12.5	11.1
6	–	150.0	66.7	42.9	31.6	25.0	20.7	17.6	15.4	13.6
7	–	233.3	87.5	53.8	38.9	30.4	25.0	21.2	18.5	16.3
8	–	400.0	114.3	66.7	47.1	36.4	29.6	25.0	21.6	19.0
9	–	1000.0	150.0	81.8	56.3	42.9	34.6	29.0	25.0	22.0
10	–	–	200.0	100.0	66.7	50.0	40.0	33.3	28.6	25.0
11	–	–	275.0	122.2	78.6	57.9	45.8	37.9	32.4	28.2
12	–	–	400.0	150.0	92.3	66.7	52.2	42.9	36.4	31.6
13	–	–	650.0	185.7	108.3	76.5	59.1	48.1	40.7	35.1
14	–	–	1400.0	233.3	127.3	87.5	66.7	53.8	45.2	38.9
15	–	–	–	300.0	150.0	100.0	75.0	60.0	50.0	42.9
16	–	–	–	400.0	177.8	114.3	84.2	66.7	55.2	47.1
17	–	–	–	566.7	212.5	130.8	94.4	73.9	60.7	52.6
18	–	–	–	900.0	257.1	150.0	105.9	81.8	66.7	56.3
19	–	–	–	1900.0	316.7	172.7	118.8	90.5	70.1	61.3
20	–	–	–	–	400.0	200.0	133.3	100.0	80.0	66.7
21	–	–	–	–	525.0	233.3	150.0	110.5	87.7	72.5
22	–	–	–	–	733.3	275.0	169.2	122.2	95.7	78.7
23	–	–	–	–	1115.0	328.6	191.7	135.3	104.6	85.5
24	–	–	–	–	2400.0	400.0	218.2	150.0	114.3	92.6
25	–	–	–	–	–	500.0	250.0	166.7	125.0	100.0

* At intersection of price cut row and current gross profit column, find percentage increase in unit sales required to maintain the same absolute gross profit as before the price-cut.

He may decide, however, that the market for shirts is so price-sensitive that it would not stand a 5 per cent price increase. So what methods could he use to aim for that 50 per cent extra turnover he needs on quiet days to make the same gross profit? (Given that he will have less customers pass his stall on quiet days, he'll have his work cut out.) He could offer the 10 per cent discount on two shirts sold together rather than on single shirts, i.e. the near classic 'Shirts, only £15.00; save £3.00. Two for £27!

Alternatively, he could see if his shirt supplier can let him have a selection of ties at, say, £1.50 each. Our trader could then offer *added value* to the shirts and not cut his price at all. He would create the promotion of one free tie, worth £3.00, with every pair of shirts. That may be sufficient to generate the extra turnover required to meet the cost of the ties. If he is getting full price for his shirts and bringing in £4.50 gross profit per unit, he need only sell sixty shirts, only ten more than 'usual' (sixty shirts at full price yields £270 gross profit, thirty ties cost £45, thus gross profit is $270 - 45 = £225$).

By running this simple sales promotion the trader has:

- Added value to the shirts
- Not cut his price, so that customers calling on market days do not pressurize him for his discounted prices on 'good' days.
- Not devalued his shirts.

Remember his two options – selling forty-three shirts at the higher price or sixty shirts to only thirty customers with the tie promotion. Either way, on quiet days, these options must be easier than selling seventy-five shirts at the 10 per cent reduced price; especially if there are less customers on non-market days.

2.4. Consumers and price

Knocking a few pence off the price of a product is not the universally most attractive method of attracting customers.

Marketing reported back in September 1979 that expenditure on sales promotion in the previous year was estimated to be at £2.165m, including half a million spent on discounting.

While the figures are out of date, the precepts in the article remain as valid today, sadly, as they did then. The report suggested that:

> . . . a large part of that money (£500m) is being wasted . . . The first reason for this is that retailers have tended to concentrate their promotion activity on price cuts which are all too easily initiated and

have no element of novelty. This has led to boredom among shoppers who see most stores as offering the same deals.

The article quotes research by Harris International Marketing as the basis for this point of view. The research indicated that 'only about half its respondents felt strongly enough about low prices to cite it as a reason for choosing that shop' and 'only eight out of every 100 respondents actually deliberately buy brands that are reduced in price.' Other research by the Taylor Nelson Monitor seemed to point in a similar direction.

On the other hand, 'techniques like free gifts, competitions and self-liquidators, for example, show dramatic increases in popularity'.

The main reason for the lack of enthusiasm for price-cuts seemed to be 'a mist of confusion and suspicion among housewives about the genuineness of the offers'. The Harris research 'reveals that shoppers' awareness of prices is dropping; they cannot remember from one shopping trip to the next how much they paid for certain items as prices fluctuate. This makes them anxious and confused and ultimately suspicious of the special offers with which they are bombarded'. The article quoted underlines 'the need for greater emphasis on value for money rather than low prices', and suggests that 'retailers must closely examine their promotional policies'.

Right in the middle of our free enterprise system is the quest for competitive advantage. As soon as consumers show any sign of buying a product in any volume, an opportunity is created for a competitor to divert that demand towards a similar product, but one that offers a greater advantage to the user. Sales promotion is concerned with actions which give that all important edge over competitors.

In the marketing sense competitive advantage is achieved by three basic means. A product must perform better than its competitors, do a comparable job at a lower price, or be made more attractive than its competitors to a degree that may transcend considerations of performance and value.

A product can be made more attractive by features inherent in the design of the product itself, or, as with packaging, something 'external', which can be added without affecting the performance and price of the product. How about packing a cocktail drink in a silvered shaker rather than an ordinary bottle?

There are sales promotion techniques that can lend momentum to all three aspects of competitive edge. They can be applied to a smaller degree to product performance rather than to value and attractiveness.

One of the biggest challenges facing marketeers in the 1990s is finding that added value, and it must be added value that is really relevant to the target audience identified. Take the following example.

A car polish manufacturer might offer a free car-care manual to anyone who completes an entry form on the pack and sends it in. Anyone wanting to buy a car polish, but lacking a current brand preference, could find such an offer sufficiently attractive to make the promoted polish have a higher value than equivalent car polishes that appear to offer identical product performance.

Much, although not all, of the persuasive power of the promotion is directed at new users, whereas a price reduction or an extra-product offer, whether to regular or new users, incurs extra costs with *every* sale. The car-care manual only costs the manufacturer anything if the consumer actually sends in for it, but the offer may attract many others to buy, even though they then take no further action.

Non-price promotions also have another consideration as far as the consumer is concerned. It is possible to offer items that are truly relevant to the established needs of the consumer. In the example of the car polish it is reasonable to assume that people who polish their cars will be more than usually interested in maintaining them properly. Thus offering a car-care manual sharpens the appeal of the product for potential buyers with an inclination to spend time and money on their cars. Now, depending on the polish manufacturer, the car-care manual can be an excellent vehicle to promote other products in his range, e.g. window cleansers, screen washes, upholstery cleaners, antistatic cleaners for plastic dashboards. What is more, the manufacturer also gets a mailing list of key customers, which could open up a whole new field of direct marketing opportunities. See Chapter 9.

In addition, and often almost as important, the short-term offer of a car-care manual will contribute, in the minds of regular users, to the longer-term regard in which the product is held. The tactical sales building effort thus makes a substantial contribution to the strategic positioning of the brand in the minds of the target audience.

2.5 A better alternative – set the objectives and decide on the techniques

In Chapter 1 we established that the role of promotion is to encourage purchase by temporarily improving the value of a brand, and as such is part of the marketing mix, tying in with advertising, product performance, and pricing. You will now have made decisions about the appropriateness of using sales promotion; but rather than leaping into a technique that seems attractive or fun, you should first stop and decide what you want to achieve, and then select the appropriate technique. Don't simply jump on the bandwagon of a technique that feels exciting or seems to be working for someone else.

Later in this book many techniques will be discussed and the reader is directed towards those sections as appropriate. Let us first, for the moment, consider the all-important *objective*. Why do you think you need a sales promotion to 'temporarily add value to your brand'? Well, the answer probably has something to do with market forces. These forces include, for example, competitor activity: perhaps you need to respond to a competitor's promotion, or you need to do something about a new entrant to the market. The market forces as such may have taken the form of a distributor's activity; perhaps your brand has been de-listed and you want to win the retailer back or improve the volume turnover by other retailers where you are stocked.

Table 2.2 shows those objectives certain consumer sales promotions *might* achieve, depending on your circumstances. If you wanted to increase your brand's awareness among certain customer groups, you might choose to use a personality: Leslie Crowther was used for Stork Margarine, Daley Thompson for Lucozade. In more specialist markets some professional people are used as personalities to promote a given brand: Kenny Roberts, three times World 500cc motorcycle champion, promoted PJl oils. So you see, by choosing your personality carefully, you can target your promotion to a quite well defined audience.

Money-off coupons are used by manufacturers to encourage sampling, repeat purchasing, or cross-purchasing (where one pack carries a coupon for a sister brand, perhaps). Distribution by door-drops is now declining, although similar leaflets are frequently used in the press – above-the-line or on pack. Retailers often do not favour manufacturers' coupons, but devise their own coupons to bring more customers to their store or to build volume of their own brands.

Rebate schemes, where proofs of purchase (packet tops, specific tokens or ring pulls from canned drinks) are redeemed against cash, money-off next pack, a free pack, or a gift, encourage repeat purchasing. Occasionally such repeat purchasing may continue beyond the promotion period where the product's performance matches the consumer needs. Beer and lagers sold in fours usually require consumers to redeem, say, thirteen or seventeen ring pulls to qualify, i.e. asking customers to buy one more pack than the three or four required to save twelve or sixteen ring pulls, but a perceived lower number of ring pulls than sixteen or twenty, the total number of ring pulls actually purchased.

Free product, while enticing sampling by new customers and consolidation of existing customers, can be expensive to produce. However, particularly for new product launches, samples can hold the key to success.

Self-liquidating offers, i.e. those where customers make a payment for the gift and so cover the cost of the promotion, are attractive to

Table 2.2 *Promotional objectives*

	Self-liquidating premiums	On-pack premiums	In-pack premiums	With-pack premiums	Container premiums	Continuing premiums	Trading stamps, gift coupons, vouchers	Competitions	Personalities	Couponing	Sampling	Reduced price pack	Banded packs	Related items
Launch or relaunch						X		X	X	X	X			
Induce trial								X	X		X			
Existing product – new usage								X	X	X	X	X		
Gain new users					X	X	X	X	X	X	X	X	X	
Retain existing users					X	X				X	X			
Increase frequency of purchase					X	X								
Upgrade purchase size	X	X		X	X						X			
Increase brand awareness								X		X				
Expand distribution								X	X		X	X	X	
Increase trade stocks				X							X	X	X	
Reduce trade stocks								X					X	
Expand sales – off-season								X			X	X	X	
Activate slow moving lines								X			X	X	X	
Gain special featuring in store	X	X	X	X	X			X			X	X	X	
Increase shelf facings		X		X							X	X		

many marketeers because they can communicate something about the brand or the store, and tend not to cost too much. For example, a wholemeal flour packet could carry an illustration or sketch of a housewife wearing a like-branded apron. This apron would be available at cost with a small number of proofs of purchase. Consumers could identify the gift with the brand and would get a regular brand reminder hanging on the back of their kitchen door.

As a further suggestion, pretty well everyone who applies for an apron has identified themselves as a user, so each could be mailed a few months later and invited to send in their best recipe using the flour. The best ten receive a worthwhile prize, say traditional scales and brass weights. You now have a good idea how your brand is used most – cakes, bread, puddings, biscuits, etc. Further, you could get a panel of cooks – perhaps the local catering department at your local technical college – to try the most promising ideas. You will then be ready and able to run a further promotion offering 'The best customers' recipes' when you next have a specific need to increase sales.

Again, you have communicated something positive about your brand and at a cost far below many advertising campaigns. What is more, with this sort of promotion, you have also collected some useful information about your key customers. You know where they are distributed across the country and what foods they are proud of preparing with your flour. On the down-side it is difficult to forecast quantities: too few and the promotion is expensive and ineffective, too many and you will run out of stock of your offered items, antagonizing hard-won customers by delaying fulfilment.

If you do not feel your customers will buy your offered item, then you may need to look for an appropriate free gift. Coca-Cola and their franchisees have run some excellent branded free-gift campaigns based on ring-pulls. The small items (sweat bands, hats, key rings, tee-shirts) were available with fairly small numbers of ring-pulls, and more expensive items (sweat shirts, bomber jackets, can-shaped kitbags) with very large numbers of ring pulls, or by lesser numbers and a cash equivalent. Such free offers build repeat purchasing, but product sampling may be achieved by offering the free gift in (or on) pack. Breakfast cereals show some classic examples of in- and on-pack promotions, e.g. the box presents an exciting board game, and the dice is in-pack. Unfortunately, increasing costs make it difficult to find a really worthwhile free gift. Get the gift wrong or have one of poor quality and your perceived brand quality slides downhill.

Remember, whatever technique you end up employing, make sure you are clear on *what* it is you want to achieve and *why*. Find out first what is going on in your market place, decide what results you need to achieve, *then* decide how you might get there.

2.6 Some original added-value techniques

2.6.1 *Nippon Telephone and Telegraph*

The state-owned monopoly was launched into the private sector in 1985. In the following year NTT employees were on the streets of Tokyo selling telephone cards – and they sold like hotcakes. NTT realized that the Japanese are inveterate present-givers. Wedding guests in Japan must both give and receive presents. There are even two gift-giving seasons in Japan: summer and winter. The gifts exchanged are invariably fairly modest and the most popular are those intended to be used, such as soap or salad oil. But now NTT phone cards are the most popular.

NTT cards are made from a flexible plastic film that can carry a picture. These pictures, ranging from Sumo wrestlers to cherry blossom Valentine's day hearts, have made the cards the perfect gift.

NTT has produced 250 different kinds of card and has ten styles that customers can print themselves – the ultimate business card. What this has done is to add value to a telephone call, and a call that has not even been made.

Sales of the cards have been staggering. In 1985, with just 3 months' worth of sales, Y65m worth of cards were sold. In the year ending March 1985 sales had expanded to Y7bn. To March 1986, sales had quadrupled to Y30bn. The telephone company admitted that a significant proportion of the cards were never used because they have become collectors' items. A Y5,000 (approx. £20) commemorative card bearing a picture of Osaka Castle issued 3 years previously was worth a staggering Y65,000 in 1986, if unused; a used Osaka Castle of the same vintage was worth Y28,000. At the last count, there were estimated to be more than 30,000 serious collectors in Japan.

2.6.2   The Post Office: 'Go buy the book'

By and large, the higher the consumer's average stockholding, the higher the rate of usage. This certainly applies to stamps, and the Post Office, on launching books of stamps, i.e. ten stamps of a given class in one book rather than just 50p. worth of stamps – after all, who uses all those odd penny stamps at the end of the 50p. books? – was anxious to increase consumers' propensity to buy stamps by the book rather than singly. In the same way as for NTT, there are obvious cash-flow advantages by increasing consumer stockholdings (and decreasing transaction costs by selling whole books).

A series of 15p. discount coupons was distributed via national daily newspapers. Tests had shown that consumers were very receptive to discounts on stamp books; a coupon for 15p. off a £1.50 stamp book appeared to be a sufficient cost reduction. Tests also showed that daily newspapers were likely to be the most cost-effective medium.

As a result of the promotion, sales of stamp books increased by a staggering 300 per cent, and more than 30 million extra stamps were placed in the hands of the public. Sales of single stamps were unaffected, but sales of standard stamp books after the promotion increased, showing that the public had been educated to the convenience benefits of 'buying the book'. In addition, the total volume of social mail, which is normally very stable, increased by 20 per cent year on year during the quarters in which the promotion was run.

2.7 Summary

1 Price reductions are a direct cost to the business and reduce profits accordingly.
2 Other forms of publicity, especially sales promotion, can sometimes achieve a similar increase in sales without the same loss in profit.
3 Added-value promotions can enhance people's perception of the brand, whereas price reductions may reduce it.
4 A huge increase in sales volume may be necessary to recover profit lost through price-cuts. In an example on p. 23 a 10 per cent price-cut meant a 50 per cent increase in sales volume needed to achieve the same profit as before.
5 Price cuts must therefore only be made for quite specific reasons and in full knowledge of the implications. Alternative ways of achieving objectives should always be considered.
6 Various forms of sales promotion to add value are one way of achieving positive results. Some of the techniques and a few examples are discussed here (see Chapter 8 for a fuller exposition).

3 Promotional strategy

3.1 Analyse, plan, implement and evaluate (APIE)

In the first chapter we looked briefly at how 'average' industrial companies and consumer companies apportioned their promotional resources. We referred to the fact that just as in baking a cake, so with promotion, the mix has to be right. In this chapter we shall look at ways in which one can decide on the most effective promotional mix for a particular marketing situation, drawing on the whole range of above-the-line advertising and below-the-line promotional techniques.

We can look at the promotional mix in a way that's as easy as pie: APIE in fact. This mnemonic stands for Analyse, Plan, Implement, and Evaluate. Find out where you are and work out how you got there (Analyse); decide where you want to go from here (Plan); put that into practice (Implement); and, in order to measure your success, work out how well you did against your plan (Evaluate).

Let us look in more detail at each of these stages.

3.1.1 Analysis: where are you?

The first place to look, and the cheapest, is at your own sales data. Look at it objectively and you will find a whole mass of hidden information. Have you discovered the 'Pareto Effect' in your company? This is also known as the 80/20 rule – about 20 per cent of customers account for about 80 per cent of business. The Pareto Effect is found in almost all markets from capital industrial goods to banking and consumer goods. Things tend to come in lumps, not evenly spread. Is it the case for your business? How important is it to know?

Well, for one thing, knowing which customers are in the 20 per cent bracket does not mean a company should drop its 80 per cent! The sales volume of these customers makes an important contribution to overheads. In addition, the 80/20 rule would probably still apply to the remaining 20 per cent. One could go on until there is only one customer left! However, in carrying out this kind of analysis it should become clear where you should be placing your greatest effort. There is, however, a serious danger. This form of analysis is static: in other words, the best *potential* customers may well be in the 80 per cent, or even in the larger group of non-customers. It is obvious then that while such analysis is vital, great care is necessary over how it is used.

By analysing your own company sales data thoroughly you will begin to see more details about your own company as well as important data about your customers. You will begin to uncover who bought what, when, where and how frequently. What pack sizes were most popular/profitable? This data is already sitting in someone's office, though maybe not in the format you might ideally want. Getting other data is going to cost you in time and revenue.

You may already, from your own data, have answered the what, when, where and how questions about customer purchasing, but you will need to ask some more questions to find out why they buy, and often more importantly, why not. You may be able to buy some research off the shelf or may have to commission your own. Alternatively, you could get out and talk to some people in the trade: this sort of field work is generally under-used by marketing people. Trade profiles are also valuable. Taking a close look at what competitors are up to is all part of the analysis exercise.

For further guidance on how to develop marketing plans – the reader is directed to an excellent work of that title by M. H. B McDonald.[1]

Once you have analysed your data thoroughly you will be able to quantify your objectives. Decide what you want to achieve. Try to be specific about it too. Write some numbers down. It is no good saying 'I plan to increase sales next month/year'. By selling one more pack than you did last time you are there! However, saying 'I plan to increase my sterling share of the veterinary inhalation anaesthetic market share from 36 per cent (Quarter 2, 1989) to 42 per cent (Quarter 3, 1989)' is a quantifiable objective. You have defined what type of share you are after (volume share relates to the number of units sold, while value or sterling share refers to your share of the total money spent by customers on that group of products). You have described the market concisely, defined where you are now and where you want to be *and* by when.

So, having identified where you are and where you want to go, you will need a plan of action.

3.1.2. Plan: This is how you are going to get there

It is said that the Japanese are great planners. They communicate with each other and agree, collectively, on the appropriate course of action. Whilst they spend a considerable time planning, their implementation phase is often much shorter. Consider the two scenarios in Figure 3.1.

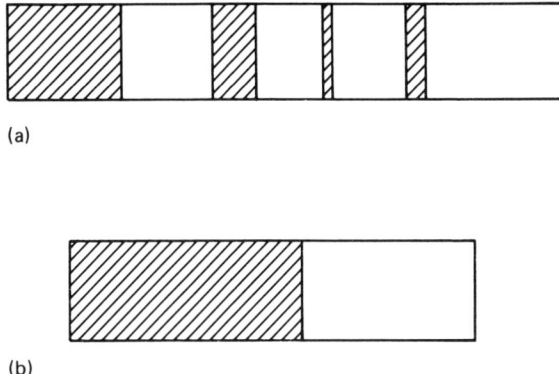

(a)

(b)

Figure 3.1 *Planning scenarios: (a) short planning phase, long implementation phase, with plenty of opportunity to go off course and redirection necessary; (b) long planning phase, short implementation phase, time to completion much shorter*

In (a) the plan has not been thought through well enough before everyone went racing off doing their bit. The result was that a number of 'reappraisals' were necessary along the way. The end result, once achieved, was inefficiently arrived at compared to (b), where more time was spent thinking through the options before acting. So if you work in production and you get a salesman screaming for a new pack tomorrow, show him the example above: it may make him rethink his options. The Japanese may have something.

Your plan itself will need to pay due regard to 'context'. You will need to ensure that your planned promotion follows an agreed brand strategy. There will be no point putting together a promotion that is at a tangent to your advertising, without good reason, supported by data.

Your plan will also need to define the proposed solution to meet your objectives, both in terms of the commercial mechanics – what exactly the consumer has to do, what the company is going to do about, physically, counting 50 ring-pulls from 25,000 customers (the marketing departmental secretary cannot be expected to do the job, unless you want to lose her!) – and also in terms of the creative communication. In other words, you will need to clarify exactly what the promotion is planning to communicate to customers. Is the competition you are planning designed to be a 'fun' thing for the whole family to enter? It should be if you are promoting a breakfast cereal. Or is your competition intellectually challenging? If it is, don't put it in a tabloid newspaper.

3.1.3 Implementation – making things happen

In any organization you are likely to have the 'thinkers' and the 'doers'. If you are really fortunate, the majority will have a good blend of both attributes. No matter how competent your 'doers' are, they cannot be expected to perform well unless you have done your planning thoroughly and set your objectives clearly and realistically.

When you are running any form of below-the-line promotion, from attending a commercial exhibition to producing an on-pack premium offer, you will have to make sure that everyone keeps to the plan and that it runs on time. To this end you may have to control some outside suppliers or services. If you are employing an outside sales or merchandising field force, have they been briefed clearly at the outset? Have you set some guidelines or 'stage goals' so they can see for themselves that they have implemented your plan appropriately? Suppose, for example, you have employed Manpower Services to call on, say, hoteliers and restaurateurs to promote your new 'Cash & Carry for Caterers' in their neighbourhood, and you have set them a target of twenty businesses a day to call on. Who checks as it goes along that they are implementing that plan appropriately?

3.1.4. Evaluation – well, did it work?

Only by establishing realistic and quantifiable objectives at the outset can you have any real measure of success. Be honest with yourself when you come to measure your success. National Pet Week was launched for the first time in the UK in May 1989. One of its primary objectives was to increase the public awareness of what constitutes responsible pet ownership. Measuring air-time recorded on National and Regional TV was NPW's method of evaluating their achievement of the objective. Indeed, on the face of it, $3\frac{1}{2}$ hours of air-time was a creditable performance – such air-time as pure advertising would have cost millions. However, just as absolute media spend is no measure of the success of an above-the-line advertisement, so $3\frac{1}{2}$ hours of broadcasting does not measure whether or not the *public awareness* of what actually constitutes responsible pet ownership is increased. The realistic evaluation of the achievement of that particular objective can only be firmly established through attitudinal research of the public. Measuring the effectiveness of public relations is dealt with in more detail in Chapter 13.

If you can define quantifiable objectives, evaluation after the event is simplified. If your objectives are nebulous, then make sure you are realistic and honest in your appraisal and don't measure something only indirectly related to your goal. Better yet if you make sure your objectives are *not* nebulous but very clear-cut. Best of all if you can be sure at the outset how they will be measured and the necessary activity put in hand at the beginning.

3.2 Making promotional decisions

- Should we advertise on TV?
- Should we have a lavish, full-colour brochure about us, our products or services?
- Should we exhibit at one or more of the larger departmental stores, or the next international symposium?
- Should we cancel all our advertising and hire more salesmen?

How do we decide?

Well, first, we must be clear that all these things, each good in its own way, cost a lot of money. Second, all of them are basically no more than methods of communicating with customers – each good in some ways, not so good in others. Advertising on TV is expensive, but if you are trying to reach, say, 10 million housewives, then the cost per 1000 of your audience is probably very reasonable. However, if you were after a small group of people – doctors, say, or farmers or warehouse managers – rather than all homes in the country, TV is not a particularly good option (except perhaps if you were after farmers and you bought media right in the middle of the lunch-time farming programmes in some regions).

You want to do more than deliver a simple message. You may want, for example, your prospective customer to see your product operating, or handle it, ask questions about it; or you may have a service that can be varied to suit his situation and you need to discuss it with him. How good is television then? Not much – you will need a salesman, even though the cost of communicating with each prospect is much higher; or maybe get your prospects to come to you, say at a trade exhibition or a 'travelling circus' that you invite them to at various places around the country.

However, whether you are trying to appeal to a mass market or a finite group of customers, there are often many occasions when you will need to consider different promotional techniques and vehicles to get your product or company across and satisfy those customer needs profitably.

As mentioned earlier in the book, you will have to have made some pretty fundamental decisions about your marketing mix to make sure that all facets of your business, the products, the prices, their distribution (place), are all in harmony and can be brought together with the right promotional mix. Within the promotional mix we are concerned with how best to show off our products to our customers, current and potential, in the most appropriate fashion. This heading sometimes includes matters such as visual design and packaging. But primarily we are concerned with methods of communicating with our customers, by methods such as personal selling, advertising, sales promotion, and public relations.

While the scope of this book is about below-the-line promotion, the role of advertising as part of the promotional mix, and the interdependency of above- and below-the-line promotion means that it cannot be ignored. Above-the-line is usually concerned with *attitudinal* matters, below-the-line with *action*. Advertising generally delivers a message to a great many people very quickly but presents problems if we need to discuss an issue or if the message needs modifying to suit each customer. And of course advertising cannot overcome minor objections raised nor negotiate a contract, carry out an on-the-spot analysis of a customer's needs, or arrange a trade-in. Only in special circumstances can 'direct response' advertising take an order.

'Personal selling' enables a 'dialogue' to take place, and it is known that two-way communication (where the customer can ask questions and the salesman can react to the particular situation) is more effective than one-way communication such as advertising. On the other hand, a salesman can deal with only a small number of people, and each 'contact' costs a lot of money. Furthermore, it takes a long time for the sales force to get round and talk to everybody we need to communicate with.

'Sales promotion' is a term covering a whole variety of things, including cut-price offers; 'premium offers' (steak knives, drinking glasses, tights or world cup medals); competitions (win a holiday in the Bahamas); personality promotions (the Dutch dairy girls are visiting your town); and trading stamps. Sales-promotion techniques are good at producing activity and interest at the point of sale. Cut-price offers, for example, induce people to take one product off the shelf rather than another, and go to one petrol station rather than another.

The other strength of sales promotion is that it tends to get dealers to play a rather less passive role than the one they normally adopt. Indeed, many sales-promotion campaigns are deliberately designed to stimulate 'the trade' into greater activity in support of a particular product or range of products. Sales-promotion schemes can be aimed solely at people in the trade or at members of the sales force.

'Public relations' is also a very broad term, and one of its main facets is press relations, which is concerned with disseminating (mainly favourable!) information about a company and its products through 'the media' (radio, TV and the press especially) not by paying for space, as with advertising, but by providing news items or stories that the media will feel are of interest to their readers, listeners or viewers.

An advertisement says precisely what we want it to say and we know that it *will* be published and *when* it will be published. Sending a press release to a newspaper, on the other hand, is no guarantee that our story will be published nor that if published it will be used in the way we would wish. An advantage is that favourable comment in the editorial columns has the weight of authority of the publication behind it and so is more believable than an advertisement where people know that it is *us* saying how wonderful our product is.

Whatever your preconceived notions might be about why your customers buy, there is no substitute for being open-minded about the issue, researching customers' reasons for purchasing and continuing to explore new avenues to maintain that competitive differential – that 'thing' that makes you different from the competition and influences your customers' buying decisions. There are numerous examples, particularly in the scientific/technical field, where manufacturers have a particular story to tell and the customers are jolly well going to hear it! But the manufacturer who realizes that technical specification is not the only criterion and starts to help his customer run his business usually gets the contract.

One example comes from the medical field. A major pharmaceutical company with a reputation in anti-anxiety products, anti-depressants, and sedatives, researched and produced a major new pain-killer. A morphine derivative that did not cause euphoria or addiction, could be taken with alcohol and did not cause nausea. Sounds ideal! It was. It had a unique mode of action where molecules of the drug selected out and blocked those receptors in the brain that were responsible for causing the sensation of pain: just as morphine does. However, during recorded in-depth interviews with general practitioners, it was realized that the humble family doctor didn't want to know about neuro-receptors but wanted more straightforward, practical information.

Despite this, and against their agency's best advice, the manufac-turers went ahead and launched on the basis of the technical story. The launch was not successful (and the agency lost the account!). Only when the promotional message was corrected, did the product achieve the success it deserved.

The very best techniques of publicity cannot make up for a shortfall in open-mindedness and a willingness to listen to a good cross-section of customers. There is no substitute for getting the strategy right first. See Figure 3.2.

Once you have done your groundwork, you will be in a pretty good position to decide what message your customers want to hear, and will

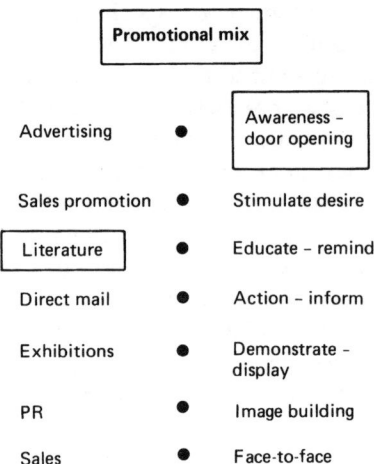

Figure 3.2 *How various types of promotion and publicity can make their own special contribution to the marketing mix*

also be able to decide how best to get that message to them. In the case of general practitioners, there is little substitute for having a salesman visit the practice, meet the GPs, discuss the various issues of importance and then for the salesman to gain a commitment from the doctors to prescribe the product. Once achieved, perhaps the salesman may then have to nip round to the local pharmacists and make sure they have it in stock to meet the prescription demand.

3.3 Why strategic planning?

Many promotional decisions have been taken as a purely short-term activity, usually in response to a particular set of circumstances, such as sudden competitive activity or unusually high stocks. An immediate reaction was necessary, usually without any particular strategic focus. As certain techniques proved successful, many companies began to repeat their promotions with such frequency that promotions became written into the annual marketing plan. In this way promotions were marked out in advance, money allocated, and agencies or consultancies called in to create the ideas and organize the promotions. Such *ad hoc* activity is no substitute for long-term planning.

Strategic planning has major benefits:

- You can develop a consistent drive towards the achievement of some fundamental objectives, all parties and activities directed towards a common goal.

- You will create a momentum, where each promotion increases the acceptability and effectiveness of the next, collecting customers and generating loyalty.
- Tactical opportunities will be marked off as they are achieved, while all the time you will not lose sight of the plan.
- If you are a manufacturer, you will be able to demonstrate to the trade, either before or after the promotion, clear and understandable evidence of a real marketing effort, geared towards the achievement of valuable objectives for both parties rather than a handful of 'gimmicks' that the retailer or distributor (who is also likely to be a sophisticated promoter himself) finds hard to commend yet easy to deplore.
- You can establish a bond between your brands and your regular consumers. The days of mass marketing are gradually falling behind us, and you are rarely closer to your customer than when you promote. Consistent, strategic promotion can tighten that bond as you reach further down that continuum to your audience. Remember Pareto's law – probably 80 per cent of your sales are accounted for by 20 per cent of your customers. Strategic planning enables you consistently to make the most of the appealing features of your product or service, and to avoid antagonizing loyal customers by thoughtlessly inappropriate activity. (It is probably cheaper to keep your existing customers than find new ones!)
- Finally, you will be able to make better use of your resources and maximize your opportunities. At some stage in your business year you will have to prepare annual budgets. Strategic planning permits an overview, allows you to take the long-term assessment of where you are heading. Instant promotions, in reaction to special circumstances, may be necessary, and delay for thorough research is then often unacceptable. However, strategies that span the years are worth researching thoroughly.

The above half dozen points would be well understood in the advertising world. However, only now are they also being applied to below-the-line promotional decisions. We shall pick up the strategic issue again in Chapter 8, as we look at sales promotions in more detail.

3.4 Setting the budgets

In 1981 Patti and Blasco[2] published some data based on a survey of big spenders on publicity in the United States. Until then studies conducted in the USA, Europe and the UK all suggested that, despite the best efforts of the academic researchers, businessmen still tended to set promotional budgets primarily by rules of thumb. Patti and Blasco, however, reached the significant conclusion that the gap between theory and practice in promotional budget-setting was closing. They suggested that companies using the more advanced budget-setting techniques tended to be better at setting and allocating the budget in a manner that minimized costs and maximized profits than those that did not. You need to work pretty hard to make £1000 *bottom-line* profit, but it is all too easy to waste that amount on the misappropriation of the publicity budget.

Most text books advocate logical and rational methods of budget-setting (most frequently 'objective and task') as the best approach. However, all early research pointed to 'guesswork', 'rule of thumb', 'gut feel' as the reality of budgeting, although Patti and Blasco's study was the first to confirm a changing approach. The change was attributed to an increasingly adverse economic climate.

In 1984 the Institute of Marketing in the UK commissioned a marketing review undertaken by Hooley, West and Lynch.[3] Table 3.1 summarizes the initial findings.

Table 3.1 *Marketing in the UK*

Budgeting method	Use regularly %	Have tried it %	Heard of but not used %	Never heard of or not used %
What we can afford	48.5	16.6	10.8	24.1
Objective and task	39.8	13.4	15.0	31.8
% sales	38.4	15.7	21.2	24.7
Experimentation	13.6	20.9	28.5	37.0
Desired share of voice	11.4	12.0	27.8	48.8
Match competition	8.3	15.5	39.8	36.4
Accept agency proposal	4.2	19.9	35.4	40.5

Figures are raw percentages.

The table shows the budgeting methods used by companies responding to the survey. Note that a high proportion of companies employed a combination of methods to set budgets.

While 'what we can afford' was cited as the most popular budgeting method, 'objective and task' was mentioned by 40 per cent of respondents to this survey. Most of the earlier studies had shown only around 20 per cent or less companies employed this method.

Many respondents used a combination of methods to set budgets. Three combinations predominated:

- 'What we can afford' and '% of sales': 18 per cent.
- 'Objective and task' and 'What we can afford': 18 per cent.
- 'Objective and task' and '% of sales': 16 per cent.

If one were to review all such field surveys in the UK and the USA in the 15 years up to 1985, aggregate the results, one would find that only the above three procedures are in genuinely common use, as follows:

	Of all responses (%)
% of sales (or advertising/sales ratio)	44
What we can afford (executive judgement)	21
Objective and task	18
All others	17

3.4.1   *What is advertising/sales ratio?*

An advertising/sales/(A/S) ratio method sets the budget at a certain percentage of sales revenue or, much less often, profit. Ideally one would want to do this for each brand, but in practice, especially with multi-brand companies, one figure covers all. For example, in 1978 Beecham Products set its world-wide advertising budgets at 10 per cent of world sales. One serious flaw, however, in the method is that one must first set a ratio before the method can be used. Setting a ratio is usually done by reference to a set of perceived industry norms: 10 per cent for fast-moving consumer goods, about 5 per cent for durables, and around 1 per cent for business-to-business industries and service industries. Therefore the A/S ratio method is no more than a collective executive judgement.

Don't be too hasty and dismiss the intuition of experienced managers, however; it can work in practice, especially when the supposedly scientific methods look illogical, as further reading in any standard advertising or marketing textbook will reveal, and almost totally inflexible. If this approach is used regularly, it will gradually merge with methods based on 'ratios'.

3.4.2   *Objective and task*

Objective and task reverses the logic of the former methods: rather than defining the budget first (and then wondering what to do with it), one starts by defining the task to be achieved and then costing the means of achieving it. There are, however, two practical difficulties with this apparently easy answer to setting budgets.

First, there is ample evidence that companies find it difficult in practice to articulate the kind of clear, unequivocal, measurable, actionable objectives that could define the tasks. For example, it may be quite easy to agree to mount a trade exhibit at a congress or symposium but who actually defines at the outset how big the firm's exhibition will be? Who from the likely audience do they want to attract, and how many, and why? And how do you quantify your success? Orders taken? That is of little value if delegates cannot actually place orders on the day!

Second, objective and task does not specify how the cost of achieving it will be calculated. It is easy to tot up the costs of a given campaign, but quite another to devise one capable of meeting precise objectives. (For example, if one were planning to produce product literature for the sales force to use, how do you decide on the implications of a mono (black and white) leaflet or full colour glossy brochure as far as attainment of specific objectives is concerned?) The temptation to revert to more mechanical methods is obviously very strong.

3.5 Evaluating campaigns

Having analysed the market, planned a campaign that matches your strategic objectives, and decided on your budget, you will be understandably keen to put the whole thing into action and watch the desired effect taking place. However, when that 'desired effect' does not take place, it is a little late to start wondering why? You are probably already committed, money would have been spent. So, rather than diving in head first, it is prudent to dip your toe in the water and test the temperature by doing some preliminary research. You may decide not to go in at all, and to look for a warmer pool: it is a bit late to make that decision when you are submerged.

Assessing the benefits of research is not easy (see Chapter 6), as they vary tremendously according to four main criteria:

1 The type of research (qualitative or quantitative).
2 The nature and extent of the issues being addressed.
3 What the outcome would have been *without* the aid of research.
4 The skill of the organization chosen to undertake or manage the research.

As the name implies, quantitative research is essentially a survey of a relatively large group of customers, which seeks to establish opinions, attitudes and preferences on a percentage basis. It is subject to statistical sampling methods and can be used to predict consumer behaviour on a large scale by extrapolating the results from a statistically valid sample to the market place as a whole.

Qualitative research, on the other hand, works with a relatively small number of consumers, who are interviewed in-depth in a largely unstructured way. Its major function is to provide an *understanding* of the market place and the consumer within it, so it answers the questions of 'why' and 'how' particular brands and concepts appeal to different people.

It is now commonplace for up to 1 per cent of the advertising promotion budget to be spent on market research, while a marketing services director at a top London agency once estimated that only 0.1 per cent of the total below-the-line spend was used researching the plans to predict their effectiveness or acceptability when implemented to the global market. This is clearly unsatisfactory and suggests there is need for more research than is currently being done.

Research can be used to establish the following useful data:

(a) Awareness of promotion.
(b) Level of participation.
(c) Likelihood of product purchase.
(d) Quality rating of promotion.
(e) The effect on brand image.
(f) Relevance of the promotion to the consumer.
(g) Any potential improvement or ideas for future activity.

Depending on the budget available, there are many techniques that can be used to check a promotion, either while it is running or after it has finished. Such techniques range from telephone sampling right up to large in-home surveys. Often, however, specially commissioned research is not necessary. Existing retail audit consumer panel data and other routinely collected information suffice, including feedback from your field force.

3.6 Let's learn from Quaker Oats

Some 85 years ago readers of the magazine *Home Chat* were offered a free set of bone china cereal dishes in exchange for tokens from Quaker Oats' packets: four dishes for 35 tokens, six for 50. Even in those days that represented an awful lot of oats, so readers were invited to reserve their sets by sending in 2 shillings, a sum to be refunded when tokens were submitted.

While relative values of shillings and bone china have changed over the years, Quaker Oats remains committed to sales promotion as a marketing tool. Spending over £4m annually below-the-line, Quaker now runs around forty promotions a year across its product range of foods, from cereals to snackbars to baked potato fillings.

With such diversity of products there is no common strategy applicable to all Quaker brands. Each individual promotion will have a specific objective – to build volume sales, for example, to lure back lapsed users, or to encourage trials of a new or relaunched product. But each promotion follows a strategy that is designed to reflect the positioning of the brand it supports.

Because Sugar Puffs competes in the child ready-to-eat cereal market, promotions to support it are of paramount importance to match competitor activity. Most promotions are advertised on TV, and the relatively long lead times mean it is necessary to try to predict children's rapidly changing likes and dislikes a considerable distance into the future. Research helps to give gazing into the crystal ball some clarity.

In 1976 Quaker's agency, Boase Massimi Pollitt, came up with the idea of the Honey Monster. The character has been an enormous success with children, who perceive the creature as friendly, harmless, and a bit mischievous. Over the next 4 years to 1980 promotions for the brand consisted of free mail-ins and self-liquidators, e.g. Honey Monster soft toys, watches, tee-shirts. According to Quaker, the response was in line with what one would expect from self-liquidators, but the company was not necessarily selling more product. However, it was doing a brand-reinforcement job by putting a permanent reminder of the brand in the home.

Mail-ins were free, and items offered included magic pens, jigsaws, calendars, beach-balls, pencil cases, all linked to the Honey Monsters. The beach-balls and pencil cases were particularly popular, because, as research had shown, they were something children could relate to and something they could visualize immediately.

From 1980 onwards the research, conducted regularly to keep pace with children's fickleness, promoted a move to a more successful device: the pack insert. Research had confirmed that children liked something free and immediate. It was known that the child sector was dominated by child requests, and TV advertising could generate that request. However, Mum, while responding to the initial request, would need to buy a few more to accumulate the requisite tokens. Children's interest might wander meanwhile and the promotion fizzle out. Children live very much for the moment, so the immediacy of the pack insert was a natural progression. Such promotions would also achieve higher volumes.

So, of four promotions run on Sugar Puffs today, one might be a free mail-in, but most are pack inserts. Again, experience and research used together confirmed the absolute winner: stickers in-pack. They seemed to fire the imagination. They are affordable, and children love collecting and swapping. One of Quaker's main criteria when researching for a child-insert promotion is to find something that is playground currency and is collectable.

When it comes to adult or family cereals, the added values are of a different order. Harvest Crunch, an expensive, upmarket brand, is a cereal that consumers tend to see as a treat. One autumn, Quaker decided to change the 1.25 kg packaging from an unwieldy carton to a polythene bag, and took the opportunity to run an offer of 1.5 kg for the price of 1.25 kg, presented in a decorative tin branded for future storage. The storage tin had a tremendous on-shelf impact, and people were buying two or three to give to friends. In 8 weeks total sales of Harvest Crunch equalled the total for the previous year. No wonder that promotion was joint winner of the Institute of Sales Promotion silver award in the food products free offers category that year.

Incidentally, the free storage tin was run only on the standard variety of Harvest Crunch, which was being relaunched with a new recipe containing sultanas as well as raisins and hazelnuts. But both varieties were promoted with cash-back offers at the same time. This method was used to redress the pricing issue and the treat aspect of the brands, and as a way of getting people to buy more than one pack.

All the way down the line, Quaker admits that researching its promotions is crucial to the development of effective campaigns, especially campaigns aimed at children. What is more, on a free mail-in, for example, Quaker would also research the mothers, because they are much more involved than with a pack-insert. Further, if any Quaker product's promotion was going to be advertised, then the promotions department would work closely with the advertising agency, PR consultancy and promotions consultant to ensure that whatever activity was planned matched the promotional strategy and reflected the same image for the brand.

3.7 Evaluation – how the professionals do it

Just as the proof of the pudding is in the eating, so we have an evaluation at the end of a pie (or APIE!). We have *a*nalysed where we are and where we need to go, we have *p*lanned an appropriate route – even sent out a search party ahead to test the plan (we've researched)

– and we have implemented that plan to the very best of our abilities and marched off into the sunset. We should be well satisfied with our work, shouldn't we? Just before we sit back with a large Scotch and a smug grin, we must remember that our day is not yet over. We must evaluate our work to make sure we have actually reached our planned destination. If we do not take stock of our efforts we shall not know whether we have really made the best uses of our resources, not know, if we repeat a similar exercise the following day, whether or not we shall be repeating any mistakes. Just as two wrongs do not make a right, we must make sure that we check the accuracy of our earlier navigation. Only in this way can we keep on course.

How you measure your success depends on what your objectives were at the outset. If you have made your objectives clear at the start, then your assessment of your achievement is that much easier.

The Institute of Sales Promotion gives awards to those promotions in the country that are especially successful. Each year these top performers are worth reviewing, because it is helpful to learn from other people's successes (and far less costly than one's own mistakes!). The judging of the promotions is generally based on three criteria:

- The selection of techniques in relation to the stated objectives and the likely capability of the promotion in motivating its target audience.
- The standard of creativity used in communicating the promotion.
- The promotion's effectiveness in achieving its objectives.

3.7.1 How Guinness did it

One outstanding example came from the 1982 awards. The judges were unanimous in selecting, for the prestigious *Marketing* magazine Grand Prix award, the Guinness 'Watch the Birdie' promotion, which was the gold award winner in category four – alcohol and tobacco. The judges' view was that, in this difficult market, this promotion had performed particularly well in terms of brand image, repeat sales, visits to outlets and motivation of participants.

Analysis had shown that draught Guinness was regarded as a specialist drink and an acquired taste; traditional Guinness drinkers form a declining market, so there is a need to recruit new consumers. On top of this, brewers consider draught Guinness and draught beer to be in competition, and this attitude can hinder effective promotion of Guinness in pubs. Guinness is also of course sold at a premium over other beers.

The 'Watch the Birdie' promotion's planned objectives were to improve drastically the visible in-pub presence of the product; to increase throughput levels and ensure that this increase was true incremental volume; and to reaffirm the toucan as being synonymous with all Guinness products.

During the implementation phase, participating licensees were supplied with a Hanimex 110F camera, with built-in flash and two 24-frame films. The point-of-sales kit supplied at the same time included pre-paid film-processing envelopes on competition entry envelopes. At his discretion, the licensee took a photograph of his customer skilfully portraying in an 'apt, original and amusing' way the unique character of the draught Guinness drinker, while downing a pint of the product.

The customer reserved a space on the gallery poster, and the photograph was then processed and affixed to this space. On conclusion of the activity, the licensee and his customers chose their entry for the national competition and submitted it to the judging panel. The winning photo earned a £1000 cash prize for the customer and also for the licensee. In addition, a free celebration cask of Guinness was given to the winning pub. There were two second prizes of £500 and seventy-five third prizes of £75 each.

During the analysis phase, Guinness recorded that some 1.2 million photographs were processed (equivalent to 1.2 million pints) and over 24,800 entries submitted. So, obviously, the visible in-pub presence of the product was drastically improved (after all, who could resist scanning the rogues' gallery poster?), the toucan being ever-present at the point-of-sale too. That high level of entrants suggests that licensees now had a positive attitude towards Guinness making further promotions more acceptable. Naturally everyone in the distribution chain was happy with the increase in true incremental volume too.

What was also extremely interesting and particularly useful to Guinness was found when all the 1.2 million photographs were analysed. These revealed that not only were new and younger drinkers being recruited but also there was a significant female participation.

So you see that by careful analysis of your market at the outset and thorough evaluation after the event, you can draw together some useful information to help you in that essential strategic planning process.

3.8 Summary

1 An effective promotional mix depends on careful management, using the stages:

Analyse.
Plan.
Implement.
Evaluate.

2 Planning needs to be on a long-term strategic basis, and not just to deal with immediate tactical situations
3 The most useful budget-setting techniques are advertising/sales ratios and the objective and task system.
4 Examples of promotional campaigns by Quaker Oats and Guinness are given.

References

1 McDonald, M.H.B. (1989) *Marketing Plans* (2nd edn), Butterworth-Heinemann.
2 *Journal of Advertising Research* (1981), vol. 22, pp. 23 – 29.
3 The report, 'Marketing in the UK: A Survey of Current Practice and Performance', is summarized in *Int. Journal of Ads* (1985), vol. 4, pp. 223 – 231.

4 Getting organized for a below-the-line campaign

4.1 In-house or bought-in service?

Few athletes would dream of stepping on to the track without being well prepared and trained for the race. Getting fit for marketing demands a dedicated, well thought through plan of campaign. That was the subject of the last chapter. Without a strategy, you may be obliged to watch your competitors passing the winning post ahead of you and reaping the rewards.

But all the best-laid plans are useless unless applied effectively. Implementation is a key ingredient in APIE! Effective implementation relies on getting organized for the work. As with above-the-line advertising, where it is generally accepted that in order to maximize your efficacy you need the support of experts, so with below-the-line work. Those experts could be on your company's direct payroll or they could be contracted from an outside agency.

The route you choose depends on a variety of factors. For example, if you are only concerned with one or two major campaigns a year, then keeping a person on your payroll all year is not cost-effective. There may also be problems if you need to change your type of publicity or generate some fresh ideas. Does your employee have that breadth of experience to come up with the right results every time? Maybe it would be better to bring in an outside supplier when you want something done. In between jobs you will not have the personnel overheads to carry.

Outside suppliers put their resources at your temporary disposal and you only pay as you go. No need for you to employ a wide range of specialists; your supplier can do that for you. But there is a problem. Nobody knows your business better than you, so how are you going to bring suppliers on to your wavelength and, as importantly, your customers' wavelength? Well, that's all down to you! You must brief your suppliers accurately and clearly, so that they have a chance of coming up with the goods that match your needs. As you can already see, the in-house versus bought-in debate has many aspects to it.

Suppose you decided that you wanted to use the Post Office to carry your message along the continuum to your customers (see Section 1.1).

You may want, for example, to mail all warehouse managers with details of your fork-lift trucks, telling them that you will run a free training course for four drivers with every unit purchased before a given date. Buying an outside list of warehouse managers from a broker may seem the perfect vehicle for reaching your target audience. Yet how far can this list or any other similar list be trusted? Have they been thoroughly tested and validated, and if so by whom? Out of date or inappropriate lists can prove an extremely expensive mistake.

Since your company may not already have an up to date list you can do one of two things. You can build your own list, say, by running an advertisement (with a freepost contact) in a journal (or journals) known to be well read by warehouse managers and offer something of particular value to them (maybe a staff rota wall planner). You can analyse enquiries received, compare them with your known customer list and build your list that way, though obviously this is expensive and time-consuming, and certainly not worthwhile for one direct mail campaign. Alternatively, you may find an outside agency that specializes in your area. The agency would need to be totally committed to ensuring that the information it held was accurate, relevant and current. Perhaps you would need to ask them if the lists were subjected to any telephone research or validation programme. Such direct marketing will be explored more deeply in Chapter 9.

You may find that when an all-important exhibition looms on the horizon, or a competitor springs a coup that starts to eat into your market share, a hastily put together response may seem to be the only solution. Yet diverting valuable staff from their own specialized areas of business into a last-minute marketing campaign is anything but cost-effective. It could be that a good agency has the resources necessary to respond swiftly and skilfully to all marketing solutions.

One problem with many outside agencies, particularly those servicing clients with technical products, is that ill-conceived design and copywriting are produced. Design companies, advertising agencies, and PR consultants may not have the relevant experience or expertise to put together a publicity message that has both impact and appeal. Often you may find that your technical staff will prepare the technical brief, or if you are lucky, actually write reasonable copy, which can then be turned round into more appealing text by the agency staff. In this case, the agency's creative staff need to work in close liaison with the client to ensure that the message is not only accurate but also solicits the desired response.

Considerable caution must be exercised in using an outside organization: quality and capability vary considerably. There is also often a high staff turnover, which makes continuity of style and quality difficult.

As with so many other publicity activities, the right solution is perhaps to establish exactly what publicity services you need first, then to pursue only those that are essential. A technical leaflet or a maintenance manual, for instance, is as essential as the product's raw material or the machine that makes it. If you make your products with first-class raw materials, and employ the latest techniques and machines to manufacture them, it also warrants first-class literature, and the rate for the job must be paid to those people who can produce the goods for you. We shall return to this subject of literature in support of your promotional activities in Chapter 10.

4.2 Possible organization of an in-house facility

An organization is a more or less permanent grouping of people established to undertake specific tasks in order to achieve a given set of objectives. However, the objectives may not be explained or agreed at the outset, and occasionally, especially after the passage of time, the original objectives may have been lost, ignored or modified. Therefore, if you do plan to run your own below-the-line promotion campaigns in-house, you will need to set some clear guidelines for the people in your organization to follow.

In the larger companies responsibility for the organization and implementation of much of the promotion mix, outside the field force, is likely to fall on one person or a combination of three people:

- The brand or product manager.
- The marketing services manager.
- The promotions manager.

All these people will ultimately report to the person 'responsible' for marketing – the marketing manager or marketing director. The organization chart or organogram of such a structure would look something like Figure 4.1.

Depending on the size of the organization, the precise hierarchical structure and titles may be altered slightly. For example, one could have the situation where the product manager A (Figure 4.1) would be a group product manager responsible for a smaller range of brands, or, in the case of the largest companies, one brand only. However, for clarity and simplicity's sake, let us consider the organogram as presented.

The commercial activities of most companies were organized on the basis of specialization up to the mid-1950s. Then came the generalist discipline of marketing and its particular organization. The central

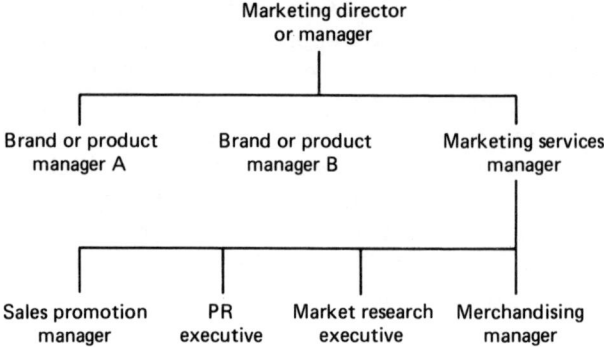

Figure 4.1 *Possible organogram for a marketing department where below-the-line promotion is mainly in-house*

concept of marketing orientation was that the brand manager was the 'managing director' of his brand, and this concept cut straight across the boundaries of the specialist. So advertising, public relations, and product development managers tended to be dropped from the organization chart, but often re-emerged as product group managers or marketing managers. The sales department, in many cases, became merely the tactical arm of the strategic marketing body. The marketing organization was then well structured to implement its principal publicity tool – advertising.

As we saw in Chapter 1, during the 1960s below-the-line expenditure began to grow in relative importance; the marketing organization set out to manage it. Sadly, everyone wanted to be close to the glamorous advertising decision, and no one wanted to have too much to do with the boring sector below-the-line. So the organization delegated downwards and the Cinderella of promotion below-the-line went to the junior members of the team: assistant brand managers and the like.

Three major factors developed in this phase of promotions management.

1 The newly recruited assistant brand manager, straight from the college or the sales force, had little experience in one of the most complex-to-manage of all marketing tools.
2 It was a booming period for marketing personnel, so frequently the same job would pass through many people in the same year.
3 Advertising mistakes were relatively easy to hide, whereas sales promotion mistakes stood out like a sore thumb – budgets exceeded, storerooms filled with unwanted premiums, dissatisfied consumers complaining.

Some major disasters marked this sad period – the bigger the company, the bigger the disaster. As a consequence, and against the general management trend, the specialist began to creep back into the field of below-the-line promotion. The sales-promotion manager arrived. (At the same time, and dependent on the needs of the market in which the company was operating, other similar specialists arrived. Among these were the exhibition manager, entertainments manager, PR manager, and so on.)

The essential role of the sales-promotion manager rests with accountability. He/she is the one person in the company who is strictly accountable to senior management for the performance of the promotions according to the agreed plan, primarily in respect of ensuring that budgets are not exceeded, that the administration of the offer is excellent, and that the quality and supply of promotional goods are fully up to expectation. Moreover, the SP manager's organizational ability can engage him (say he is a man) in a number of other key areas. He can take part in the formulation of the sales-promotion plan for individual brands; this may or may not cut across the brand manager's job, depending on the organization. He can also act as a liaison between the sales department and other departments of the company, to ensure that a coordinated launch plan for the promotion is agreed and fitted into the factory schedules necessary to deal with the promotion well in advance, and that all the necessary paperwork is in order. In nearly every case the SP manager will be concerned with the measurement of results of the promotion, from the organization of the handling-house returns to the coordination of data (sales data audits) from other sources. Some SP managers also contribute to the creative or lateral thinking process that evolves the concepts and execution of the various sales-promotion techniques. However, human nature being what it is, remaining impartial to one's own idea is often very difficult.

It is for this reason that a sales-promotion consultant may be engaged to work in parallel with the SP manager. The latter has an administrative responsibility that is geared to the sensible disposal of the company's resources. The sales promotion consultancy, like virtually any other external service company, provides to a great extent the imaginative and 'entrepreneurial' quality that a large company buys in.

The third party to any publicity decisions on a brand is the brand manager. As mentioned before, these people are the 'managing directors' of a brand and as such are concerned with the four Ps (Product, Pricing, Place and Promotion) of marketing their brands. However, brand managers are often the young line managers keen on gaining wide experience through working on other brands, and possibly dipping into the sales force (unless they were recruited from there initially) or moving between divisions or even companies. The result is the 'chopping and changing' nature of many below-the-line campaigns: a new promotion is unrelated to the one before and the one to follow, each promotion like a sandcastle washed over by the tide of new brand management. Hence the need for having a clear strategic plan that stands the test of a new brand manager.

This is not to say that a fresh approach does not have its merits. The brand's promotion must not get stuck in a rut, and new ideas and techniques are all worth considering. The fresh approach needs, however, to be balanced by the experienced hand.

That experience can come from the SP manager or the brand manager's boss – the group product or marketing manager. Having such an overview, the more senior manager or the SP manager can ensure that the publicity programmes developed can encompass a number of the company's brands if appropriate. Multi-product promotions may often be the most efficient and successful means of promoting the company's goods. Naturally multiproduct promotions will need the support of individual product managers, but such schemes may never be initiated if responsibilities are uncoordinated.

4.3   Selecting an outside supplier

It is assumed that you need to go outside your organization to run your promotions. The question that immediately arises is – which agency? The answer depends entirely on your needs. If you need some highly technical literature produced to support your products, it is likely that you will get the piece written by your own experts, then go outside to get it designed, artworked and printed by an outside agency. Perhaps you need to put on an impressive display at an exhibition; again, depending on the size and complexity of your exhibit, you may put the whole job with specialists, having given them a simple but thorough brief. If you are running an on-pack promotion, it is probably worth getting a design house to look at the job for you; after all, the pack speaks volumes about the product and there is no point damaging a brand by a clumsy piece of design.

However, who you turn to will largely depend on a selection of factors, the order of importance varying from one situation to another.

4.3.1   *How much are you spending?*

If you plan to spend £10,000 on your chosen piece of below-the-line promotion, there is no point trying to get the best level of service from an agency whose clients are mostly in the £1 million and upwards class.

4.3.2 Relative accessibility

If there needs to be frequent consultation and regular contact, it may be felt necessary to have the agency located where much contact is easy – not necessarily in the same town, but at least at the end of a good rail or even air route or linked by a motorway. Do not be surprised by the suggestion of an air route: we are in global markets now and pan-European sales promotion is becoming more frequent.

4.3.3 Specialism

This is a big issue, and one that can be looked at in two ways. On the one hand, you may feel that your business is such that you would prefer to speak to an agency that has had former experience of your markets. Some groups specialize in the financial-services area, so are probably competent to handle the statutory advertising of financial products. There are some agencies who specialize in 'industrial' or 'business-to-business' markets; others even concentrate on particular product areas, such as medical or veterinary, and agricultural. These agencies offer a fairly wide range of services and can handle your above- and below-the-line activities – so-called one-stop shopping from a full service agency.

On the other hand, you may require the specialization of a firm that has developed an expertise in one particular form of below-the-line activity. You will find that some firms can organize a conference for you, others run hospitality events attached to major sporting attractions, still others organize incentive schemes for representatives. Many sales-promotion firms, which originally started up to fulfil the needs of manufacturers that wanted to run sales promotions but did not have the resources or skills to run the programme in-house, are now widening their range of skills and services.

4.3.4 Type of help needed

You need to be very clear on the type of help you require.

Creative
You may need to employ an agency that can produce some good, original ideas to support your brand. Then, having got the idea and the design right, you may feel happy to go off and run with it, perhaps producing the new packs and running the promotion in-house.

Administration
Handling 50,000 enquiries could give you a logistical headache, and you might end up antagonizing your prime customers by not fulfilling their expectations promptly. If this could happen, then you would need to organize a handling house to deal with the enquiries.

Under the heading of administration also comes careful attention to the business paperwork of your chosen supplier. Frustrations often expressed by client companies concern inaccuracy of copy, delays in delivery of materials, e.g. literature, and inaccurate invoicing. When there is a large volume of work going through (across the spectrum of below-the-line activities), a firm grasp of logistics can be vital.

Sourcing materials (gifts)
One stumbling block often limiting a promotion might be sourcing the appropriate gift in sufficient quantities and at the right price. There are specialists in this field too. Many have a surprising ability to find just the right idea that matches your brand identity, one perhaps you had not even thought of.

Marketing
While you may feel that your company has got to grips with the marketing concept and that the philosophy has permeated throughout the whole organization, there may be occasions when outside help is needed to research a market, run a market analysis, provide know-how in targeting audiences, or assist in defining a market segment. It may be that the agency, while not having such specialists on its staff either, would have access to a reliable pool of valuable expertise and information that you do not.

You must define exactly what you want and write down your objectives clearly before you start looking for outside help. These initial deliberations are crucial. A small mistake at this stage could be magnified into a large one at the end. Defining your appropriate criteria at the outset is an analysis that serves as the basic yardstick against which to measure potential suppliers.

You will need to draw up a shortlist of suppliers likely to be able to meet those requirements defined earlier. Potential sources of information include:

- The Incorporated Society of British Advertisers (ISBA).
- The Institute of Sales Promotion (ISP).
- The Institute of Practitioners in Advertising (IPA).
- The Advertising Agencies Register.
- *Advertiser's Annual*.
- 'Trade' journals, including *Marketing, Marketing Week*, and *Precision Marketing*, where many firms advertise their wares.

Whittle down this list of suppliers by a strict adherence to the criteria you originally set until you have about half a dozen likely candidates. Then you will need to get these agencies to 'do a presentation', i.e. to demonstrate to you the potential that they have to offer.

Shortlist your favourite two, maybe three, agencies. At this last stage, rather as one might select a prospective employee, it is possible that the search for the final one may concentrate on compatibility: which group and its staff are most likely to fit well with your staff and form a good working team.

The ideal system upon which to build a firm business relationship may be found by using two general rules:

1 Relationships require commitment from both sides, similar to that between a client company and its appointed advertising agency. Preferably this should be expressed in a legal contract (the ISBA issues a standard form of contract).
2 Analysis of promotions, planning, and idea-generation should be paid for on a fee basis. Supply is often best kept quite separate; the promotion company might, however, have the resources for subsequent fulfilment, quoted beforehand.

Full service agency versus sales-promotion agency
It is difficult to make a decision between the two, but it will depend on your own needs at the time. A specialist sales-promotion agency may be better at some aspects of its specialism, simply because it is dedicated wholly to it. On the other hand, there is something to be said for having everything produced 'under one roof'. In theory this should lead to a greater degree of (highly desirable) coordination between all above- and below-the-line activities, but in practice the various activities will take place in different departments of the agency anyway, and internal rivalries or inefficiencies can still lead to ineffective coordination procedures. The client still has to ensure cohesion at the end of the day.

The appropriate answer really does depend on the companies and personalities in question, and on the precise nature of the tasks being carried out.

4.4   Recent trends in sales-promotion agencies

One notable feature of the SP scene at the moment is its evolution into a wide spectrum of ancillary service areas. Artwork and print studios, now operated by virtually all the big consultancies, were an early development, helped along by the volume growth in business. During the mid-1980s many consultancies also moved into public relations, conferences, audio-visual production and travel. This evolving diversification generates mixed feelings. On the one hand, the acquisition and setting up of specialist subsidiaries can be seen as bringing a healthy input of new talent, as well as making the business base broader. On the other hand, one could fear dilution of the industry's specialist skills, leading to a return of the disguised cross-charges from which the industry has just withdrawn.

A consultancy group's subsidiaries do not necessarily present a conflict of interest, especially as most subsidiaries are profit centres in their own right and have their own client lists. One reason for consultants' diversification is the ready availability of youthful, specialist companies, formed by people who have grown up with sales promotion and understand its mechanisms, particularly in fast-moving consumer goods (FMCG) industries. Another reason, particularly in recent years, is the growth in new markets for sales-promotion services that require specialist knowledge. Among these new markets for SP consultancy's expertise are travel agencies, postal and delivery services, computer hardware and software suppliers, building societies and banks. All these industries are relative newcomers to the world of sales promotion.

As many consultancies themselves grow and mature, they gradually reach a size at which they are subject to the same breakaways and spin-off movements as advertising agencies. Many consultancies of course concentrate on developing their own business first before looking at diversification. Broadening their activities too soon could spread their management resources too thin, as well as placing more demands on finance.

The subject of conflicting interests often arises. You may not be too confident dealing with an outside supplier who recommends that you attend every trade exhibition across the country when you know that that supplier also has an exhibition-organizing subsidiary down the road. The sales-promotion consultants' own code of conduct is very strict on the subject of conflicting interests. To qualify for the Institute of Sales Promotion's register as a consultant, applicants must satisfy the membership committee that a major part of its business is sales promotion and not purely some other element of the below-the-line promotions mix. The applicant must also provide objective and impartial advice that 'does not give preference in its recommendations to any medium, component or technique dictated by aptitude or specific interest'.

The ISP rules were drawn up to exclude premium suppliers, whose promotions necessarily used those products from which they derived their income. The rules equally, offer a safeguard to users of the newly emerging conglomerates. However, the role of any sales-promotion consultancy is to create whatever promotional activity best communicates an enhanced value for its clients' products.

4.5   A guide to briefing an agency

Once you have gone through the process of deciding you need some outside help with your publicity, you have a rough idea what you want to do, and you have been through the process of choosing an agency or consultancy, what next? You will need to tell the agency what to do – to brief it. Now a brief should be the means of uniting the person who sees what should be done with the person who sees how to do it. A brief is therefore a communication between two groups intended to bring each of them on to the same wavelength and the same heading; and it needs to be written down because then, on evaluation, there is no dispute over what the intentions were at the outset.

One of the traditional prime reasons for writing a brief was that it helped clarify to clients what it was that they were trying to achieve. After all, if the client didn't know, what chance had the agency of coming up with the right means of getting there!

Written briefs were also essential in those days when consultants were called in to handle one-off pieces of publicity, and perhaps three or so groups were called in to respond to the same brief. However, as mentioned earlier, your strategic plan is an essential first place to start, and you probably built that plan through the teamwork of your organization. The promotion specialist is an important addition to that team, and often he/she has made a valuable contribution to the strategic plan. Remember, however, that nothing in a written brief remotely approaches the value of the awareness, commitment, and deep grounding that comes from established involvement.

Naturally getting to know a new agency has to start somewhere, and a comprehensive brief is still the best way. Even if you have been working with a certain supplier for some time, introducing a formal brief does make you recheck the fundamental assumptions of the strategy. It will also make you periodically take into account the changing tactical opportunities and needs in the market place.

Whether you are bringing in your consultant or agency to play a strategic or tactical role, there has to be a beginning. So make that first brief thorough. You will certainly need to outline the market you are in and you will need a clear set of objectives to work to. It may also be important to state a few other crucial facts, especially for on-pack promotions: pack volumes, the mechanical limitations on pack featuring, and legislative constraints, what the timing should be, past activities and so on.

On any product you will need to be completely clear about three things:

- What can and cannot be achieved by promotions.
- What precise contribution you will want promotions to make across the year as a whole.
- The specific objectives of the promotion(s) you are about to plan:

  (a) Are they really achievable?
  (b) Are they decisive and quantifiable?
  (c) Can they be post-evaluated?
  (d) Is the budget itself realistic?

That is, you will need to establish your promotion strategies and a tentative evaluation plan.

So how do you know whether the brief that you have just painstakingly written is good enough. Here is a checklist to help in your assessment:

1 A brief is a working document produced by your company for restricted circulation internally and externally. Does it present a clear insight into your company and its product(s), its current and planned direction; and does it give a meaningful and common base for developing and assessing relevant and effective promotions?

2 Is your brief totally appropriate for its task and its audience, and is it concise?

3 If the above are satisfied, then the key criteria to be met are:

   (a) Is the brief analytical as well as descriptive? That is, does it outline the causes of the situations it describes as well as the situations themselves, the main motivations and influences as well as actual behaviour?
   (b) Does it look forward and explain the likely future situation as well as present and past? This will provide some indication of the context in which the planned activity should take place.

(c) Is the body of the brief primarily qualitative and the necessary data in appendices? This will keep the main body of the brief clear and uncluttered.

4 Does the brief answer these three questions?

(a) Where are you now?
(b) Why are you there?
(c) Where do you want to go and by when?

Then the agency can answer a fourth:

(d) How do you get there?

In answering these questions you will need to start with a short summary of what you are looking for and end with a timetable for developing the promotion(s) under discussion. Other specific contents will vary according to the scope of the activity being planned, but are likely to include the following:

Where are we now?) Why are we here?)	– product type	usage/related items/ consumer benefits/ interest levels/attitudes
	– the market	structure/movement/ competition
	– the brand	strengths/weakness/ opportunities/threats
	– promotion history	philosophy/results/ implications
Where do you want to be?	– promotion strategy	general/specific
	– parameters	financial/volume sold, etc.
	– judgement criteria	qualifiable

One final observation. Do not be tempted to write into your brief every conceivable objective that promotion might achieve and, above all, be truthful. Do not use language to disguise but to illuminate. If you are actually trying to sell more at less cost, then say so. (After all, who in business is trying to do anything else at the end of the day?) Only in this way will you be likely to get the best out of your consultant or agency.

4.6   Kanute Bathroom Products (KBP)

The following entirely hypothetical example is an outline brief one might write to an agency.

Kanute Bathroom Products

As early as 1915 this Danish company opened for business selling baths and washbasins in England. It rapidly developed a reputation for highly attractive ceramic bathroom products. Kanute also developed strong business interests through 'Pores SA', a subsidiary specializing in saunas successfully sold mainly in Norway and Sweden. Its Northern European interests were less successful with Pyne Inc, a firm based in The Netherlands specializing in bathroom cabinets made from elm. KBP have recently acquired Poseidon Showers Ltd, a UK-based company specializing in the manufacture of electrical shower units. Since KBP's takeover, a new range of Poseidon showers has been developed. The purpose of this brief is to produce an outline promotional plan to launch the new Poseidon range.

1   THE MARKET: UK SHOWERS

(a) Poseidon products are sold through a number of outlets before reaching the public. Figure 4.2 illustrates how the sales operation occurs.

(b) There are fourteen general wholesalers, of whom about half a dozen are able to promote Poseidon products nationally.

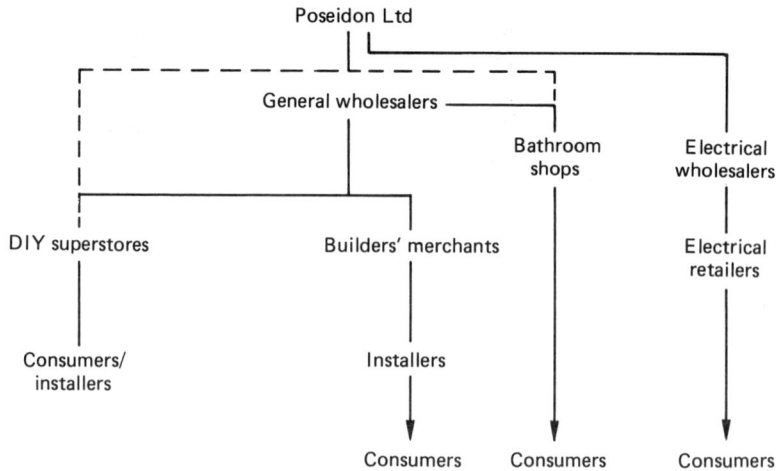

Figure 4.2   *Poseidon sales operation*

Figure 4.3 *Poseidon sales structure*

(c) The general wholesalers form the major link to DIY super-stores, builders' merchants and bathroom shops, although Poseidon does sell direct to some of the larger dealers.

(d) The Poseidon sales structure, reorganized after Kanute's takeover, is shown in Figure 4.3.

(e) The field sales manager, with four representatives, is to be dedicated to the electrical wholesaler/retailer operation to improve Poseidon's position in this sector.

(f) The merchanting manager services the needs of the major DIY superstores and has the occasional help of the 'electricity' team at trade shows and exhibitions.

(g) The national accounts manager services the needs of the general wholesalers, which in turn sell to the specialised bathroom shops.

(h) The regional sales manager has responsibilities for Northern Ireland and manages the two younger sales representatives in the builders' merchants division. The other five report direct to the national sales manager.

(i) The general wholesalers each run five to ten salesmen, who sell over 2000 lines in all. Some also operate telesales.

2 GENERAL INFORMATION

(a) Shower heaters are sold through five major types of outlet.

(b) Table 4.1 shows these types, their importance to the market and Poseidon's position in each.

(c) Poseidon's brands include 'Cronus' and 'Rhea' – two original designs from which the important Poseidon C was derived. The Poseidon C has been married to the Amphitrite range of taps and shower accessories quite successfully for many years.

Table 4.1 *Poseidon's position in main outlets, 1989*

Classification	No. of shower units	Market share (%)	Poseidon brand position
A DIY builders' merchants, bathroom shops	123,000	24	4th
B Electrical wholesalers	45,000	$8\frac{1}{2}$	6th
C Electricity boards	234,000	$44\frac{1}{2}$	7th (of 7)
D Others (mail order, dept. stores)	45,000	$8\frac{1}{2}$	1
E Direct – the Trojan "instaflow"	78,000	$14\frac{1}{2}$	–
Total	525,000		

3 PRICING

(a) Poseidon generally undercuts the Greek manufacturers' 'Athens' range, but is in turn undercut by other manufacturers. Product comparisons are difficult, as specifications vary considerably. Poseidon is competitive but its products are not the cheapest.

(b) Poseidon believes that purchasing decisions do not rest with price alone; the market is not therefore too price-sensitive.

(c) The average unit price is in the range £100 to £200, although installation could range from £50 to £400, depending on the complexity of the job. Specialist companies usually supply curtain rails and curtains, from about £25 to £100.

(d) While Poseidon's approximate unit price is around £185, trade discounts can be as high as 35 per cent off RRP.

4 REGIONALITY

(a) More showers are sold in the South East, which has nearly 40 per cent of the market, than in the rest of the country.

(b) Poseidon's top areas are North West and Midlands.

(c) Poseidon's position in the South has been badly affected by vacant representative territories recently. There is an important need to restrengthen the position here in 1991.

(d) Kanute Bathroom Products also has a strong position in the North West and the Northern territories. Kanute's major competitor, Edmund Ironside Baths of Ashington, a company based on traditional products, has its major strengths in

Wessex. It is believed that Edmund Ironside Baths is soon to launch the 'Assandon' shower range.

5 SHOWER PURCHASING

(a) The main reason to purchase showers is economy, as compared to baths, followed by convenience.
(b) Shower replacements form 15 per cent of the market.

6 ADVANTAGES OF ELECTRICAL SHOWERS

(a) Conventional showers come from the mixer tap apparatus over baths, and depend on a main hot water supply being operative in the dwelling at the time the occupant wants to shower. Electrical showers do not depend on the main hot water supply.
(b) Heavy trade advertising in the late 1970s has created a demand for separate electrically heated showers, either over the bath or located separate from the bathroom.
(c) Easy to overcome location and headroom problems.
(d) Stabilized water heaters are recognized as being safe.
(e) Operational temperatures are easy to select.

7 NEW POSEIDON SHOWER FEATURES FOR 1991 LAUNCH

(a) The new range will update the current range and be featured as the new Trident range.
(b) This will have three main advantages:

    (i) Ease of control of temperature.
    (ii) Ease of control of force of shower, due to new 'mitral' valve design.
    (viii) Multi-shower head gives more refreshing showers.

(c) Temperature control with unique LCD visual display – exclusive to all Poseidon units.
(d) Safe-sure flushes heat out of shower, so that it is safe for the next user – and will operate at their temperature. This safeguard is only featured on the Poseidon C. 'Trojan', 'Troy' and 'Attica' are the only competitors' products to have this feature. The 'Attica' equivalent costs £220.
(e) Water pressure indicator displays water pressure on LCD. This is a key trade benefit. Only Poseidon A4 has this feature.

(f) Wide selection of entry points for cables and pipes. Top entry provided better finish. Key trade benefits as installation costs reduced, less materials are needed. Neater finish for customers. Only Poseidon C has these features.

(g) A 5-year warranty is available at £37.50. Only 'Attica' and 'Athens' can match this offer. Estimate 15–20 per cent redemption.

(h) Good after-sales service for trade, good availability of spares, etc.

(i) All Poseidon showers can be repaired without taking unit off the wall: a good benefit for installers.

8 WHAT ARE BUYERS LOOKING FOR IN A SHOWER?

(a) *General wholesaler*

   (i) Brand awareness by bathroom shops.
   (ii) Ready demand for the product – easy to sell.
   (iii) Sell at printed price list to make margin. Good terms vital.
   (iv) Availability.
   (v) Reliability.
   (vi) Good after-sales service.
   (vii) Good features on the units themselves.
   (viii) Good point of sale support – showcards, leaflets.
   (ix) Exclusivity – not too many wholesalers selling Poseidon in competition.

(b) *Key accounts/bathroom shops/merchants*

   (i) Product and product performance.
   (ii) Price has to be acceptable – with good profit margin.
   (iii) Demand.
   (iv) Good point-of-sale support – showcards, leaflets.
   (v) Availability.
   (vi) Reliability.
   (vii) After-sales service.

Store staff generally have 'preferred brands'. Therefore it is important that the staff appreciates the benefits of the Poseidon range compared with the competition's.

(c) *Installer*

    (i) Reliability – confidence in the product.
    (ii) Ease of installation.
    (iii) After-sales service.
    (iv) Demand.
    (v) Special deals/prices.

9 THE IMPORTANCE OF THE INSTALLER

(a) The installer can be a building contractor, plumber, electrician or DIY, or a specialist shower company.
(b) He buys from electrical wholesalers, builders' merchants, bathroom shops, DIY superstores (UBM, Texas, etc.).
(c) The professional installer lost confidence in the Poseidon range in 1990, and a key objective for 1991 is to rebuild his confidence. One of the problems has been complicated controls, which is overcome by the new range.
(d) Following our field work, and Poseidon research, it is agreed that the installer is probably now influential in a *minority* of brand decisions, with the consumer having a more significant effect on choice.

10 POSEIDON 'TRIDENT' RANGE IN 1990

Poseidon 'Coast'	Budget heater, different fitting kit, low price
Poseidon 'Sure'	Same styling as Poseidon Economy, low price
Poseidon C	Better styling, more expensive. 60 – 65 per cent of Poseidon sales.

The Poseidon 'Chronus' and 'Rhea' have now been replaced by 'Poseidon C'.

Electronic heaters will be launched in the last quarter of 1990.

11 GENERAL

(a) Factors generally stock Poseidon and one other brand. They have to buy 400 showers to get best terms – but deliveries can be split.

(b) Bathroom shops are serviced twice a week by wholesalers. They can buy volume, e.g. five units instead of one to take advantage of a deal.

(c) About 25 per cent of all households have a shower, and about 2 million have electric showers.

(d) Showers are in top three of next purchase items on household expenditure.

12 KEY PROBLEM AREAS

(a) The peak period for purchasing showers is March to September.

(b) Pre-sell to the trade begins January/February.

(c) Although the new product is available by 1 March, it will not be fully through the distribution system for the consumer until April/May.

(d) There is therefore a problem in ensuring competitors do not block the pipeline before the new range is available – and at the same time we still have to ensure we sell-in and sell-out the existing 'Chronus' and 'Rhea' showers.

(e) Timing and content of consumer advertising are also critical in the launch programme. We cannot wait until the new range is in total distribution before starting our 1991 advertising campaign, owing to the seasonality importance of sales – both to the consumer and to the trade.

13 CAMPAIGN OBJECTIVE

(a) The general objective behind the campaign approach is to increase Poseidon's total share of the shower market.

(b) Throughout the campaign our single-minded objective will be to sell Poseidon as a brand of electric shower heaters to all sectors of the trade rather than selling electric showers as a product category.

14 CAMPAIGN STRATEGY

(a) Our strategy is to integrate both advertising and below-the-line activity so that visual awareness of the Poseidon brand and its features is translated into brand preference at point of sale.

(b) This will be done by making the product available through both distribution and display.

(c) Display will play a very important role, as the new product benefits have to be immediately visible to ensure they are communicated to the buyer – trade or consumer – with or without the help of salesman.

(d) Because of the multi-level distribution chains a different approach for each level is necessary, but it is important that the launch of each level is synchronized in the most effective and efficient way.

15 THE TASK

It is now October 1991. You are required to produce an outline promotional campaign to launch the new Poseidon range.

Your proposals should take account of both above- and below-the-line activity. The above-the-line proposals may be merely indicated, whereas the below-the-line aspect should be considered and presented in more detail.

A total promotional budget of around £250,000 is likely to be available, but will only be released if the expenditure can be seen to be justified.

4.7 Try it for yourself

It is a useful exercise to ask yourself what additional information you might need if you were the agency being briefed. Try also to prepare a brief along similar lines for one of your own jobs, and see how easy or difficult it turns out to be.

Practising the preparation of good briefings, as with most things, is the key to success.

4.8 Summary

1 Whether to use outside suppliers or specialists in-house raises a number of considerations, and the 'right' answer depends on how you rate them in your particular circumstances.

2 If you decide to use outside suppliers, they need careful selection, taking into account:

(a) Your 'spend' and their size.

(b) Accessibility.

(c) Their ability to provide the specialism you need.
(d) The type and depth of support you need.

3 Briefing a supplier properly is one of the keys to success. A guide to briefing is given, along with a hypothetical example.

5　The main target audiences

5.1　Classification

One often hears about 'Mr Average', 'Joe Public' or 'the man in the street' as a way of defining a customer. But does such a being really exist? Even if one were to define 'the average' person as a customer, there would be little point, because there would be so many variations from that 'average' among the 55m or so people in Great Britain that a large customer group would probably be missed. As there is not an amorphous mass of people, all identical, all wanting the same needs satisfied, it is important to identify a specific target audience for your activities.

Earlier we talked about the continuum between a manufacturer of a product (or supplier of a service) and the consumer (or user) of that product (or service). In order to make that line as straight and direct as possible it will be important to define where it is going, and what it is aimed at, rather than letting it snake into the horizon, hoping that it might hit the target. We need to identify that ultimate goal and target all the activities of our organization, through the marketing mix, to the successful and profitable satisfaction of the specific needs of that target group of customers.

But as well as end-users there will be others with whom we must communicate.

Starting at the manufacturer's end of the continuum (see p. 6), we have those employees who make, pack, and despatch our product. There is greater fulfilment and sense of purpose for them if they know to what ends their activities are directed. Chapter 13 deals with the methods that could be used to communicate that information to all company employees.

You probably have a direct sales force that goes out into the market place, represents your company and presents products to prospective buyers. Its members need to be clear where those customers are and what they want to hear. The sales force is therefore an important target audience for your below-the-line promotional activities. You will need to sell your products to the sales people first if you expect them to go out and sell effectively.

The sales force may not sell to the end-consumer but to an intermediary, who will then sell the product to a consumer. Such 'trade' intermediaries include wholesalers, merchants (and their sales staff), retailers (and their sales staff), in fact any group who do not 'consume' or use the product. Each of these groups of people are also target audiences, and they need to receive relevant publicity about your product or service if they in turn are required to sell that product effectively to the consumer. Human nature being what it is, it is likely that these intermediaries need to receive much more than just information. They will probably perform their tasks much better if they have some incentive or inducement.

5.2   The need for segmentation

Users and intermediaries may themselves represent too wide a group to be effectively targeted. Sub-dividing our total target group into smaller sub-groups is called segmentation.

We can sub-divide the population according to a variety of personal characteristics, e.g. age, sex, or socio-economic status. Dividing audiences in such a fashion is called demographics. If we then divided a given group according to where they lived, we would have a 'geodemographic' segmentation of the population. Geographical segmentation need not be limited to one country either; we may want to target our specific activities to a defined demographic group across Europe.

Segmentation by personal taste is often important. With products such as food, not everybody's tastes are the same, and a product that satisfies most people will leave others not completely satisfied. People less than completely satisfied by the 'standard' product form a ready market for a product formulated rather differently to meet their particular requirement. The instant coffee market has different blends to suit different tastes, not only in terms of palate but also in terms of price. Remember the example of apples from Chapter 2? Some instant coffee blends are positioned as being expensive, upmarket brands. Some people want to be seen to be paying more.

In societies where there are different ethnic groups, it will often be necessary and profitable to produce distinct product ranges to suit their different tastes and needs.

With many simple consumer products, such as cigarettes, drinks and toiletries, people may have strong brand preferences, even though the measurable physical characteristics of the various brands are virtually indistinguishable. Brand name, packaging, promotion, etc. are used to give the brand an 'image' that enables individual psychological and emotional preferences to be expressed. This approach is described as segmentation by life-styles.

People buy the same product for different reasons – to acquire different benefits. One customer may buy a car because it is safe, another because it is roomy. Targeting customer groups in this way is 'benefit segmentation'.

Given that a company will only have finite resources to use in publicizing their products or services, it will be important to direct these resources to the group or groups of people likely to have the greatest impact on sales performance.

5.3   An opportunity brewing for sales promotion

In March 1989 the Monopolies and Mergers Commission in the UK recommended that the brewing industries complex monopoly be dismantled in the name of increased competition. There were essentially two radical proposals:

- The number of pubs owned by any one brewer to be limited to 2000. (This could force the sale of 22000 pubs if adopted.)
- The tied-house system be abolished so that pub tenants should be able to sell at least one draught beer from a second brewer and should also be able to shop around for supplies of wines, spirits, soft drinks, ciders and alcohol-free and low alcohol beers from the most competitive source.

As a result, the predictions for business to become significantly more competitive seem to be well founded. Sales promotion companies can expect a period of high activity – directed at consumers, and increasingly at landlords.

With the loosening of the tied-house system, tenant landlords are likely to become key decision-makers over which brands are given space behind the bar. While it is impractical for tenants to buy wines from one source, beers from another and soft drinks from a third, they are expected to change to one-stop suppliers that offer good product ranges and service at the most competitive price. This new era of sophistication means that tenants will become more powerful, will be better paid and have better status. Pubs will be run by intelligent business men and women who will be wooed with better service and far better promotions.

Sales-promotion firms operating in this market are working on ways to improve the targeting of various breeds of publican. There is generally a diverse range of people, from retired servicemen to professional club stewards to sharp urban business men and women.

Promotions will soon be able to be aimed exclusively at, say, sports clubs, pub restaurants or working men's clubs.

Accurate targeting will be perhaps still more important when it comes to promoting niche products. Pimms presents a good example. The campaign aim was, in its second year, designed to improve distribution and extend the seasonality of the drink beyond 'Wimbledon fortnight'! A consumer pull-through promotion featured small booklets of anecdotes for consumers, and a series of jazz nights in selected outlets. Obviously Pimms is not to everyone's taste, and would not be well received in certain outlets. It must be targeted carefully to attractive pubs in upmarket or tourist locations ('Yuppie criteria', as one agency MD put it!).

Targeting the right pubs is particularly difficult because, for the most part, brewers have been slow to invest in the necessary on-trade market research. Some brewers were content in the past to use second-rate ideas too. Complacency set in during the 1960s and 1970s, when the market regularly grew by around 2 per cent year by year. Beer sales gradually levelled off in the 1980s and competition increased. This pattern seems set to continue into the 1990s, and there are signs that competition is such that more brewers are prepared to invest in retail market research to identify customer and outlet profiles and to make sales promotions in pubs more effective.

Ind Coope, a subsidiary of Allied Breweries, has built up a sophisticated database of outlet profiles within its estate of managed pubs. Outlets are divided into nine 'core-styles', ranging from community pubs in urban locations to country inns and disco pubs. By doing this exercise, Ind Coope limits the risk of alienation of customers with inappropriate promotions or inappropriate products. For example:

1   John Bull Bitter 'pool and darts nights' are aimed at community pubs but have no place in country inns.
2   Lucozade, not normally a product associated with pubs, was promoted specifically at pubs with an 18- to 24-year-old clientele and at pubs near sports and leisure centres.
3   A children's milk-shake promotion was successfully carried out in pubs with family rooms.
4   A low-calorie drinks promotion with giveaway calorie counter booklets for purchasers of Britvic Citrus Spring drinks was aimed at pubs with a higher proportion of female customers than usual.

Whitbread, another major brewery, has done a similar profile exercise, segmenting its 1050 management houses. Blanket promotions across 1000 different pubs are a thing of the past; such promotions would have been bland and not particularly cost-effective. Whitbread is not alone in recognizing that the regular six-pints-a-night-drinker is a dying breed. Whitbread is concentrating its efforts on occasional customers to make sure they put a Whitbread outlet on the shopping list of places to visit. To cater for this market, Whitbread are prepared to make radical changes to individual pubs. Each pub is considered as if it were a greenfield site. The location, the competition, and the potential, as well as the actual clientele are all reviewed before decisions are made on what sort of pub it should be.

By the nature of the business, brewers have to operate marketing strategies the opposite way to those used by most other retailers. Multiple retailers first develop a store concept and then find suitable sites for it as, if their store does not work in a particular area, it can move relatively easily. For brewers, however, the difficulties attached to getting licensed premises means they are saddled with the site and have to adapt the product accordingly.

The maxim 'knowledge equals power' applies as much to brewing as it does to other markets. The businesses that are best informed about their markets and how they can be segmented are the ones most likely to survive in the competitive world.

5.4 Geodemographics in search of new business

We have seen that there are several ways of defining a campaign's target market or audience: not only in terms of demographic factors, such as age, sex, social grade, region of the country and presence of children, but also in terms of heavy usage of particular products, and in terms of ownership of characteristics on which your product depends. (For example, if you market hair-care products, there is little point publicizing your products to bald men!) Which factors are most important naturally varies from company to company.

The division of markets by socio-economic groupings is widely used in marketing to define target markets as accurately as possible. In the UK the National Readership Surveys (NRS) classification of the population is one of the most basic definitions of a target group. The structure of the UK population by social grade is shown in Table 5.1. While this form of market targeting is used quite widely for advertisers in the press, it is nevertheless a useful parameter for targeting all publicity campaigns.

In the *Director's Report*, July 1988, published (monthly) by the Henley Centre, it was suggested that as the UK has divided into 'two nations' – the haves and the have-nots – businesses, not surprisingly, have tended to market to the haves. However, the report

Table 5.1 *UK social structure*

The National Readership Survey (UK) for classification of social grade		
Class/Grade	*Percentage of population*	*Description*
A	3	Higher managerial, administrative, or professional
B	13	Intermediate managerial, administrative or professional
C1	22	Supervisory or clerical and junior managerial, administrative, professional
C2	31	Skilled manual
D	19	Semi and unskilled manual
E	11	Those at the lowest levels of subsistence: pensioners, widows, casual workers, the unemployed

asked whether firms should turn their attention to the have-nots, who represent a sizeable proportion of the population, and provide brands, products and services to suit their needs?

Analysis of data collected for their 'Planning for Social Change' (PSC) survey indicates that while there are great discrepancies in income between social classes AB and DE, the difference in discretionary economic power (i.e. the money that is left after housing costs, food, bills, savings, etc.) is not as big. This means that for some products, e.g. magazines, snacks, and leisure activities (such as pubs, gambling and cinemas), the low paid have significant importance. See Figure 5.1.

Several companies have developed slightly different systems of geodemographic analysis. Such market segmentation systems enable consumers to be classified according to the type of residential area in which they live. Systems include ACORN, Super Profiles, Pinpoint and Mosaic; all are based on census data and their updates. ACORN (A Classification Of Residential Neighbourhoods) links people's addresses to their likely life-style and hence to their potential purchasing habits.

The ACORN classification of residential neighbourhoods divides areas of about 150 households (census enumeration districts) into thirty-eight different neighbourhood types. The classification takes into account forty different variables, e.g. demographic, housing, employ-ment characteristics of the residents. The thirty-eight neighbourhood types aggregate into eleven neighbourhood districts. The use of the electoral roll means that names and addresses can be produced for any given ACORN area.

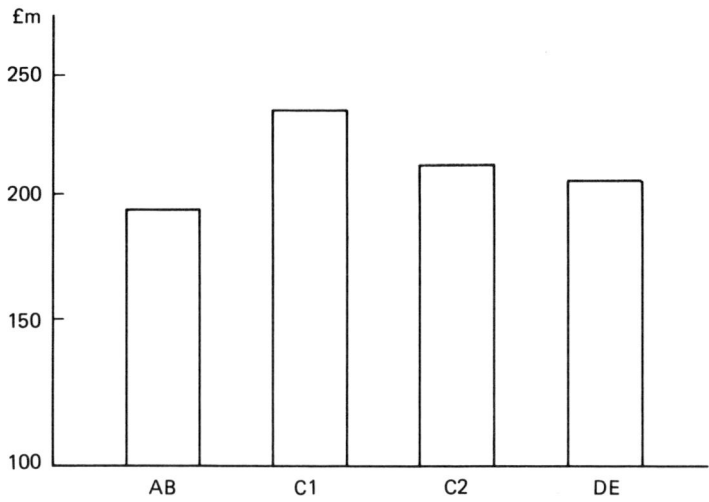

Figure 5.1 *Personal weekly spending money in 1987. Source: Henley Centre, Analysis of PSC Survey*

The eleven ACORN neighbourhood groups are the following:

Group A – agricultural areas.
Group B – modern family housing, higher incomes.
Group C – older housing of intermediate status.
Group D – poor quality, older terraced housing.
Group E – better off council estates.
Group F – less well off council estates.
Group G – poorest council estates.
Group H – multi-racial areas.
Group I – high status, non-family areas.
Group J – affluent suburban housing.
Group K – better-off retirement areas.

While address lists have obvious application to direct mail, knowing an area by its principal housing type helps in the selection of regional publicity campaigns. Suppose you wanted to set up demonstrations of your product in shopping precincts and you knew your product had particular appeal to, say, modern families on higher incomes. ACORN would be able to tell you where best to position them.

Another method by which you may be able to find out information about who your target group of customers are, without commissioning your own market research survey, is to use information provided from continuous surveys conducted by research firms that sell their findings to any company that wants them. One of the most important is the

Target Group Index (TGI), which is available both in the UK and the USA, and which analyses a large number of product groups in terms of their users. The products covered include many of the major markets, such as beer, cars, detergents, washing machines, soups and slimming products, and the analyses are in terms of the demographic profiles of the heavy, medium and light users, their reading and TV viewing habits (to help with media selection and in several other ways, particularly around life-style criteria).

Using such geodemographic analysis techniques, one can build up a clear picture of a target audience. This may have impact on the whole marketing mix, not just on the publicity component. Let us take an example from the financial market; the company name has been changed to protect confidentiality.

5.4.1   Target audience: example

Shekel (a financial company) approached an agency with a simple brief: to generate sales for Shekel's term share accounts. The brief contained little information about the target audience. Shekel thought that the majority of existing savers (at least 80 per cent) were around retirement age, although it admitted this figure was based on a small sample.

The agency examined TGI and produced three questions of interest:

- Have you yourself any current investments in a building society and, if 'yes', is it a term account?
- Have you investments in unit trusts (not linked to insurance), either yourself or jointly?
- Do you have a deposit or savings account at a bank?

The first two questions were researched further. The three questions highlighted two types of saver – the young using savings accounts and older people using deposit accounts. The TGI information relating to building society usage revealed more information about term account and unit trust ownership, as shown in Table 5.2. In summary, the data indicated a prime target audience of ABC1 adults, 55 years or more. Older C2 adults were a secondary target audience.

In order to learn more about the prospect most likely to respond to Shekel's publicity, the agency looked further at the TGI life-style questions. Relevant questions were selected and the variation from the norm was recorded for the primary target audience, ABC1 adults, 55 years or more. Data for ABC1 men, 55 years or more, was similarly classified. The results of this analysis (Table 5.3) show that the

Table 5.2 *Building society term account and unit trust ownership*

	Target audience profile
By sex:	Some bias to men
By age:	The two most important groups are 55–64 and over 65 years.
By social grade:	AB and C1 have highest index figures, although C2 adults need to be considered as a secondary group, due to the sheer number (12.5 million adults).
By income:	Slight bias to richer households.
By married/children:	Some bias to many years of marriage, with few children in the household.

Table 5.3 *Life-style analysis of likely Shekel prospects*

	ABC1 Adults 55+ Index vs pop.*	ABC1 Men 55+ Index vs pop.
Agree with		
– Like to be well organized and follow a routine	112	117
– Like to be well insured for everything	114	118
– Don't like the idea of being in debt	106	106
– I am a very good manager of money	125	120
Disagree with		
– Want to save but find it difficult	137	144
With inflation there is no point in trying to save money	105	110

* Index is a comparison of a particular group of adults to the population (pop.) as a whole using the base of 100 for the population as a whole.

individuals Shekel seeks to influence are fairly conservative in nature and believe they are good managers of money. The results were able to influence decisions across the marketing mix, because, rather than target the 65+ age group, Shekel was able to switch targets to ABC1 adults, 55 years or more: an important group of people who are probably at their peak of earning capacity and still have up to 10 years in employment. This is useful information which could be used in the following way.

Product

The term share accounts could be redesigned to appeal to the prime target audience, particularly in the period of saving to give the maximum capital growth, say, rather than income generation.

Price

In respect of Shekel, this part of the marketing mix could be taken to refer to return on investment. The research had shown that there was no strong disagreement among the target group with the notion that inflation limits the value of savings. Shekel's term share account's past performance should reflect the possible advantage of savings *vis-à-vis* inflation.

Other areas that would need to be addressed would be minimum investment clauses, withdrawal penalties and the period of savings. These issues differ in their level of importance between 55-year-olds and retired people.

Place

The prime target audience is likely to live in a different area than the assumed target of 65+ year olds. This will have obvious implications for the approach that Shekel might take in search of new customers. Further, they are likely to have different reading habits, approach the high street in a different frame of mind, and, as mentioned, have a different life-style, particularly in that they are still wage-earners, and debt holds less fears.

Promotion

The language used and style of all written communications need to address the target group – whether they cover advertising, direct mail, product leaflets, merchandising (say, at a building society counter), and even telephone selling. As the product has been designed to suit the target group, so too should the promotional message. Any illustrations used should be similarly appropriate to ABC1 55+ adults rather than purely 'retired people'.

So you see, researching the target audience thoroughly can have a significant impact on the success of your below-the-line publicity. Even the best executed techniques fall by the wayside if they are off target.

5.5 The links in the chain

Most marketing activities form part of a chain, e.g. from manufacturer to area distributor, to retail outlet, to end-user. Each of the links in the

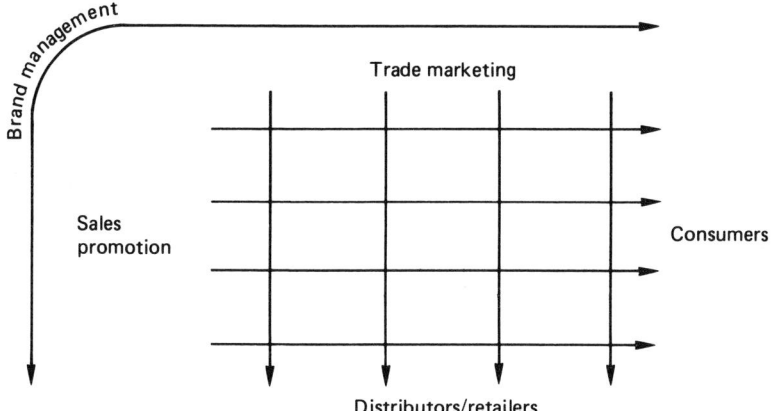

Figure 5.2 *Brand managers work through trade marketing and sales promotion groups, each addressing the needs of quite different target audiences*

chain will need its own communication and so may be an important target for below-the-line promotion.

There may be an overlapping grid of promotional activities as in Figure 5.2.

5.6 Why is a sales force a target audience for below-the-line activities?

Let us first clarify what is meant by a sales force in the context of being a target audience for your below-the-line activities. A sales force is any group of people in the continuum between manufacturer and consumer of the product or service who are concerned with the exchange of that product or service for profit. So, in this context, a sales force could include your own staff who sell the product to a wholesaler or retailer. In turn, wholesalers may have their own staff selling your product to retailers or other users of the product. Again, these retailers could have their own staff selling your original product to the ultimate customer or consumer.

The term 'user' has been employed to convey the fact that wholesalers may not necessarily sell the product only to retailers. For example, wholesalers to the catering trade sell their products to, say, hotels, which in turn sell-on to their patrons. Understanding the links in your supply chain is crucial to the ultimate success of your business, and it will be important to keep a balance between those efforts you make to sell-in your product to one group in the chain and those efforts you make to pull-through your product. Given the interest rate impact on borrowings, no traders will be keen to buy-in high stocks of products unless they are fairly certain of being able to sell them on again promptly.

Because wholesalers and retailers, by their very nature, will be handling a wide range of suppliers' products, yours are likely to be one of many. You will therefore need to be very clear about what features and benefits of your products influence the various links in your continuum. A range of colours might be perceived as a benefit to the ultimate consumer as far as your products are concerned; but a retailer might not be so pleased because he may have to stock a wider range than he might have space for. Next-day delivery direct from your warehouse might be the benefit that persuades the retailer to stock and promote your product in preference to a competitor's.

A retailer's own shop assistants may never know about the business dealings that have gone on behind the scenes; all they are aware of is the product in their shop. Do they know about the next-day delivery direct from your warehouse? When they have a busy Saturday afternoon and a customer who wants a 'blue one' but they have only green ones in stock, who loses the sale? Everyone! So, even if you have developed the right marketing mix and taken great pains (and expense) to deliver the necessary level of service in support of your products, there is still a target audience that needs to be addressed if the final link in the chain, the humble assistant, is not to fail.

Given that you have identified your own staff, and various intermediates' staff, right down to the shop assistant (and the customer target audience), how do you go about influencing each group in the supply chain? Let us consider each in turn:

5.6.1 Your own sales staff

Involve them early
Your sales staff are on your side, so keep them there. You will probably have already used their experience in defining what makes the sale, what benefits their day to day contacts respond to. Bringing the field force early into what has been planned will help them to plan their part of the execution or implementation phase. If you have designed the latest phase of publicity activities down to the last detail and expect the sales force to implement those plans, always remember that they may already have a full diary of appointments; so it is no good trying to pull two representatives in to help with a trade exhibition in Brighton if they have firm appointments already booked in Newcastle the same day.

Make the plans clear and your promotions easy
There is no point trying to complicate the issue by offering quantity discounts on twelve different lines a dozen different ways. For example:

PRODUCT A   two free on ten purchased.
PRODUCT B   three free on thirteen purchased.
PRODUCT C   five free on twenty-four purchased. . . and so on.

While the accountants will be happy that on a cost-of-goods basis the offer is at the same ratio to gross margin for each product, the sales force and the trade will not thank you for it. Why not try to standardize on, say, '10 per cent extra free product on all orders invoiced in . . .'

Wherever possible, add value to your brands
While this has a positive effect on the end-consumer, it will also have a positive effect on the sales team. If cutting price or dealing on quantity becomes the norm, the trade will begin to devalue the brand and the sales staff may all too easily drop into bad habits. It is much better to give your sales team some 'added value' to sell, rather than to give away discounts.

Give your sales staff the tools to get results
Salespeople like to make sales. One of the big rewards that comes from the job is to see customers buying from them. So give them the promotional tools that make their job easier and watch the impact on your turnover.

One good example comes from the business-to-business world. A company was operating in a highly competitive market and had reached a point where, with around 10 per cent market share, it could get no further. There was no real differential from competitors, but its service package made the difference. However, the sales team had reached a point of virtual despair; they could win no new business contracts. The R & D programme had no new products due for launch for a couple of years, and existing customers were not a source of extra business. The service package was second to none, yet there were still potential customers to be won. How was the company to influence these potential customers?

The solution came from a very straightforward approach. The potential customers, while recognizing that the service package seemed to be worth changing their product specifications for, still needed further convincing. Trade magazines had a wide distribution throughout the whole industry, but one was unique in being produced as a video. The producers of the magazine were contracted to interview one of the company's existing good customers as part of an industry profile feature. A 10-minute film was produced, demonstrating the product in action, and also permitting an independent third-party endorsement to be shown direct to the whole industry.

Within a month, after the sales team had done its work, 6 per cent more contracts were signed. While details of the company remain confidential, it does exemplify the power of editorial publicity. See Chapter 13.

Reward the salespeople's efforts

More can be achieved by the positive reinforcement of successful action than by threat or fear or punishment. This is the basis for a massive incentive business. Set targets that are realistic and achievable, get them agreed at the outset, and reward those who achieve or exceed expectations. There is a school of thought that says that reward for reaching targets is to be found in the contracted salary for the job alone, extra rewards being due only to those exceeding targets. Only you can decide what motivates the people in your employ. Staff incentives will be picked up again in Chapter 8.

5.6.2   Trade staff

This group of people needs special attention, not least because its members are not on your direct payroll and may not necessarily do what you want them to, just because your company says so.

Why should they stock your product instead of someone else's?

- It may be that *their* customers want them to.
- It may be because they make more money out of your products than out of others.
- Perhaps it is because they like you.

Whatever the reason, it is important that you find out why, just in case you stop doing it! It may be that you have created such consumer demand that if this particular trader doesn't stock and supply the product, another will. Perhaps because of this the trader realizes he has a good turnover with your product, and he may forgive the small unit margin you allow. Alternatively, you may have been able to agree extra credit terms, improved your delivery frequency, or actually offered extra margin so that he takes the product on board. Perhaps it is because you always remember to invite him to the Varsity Match or send him a Christmas cake each year that he carries on doing business with you.

Remember, you may deal with a dozen different wholesalers but each wholesaler may only deal with a few suppliers of your particular product. So what is your competitive differential?

Make doing business with you easy
This means paying attention to the whole marketing mix. Attend to product quality and performance and reduce the number of product returns that your dealers have to handle. Make sure you are offering competitive value for money, in whatever form that is required by your supply chain. Ensure your distribution and availability are such that you do not keep missing sales through inability to supply: you may not get another chance. Keep your promotions simple and relevant to the target audience. Finally, address those service issues that ensure your customers come back for more.

Incentives for trade-sales staff
With probably thousands of different lines for wholesalers to carry, how can you make your products stand out among the many? If you knocked a pound off the recommended price, that would reduce your profits, and as the trade takes a margin off its sales, that would reduce its profits too. We saw in Chapter 2 how to calculate the extra turnover required to replace that lost profit both to you and your trader. What is more, you would need to communicate that pound off to the consumer for it to have any effect. How will it stand out among the mass of other 'money off' offers?

But suppose you offered a pound voucher to the wholesaler representative who took the order? Given the choice between a competitive product and yours, which would the representative favour? You will need to sell the idea to the wholesaler management first, and the scheme must be easy to operate, but that would be 'added value'. In its simplest form that voucher could be a record or book token, but it could be one of any number of incentive vouchers redeemable against a mass of products in high-street shops.

Education as an incentive
Just as the people working on your manufacturing production line will respond favourably to being informed about the external company activities, so will all the wholesalers' staff. If you take time to explain (usually over a free lunch) in straightforward terms what your products are intended for, and perhaps how consumers use them, then you will begin to find that the chap who drives the fork-lift truck will take that little extra care the next time he has your product on the

'picking docket'. Similarly, trade representatives will also respond well to your offer of a buffet supper and a presentation of the technical aspects of your products that are of relevance, and you will be helping them to sell your products on.

5.6.3   Shop assistants

As mentioned earlier, they are a key link in the chain, and the last hurdle to getting your product actually into the hands of consumers. There are a number of important issues that you could address.

Education
If a consumer comes into a chemist's shop looking for a commodity, say something for a mild muscle strain, he/she has a choice of ointments, sprays or liniments. If the customer has no particular brand in mind, what can the sales assistant do?

(a) Suggest the customer goes to look for himself on the shelves?
(b) Recommend one that someone came in for last time?
(c) Recommend one that he has used himself recently?
(d) Recommend one that he/she been specially informed about?

In this situation, where the customer is open to direct suggestion by the shop assistant, foreknowledge of your product by the assistant is essential.

This can be built up, with the retailer's approval, by distance-learning techniques, just as Wyeth has done with its Algipan range. A very simple questionnaire was sent to assistants through the pharmacist. The assistants were given product information, a simple multiple choice questionnaire, and a branded safety pocket knife (useful for opening boxes of products when replenishing shelves). Each assistant returning a correct questionnaire was given a certificate of competence, a record token, and a personalized name badge – while not branded with a name, the badge did reflect Algipan's new pack design.

Reward-linked learning is a particularly useful technique when you are trying to influence a large target audience at a distance – the case with shop assistants.

Other incentives
We are all pretty familiar with the token schemes run by the petrol companies. A similar scheme is sometimes easy to operate for shop assistants. If the people who are in a position to detail your products to

potential consumers are the same that open the outers of product and restock the shelves, it is relatively simple to include 'trading-stamps' in the outers for shop assistants to collect in exchange for selected incentives. While the logistics of the scheme need to be thoroughly worked through to be fair to all assistants, such a scheme can have a remarkable effect on increasing turnover. One scheme, still operated by a UK veterinary company, lets veterinary nurses collect tokens in packs of vitamins and mineral tablets for dogs. The tokens are exchanged for toiletries, wine, or tins of biscuits. The nurse often influences the sale, not the veterinary surgeon.

5.7 The decision-making unit

Occasionally one may find, particularly in business-to-business operations, that there is a single product used by one group of people clearly defined as the target audience. However, the product is not actually bought by them, the buying decision being made by committee or decision-making unit (DMU). It will be important for the sales team to make effective contact at all levels in the DMU.

In industrial selling particularly the purchase will be influenced by the DMU. Design engineer, works manager, buyer and finance director, could make up one type of DMU. The salesperson would need to communicate with them all, highlighting different aspects of the product to appeal to the separate target audiences: the design engineer is concerned with specification and performance; the works manager similarly concerned but also from the point of view of overall efficiency, for example the product's ease of installation and service; the buyer with price and payment terms; and the finance director with cash flow, depreciation, capital deployment and so forth. In each case the product's promoted benefits vary.

Finding out who are the members of a decision-making unit, what their precise roles are, and how they can be influenced, is essential for successful sales. Although this is especially true in industrial markets, it may well apply in other situations. For example, insurance and double-glazing salesmen know that it pays to talk to both partners in a household, as they both play a part in the decision to buy. Even in everyday purchases such as breakfast cereals, various members of the household, especially children in this case, have a strong influence, a fact recognized in the way such products are promoted. Refer to the example of Quaker cereals (p. 46).

Within any decision-making unit one may find some (or even all) of the following categories:

1 *Users*: those who will actually operate the word processor or the fork-lift truck. They are likely to be consulted by those authorizing the purchase, and certainly can have an effect on post-purchase satisfaction and hence future sales. Free training for users can be used as a promotional tool, although such training is becoming mandatory, especially in the computer world.

2 *Buyers*: the professional purchasing people. Their influence is high when there are regular repeat purchases, particularly of raw materials or standard components. Other voices dominate, however, if there is high technical input or heavy capital needed.

3 *Influencers*: these are people who may not be directly engaged in the buying process yet may be referred to as 'opinion leaders' in their field of expertise. General practitioners are unlikely to prescribe a drug without some recognized third-party endorsement by such specialists or consultants.

4 *Deciders*: decisions may be taken 'down the line' for low cost or routine purchases but are usually at top level for those where big money is needed; however, there can be surprising departures from this norm. It is often the case that tens of thousands of pounds can be spent on an ill-conceived media schedule or a poorly planned promotion, but approval for £200 worth of capital – say for an overhead projector – would need to be obtained from the board.

5 *Gatekeepers*: those who 'get in the way', e.g. buyers who resist the desire of a salesman to approach the engineer. Such 'gatekeepers' are occasionally fearful of having their decision-making authority diluted or taken away. Direct-marketing techniques can usually get around the gatekeeper.

6 *Specifiers*: architects specify building materials, design engineers specify components, and, once decided, it is very difficult to have the specifications altered later. If your product does not 'meet the spec.', then it may never be accepted. Such situations have to be recognized and the specifier convinced early on that a specification embracing your product will satisfy his requirement.

Each member of the decision-making unit therefore presents a different target market, each seeing your product from a slightly different viewpoint. You may need to use quite different arguments to convince each member about the suitability of your product. Indeed you may have to use quite different techniques, spanning the whole promotions mix above- and below-the-line in order to reach them all before a decision to purchase can be reached.

5.7.1   NHS decision-making

One excellent example of a decision-making unit can be found from Nicholas Laboratories Hospital Division's experience of approaching the National Health Service hospitals to tell them about their 'Kylie' bed sheet. This article was an incontinence blanket placed directly under patients. The top surface was hydrophobic and allowed any fluids to pass directly through to the hyperabsorbent backing material. In this way the patient remained dry and the skin in far better condition than with the usual disposable absorbent pad. The 'Kylie' was re-usable, and tests had shown that it could be machine-washed in hospital laundries so frequently that the 'cost-per-use' was much less than for disposables. Eight groups formed the decision-making unit for any given district hospital group:

(a) *Ward nurses* needed to be shown the product in action to prove to themselves it worked, and that it was easy to use.
(b) *Staff nurses* running busy wards needed to be sure that bedmaking took no longer with the 'Kylie'.
(c) *Doctors* needed to be sure that bedsores were not aggravated: indeed, the Kylie was shown to improve the condition.
(d) *Hospital administrators* needed to be confident that the 'one on the bed, one in the wash and one in store' concept was a justification for three Kylie sheets per patient – night.
(e) Naturally the *hospital laundry* needed to be satisfied that it could handle the extra bulk, that drying time fitted into its work routines and that the costs were acceptable.
(f) *Finance committees* were also a prime target audience, because they needed to be convinced that the extra costs were justified.
(g) The *stores manager* needed to make the appropriate requisition and inventory, and had to be convinced that the new bulky item could be handled satisfactorily by his system.
(h) *Community nurses*, while not necessarily in the final decision, needed to be approached so that they were aware of the product and its use as patients left hospital.

Despite addressing each group and satisfying their varied needs, Nicholas Laboratories still had a tough job on its hands. As David Edwards, senior product manager, explained:

The Kylie bed sheet is an expensive item to purchase but easily justifiable on a cost per patient–night basis. The common incontinence pad it is designed to replace is a low unit cost *revenue* expense, as far as the hospitals are concerned. A hospital would need to make a considerable *capital* outlay on the Kylie bed sheet to equip itself fully. Because they are essentially different budgets, a significant revenue saving is not immediately transferable to a capital budget.

5.8 Summary

1 General statements about the targets for publicity are inadequate. Target audiences must be defined as precisely as possible.
2 Market segmentation, by 'geodemographics' or other means, is an important way of doing this.
3 The links in the distribution chain may be important targets.
4 There must be strong communication with salespeople, not only in our own company but also in our distributors', retailers', etc. sales teams.
5 In industrial markets the people who make a purchasing decision – members of the decision-making unit – may all need to be targeted.

6 The measurement and control of below-the-line promotion

'Below-the-line expenditure in the UK is now estimated to have reached £5 billion a year – but well over £1 billion of that is wasted on ineffectual and unmeasured promotions,' said *P R Week*.[1]

What are *you* doing about it!

6.1 What are you trying to achieve in the first place?

One of the first steps towards measurement and control of your below-the-line promotion expenditure is to be both clear and honest about what you are trying to achieve. As we saw when we were briefing an agency to help us with our promotional campaign (p. 61), some fundamental heart-searching analysis about objectives was essential to successful campaign planning. The measurement of the achievement of these objectives in an equally clear and honest way is similarly essential to the control of the funding of that campaign. Only if you have checked this for yourself can you be sure whether or not a similar promotion exercise should be repeated again. There is absolutely no point in spending vast sums of money – profit – on, say, high-gloss, expensive technical literature, when nobody reads it, or worse, having read it, finds it totally unsuited to its task.

Above-the-line expenditure on advertising probably represents the largest amount of promotional money spent, often with no precise measure of what it can be expected to achieve. Advertising is a means of communication. Therefore, its results can only be measured in terms of communication goals, in terms of the cost per advertising message delivered per customer for a given result. Advertising changes attitudes, and this change can be measured, provided of course you know the prospective customers' attitudes at the outset and how you would like them to change (realistically). Then you will have to use the appropriate medium *enough* so that the audience receives that message a sufficient number of times to establish that changed attitude.

In other words, an advertising goal is a specific communication task, to be accomplished among a defined audience to a given degree in a given period of time. The lack of progress in the development of campaign evaluation is generally to be put down to the lack of defined specific goals, or, alternatively, to the setting of goals that are unrealistic.

But what of below-the-line promotion? The decision to convert that favourable attitude, so carefully developed by above-the-line means, into favourable behaviour, i.e. to buy the product, depends on a number of things. Consider why a consumer might buy a product in a food shop:

- 'That looks better than my usual product . . .'
- 'This one is cheaper . . .'
- 'That looks worth saving tokens for . . .'
- 'My neighbour suggested I try . . .'
- 'I saw that advertised . . . I'll give it a try . . .'
- 'This is new . . .'
- 'What a good idea, that'll save me time . . .'
- 'There is more in this one for the same price . . .'
- 'I might as well use the coupon . . .'
- 'The kids eat it . . .'

Typical influences in the industrial situation also give an idea of the complexity of the buying decision:

- 'This matches the engineer's spec . . .'
- 'My MD plays golf with the supplier MD . . .'
- 'Saw it at an exhibition . . .'
- 'Salesman convinced me of its quality . . .'
- 'Read about it in the press/mail/advertising . . .'
- 'Swiss machines are always more reliable . . .'
- 'My car is OK, I guess their trucks are too . . .'
- 'They took me to the Middlesex 7s . . .'
- 'All our other machines are of this make . . .'
- 'We get a better service deal with them . . .'

So you see the usual price – supply – performance – service criteria are not the only bases for decision-making. To take expenditure on above-the-line advertising or below-the-line promotion, or even on the marketing function, and expect to be able to relate it directly and precisely to sales is clearly unrealistic. It is made more complicated by the fact that for many products, particularly industrial products, the gestation period between 'cause and effect' can be very long – one authority has estimated an average time-lag, depending on the product, of between 1 and 4 years.

By being clear and honest about what you are trying to achieve by your below-the-line promotion campaign, you are well on your way to realistic and meaningful evaluation of the below-the-line expenditure. This will help limit the considerable wastage in below-the-line promotion.

6.2   What are your criteria for value for money?

Philip Kotler, a Montgomery Ward Professor of Marketing at the Graduate School of Management, North Western University, Illinois, wrote:

> The core concern of marketing is that of producing desired responses in free individuals by the judicious creation and offering of values. The marketer is attempting to get value from the market through offering value to it. The marketer's problem is to create attractive values. Value is completely subjective and exists in the eyes of the beholding market. Marketers must understand the market in order to be effective in creating value. This is the essential meaning of marketing.[2]

When you are spending money below-the-line on your promotional campaigns, you will be trying to 'add value' to your products or services. You will be trying to show your company and its products or services in the best possible light to make the target audience turn to you rather than a competitor. You must therefore have some *value* that is perceived as better for that target group than your competitors'. What you will be trying to do is to get value from your promotion by adding value to your product, but you will need to get more back than you have given away to increase your profit.

For example, you may be producing a hair shampoo that costs the consumer £1.00 for 100 ml. Suppose, in order to make your product stand out from the rest, you produce a 125ml bottle and sell it for the same price as the 100 ml one, i.e. £1.00. To the consumer the extra 25 ml is worth 25p. To you, the manufacturer, the extra shampoo and the increased packaging/labelling costs to communicate the offer might only have been, say, 10p. In this way you will have been able to add 25p *value* to your product but it would only have cost you 10p.

Alternatively, you could have reduced the price of your product by 10p., i.e. '100 ml for the new low price of 90p.' From the consumers' point of view you have just devalued your product. (In this example you will in fact probably have some additional on-costs in communicating the new low price, such as new labelling, so your costs are likely to be greater than the 10p. off your income per bottle.) Either way, you would be reducing your gross margins on the unit, be it a new 125 ml bottle or the cheaper 100 ml standard, by the same amount, and you would have to sell more units to make the same gross profit (refer to Table 2.1).

It is therefore by looking at the increase in sales units generated that we can get one measure of the value for money on this example's publicity expenditure on the below-the-line promotion of the new pack. Is the extra 10p. the new 125 ml pack is costing you worth more to you in terms of what it has done to the perceived value your customers hold of the product than the effect that 10p. off the gross margin will have on your profit? Even if the 'added value' of the extra 25 ml free had the same effect on sales volumes that the 10p. price cut would have, the added value might be more useful, in terms of giving the brand an improved value-for-money tag in the consumers' mind.

Value for money in below-the-line promotion campaigns means different things to different people. Take, for example, an industrial company with a sales team of just a few people who cover large international territories, doing business through distributors. The cost of mounting a display on a reasonable exhibition stand at an industry trade fair is very high. Suppose this company exhibited, and during the 3 or 4 days of the trade fair only a handful of people were talked to, one may be justified in saying that the event was an utter disaster. Suppose, however, that among the handful of visitors were two or three of the key people from the distributors in overseas territories who went away happy, having seen the range of products and had some fruitful business meetings. The cost of exhibiting compared to two or three overseas visits by key sales staff begins to look more reasonable. What is more, it may not have been possible for those salespeople to meet key distributors in their home countries in the same few days as on the exhibition. The sales-people have saved time and are now free to pursue other goals.

Time-share companies discovered that if people could actually stay in the apartments on holiday, they were more likely to buy. Therefore, in order to encourage people to go abroad, time-share companies run simple competitions where one of the prizes is a week's free accommodation in an apartment.

Club La Costa ran a simple 'match the photograph with the place name' competition and offered a big first prize (a free time-share apartment) to encourage participation, and 500 second prizes of a free week in an apartment anywhere in the world. Over 80 per cent of second prize winners went to the London offices to collect their prize – and to receive the 2-hour hard sell – and four out of five took the free holiday week. Of those enjoying a week in the time share, 20 per cent bought a time-share agreement. This represented such good value to Club La Costa that it repeated the competition again in the same year. Among the wider selection of prizes were 2400 giving 1 week's free accommodation.

To time-share organizations, the cost of such competitions represents good value for money, because they are largely responsible for getting people to visit their showrooms or apartments. For them, this is important, because time share has had such a poor reputation among the buying public that even a considerable expenditure above-the-line is unlikely to have such a good effect in getting people to purchase the product, even though the public's attitude may be improved.

6.3 Evaluation of sales promotions

When we looked at the difference between adding 25 ml free product on 100 ml of shampoo at a cost of 10p. and compared that to the (virtually) same cost of reducing the price by 10p, the criteria of value for money dealt with the consumers' reaction to the brand's value in their minds. However, there are more fundamental issues to consider in the evaluation of sales promotions. These fall into six main areas where data is available to help you with more tangible evaluations, particularly within retail markets, although some are more widely applicable.

6.3.1 *What do the sales force say?*

You have developed a promotion on your products which you hope will have the desired effect of firing the enthusiasm of your sales force, the trade, and ultimately the customers. Before your new promotion packs have left the factory, your salespeople will have been busy. Has the promotion helped in negotiations? You can expect one of three answers when you ask the sales force how it has got on:

(a) The promotion has antagonized the trade and is unlikely to be taken up sufficiently to have an impact on customers.
(b) The promotion has generated a terrific response in the trade: enthusiasm abounds and pre-selling has been brisk. Provided the customers like it too, everyone will be delighted.
(c) Neither of the above – the trade is non-committal, so wait and see.

Provided you have analysed the market well and planned the promotion carefully, implementation should be straightforward and this early stage of evaluation should not give you too many surprises.

6.3.2   What are your sales figures like?

Once you have established from your sales force how the trade is responding, your sales drive will be in full swing. Keep an eye on your factory gates; if they don't close for the rush of lorries taking product out, then you are achieving two things:

- You are stocking the trade
- You are pushing your competitors out of the limelight.

While stock-in to the trade is no assurance of consumer appeal, you will have more product on shelf, at least during the promotion period. Stock pressure and display facings generate sales-out in themselves, even if the consumer is not actually responding to the promotion *per se*. If you have achieved ex-factory sales, you are fairly certain of some success.

6.3.3   What are your store checks and display records like?

You may go out yourself and do random samples of representative examples of the major multiples. In this way you will get a feel for the national picture. Similarly, your sales force may be undertaking surveys of shelf displays at each call. If randomly checked by regional supervisors, the reports can be relied upon to give you a picture of the impact your promotion is having.

Equally, when in the stores, you can ask the store managers to give their reaction to the promotion in terms of the level of call-off of stock from stockroom and depot on to shelves.

6.3.4   Perhaps you have a promotion requiring redemptions.

If your promotion necessitates the collection of tokens in return for a free offer of some description, the measurement of redemptions gives you a guide to consumer uptake. Coupons can be another source of information, although because they are redeemed by the retailer first, the timescale is a little longer. (If you do get a flood of coupons early in the promotion period, you probably have considerable mal-redemption, which needs investigation.)

The rate of redemptions you get from a promotion depends on the number of proofs-of-purchase you require (high and low numbers are relative to the normal repeat-purchasing of the product) and on whether or not there is a closing date. See Figure 6.1.

When looking at your redemption rates, first decide if your promotion is behaving much as you expected, or whether there is something wrong. Unexpectedly heavy redemptions can have dangerous implications on your budgeted expenditure. On the other hand, provided sales are good, low redemption may not be too much of a problem.

6.3.5 What happens to your sales after the promotion ends?

Any below-the-line promotional exercise should not be viewed in isolation from the rest of the publicity or marketing mix, or from the strategic and developmental plans of the business. So one cannot realistically look at just the period of a promotional activity without reviewing the whole financial year.

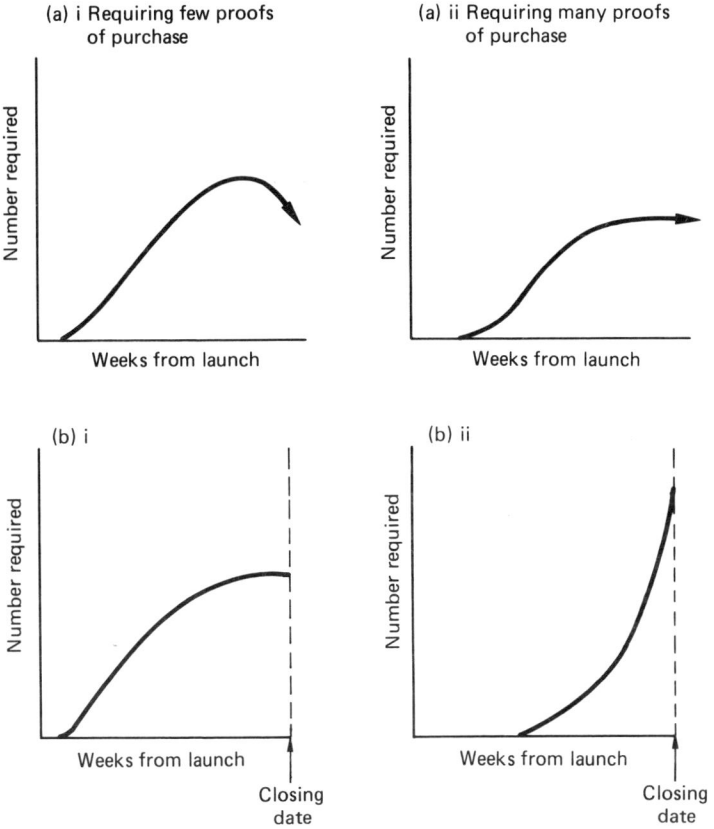

Figure 6.1 *Typical redemption patterns for: (a) open-ended promotions and (b) closed-ended promotions*

The promotion may have effects (called 'lead effects') on the period running up to the promotion, e.g. customers put off buying in a high-street store until the 'sale'. 'Lagged effects' are experienced immediately after the marketing effort, and can have both positive and negative effects on sales. Suffice to say that it will be important to view the general sales picture rather than the picture during the period of promotion alone.

6.3.6   Audits

Usually the last information source to come in is the data supplied by the various audits, depending on the industry. Neilsen is well recognized as the standard for retail audits. Intercontinental Medical Statistics (IMS) and 'Script Count' are recognized in the medical field . IMS also runs a comprehensive audit of wholesaler sales to veterinary surgeons: towards the end of 1989 it launched 'Flexivet', an adapted system based on the pharmaceuticals industry, which is a computer-based audit. Subscribers could look at data in a variety of ways – by region, by product group, and so forth. The attraction is that subscribers receive their data by telephone linkage through personal computers, and can therefore manipulate the figures at will. Such systems are becoming commonplace in many industries.

With retail and consumer audits one can find out, in a statistically balanced way, what happened to:

1   Sales to consumers out of the store.
2   Distribution.
3   In stock and out of stock
4   Brand shares.

Other useful information can also be gained. However, by this time your promotion is usually over, so there is little you can do to apply the information immediately, correct a mistake, or to maximize an opportunity as far as that promotion is concerned. Remember, though, the audits do complete evaluations for you and can be used to guide the next phase of the plan.

What else can you do to evaluate your publicity campaign? The five areas on pp. 97–99 describe the basic approaches to evaluating your campaign in terms of sales, but there is more that you could do to augment your understanding of what happened. For example, you could consider the following:

1 *Consumer attitude or behaviour tests,* either specially commissioned or from a panel that covers a variety of issues through continuous reporting.
2 *Trade attitudes* are important to research. It would be sensible to find out what the trade is thinking about the market in general, and also about you in particular. It has to be said that few manufacturers are keen on embarking on such research. Remember that:

   (a) A salesman may not be told the truth. The trade may think more of you than it would admit to a salesman just before negotiating on price.
   (b) A salesman may not hear the truth. Some salesmen mentally dismiss negative feedback from the trade in the hurly-burly of selling. Occasionally the salesman may have a particular gripe, which he will magnify in its importance to try to get head office to do something about it.
   (c) A retailer may not tell your company the truth if he suspects it might be turned back on him as a selling argument. Independent researchers are essential in getting the trade to talk objectively about the market.
   (d) Occasionally retailers can get the wrong idea about a market and the products in it. If you don't know what the retailer thinks, you will not know how right or wrong he is.

3 *'Satisfaction checks'* can be used to ask consumers, in the interests of better marketing, to give their reaction to the premium and the promotion as a whole. Responses to such questionnaires are usually high, and very valuable.
4 Any unsolicited communication from a consumer should be taken note of, whether complaining or praising. In research terms of course a few letters for or against mean nothing; however, they can carry considerable weight in the company.

6.4 Lead and lagged effects: their influence on success

Once you have finished with a sales promotion, you will be back to selling plain stock again. You may be basking in the success of a substantial sales gain during the promotion, but what happens next? Do you fall back to your pre-promotion level? Do you retain some of that incremental volume? Or do you sink below the pre-promotion level? It can be at this point that the value of your promotion is reduced, or completely negated. Figure 6.2 shows what can happen,

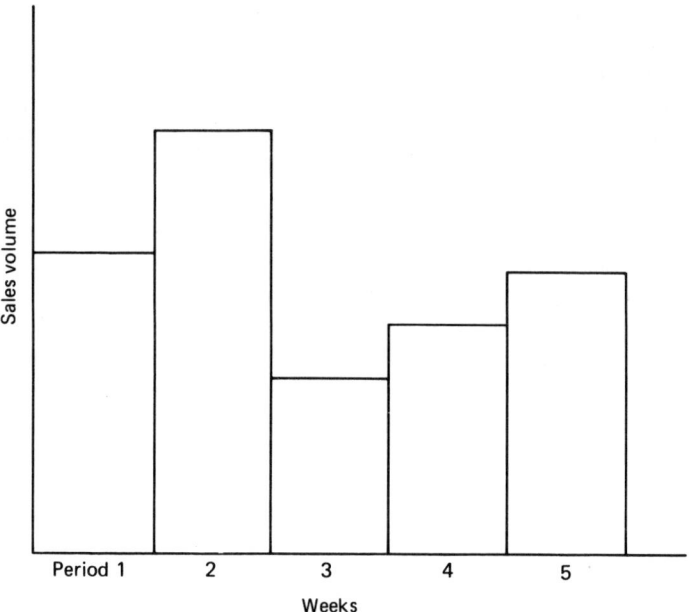

Figure 6.2 *Schematic illustration of lagged effects following a 'successful' promotion in period 2*

and indeed often does. It is not, fortunately, a general rule. It does serve, however, to emphasize the point made earlier in the section – always take the long term view of your position before, during and after your promotion.

In this figure sales were substantially greater during the period of promotion (period 2) but the gain was brief. In the subsequent two periods sales fell sharply, below normal sales levels, recovering only in period 5. The average sales over the five periods were no greater than those achieved in period 1, before the promotion. There was probably no real gain achieved from the promotion: in fact, in budget terms, it may have produced a painful loss.

There are a number of reasons for negative lagged effects:

(a) Sales into the trade during the period of the promotion may not have been fully worked through by consumer pull. Thus, in the subsequent periods, the trade reduced its orders to let the extra product work its way through.

(b) Retailers may have considered that they have done well enough by your promoted line in period 2, and decided to favour a competitor who may have had a promotion running during period 3.

(c) Perhaps the sales promotion was designed only to generate immediate sales and had no follow-through to encourage repeat purchasing, business which would have substantially helped the situation in subsequent periods.

Some promotions, particularly those aimed at enticing new users to try a product (or lapsed users to try it again) can have positive lagged effects in subsequent periods, particularly if the performance of the product in use meets the consumer's expectations and the product is repurchased in those later periods. Ignoring positive lagged effects leads to underestimating the effects of the publicity efforts and to employing lower budgets than one might have done. Since many lagged effects are negative and can limit the success of a promotion, ignoring them can have the opposite effects.

Lead effects, while less familiar, are as important. They occur when sales increase or decrease *ahead* of the publicity that causes them. An example would be Harrods' customers putting off buying until the sale. Positive lead effects are rare, because sales are hardly ever higher before a promotion than during one. One example might be when a manufacturer is launching a new model, and part of the promotion of the new model would be to sell off the earlier model at a reduced price in order to clear the showroom. The price of the old model might be sufficiently attractive for the number of units sold in the month preceding the new model's launch to exceed the first month's sales of the new version.

An area gas board ran one promotion in early 1986 that, on the face of it, was a success. During a 2-month period in early spring sales engineers were paid extra commission on all new gas boilers fitted during the promotion. The plan was to encourage the salesman to win extra business during a fairly quiet period of the year, in the hope of reducing the 'autumn rush', when consumers realize their old boiler needs replacing as they turn it on for the first time following the summer. During the promotion period new boiler sales and installations were an all-time high.

However, on closer analysis, it was discovered that virtually 40 per cent of sales during the promotion period were due to lead effects. Sales engineers were holding back orders until the promotion, and encouraging customers to postpone purchases until the promotion. The promotion led to a loss of profit even if the lead effects were ignored. The increased commission offered to the sales engineers during the promotion seemed to have the biggest adverse effect on profit. Announcing the future commission arrangements too far ahead of the promotion allowed the sales engineers to delay customers ordering, so the gas board paid out commission on orders that it need not have done.

Incidentally, while mentioning salesmen's commissions, one can learn from the mistake made by one company, which paid out commissions calculated on the basis of size of monetary value of contracts for supply. The company agreed to pay the usual (for the market in question) retrospective discounts 'up-front' (i.e. if the customer signed a contract for the supply of, say, £10,000 worth of product, the company would pay £2,000 at the outset). Representatives were paid a commission on the absolute size of the initial contract of supply. Customers were encouraged to overestimate their needs, agree to over-large contracts, and receive substantial boosts to their cash flow in up-front discounts. The salesmen enjoyed significant commission payments. After a year, when a few customers had only taken around 60 per cent of their contract, the problem was out in the open. However, the impact of this loophole was minimized by three factors:

(a) The calibre of the salesmen, who did not abuse the system too much.
(b) The vigilance of the sales manager, who knew the customers well enough to know when a contract looked over-large.
(c) The manufacturer limited the promotion of up-front discounts and commission payments to one range of products where that segment of the market was already well satisfied by the many existing competitors.

Even from a 'standing start' with the launch of a new range of products, this company gained a 9 per cent value share of the market segment within 18 months of launch (name and industry withheld for reasons of confidentiality). However, how would your company have survived with such a promotion?

Remember, always, that lead and lagged effects have an impact on your publicity campaign. A question that is always very difficult to answer but is worth asking yourself every time is 'How good would your sales *and* profit have been OVERALL if you had not run the promotion campaign?'

6.5 Coupon redemptions: more than just a promotional technique

The distribution of coupons has been widely used for decades as a method of sales promotion. Coupons form an alternative currency that consumers can use to offset the cost of their shopping; coupons can also be used as a means of added value to a product. The use of coupons will be explored more fully in Chapter 8. However, for the moment, we can look at coupon-redemption as a way of making life a little harder for us. If we consider the standard '5p. off your next purchase' coupon, clipped from an advertisement in a magazine, redeemed at the supermarket against the purchase of your toothpaste, and ultimately sent back by that retailer to you for settlement, it will yield considerable information.

Suppose you inserted one advertisement in several magazines and each advertisement carried a coupon, just like any other for that brand, but for each separate magazine where the coupon appeared it carried a simple, discreet code number, say WO/10/91. This would mean that it was carried in *Woman's Own* in October 1991. Similarly WR/12/91 would mean *Woman's Realm*, December 1991.

If you used a redemption closing date of, say, 3 months post-insertion of the advertisements, by mid-1991 you would be able to review your coupon redemptions and make rational decisions about:

(a) Which journal created the best response (a guide on media selection for advertising toothpaste).
(b) Which month, October or December, had the best response rate (an influence on media scheduling).
(c) Which stores were favoured by coupon collectors, Tesco or Sainsburys, for example (useful for your national account people).
(d) Depending on the frequency of returns by the stores, the time between the advertisement appearing and the consumer using the coupon.

Such information will help you plan future campaigns. Remember that if a consumer returns a coupon to you, then that consumer is communicating with you – so you should listen.

Of course coupons clipped from magazine advertisements are not the only techniques that you can use to research your market and the people buying your product. Proofs of purchase collected by consumers and sent in offer you more options for research. Do people who collect ring-pulls from your brand of beer buy the product more from supermarket off-licences, pubs, or off-licence chains such as Victoria Wine? Perhaps if you knew, you could make decisions about how to run linked trade promotions, or the best place for point-of-sale merchandisers announcing the next promotion where ring-pulls need be collected.

By extending your promotion exercises to gain information about your distributors, retailers and consumers, you can offset the cost of the promotion against market-research costs. It may well be that the data on buyer behaviour coming out of your promotion will be quite useful to the planning of your future operations, but that that data would be too expensive to obtain by pure market research alone.

Although not a coupon in the sense of being alternative currency, BMW Cars used a 'coupon' in the guise of a Parker pen cap. In preparation for a motor show some while ago, BMW sent the pen cap of what was easily recognizable as a prestigious Parker fountain pen to all the people they had on their mailing list registered as owners, a few weeks before the event. With the cap went a simple announcement that the barrel of the pen could be obtained by visiting the BMW stand at the Motor Show. While this proved to be an excellent technique for getting people on to the BMW stand to see the latest models and arrange their test drives, it was also a good way of bringing BMW owners together so that the company could research their response to the new product features on the prototypes on display.

This proved to be a technique of research into likely prospective buyers' attitudes that was far cheaper and more in-depth than other schemes using direct mail alone could have been; and of course the people on the exhibition stand were better trained to research buyer opinions than the average distributor would have been. In this way BMW was better placed to decide on new product innovations before their incorporation into full production, and at a lower cost than by other research means. This new information gained could offset the considerably higher costs of the exhibition, which was more lavish at this show than at former events.

6.6 Competitions: as research tools, you can win both ways

In the example quoted earlier Club la Costa used competitions as a way of getting people to sample its product. But competitions can also be used to research a market and gain useful information, usually by asking the entrant to list a number of product features in priority order. This is a frequent ruse used by manufacturers to help sort out a mixture of possible product features where there is no clear major benefit that should be promoted. It can also be used to highlight the range of a product's features by offering a prize for the competition that is attractive enough to lure sufficient people to run through the mechanics of the competition, even if they don't get round to entering.

Tie-breakers can be used, not only as a way of deciding on the ultimate winner, but also as a way of generating slogans or other copylines. Of course the virtually ubiquitous 'I use (product X) because . . .' (completed in no more than ten words) gives a good guide on why consumers – or at least entrants – use the product, and the reason may be one of the features listed in the competition.

Other competitions can be quite simple to operate. The entrant may only be asked to caption a picture or name a dish. Picture captions are occasionally used by tabloid newspapers as a way of generating amusing copy for future issues. Naming dishes helps food companies to choose attractive names for future products, especially in the convenience and ready-made sectors of the market.

One competition used in *Family Circle* (a general woman's interest/family magazine sold through supermarkets) many years ago was quite inventive in its operation. It asked readers to look at around twenty-five different pictures that were parts of various companies' product logos. They then had to flick through the journal to find on which page an advertisement for that product was reproduced. Such a competition was obviously of great interest to advertisers, because it increased the advertisement readership, making *Family Circle's* advertisement manager's life a little easier. The competition then asked entrants to define 'the ideal gift', costing no more than £100, this magazine should feature in a future competition, and explain, in no more than ten words, why. The winner, who received £100 as prize money, suggested 'A picnic hamper because a picnic is a family circle'. A number of other entrants had also suggested picnic baskets and hampers. Sure enough, in April of the following year, ten picnic hampers were offered as prizes in a successive competition.

In this example, the first competition was a good idea, as it attracted potential advertisers' attention, and also generated considerable interest among readers. By getting readers to suggest the prize, *Family Circle* generated high reader interest in the next competition, as the prize was highly valued, as well as good brand endorsement for the magazine.

While spin-offs from competitions are useful marketing tools in their own right and can spread the cost of the effort, one needs also to be particularly aware of the level of returns from a budget-control point of view. You will need to decide whether you wanted a large return or not. After all, the impact of the competition may be much greater as a promotion *per se* than the level of responses might suggest. Generally speaking, if one were to offer one big prize, then the number of entrants is likely to be less than if a number of smaller prizes were offered, and entrants feel they have a greater chance of winning. Remember too that those competitions which may deter the average punter are likely to be targets for the so-called 'professional' entrant. A soup manufacturer once offered six cars as prizes in one competition; the response rate was very low, however, and four of the six winners 'never ate soup' and were dedicated competition entrants.

However, big prizes do create considerable impact around a product. Unfortunately, with almost all tabloid newspapers advertising millions of pounds' worth of prizes in their bingo schemes, it is becoming difficult to create significant impact on a small budget. *Readers Digest* seems unable to sell books and *Which?* enroll new subscribers without offering £$\frac{1}{4}$ million every time. If your target group is a little more tightly defined, you may be able to create impact among it on much more modest budgets. It must be said of course that both *Readers Digest* and *Which?* are investing heavily in the generation and maintenance of their mailing lists.

By offering more moderate prizes and many smaller prizes, you are likely to attract more entrants to your competition. If that is what you plan to do, remember that you may run up more costs in checking the larger number of entries, though you could get a useful mailing list of customers, depending on your market. (Only a small percentage of your chosen target audience are likely to enter a competition and that percentage may not be representative of the whole, so beware!) By changing the prize value therefore you can affect the make-up of your competition entrants and control your expenditure on the competition.

6.7 Measurement parameters: what to look for

It is often not realized, particularly among industrial companies, that the cost-effectiveness of above- and below-the-line promotion can be measured. It is one of the essential factors of successful marketing that money should not be spent on unnecessary or ineffective commodities whether they be components or services, and the same principle of course must apply to promotional expenditure. How can a company decide whether it is spending its promotions budget wisely unless it has measured as far as possible the results of money previously spent in the same activity?

There are a number of useful techniques that can be used by companies to analyse the value of their work, and guide them in planning future programmes. As various below-the-line promotion techniques are discussed in subsequent chapters, specific elements of evaluation will be addressed at each stage. However, in general terms, when one is considering any evaluation procedure, there are a number of measurement criteria that can be used to assess how well one is doing (or has just done).

6.7.1   Ex-factory sales

One should look at these weekly if possible, by pack size (flavour, perfume, as well), by area, and by outlet type, with particular emphasis on special promotion packs. Look at both units and sterling sales for the period of 'x' weeks before the promotion, the period during the promotion, and for 'y' weeks after. These data can then be compared with the same periods for the previous year.

6.7.2   Consumer sales

Again, one should ideally look at these figures weekly if possible, otherwise monthly. Two-monthly is too long, as there is no time to change tack. Look at sales by size, area and outlet type, singling out any special promotional pack in units and sterling for the previous 'x' weeks or months, the period during the promotion, and for 'y' weeks or months post-promotion. Again, it is sensible to look at these data for the same periods as for the year before.

6.7.3   Brand shares

You may be able to get reliable research data that will give you brand shares for your market. Look at these shares for your own brand compared to competitors' shares in relation to the total market for the time span mentioned above, and with the same period the year before.

6.7.4   Distribution

Depending on the product and the market, one may be able to look at the distribution of one's own brand and the competition's and of the total product category by outlet and sterling for the usual periods of measurement outlined above compared with the same period a year ago. Distribution is important. After all, if you have not got your product on the shelves, how will customers buy it?

6.7.5   Cost factors

These are many and varied because there are so many cost implications to consider, particularly the hidden and not so obvious ones. Here is a selection of cost factors to look out for:

(a) Hire of extra salesmen, merchandisers, demonstrators or personality girls, their hire fees and expenses.
(b) Promotional media advertising, consumer and trade, including production costs, if *extra* to the theme advertising budget.
(c) Special promotional display material, not forgetting artwork, production of plates, dispatch, etc.
(d) Collateral material, such as printing of leaflets, coupons, catalogues, special promotion packs, salesmen's presenters.
(e) Premium items, competition prizes, judges' fees. Remember, some gifts may incur a tax on the recipient. It is worth getting your VAT Office to advise you *beforehand*.
(f) Outside service fees, consultants, handling houses, direct-mail houses (if you get a particularly good response to your campaign, your variable costs, such as costs of reply-paid card returns, will increase too).
(g) Special packaging, labelling, postage.
(h) Extra administration and handling costs.
(i) Extra production costs.
(j) Trade-handling allowances, extra discounts.

6.8 How to control expenditure

Measurement of expenditure, both honestly and accurately, is the first step to control. And control itself is the key to profitability. The best way to make a profit is to stop wasting it. Controlling costs does not necessarily mean just reducing the actual amount of money parted with either; making each pound spent work hard and getting value for money are equally important in the profit achievement.

The quote at the beginning of this chapter suggested that one-fifth of the money spent below-the-line was being wasted. Within the consumer products area something is being done to counteract this problem. In the mid-1980s Audits of Great Britain joined forces with SPAR, an American company specializing in the analysis and evaluation of sales promotions, to offer a specialized reporting service. SPAR's analysis reporting system had been developed over the previous 18 years in the US as a means of quantifying and reducing wastage. It has been refined through more recent application in Canada and Australia, and has been implemented in the UK.

The primary input source is a company's own data, although other relevant market data can be input. It covers a range of below-the-line techniques, including short-term discounts, display allowances, tailormades and consumer packs.

It is estimated that manufacturers can expect a minimum 15 – 20 per cent bottom-line payback on their below-the-line expenditure. Therefore a company spending, say, £1 million a year on promotions can expect to save at least £150,000, which can be profit or be reallocated to other areas of the marketing budget.

The basis of the system is a flexible artificial intelligence model, which produces the SPARLINE – an estimate of what sales would have been without a promotion. In other words, lead and lagged effects are evaluated. Once the SPARLINE has established what sales would have been in the pre-promotion, promotion, and post-promotion periods, these can be subtracted from actual sales in all three periods to determine true incremental volume for that promotion. By applying the relevant margin and subtracting costs, one may obtain a true picture of incremental profits.

As one would expect, the reality is complicated by the number of promotions being run at the same time and the multitude of real-life factors that can affect what sales would have been in the absence of a promotion. All necessary variables, such as general sales trend, seasonality, competitive activity, advertising, strikes and even end-of-year sales drives, are reflected.

With information provided by AGB – SPAR, a manufacturer can establish which promotions work best, which pack sizes respond to specific stimuli or what frequency of promotion is necessary. One can even pinpoint individual customer groups' responses to a particular promotion.

Virtually all manufacturers and retailers are familiar with the bar code system, which has allowed the use of electronic equipment at the point-of-sale to record a wide variety of data of use to manufacturers and retailers alike. Such an electronic point-of-sale (EPOS) system has in fact yielded another important marketing feature – not just information allowing good control of below-the-line promotion but providing more than significant improvements in stock management and control too. With EPOS systems, items no longer need to be priced individually – price changes can be made at a central computer. Inventory control is improved with up to date information on the quantities and sizes of each item sold each day. With improvements in inventory, retailers can move to shorter lead times on ordering and supply. Thus suppliers need to become more flexible on timing and quantity of deliveries, as well as the variety of products.

EPOS systems also enhance marketing information: each customer, date and time of purchase, items bought, prices paid, promotional deals, size of total shopping, and means of purchase. The retailer is therefore in a much better position to monitor the effectiveness of specific promotions, or new product introductions, and can make better decisions about the allocation of shelf-space to specific brands. Coupled with data on margins, decisions can be taken on the relative attractiveness of different types of product as far as allocation of shelf-space is concerned. Adjustments can be made on a store by store basis as necessary.

Ogilvy and Mather, a large London advertising agency, made a detailed report in 1986 on the subject of electronic point of sale in the retailing of packaged goods sector. It concluded that benefits decisively outweigh the costs.

Sales promotion, says the report, will rival the importance of display advertising with the use of EPOS. Certain promotions may be more difficult under the system: different sized or shaped new stock will need their own codes. Some manufacturers were slow to bar code their products, but some retailers would only stock bar-coded items, which soon encouraged manufacturers to get up to date.

With EPOS, some promotions will be easier to run, such as redemption of coupons based on scanner data at the check-out. Multi-pack promotions can be programmed into the computer, making it easier to run 'two-for-one' schemes.

However, the report did highlight another benefit over and above the inventory control/marketing data benefits described above. With EPOS, retailers are beginning to realize that they can change their own marketing strategy from publicizing low prices to improved customer service. The 'shopping experience' – speed and convenience – will be the message at national advertising level, and this will be supported by tactical local advertising, emphasizing price promotions. More customer information in store could be provided by means of viewdata. As consumers become more sophisticated, it is likely that convenience will be a premium in the future, not low prices. Fast check-outs are already beginning to be recognized as a major benefit, satisfying consumer expectations.

6.9 Summary

1 Success can only be measured if realistic objectives are set before the campaign starts.
2 It may also be necessary to measure the present state, e.g. of customers' attitudes, beforehand, so that comparison can be made by further measurement afterwards.
3 Below-the-line promotion will frequently be intended to add value. It is important to check whether the campaign demonstrates to the target audience that the added value is present.
4 Measurement is possible through:

(a) Sales-force feedback.
(b) Sales figures.
(c) Store checks.
(d) Redemptions.
(e) Sales after the end of the promotion.
(f) Audits.

5 Note must be taken of 'lead and lag' effects in assessing results.
6 Redemptions and competition entries can be valuable sources of information.
7 Monitoring techniques such as AGB – SPAR and information provided by EPOS can also help to monitor results.

References

1 *P R Week* (1985), 5 September, p.10.
2 Kotler, Philip (1977), *Marketing Management*, Prentice-Hall.

7 The particular problems of corporate promotion

7.1 Corporate marketing: an expanding business

Not all promotion is concerned with products. Often it is the *company* we wish to promote.

Through a combination of hospitality, sponsorship and promotional functions, a company can successfully project its 'image' to customers, shareholders, workforce and a range of other publics. Used strategically and discriminately, corporate-marketing techniques will establish and build in relationships with customers, create areas for products and sales, and strengthen the perception of the company by those targeted. Marketing a company image will call for all the facets of the marketing mix, as well as above- and below-the-line promotional techniques. As usual, it will be important to keep advertising working in harmony with below-the-line promotion, each interdependent on the other.

Since hospitality, sponsorship and other promotional functions and events are funded from below-the-line, let us here take an overview of the particular problems of corporate promotion by these techniques.

Over £400m is spent each year on corporate entertainment in the UK. This figure is on the increase according to a survey conducted in October 1988 by 'Audience Selection Key Directors Omnibus Survey', a telephone survey of managing directors of the top 20,000 companies in the UK. (See note on p. 134.)

Nearly four-fifths of all companies in the country are engaged in corporate marketing through corporate hospitality, sponsorship or promotional functions and product launches. Most companies that have made some commitment are increasing their activity: 34 per cent of companies developing corporate-marketing strategies were increasing expenditure in 1989, and only 6 per cent planned reductions, the decrease coming in companies with over £5m annual turnover. Of the companies surveyed, only 22 per cent did not engage in corporate-marketing activities of the kind mentioned. Most of these companies were manufacturing companies with a turnover less than £5m. On the other hand, companies with a turnover greater than £20m were almost all into corporate marketing of this kind.

The 78 per cent of companies that did undertake some form of corporate promotion spread their budgets between hospitality, sponsorship, sales promotion, and product launches. Corporate hospitality was the favoured activity by 54 per cent of the sample, 51 per cent committing themselves to sales-promotion budgets, and 44 per cent to sponsorship.

Sponsorship is gaining strong ground. In 1988, 44 per cent of all companies surveyed invested in some form of sponsorship, common expenditures being £10,000 per annum; though companies with a turnover of £5m or more could be spending up to five times this amount. The survey highlighted sponsorship as a particular growth area. Over 80 per cent of companies maintained or increased the amount of money spent on sponsoring events in 1988 over the previous year. Most companies forecast that their 1989 expenditure would be the same or higher still. Three-quarters of those companies that raised their level of expenditure on sponsorship in 1988 over 1987 said that they would do so again in 1989.

Promotion expenditure on product or company launches or functions is also growing. Roughly half of all companies increased their budgets in 1988 over the previous year, while the other half maintained them. This trend was expected to continue in 1989, with only 4 per cent intending to decrease their expenditure in this area.

In terms of events used by companies to entertain, promote, or sponsor, golf is clearly the favourite, and horse-racing second by a short head. Sports events feature highly as venues for corporate marketing, especially among those companies whose total annual expenditure in this field is quite high. Cultural events, such as exhibitions, theatre, opera or ballet, are less popular for entertaining, but are used in corporate-marketing plans for sponsorship. In general, this survey indicated that there is every belief in corporate marketing as being an important function. The future looks healthy in all areas, especially sponsorship.

Table 7.1 shows the top ten attractions in popularity by company size. Golf, horse-racing and trips abroad are clear winners in all companies surveyed. However, the survey also showed that marketing managers are becoming more sophisticated in the way they measure the worth of particular activities.

Golf was the most popular attraction, with 42 per cent of the total sample engaged in either sponsorship, hospitality or promotion; however, only 20 per cent of the sample said it was their most successful activity. Horse-racing was not as favourable as it might seem; while it was the second most popular activity, with a third using it as a centre-point to corporate publicity, only 8 per cent rated it as their most successful activity. Table 7.1 shows the five most popular

115

Table 7.1 *Top ten sponsoring attractions in popularity by company size*

£1–5m	Annual turnover £5–20m	Over £20m
1 Golf	1 Golf	1 Golf
2 Horse-racing	2 Horse-racing	2 Horse-racing
3 Trip abroad	3 Trip abroad	3 Trip abroad
4 {Football, Boat trip}	4 Boat trip	4 Boat trip
6 Cricket	5 {Football, Rugby}	5 Cricket
7 Motor-racing	7 Cricket	6 {Motor-racing, Theatre}
8 Stately home	8 Motor-racing	8 {Rugby, Stately home}
9 {Rugby, Opera}	9 {Theatre, Stately home}	10 Football

attractions as being golf, horse-racing, trips abroad, boat trips and cricket; but the five activities rated the most successful were golf, horse-racing, trips abroad and, sharing fifth place, rugby and boat trips. See Table 7.2.

Table 7.2 *Attractions voted most successful by company size*

£1–5m	Annual turnover £5–20m	Over £20m
1 Golf	1 Golf	1 Trip abroad
2 Boat trip	2 Horse racing	2 Cricket
3 Football	3 Trip abroad	3 {Golf, Horse racing, Football, Theatre}
4 Cricket	4 Rugby	
5 {Trip abroad, Opera}	5 {Theatre, Opera}	

While golf was enormously popular with companies over £20m turnover – 60 per cent said they used it, compared to 27 per cent among companies with under £5m turnover – the larger companies placed golf a poor third behind trips abroad and cricket in the success league. Horse-racing had a strong following among the larger companies, 57 per cent using it, compared to 18 per cent of smaller companies, though, like golf, it was not considered a particularly successful activity for the larger companies.

7.2 There is more to corporate marketing than just events

The contest between retailers and manufacturers of branded-food products has developed into one of the fiercest battles in Britain's hotly competitive food sector. At stake is the balance of power within one of the toughest markets in the Western world. Towards the end of the 1980s that balance lay firmly with the food retailers. Britain's top eight retailers accounted for over 60 per cent of all UK grocery sales. So how did this situation arise?

Success is rooted in the retailers' commitment to service, innovation, quality and value. Their power over manufacturers, however, stemmed from their success in getting some of the best and most competitively priced products into their own stores under their own label, and continued to steadily strengthen their own images.

The business of selling a food product with a retailer's name, not a manufacturer's brand, has become almost a religion in Britain. Unlike the US, where retailers pushed out simple unadorned own label packets, with no above- or below-the-line support, British retailers grew to see own-label foods as an extension of their high image and respectability among their customers. Not surprisingly, growth in own-label in the US has been much less prominent than in Britain. Figure 7.1 shows the rapid rise of own-label market shares to 1984.

The economic recession of the early 1980s stimulated own-label penetration to well over one-quarter share of the packaged grocery market. For the retail trade, the main purpose in this move towards own-label has been to secure better margins than were available on branded products, while offering better value and a lower price to the consumer. A second objective was to swing customer loyalty towards the store and away from the brand.

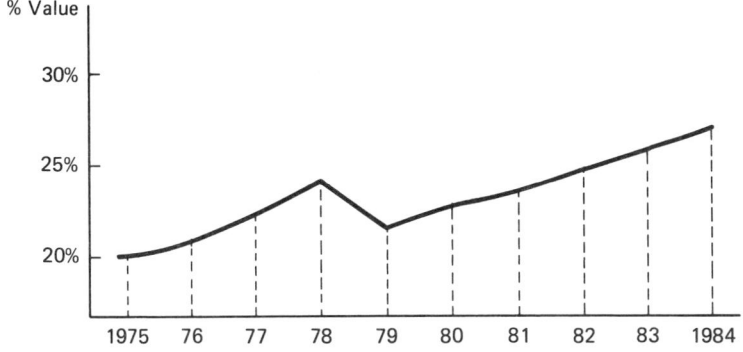

Figure 7.1 *Own-label share of packaged groceries (UK)*

As far as such stores as Spar, Mace and VG (the so-called Symbol groups) are concerned, own labels provide them with a better means of competing with the multiples on price, of developing a corporate identity and of securing retailer loyalty. In the wholesale trade the same objectives apply, but the route is to develop a brand, such as 'Peacock', which is promoted to the public.

Now, rather than fighting among themselves, more manufacturers decided to fight the own-label battle with retailers. Their weapons were cost efficiency, technological and product innovation, and strong advertising support.

Own-label products are generally 10 per cent cheaper than branded goods, although some cost as much as 30 per cent less. Brand leaders have invested heavily in the kind of equipment that will help them keep this gap as narrow as possible. They have also spent more freely on advertising and below-the-line support to build – and keep – loyalty to their brands in an effort to jump over the head of the retailer and appeal directly to the consumer. In the mid-1980s, Nestlé Unilever, Kelloggs, General Foods, all increased their promotional budgets – some by as much as 20 – 25 per cent. Their tactic was to switch to the offensive, with the aim of redressing the balance of power. 'If it doesn't say Kelloggs on the packet; then there isn't any Kelloggs inside.'

The use of own-label foods was one way retailers, particularly supermarkets, could extend their own image among consumers. But this image was developed by attention to a whole series of criteria spanning the marketing mix as it related to that particular store. From the retailers' point of view this meant addressing, for example, store layout, range of goods stocked, point-of-sale, pricing policy, as well as such issues as staff training and motivation, even staff appearance. Collectively, these all added to the corporate image of that super-market.

Supermarkets arouse remarkably strong feelings, perhaps because they are now where the majority of consumers go for their basic needs. People can become oddly attached to their favourite chain – identifying themselves quite seriously with it and dismissing the competition. Even though most people use more than one, a particular shop still holds their loyalty, suiting their idea of themselves and their wants. Everyone has a ready answer to the question of what supermarket they like best.

This feeling of belonging is partly a natural counter to the supermarket's impersonality, the fact that next to no human contact comes about in using them. (This is a structural phenomenon, not the assistants' fault: watch how customers treat those working the tills.) It is likely that most consumers prefer this no-contact approach. Yet there are stronger arguments for such preferences. Supermarket chains are alike in that their size means that they cannot cope with the irregular small-scale local product, which is the key to truly good food, although many in-store delicatessens are trying to satisfy this demand. But beyond this there are substantial differences: in range, quality, price, and shopping environment. All these features build towards a supermarket chain's personality, a corporate image that can, and does, extend country-wide.

The huge supermarket chains are of course here to stay and grow; they look set to get fewer and bigger. In 1900 chain stores had only 5 per cent of the grocery market, co-ops 15 per cent and private grocers 80 per cent. Self-service was not introduced until 1946; the first superstore of more than 25,000 sq.ft opened only in 1965. Yet the multiples (Sainsburys, Tesco, Safeway) now have over two-thirds of the grocery business, and there are approaching 500 'superstores' in Britain, with many more on the way.

7.3 Driving home on corporate image

In early 1989 Vauxhall Motors withdrew a controversial advertising campaign, at a cost of £100,000. This demonstrated how highly major car manufacturers prize their public image. The offending poster was not exactly the centre of a storm of protest either: only a single complaint had been received. Yet this was enough to warrant Vauxhall making a withdrawal – a decision due as much to Vauxhall protecting its corporate image as a 'caring company' as to fears that any adverse publicity might harm sales.

Car manufacturers tend to draw a distinction between brand image and corporate image. The former relates to the face we are most familiar with – the way products are marketed. The sleek saloons zooming through stars, dynamic landscapes, or traffic jams, TV commercials, poster and press advertising (above-the-line), and sales brochures, point of sale in showrooms, even free 24-hour test drives (below-the-line), are examples of ways of marketing the product.

Marketing the company is approached quite differently. Apart from thoroughbred manufacturers such as Ferrari and Rolls-Royce, where corporate and brand images are indivisible, the larger manufacturers tend to keep the two separated, sometimes by default, usually by design.

Above-the-line the company is usually kept abstract: a logo and a brief blurb mention at most. Nothing must be allowed to distract from the product itself. Brands such as Fiesta, Escort, Orion, Sierra, and Granada dominate. However, some of the smaller motor companies do try to present a company image in their advertising, and indeed their company name may be synonymous with the product, e.g. Peugeot 305, Renault 5, Citroen BX. Others of course will just promote the badge or name to build a company image through their advertising message. (Two notable examples come from manufacturers with small market shares. One had a simple photograph of its BMW badge on the bonnet, with the body line 'Enough said'. The other showed a small child rolled up in cotton wool, rather like a carpet. Again the copyline was simple: '. . . or buy a Volvo'.)

The fact that fleet sales – both company car and hire-firms' sales – accounted for around 65 per cent of UK vehicle sales (August 1989) has caused car manufacturers to alter their product marketing accordingly. Employees are often invited to choose from a shortlist of possible company cars, so price and fuel efficiency are no longer primary governing factors; a life-style match or individuality or getting as many product features as possible into the deal are more popular prerequisites.

Concepts of corporate marketing have also changed. In the 1970s, with strikes so frequent, corporate image in the car industry was synonymous with maintaining healthy 'industrial relations', keeping the workforce happy. Since then, corporate image has extended beyond the factory floor and out into the surrounding community, going above and beyond representing the company as solely 'the boss'. The desire to present the company as friend, not threat, has at times verged on corporate maternalism. It has been achieved by associating the company with ideals connecting it with the image it wants to put across, or schemes that will eventually benefit the company in the long term – such as training schemes or sporting activities – or serve to improve relations between, say, workforce and dealers.

The car industry is fortunate in that its history and cultural connotations can be easily applied to promotional projects. Surprisingly perhaps, not all manufacturers seem keen to take advantage of the potential corporate-image promotion offered; not surprisingly those that do tend to be the ones with a firm and committed UK base. In the 1990s one can expect the Japanese car manufacturers to take up the challenge of corporate-image promotion quite seriously once their manufacturing base is well established.

However, because manufacturers are wary that any charitable gestures could be interpreted as springing from less than noble motives, many tend to keep a low profile. Promotions include sponsorship and other forms of financial encouragement to outside organizations to get schemes going. Two companies that are extensively committed to enhancing their corporate images in such ways are Ford and Vauxhall Motors. Both have gravitated towards events they feel bear special relevance to the corporate image that they wish to promote.

For example, Ford's external corporate image-building events include:

1 Charitable causes, such as Save the Children.
2 An association with the Queen Elizabeth Foundation for the Disabled, helping to train disabled drivers in specially adapted cars.
3 Making community transit buses available to groups around Ford plants
4 Spending £25m a year (1988) on national and local training schemes and academic projects. For example:

    (a) Industries rely on a flow of technically qualified technicians from colleges.
    (b) Such schemes create a company ethos to attract appropriate graduates.
    (c) Commercial and academic links fuel the exchange of ideas.

5 A favourite image-enhancement project is Ford's protection of the environment:

    (a) In the mid-1970's Ford started a 'save the village pond' scheme.
    (b) Acres of trees planted around Ford's Dagenham factory has created a miniature nature reserve.

6 Ford raised £40,000 from its sponsorship of the Beatrix Potter exhibition, which went towards arresting erosion of paths and walkways in the Lake District.
7 Ford is a regular sponsor of the National Trust's activities, including the International Conservation Awards.

Like Ford, Vauxhall has chosen to devote a large proportion of its corporate image-building to a particular area – that of motor sport. Vauxhall conducts its events through GM Dealer Sport (GM stands for General Motors, Vauxhall's parent company). Vauxhall's participation in motor sport is represented by GM-Dealer Sport; teams of Vauxhall sales representatives and its dealer force are invited to compete along with industry associates. Through a wide variety of participative motor-sport activities, Vauxhall is trying to forge relations between the company and its contacts, and also to promote the qualities of its cars. By appearing at such events, Vauxhall demonstrates its commitment to the whole spectrum of driving – as a firm of professional car enthusiasts, not simply purveyors of a four-wheeled product.

Three other areas are worth considering in regard to Vauxhall's corporate image:

1 From 1 January 1990 all Vauxhall vehicles were equipped to run on lead-free petrol. Further, the company has offered to similarly convert any of its cars sold since 1985, and has been actively seeking to contact owners. Swansea Vehicle Licensing Centre has supplied a list of around 1 million owners, including owners of secondhand cars, and Vauxhall has spent £20,000 on contacting each driver. Conversions are likely to cost the company £5m. Further, Vauxhall has equipped all new cars with catalytic converters, which filter petrol of many harmful by-products.

2 Vauxhall plans to reduce the burden on society of the cost of retrieving stolen cars by introducing unique locks on the doors of its cars. With an extra turn of the key, the door is 'dead-locked' and cannot be opened, even from the inside without the proper key. Similarly, in-car radios will be fitted with special code numbers, so that, if the radio is disconnected, it can only be reactivated by using that code, known only to the owner. These deterrents to car theft have won Vauxhall awards from the British Vehicle and Renting Association.

3 As Vauxhall is one of Luton's biggest employers, they felt it was important to give something practical and useful to the immediate community. To this end Vauxhall sponsors a creche at Luton Airport for the use of all travellers. Called the 'Vauxhall World of Children', it is supervised by fully trained staff and caters for youngsters between 2 and 8 years old.

It is not easy to identify an aspect of corporate image promotion that can be described as purely altruistic, and there are other car manufacturers that would not dream of divorcing corporate from brand image. They are out to sell cars and that's that. It could be argued that only manufacturers that already enjoy a large segment of UK car sales can afford to go apportioning resources to activities that are not immediately related to selling the product. But, then, how have they come to be selling that many cars in the first place? Cars may come and go but image remains.

7.4 Feed the image

Companies are now more aware than ever of the benefits of entertaining small numbers of clients with a meal at a restaurant or hotel. Such events often follow a briefing, seminar, or presentation. In the UK there is an improvement in the attention paid to food, particularly in the last 2 decades. It is now being recognized that there can be a link between the food, drink, venue, time of day, and the event. All can have considerable importance as components of the total effect of the event, however modest, and they all can convey an image of the company to the guests.

7.4.1 Get off to a frying start

Meetings and presentations held over breakfast are finding favour in the corporate community. Breakfast events are still unusual enough to encourage attendance, and because they are not normally served at a set time, hosts are able to make more contacts, greeting new guests as others leave. 'Power breakfasts' enable executives to confer on an important event happening later in the day. Working breakfasts are more commonplace in the USA, though many politicians can be seen conferring over the breakfast table in Blackpool's major hotels during conference seasons.

The London office of a firm of chartered accountants has long exploited the benefits of an early start. Breakfast seminars are run for both paying guests and prospective clients, covering a range of financial topics. At these events it was recognized that people realized that their minds were fresh and they tended to absorb more and communicate easily. Most people are slightly more sociable in the morning than they are as the day progresses. This firm recommends using round-table discussion groups; otherwise they felt they were negotiating an arms treaty.

Early starts mean guests can be in their offices by 10 am, leaving the rest of the day uninterrupted. One property developer capitalized on this when inviting various prospective customers to half a dozen different breakfast-time viewings of a new riverside London development. Guests could stop off on their way to work. Although traffic was busy in the early morning, guests did not have to make the journey from their offices to the wharf and back either side of a lunch; this alternative to lunch was preferred by the visitors, since heavy lunches tend to leave many wiped out for the rest of the day.

The working breakfast had the opposite effect. After an invigorating breakfast, people were set up for the day, raring to go! Breakfast can be quite invigorating, especially if it is a champagne breakfast. The prospect of downing alcohol may seem unpalatable, but champagne at breakfast – or more usually Bucks Fizz (a 50/50 champagne and fresh orange juice mixture) – is practically universal for early morning corporate occasions. It is said that 'Champagne is a hallmark of quality and a symbol of success'.

Another benefit of the breakfast event was that announcements and presentations could be made while people were still eating; people are used to being distracted at breakfast by radios, newspapers, mail and toasters. Therefore time-saving is a big consideration. If you do plan a breakfast event, here are a few tips:

1 Make sure the venue or outside caterers are prepared and have experience in running breakfast events.
2 Make sure too that your target audience can get to the venue reasonably early, without having to ask them to get up at 4 am!
3 For your key company people, consider having them stay overnight close by; there is no substitute if your own team gets caught in the rush hour.
4 The food of course is integral to enhancing a lasting impression. The frontiers of many a Continental breakfast have been elasticated to add originality to the coffee and croissants format. Try a Greek breakfast of Baklava, Greek yoghurt, black olives, caraway seed bread, feta cheese and honey, washed down with Turkish coffee.

   The English (or traditional) breakfast has the reputation of being unhealthy, containing many high-fat foods. Venues and caterers now provide good wholesome food for healthier diets and special requirements. Most will feature fresh fruit and grilled fish, served with brown bread rolls, margarine as well as butter, and decaffeinated coffee (although some dieticians say that the solvents used to remove the caffein leave residues that are more harmful than the caffein itself!)
5 Breakfasts can be self-service or, for smaller meetings, waitress service. Although breakfast serving can take place over a period of time, food should be cooked fresh as waves of new guests arrive. Sausages and kidneys may be kept warm once cooked, but eggs must be cooked fresh every time.

Breakfasts are relatively unusual in the travel trade but the Irish Tourist Board found success with its series of twenty-two breakfast presentations held around the country to promote Ireland. The average attendance was thirty-five. Breakfasts enabled the ITB to get to agency managers who would have been otherwise too busy to attend. They were very pleased with the result: a 19 per cent rise in business for the first 5 months in 1989. The breakfast meetings played a key part in that success.

7.4.2 The luncheon event

If the event is lunch, make sure the lunch is good, even if the speeches are not. It is better to invite your guests to drink champagne, if that is what the budget allows, rather than stretch the budget but only provide a mediocre meal. For the large or particularly important lunch, you are likely to choose the venue by two criteria:

- *Selection by name*: choosing a top hotel (the Savoy, the Ritz) or five-star examplars of historic grandeur, or an accepted institution in culinary circles (Groucho's, La Gavroche, Maxims in Paris). These will have immediate renown and convey sophistication; even if the meal is not as imaginative as your most critical guest would like, the mere fact of having been entertained there on your account will satiate the appetite.
- *Selection by past experience*: choose a restaurant you know and trust. You could be getting preferential treatment if it is known you return often.

Food critics might balk at such a simplistic approach, but it is best to be on safe ground, unless you are prepared to research your market first. There are many small restaurants with young chefs now providing both interesting and high-quality foods. You will have to go out into your local area and find the venue that best suits your needs.

Ray Acknerman, chairman of the Restaurateurs Association of Great Britain and food critic both in print and other media, judges a restaurant by the selection of bread: if the bread is good, he feels assured of a good meal. He also considers the choice of restaurant is very much 'horses for courses' – it depends on the aim of the occasion. However, he sees one of the essential factors governing the choice as what the host prefers: 'A meal is an ideal opportunity to show off what we as a nation have got.' This is a variety of cuisine (especially in London) rarely seen elsewhere that welcomes a culture without wanting to dominate it. Oriental, European and US restaurants all have a style of their own, and the selection can be made to suit the company's entertainment.

For instance Barclays Bank Corporate Division, which widely entertains clients, looks for suitability and value for money. 'If the purpose of the event is to discuss business, then the "gimmicky" side of a meal or venue is not appreciated,' one spokesman said. Barclays also prefers something with a specific angle that can reinforce its image.

Castrol UK chooses venues to reflect the quality and style that parallel its own.

Checklist

1 If entertaining clients for a business lunch, or perhaps before or after the theatre, choose a location with private rooms to accommodate the party. There is no point shouting over other revellers.
2 Design a menu that will tempt and satisfy your particular guests.
3 Do you want a light, buffet meal or something more substantial? Think about the season too.
4 Consider flowers, colour schemes, place cards and specially printed menus to convey whatever image, message or reason for the hospitality that the company intends. If you feel a special menu is extravagant, consider printing an outside cover that can be used at different functions, but prepare good quality, prominently printed photocopies of a special insert specific for the day, and bind it in with silken thread. The finished result can be quite impressive but not too expensive.
5 Many chefs are prepared to leave their familiar surroundings and cater for groups at a location of the company's choice.
6 When choosing a venue, make sure that the person you deal with will be there on the day and not merely be a relay to a third party. It is the detail that makes the difference.
7 The venue should have flexibility of menu and be prepared to discuss the courses individually rather than you having to accept a selection from ten or so set menus.
8 There should be quality and range of wine offered, and the staff should have worked together before. If you have a luncheon covering four tables there is nothing so irritating as having one table cleared after one course before another table: a good head waiter would be surprised if you suggested that anything but coordination existed among his staff.
9 Ensure that the venue offers a relaxed atmosphere, where food and its eating are part of an honoured tradition. According to one consultancy that designs and manages such events, 'If the bread is on the plate and the starter is on the table when you arrive, then you are in real trouble'.

7.4.3   To buffet or not to buffet?

Buffets are now the most popular kind of catering in corporate hospitality. Once only associated with wedding receptions and railway snacks, buffets are discarding their old image as 'poor relation' to sit-down eating. They are cheap and flexible, and the cuisine can match gourmet standards. The informal, unconstrained atmosphere enables people to mix freely and make contact with fellow eaters.

Buffets are usually lunch-time events, the food being supplied either by an independent caterer, or, if the event is in a hotel, by the in-house catering department. The advantages of buffets are many, and they provide a solution to the more rigidly coursed heavy lunches, which can leave guests feeling sluggish for the rest of the day. Other points to consider include:

1 Buffets take less time than a sit-down meal as hosts and guests alike can shuttle in and out. There is no waiting for all people to finish one course before starting the next.
2 Themed foods are easy to present. At the Barbican Health and Fitness Centre 2400 people were fed in 4 days: with organic foods to the fore, a health-conscious content was easy. Glucose-free and low-fat comestibles were easily prepared and made available on free choice.
3 The visual impact can be tremendous, although it is often under-exploited. *Don't* rely on quantity rather than quality. As buffets look inviting, guests are naturally keen to get started (after someone else is first to the table), so stagger the movement of guests to and from the table if possible.
4 Consider little extras such as floral displays to make the event more successful. An ice sculpture makes an impressive centre-piece.
5 Buffets allow people to widen their culinary experience without widening their waistlines. Unusual and exotic concoctions can be sampled at a nibble. The promise of a wide and intriguing choice can help achieve a high attendance at an event.
6 Buffets also have an inherent reputation of being healthier that sit-down lunches, as they are based on the predominance of salad. Beef and quiche are on the wane; light white meats such as chicken, turkey and fish – particularly salmon and tuna – are on the increase. However, do not ruin the effect by swamping every dish with salad dressings, mayonnaise or thousand island; leave the guests to take a selection for themselves.
7 People tend to drink less alcohol with buffets than is traditionally found with sit-down meals. Therefore you may be able to halve

the quantity of alcohol yet double the quality and go for a good champagne. Given that many guests may be driving away from the event, have an interesting selection of soft drinks available too – not just Perrier and orange juice.

8   However, it is not simply a beguiling bill of fare or a sober mind that makes a meal memorable. The organization of buffets is also an important factor. Poor crowd control can leave the most mouth-watering collation looking like a stampeded salad bar. A buffet caterer should take as much care over the serving as over the food itself. People do not like queueing, and the resultant irritation creates a bad impression of the food

At buffets guests may file past tables where food is dished out by staff standing behind, or they may help themselves. The snags start when too many people congregate at one point:

(a) Consider having three smaller buffet tables with identical food; people can then gravitate to the least crowded tables.
(b) Always keep the salad bowls and food trays replenished, as this stops the guests clustering around the one spot.
(c) Alternatively, keep the meats and vegetables on separate tables, so that the guests are obliged to keep moving.

9   If you are providing a buffet linked to an exhibition, give a fork buffet. Here the food is designed to be consumed by a fork only, and the plate has an extension or clip to hold a cup or glass. People are then free to wander.

10   Always consider the seating arrangements. One approach is to have tables and chairs arranged in an irregular manner, so that small groups can gather and not be restrained by a formal seating plan. Even at all-standing functions, it is worthwhile having some tables, so that hands can be relieved of glasses while cards are swapped or lighters looked for. Unhindered mobility is a key to success at buffets.

11   A final plus point. Buffets are cheaper than sit-down meals. They require less preparation, less staff, and do not necessarily need a purpose-built dining area. The food itself is basically cheaper too.

12   However, a fundamental objection. Some people object to carrying their food around the room, juggling with the glass and the plate, and having to extend a greasy hand in greeting after munching a chicken leg.

7.5   Be creative and use interesting venues

Outside catering is increasingly being used by companies to create a thematic atmosphere that will prove memorable. A number of caterers now provide a free venue-finding service appropriate to the occasion, and organize the whole package (hire charge, entertainment, flowers, etc.), as well as concocting a display of culinary talents. Using outside caterers in this way results in the company being given flexibility of surroundings, as well as having a hand in the selection of the cuisine. This method means that the hosts are not tied to a hotel venue and have the ability to act as managers towards the desired effect. With a bit of thought you can find just the right venue.

The Industrial Society uses a variety of imaginative locations for several of its seminars, as these tend to attract maximum invitation response from the delegates. One recent event was to use HMS *Belfast*, moored in the Thames, for a seminar on communications skills, followed by a buffet lunch for the delegates on the east walkway of Tower Bridge. (The walkways are covered and heated to avoid the ravages of the British climate.)

Supertravel, the UK coordinators for a group of American lawyers in London for a legal convention (held at the Tara Hotel, Kensington), used the Cabinet War Rooms for a buffet lunch. These underground rooms were used by Winston Churchill as emergency air-raid accommodation during the Second World War – a truly memorable venue for the American delegates. Supertravel has also used Madame Tussauds to host a cocktail party. They chose to name the canapés either after a character at the waxworks museum or by a name suitable to one of the museum's rooms – but who would eat 'devil's eyes'!

Deloittes Haskins Sells, a firm of London accountants, used the London Dungeon, which is set among vaulted archways near London Bridge. It has been open as a tourist attraction since 1973, providing a 'catalogue of man's inhumanities to man' – a medieval torture chamber. The insolvency department of Deloittes entertained a client company on a ratio of 3:1 to an evening buffet.

Cornell University Hotel Catering School Alumni hold an annual dinner at various venues throughout Europe. One year they went to the Natural History Museum for an upmarket buffet dinner, with quartet and candelabras. The food provided for this event included duck casserole, sucking pig, and smoked poultry platter.

One veterinary pharmaceutical company had a press launch for a new range of cat vaccines. It invited the press to the London Theatre, gave them a commercial and technical presentation by international speakers, and after a buffet lunch, invited them all to the afternoon matinee of the show *Cats*. Every journalist attending wrote something complimentary about the day *and* the products.

With so much corporate hospitality going on currently, you will have to give people a day to remember. So, if you are going to spend a lot of money hosting a corporate event, why not spend more time and effort on the creative side and get something unique? Take a leaf out of Virgin Atlantic Airways book.

Virgin, fronted by the dynamic chairman, Richard Branson, has always striven to be a unique airline. From the mid-1980s, when it was founded, the company's underlying principle of uniqueness has applied equally to its in-flight passenger service, corporate entertaining and image promotion. Virgin Atlantic firmly believes that creative corporate hospitality is more effective than entertaining at established events, such as Henley or Wimbledon.

Constantly on the lookout for new ideas, Virgin investigated a series of spectacular airborne parties. Using one of Virgin's 747 aeroplanes, 350 guests were invited to a film preview and champagne reception – at 35,000 ft. While few companies could afford the £30 – 40,000 operational costs for fuel and cabin crew, Virgin expected that the parties could produce a return in advance if they were run as sales incentives. Travel agents selling x number of Virgin flights would qualify for their party tickets, so the event could pay for itself.

Nurturing close contacts with the travel trade is a major corporate objective for Virgin Atlantic. During the summer of 1989 the company took one of its hot-air balloons on a 30-day tour of the South of England. In each town local travel agents and journalists were given the chance to fly in the balloon. Note, Virgin Atlantic spends 10 per cent of its marketing budget on corporate hospitality.

LMG William Thyne, an Edinburgh packaging company with several whisky producers as customers, used the Scotch Whisky Heritage Centre to provide a ready setting for an annual sales conference dinner for its own staff. Around forty staff members were first given a guided tour of the museum, which included a working model of a distillery, and a trip through 300 years of Scotch-whisky history. Visitors rode in electric cars through sets featuring life-size figures and evoking the sounds and smells of the different periods. These included the aromas of dried peat, heather and whisky, released by heating special oils.

After a 40-minute tour, the guests were treated to pre-dinner drinks and a three-course meal in the centre's private reception room. An elegant effect was quite easily created with dim lighting, private bar and flowers and candles on the tables. Whisky truffles, served with coffee, were an apt finishing touch. At 1989 prices, £25 a head, including room hire, exhibition tour, food and drink, the company got value for money.

7.6 A word of warning

In the summer of 1989, about a fortnight before Henley Royal Regatta celebrated its 150th anniversary, the Henley Hospitality Regatta organization went into liquidation (or, as the female answerphone voice told callers, perhaps with a sense of foreboding, 'liquidization'). An estimated eighty clients were left high and dry, with over £320,000 in total invested in hospitality at Henley. Unfortunately this was not the first time that such a scandal had rocked the corporate hospitality business, and it probably won't be the last. While most of the unfortunate companies were reaccommodated to enjoy the regatta by, among others, Corporate Hospitality Association members, it will probably be the last time many of them will entertain at Henley, or any other event.

Likewise, there have been various reports about over-capacity at some of the classic events – notably Henley – possibly leading to the demise of the popularity of many such venues. However, it should not be forgotten that many companies are more often seeking tailor-made or participation events, rather than the old round of Royal Ascot, Henley and Wimbledon.

None of this should put companies off using corporate hospitality. There are a number of things a buyer would be well advised to remember:

- Much of the hospitality buying for a company is left to someone at a fairly junior level who may be susceptible to selling practices that a more senior or experienced marketing manager or director would avoid.
- Most reputable companies do not require money up-front before packages are guaranteed (as Henley Hospitality Regatta did).
- A buyer can always check with the event organizers that the company selling the package is officially appointed or has their approval. In many cases packages for corporate hospitality can be bought direct from the organizers.
- Last, but by no means least, buyers should meet the package providers and visit their site for the event. (However, it is understood that Henley Hospitality Regatta did just that, yet still managed to deceive some!)

Only by such widely publicized affairs as this can a buyer's market evolve, and the buyer can demand and get the very best standards of service.

7.7 Corporate design

It can be quite staggering to hear how much companies can spend in developing a corporate logo. Redressing a company image often starts with the generation of an alternative, maybe more modern, logo. The cost of developing the right design of the way the initial letters of a company's name are grouped can run into millions of pounds for the design alone, though of course many cost considerably less.

While companies try to encourage a local image, important for selling locally, they recognize that collectively they have more strength. This is why so many large groups spend so much money developing and promoting the right corporate image – important not only to the 'outside' world of customers and shareholders but also internally to employees of a group which feel that their company or division is part of a much larger family or corporation. They have a sense of belonging.

It is usual for the corporation to prepare a manual to define exactly how the corporate identity is to be used by all group companies and divisions; it is not unusual for such a manual to run to two hundred pages of text and examples explaining precisely how a logo device should be reproduced on letterheads through to logos on sweatshirts. A manual is likely to contain actual examples of artwork that a division's agency can use to copy when preparing literature and so forth. Whenever you see the Coca-Cola company use its familiar red and white livery, be it on the side of a lorry, a can of its product, or a branded squash bag, you will notice it is the same; and that applies anywhere in the world, even if the ingredients' list on the can is in Cantonese. Corporate design will be important when we look at literature in Chapter 10, both from the point of view of pure publicity literature and with respect to the work now being done to improve a corporate image through the publication of company accounts.

7.8 Corporate clothing

Walking down any busy high street at 8.45 am, one can believe that corporate-identity fever has swept the high street, bringing with it armies of men and women dressed from head to toe in outfits intended to kill off competition and make the customer feel at home. It's called corporate clothing, and more and more companies have deemed it good business sense to provide their staff with specially designed and developed working wardrobes. It began with airlines and quickly spread to national supermarket and department store chains. Now staff in most banks, building societies and property-services agencies wear corporate clothing, and experts predict that by 1995 every organization with a presence on the high street will follow suit. Such a united corporate front is so important that even some betting shops are now realizing they must invest in corporate clothing to keep pace.

Corporate clothing means more than uniforms, protective clothing or even fully coordinated ranges of staff attire available off the shelf. Boundless potential can be found in exclusively designed, upmarket corporate wear. This is becoming an essential part of the whole corporate and image strategy, such is the importance of the public perception of a company. People are any organization's best ambassadors, and if you ignore the image of those ambassadors, you dilute the whole company image.

The total corporate clothing market in the UK is thought to be worth between £150m and £200m a year. It includes gas and electricity boards, hotel and restaurant chains, amusement parks, local government, opticians and car-hire firms. Actual market spend is difficult to establish in view of the speed with which it is developing, but it is estimated at £30m. While the corporate clothing market has taken off, it is seen as part of a generally heightened awareness of the importance of corporate identity. Corporate clothing has always been a part of the corporate identity programme, but in some cases it is much more important and appropriate than in others. For example, some would argue that it is probably more important for a petrol station than for an insurance company.

Corporate clothing is not just about high fashion and being immediately identifiable to an external audience – the customers. Many people not in the public eye also wear corporate clothing. It makes them feel good about themselves and about their jobs too – so that is important for the corporation.

One can see an immediate benefit for department stores to have their staff wearing similar outfits; the staff stand out from the crowd and their tailoring can speak volumes about the store. But why is it important, and what benefits does it bring, to places such as banks? Here we have conflicting views.

Barclays Bank has yet to find any benefits. In 1984 it tested customer reactions to corporate clothing in sixty-three branches. There was a 50/50 split. The big city customers wanted to see the bank's staff in corporate clothing, so that they could go into a busy branch and identify staff quickly, be it a cashier or a loans officer. In rural branches the complete opposite was found. Customers there, who were often on first-name terms with the staff, did not want to see them in uniforms; they felt it exacerbated the 'them and us' situation. Repeated testing by Barclays has not changed its mind ; the bank only expect its staff to be smartly dressed. Barclays has only relented to equip its personal bankers. Female personal bankers wear an outfit of corporate turquoise and male personal bankers wear a corporate tie: the scheme, it says, has been a great success. It has no plans to extend the scheme to the rest of the staff, partly because it would be extremely expensive.

Midland Bank takes quite a different view, considering corporate clothing to be the icing on the cake. At the end of the 1980s they instigated a project to update and redevelop their styles, because both their staff, who enjoyed the sense of belonging, and customers liked it. The 'listening bank' wanted its staff to look smart, businesslike and efficient. They felt it fitted in with the retail environment that began to emerge towards the end of the 1980s in banks and building societies. Midland staff are not obliged to wear the blue skirts, blue trousers, tweed jackets and the selection of shirts and blouses on offer, but 95 per cent have chosen to do so.

The market is, without doubt, expanding rapidly. But the distinction between upmarket corporate clothing and carefully designed uniforms is becoming increasingly blurred. The 1980s saw a revolution in the perception and use of corporate identity, but does the British public really want to see shops, banks, estate agents, and even betting shops run by crews of identically dressed men and women? We shall have to wait and see!

7.9 Summary

1 Promotion is not only used to increase the sale of products, but also to enhance the awareness of a company and people's attitudes towards it. This is referred to as *corporate* promotion.
2 Corporate promotion consists of a wide range of activities including hospitality, sponsorship, corporate design and company clothing (livery).
3 Like all other promotional activity, these methods have to be carefully selected and planned in order to achieve clear objectives.

7.10 Note

Although accurate figures are not available at the time of going to press, the recession has produced a big reduction in corporate entertainment expenditure.

Part Two

In the first chapter we looked at the broad issues of marketing, particularly the four Ps – Product, Price, Place and Promotion – remembering the S for Service. Within the area of promotion we looked at issues falling above- and below-the-line, also noting that, as is often the case, there was a grey area around that 'line'. A very large part, in terms of financial expenditure, of what goes on below-the-line is being taken up by sales promotion. But what exactly is sales promotion? We started the book with a very useful workmanlike definition that will serve us very well. Yet, ask any promotion professional what it actually is and you are likely to get a whole range of answers. The old-school grocery company will doubtless be biased towards individual techniques, short-termism and building on brand values. The expansionist consultant will say that 'sales prom' is about promoting sales, including media advertising, and maximizing opportunities and profit.

The current Institute of Sales Promotion definition is interesting: 'Sales promotion comprises a range of tactical marketing techniques designed within a strategic marketing framework to add value to a product or service in order to achieve specific sales and marketing objectives'. In reality, the whole concept of defining sales promotions has its constraints in the practical business world. To define means to put limitations on, or to apply parameters to, something. What is sales promotion to one will be direct marketing, public relations, event management or sponsorship to another. Different markets, different products, different companies all have different needs.

However, with this in mind, and for the purposes of covering the subject of publicity fully, it is sensible for us to regard all non-media advertising in the all embracing 'below-the-line' promotion term, and to sub-divide the subject into component parts. In this way it will be easier to obtain a better grasp of the fundamentals of the subject and, indeed, implement practical applications to achieve defined marketing goals. The subsequent chapters, which form Section B, take a broad view at the whole gamut of below-the-line publicity techniques. While many techniques are covered by separate chapters, it is acknowledged that in the business world there are blurred edges to many of them.

8 Sales promotion

'How do you define sales promotion? We'll do anything a client wants, short of above-the-line advertising', quoted the chairman of a leading consultancy. Some of his leading competitors would quarrel with that in one respect only – as the trend towards supporting big promotions with advertising continues, they are increasingly busy producing display advertisements, even TV commercials.

The sales promotion sector began as suppliers of premiums to marketing departments, including the famous plastic daffodils given free with purchases of washing powder. Consequently, they have always been regarded as having a nose for a business opportunity. One commentator described them as the 'can do' boys of the Thatcher era.

As new clients for sales promotions have appeared in areas such as financial services, sales promotions have spanned the boundaries of other below-the-line publicity techniques. Sales-promotion consultancies will now tackle sponsorship, product launches, and exhibitions. Many have in-house studios that are only too happy to design packs or point-of-sale displays. All this helps to explain why it is difficult to draw up a league table of sales-promotion agencies. In 1992 *Marketing* published the figures shown in Table 8.1 relating to the turnover of sales promotion companies.

8.1 Clarification of terms

Let us consider Michael. Twenty years ago Michael had the opportunity to work on a product that was quite important to him at the time, and in fact still is. The product needed to be packaged and presented properly in order to find its right place in the market. To promote and market it successfully, its plus points had to be stressed and its many weaknesses minimized. Furthermore, the product had to be communicated in the

Table 8.1 *Turnover of sales promotion companies*

	1992	1991
Turnover of top sixty-three companies	£263.25m	£249.05m
Turnover of sixty-third company	£14,000	£188,000

right way to a very specific and well-defined target audience, brought to their attention in an innovative way, then married to an incentive of some kind to make the audience really want it.

Sounds like a familiar brief for a product launch, requiring the skills of a sales-promotion or direct-marketing agency? In fact you'd be wrong. The product that was quite important to Michael was Michael, and the results of Michael's endeavours would quite obviously make a big difference to his career prospects and his future.

Without really appreciating it, Michael was using the techniques to find his first job as a graduate in a then emerging discipline, which was a blend of sales promotion and direct marketing. Obviously the letters of introduction he wrote were direct mail. The special offer was the opportunity to meet a potential new recruit to the world of communications. This marriage of sales promotion and direct marketing resulted in a six out of twenty uptake. If we all achieved a 30 per cent 'Yes, I would like to try' strike rate from our sales-promotion/direct-marketing approaches, we would all be rich. This example, for which we have Michael Ingrams of the Ingram Company to thank, serves to illustrate several points.

The blurred line between sales promotion and direct marketing probably does not exist. The experienced practitioner trying to use all methods at his disposal will easily move from one methodology to another. Twenty years ago, though, the terminology did not really exist, neither did the technology. Twenty years ago 'below-the-line' as a whole was only just emerging. Within this ill-defined categorization direct-marketing techniques were being used, though they were not called by that name. Everything that was not advertising was just called below-the-line.

The second point to come from this example relates to that blurred line. If there was a blurred line over those 2 decades, then it was between above- and below-the-line rather than between sales promotion and direct marketing. A generation of excellent practitioners has since grown up bridging the two areas.

As the classic debate has always found, above-the-line and below-the-line have many similar objectives, and may therefore overlap. Indeed, as we have already seen, the two disciplines are interdependent. By the same token, sales promotion and direct marketing often intrude into each other's territories. If, as a broad generalization, one can say that the objective of sales promotion is to increase take-off of a product or service through the addition of added value, while direct marketing seeks the same result by addressing its target audience personally either at home, or in the office, it becomes apparent that the two disciplines can borrow quite heavily from each other.

There is actually nothing frightening or terribly complex about either discipline. The best professional exponents in any field 'know their stuff' and can advise on the best course of action. Some activities start life as a sales-promotion exercise and then are carefully planned to develop into a potent database marketing opportunity.

For example, consider Sealink Auto Club. The brief was to develop a promotional technique that would generate loyalty among motorists. By joining the club, consumers could take advantage of a 20 per cent rebate on the cost of their car-ferry travel, as well as being offered various other promotional benefits. However, once Sealink had enrolled members and put their details on computer, it had an invaluable database for direct-marketing purposes.

That there are areas of overlap between sales promotion and direct marketing is clear. Sales promotion, by and large, would regard direct marketing as a specialized and potent part of its armoury, while direct marketers would acknowledge promotional techniques as a critical adjunct to their skills. Both can theoretically operate without the other, as roast beef can exist independently of horseradish sauce, but the magic is missing.

However, for our purposes, we can regard sales promotion as consisting of an offer that has tangible advantages not inherent in the usual product or service in order to achieve marketing objectives. So sales promotion is a stimulus or motivating influence to *buy* and will be treated separately from direct marketing, the subject of the next chapter. The present chapter will also deal with the subject of incentives, those payments usually made to salespeople, as inducements to perform better. Why include them with sales promotion? Incentives are included because they are stimuli or motivating influences to *sell* and balance the buyer/salesperson equation.

8.2   Can sales promotions be strategic?

If the offer featured as part of a sales promotion is carefully selected it can do much for the promoted brand. Wherever possible, select your premium to match the brand identity and theme advertising of the product being promoted. This approach helps to prevent any potential conflict between the brand images being projected by above- and below-the-line campaigns. Furthermore, a carefully planned and well-executed premium promotion, with a highly creative approach to the selection of the premium itself, can be just as effective as advertising in influencing consumers' attitudes to brands. As the main asset of any manufactured product is its brand identity, the selection of a premium must ideally enhance the image the brand-owner is building.

While a premium can play an active role in developing a brand identity – by 'creatively complementing' the brand and helping to endorse the brand position – it is also important to ensure that the premium item appeals to the product's target market. For example, United Biscuits' Penguin brand in mid-1986 offered a premium that was designed to appeal directly to the product's target market, while also visually endorsing its 'fun' identity. Through an on-pack promotion, consumers were able to collect free Penguin badges by providing proofs of purchase. This was not just a one-off, tactical promotion but the first in a series of badge offers designed to brand Penguin below-the-line. It was just another way to 'PickupaPenguin'!

Of course, Robertson's jams and marmalades were traditionally promoted by means of the Robertson's Golly, both above- and below-the-line. Collecting the Golly badges remained an institution for decades.

The job of sales promotion is not just to add value to a product or service; it must use the promotional opportunity to add brand values and to pick up on the advertising positioning. If an element of the brand's above-the-line advertising is added to the pack on-shelf, it provides an extra chance of persuading consumers to pick up the product.

Another good example comes from Elida-Gibbs' Cream Silk hair-conditioner. One premium promotion included a free silk bandeau offer with proofs of purchase. As well as adding value to the product, the premium added *brand* value by emphasizing the word silk. Further, the promotion supported the brand's current advertising copy line – 'Which one is your type?' – which promotes the fact that there are four Cream Silk variants to suit different hair types. The promotion reflected this element of choice by highlighting the different ways in which the bandeau could be worn; it was available in four colours, with each colour reflecting the packaging of one of the four product variants.

Naturally it may not be possible to tie everything together as nicely as Cream Silk was able to do. Indeed it is important to guard against allowing the need to provide a premium that is relevant to the brand to supersede the benefit to the consumer. (To take a hypothetical example, if you were trying to promote Avon tyres to the male-dominated sports-car market, you might not have much success offering Avon cosmetics as the premium – unless of course you offered the male cosmetics from the Avon range!) However, it is still possible to achieve a level of compatibility by customizing the premium item, or by adding the brand identity or campaign slogan.

So, yes! Sales promotions can be strategic.

8.3 Apply the KISS (Keep It Simple and Sell) principle

While one is being creative to add brand values, spare a thought for the consumer. Your customers are not out looking for ideas, they are just shopping, so sales promotion must not be complicated. Using creativity in sales devising promotion means a simple concept that is true to a brand's values. In order to get the idea, you should put yourself in the consumer's shoes.

When did you as a consumer last give a considered thought to a sales promotion? Possibly it was one that you took part in without realizing it: money off next purchase perhaps. Even if you had not plans to clip the on-pack coupon, the offer may have enticed you. Other promotions may have been so obviously a benefit that you accepted them without a second thought: 20 per cent extra free, say. Some you may have rejected because they were irrelevant or simply unappealing, or, worse, too complicated.

The chances are that the promotion you do remember, the one you consciously took part in – or bought the product because you meant to participate – was simple. It felt right. The headline, the proposition, the task, all were clearly for you. The product was bought; the sale was made. Another success!

A sales promotion is an idea seeking to catch the interest of consumers, not the other way round. If the idea is easy to understand, it will appeal and help to make a sale. Sales promotion – unlike advertising, which has 30 seconds, a full page of colour or nearly 200 sq. feet of poster to put across its idea – has to intrude at a time when people are not interested in intellectual challenges. They are doing a chore and would probably prefer to be doing something else. They are buying groceries or filling a tank with petrol.

Consider Figure 8.1. To arrive at a simple idea requires a great deal of thought, but too often sales promotions appear to be ideas looking for solutions rather than ideas based on a solution. Analysis comes first. It includes gathering all the relevant information that will enable quantifiable objectives to be set. Planning is the process that produces effective strategies, leading to a considered mechanic for the promotion that can be simply implemented, following a review of options. The idea is the solution to all that hard work that has gone before.

Sadly, too many people judge a sales promotion by the 'big idea' concept, rather than the suitability of that idea to achieve the desired goal. In addition, it is not just the idea that is often so ill-considered and inappropriate, so is the response method.

Let us look at some of the more popular promotional techniques:

- Prize promotions, e.g. competitions, draws, sweepstakes.

- Premium promotions, e.g. free or self-liquidating mail-ins.
- Cash refunds.

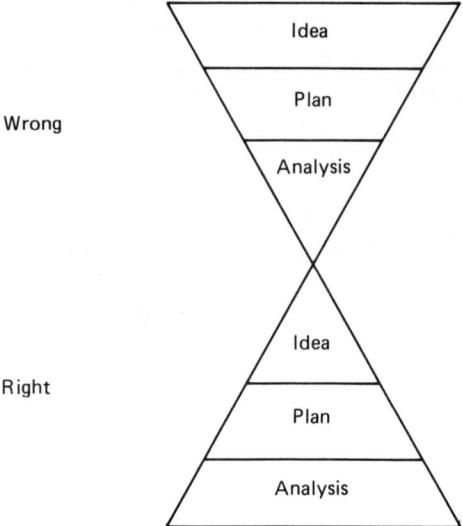

Figure 8.1 *The bottom-up approach to idea-generation*

Nine times out of ten such promotions require the participating consumers to write a letter. In other words, they have to fill in an entry or application form, address an envelope, buy a postage stamp, cut out a proof of purchase, maybe enclose money, and post the letter.

Could anything be less in keeping with the way the general public behaves normally. People do not often write letters today. When wanting to communicate with friends or relations, they are much more likely to pick up the telephone and speak to them. Look what comes through your home letterbox: not letters from friends, but rather a miscellaneous collection of bills, circulars or invitations to spend your disposable income on books, records, insurance policies and investment funds. The one big occasion of the year when people do write to each other – at Christmas, in the form of pre-printed greetings cards – the Post Office has to take on extra staff to cope with this untypical activity.

Consumers are asked to respond to sales-promotion offers in such antiquated ways:

(a) Apply on printed application or entry forms – printing has been around since the late Middle Ages.
(b) Fill them in with pen and ink. Stone Age technology!

(c) Send them in via the Post Office – a great nineteenth-century invention.

And what of the delays?

1 'Allow up to 28 days . . .' – a Savile Row tailor can make a hand-crafted bespoke suit in that time.
2 'Winners will be informed by 15 July; if you wish to receive a list of winners please send a stamped addressed envelope to . . .' Who cares?

There must be better ways of organising all these promotions, ways that exploit new and existing technologies. All the signs are that the consumer welcomes new ways of participating. Remember the success of scratch-off cards when they were first introduced as a competition mechanic. Consumers responded favourably to the opportunity to know instantly whether they had won or lost, without any need to send in and wait sometimes for months before hearing the result.

Phone-in competitions regularly attract a high level of entries – higher levels of response than competitions conducted through the post. One, run for Country Life English Butter in early 1989, received more than 60,000 telephone calls and nearly 8000 entries, such was the interest in phoning the Buttermen. Remember the example from Chapter 1, when Antiquary Whisky used the telephone not only to act as a 'promotional leaflet' but also to take an instant record of entries to the competition.

Current voice-interactive techniques and simple computer genera-tion of questions (which become progressively more difficult to answer) make it possible to identify winners of various prize levels during the telephone call. Consumers are thus able to participate live, in the same sort of quizzes as they watch in such large numbers on television.

The real breakthrough of course would be if television regulations allowed the promoter to sponsor such quiz programmes, inviting purchasers of his brand to participate by phone in parallel with the studio audience. In Italy such sponsorship is permitted, and consumer competitions built around quiz programmes generate millions of entries. Perhaps it will not be too long before such schemes are permitted in the UK.

Phone-in competitions are frequently employed in promoting and broadening the interest in radio stations. In 1991 large cash prizes were being offered by Europe's largest commercial radio station, London's Capital Radio, during weekday breakfast-time broadcasts. The *Today* newspaper would carry details of a so-called 'trigger record' each morning, and entrants, on hearing the trigger played, would phone in to Capital Radio. Ten lines would remain open, perhaps for up to 25 minutes, before one entrant was selected to answer a simple question. Tension increased as the prize was kept sealed in an envelope that the DJ, Chris Tarrant, would try to 'buy-back' off the winner. The envelope could have contained a prize of a used lollipop stick through to round the world trips, or £10,000 in cash. Here again, the telephone was used as the direct response media for the competition, giving all concerned instant results.

So while using the mail box has served as a valuable response medium, since some retailers have become reluctant to redeem coupons, unwilling to display free with-pack premiums, and store-draws have become more difficult to negotiate in some retail outlets, remember the telephone.

Further, decisions taken at the point-of-purchase about which brand to buy are much too important to dodge. Contemporary car-owning consumers are happy to drive to the high street or shopping centre, or past a few garages, to reach their 'brand', but not so happy to put pen to paper. Yet they'll pick up the phone. Similarly, with promotions in which cash has to be sent, why use the mail to transfer money to consumers when every high street has a post office and several banks, all in the business of receiving, handing out and transmitting cash?

A Post Office Pet Savers scheme, for example, offered pet owners £1 in exchange for thirty tokens from a pet food range presented at any post office counter. BBC Radio 2, during its November 1989 'Children in Need Appeal' asked people to hand in their 1p pieces in a bid to raise 100,000,000 such coins for charity – to high street banks. A similar campaign in 1992 asked people to send in the discontinued 5p pieces which were being replaced by new coinage.

Today's business world is changing more quickly than ever before. To stay ahead we cannot rest content with obsolete ways of administering promotions. They have got to be easy for people to take part in, and the interaction and exchange should be simple, fast and efficient, giving immediate responses.

8.4 Tailor-made promotions

A tailor-made promotion is a promotion mounted by a manufacturer through one retail organization. Any of the standard sales-promotion techniques could of course be used in a tailored form, though price-cuts and coupons make up the vast majority of these schemes. Within this area of tailor-made promotions fall incentive schemes, whereby a manufacturer might provide the retailer or merchant with support so that he can run a bonus scheme for his staff to encourage their selling that manufacturer's brand in preference to a competitor's.

With the increased dominance and power of the retail trade in the last decade, particularly in the grocery sector, the demand for tailor-made promotions from the multiples has led to an increase in such targeted activity. Tony Dakin[1] cites the case of Cadbury-Schweppes, which throughout a 12-month period dropped national promotions entirely, and ran twenty separate tailor-made promotions. When they came to study the results Cadbury-Schweppes found that as a direct result of the tailor-made promotions, sales were up, on average, by 25 per cent.

There are three reasons for using tailor-made promotions.

First, to help in the sales-negotiation process. By offering such a scheme, a manufacturer has something to offer in exchange for a greater commitment by the retailer. Such negotiations are very much the domain of the national accounts manager, and may occasionally be agreed outside the marketing department. Very often the agreement is made not so much on what the likely gains are, but on what the losses will be if you don't comply.

Second, to proffer a positive solution of tactical problems. While your brand may enjoy national distribution and good shelf-pressure, there may still be tactical problems with one major multiple. If you prepare the tailor-made promotion thoroughly, you may be able to overcome the problems.

Third, to make a positive move to exploit a retailer's particular characteristics. As we saw in the last chapter, retailers, particularly the major multiples, have developed quite clear corporate images. The characteristics of each company's customers differ slightly, sometimes significantly, particularly in terms of their attitude to price and other factors, and of course their general demographics. For example, the customers of Woolworth seem to be markedly more responsive to competitions than the customers of Boots, and so on.

There are seven main groups of tailor-made promotions.

8.4.1 Special-price promotions

These are the simplest form. The manufacturer makes a contribution, either by reducing prices or by offering free goods. Some or all of this price reduction is passed on to consumers. Occasionally, the retailer makes a contribution. Remember, however, what was said in Chapter 2 about price and exchanging turnover for a reduction in unit profit.

8.4.2 Special coupons – easy to administer

Coupons, often as part of a retailer's advertising, are redeemable only at their stores. A manufacturer may have to contribute to the above-the-line media costs.

8.4.3 Local events – organized by the manufacturer's salesmen

Such events are normally designed to create massive displays in-store or just outside, often built around a competition theme where the prizes, from kitchenware to motor cars, are built into the display for maximum impact. Variants include new-store opening events, where good relations with the store manager can be started.

8.4.4 Tailored spokes

In these cases a national promotion is run but a special version is developed for a given retailer or maybe just a given geographical area. The weight of the national event drives the tailored spoke on a local level.

8.4.5 Inserts in a retail theme

Where a retailer mounts its own corporate promotion and invites other manufacturers to participate. While it was a while ago, the Co-op Royal Silver Jubilee Celebration in 1977 was one of the largest examples of such a promotion. Over a 6-month period (rather than the usual few weeks) fifty-six manufacturers with more than 100 national bands participated with individual and joint jubilee promotions.

The creative execution of the promotion was a triumph of planning. A special Co-op Royal Silver Jubilee Celebration logotype was developed, with specific colours, a designer's guidance manual distributed, and so forth, such that all participating companies' entire array of activity would have a homogeneous appearance. The original objective was achieved: the Co-op's market share was protected against tough retail competition and deep price-cutting. Sales momentum was maintained too, with a combination of the Jubilee promotions and the Co-op's own price promotion programme; many manufacturers also achieved record sales during the event.

8.4.6 Packaged promotions

Not to be confused with custom packs, these are often built on a modular design and can be personalized to suit the needs of a given retailer. The local salesman is free to choose from a 'catalogue' of items, pre-designed and pre-approved by the manufacturer's marketing department, and collated for the relevant store. Because of the inherent flexibility of this type of tailor-made promotion, there is considerable scope for local initiative by the salesman and store manager, while still leaving control with the retailer's and company's head office.

8.4.7 Custom packs

These are packs produced with promotion flashes tailored to the individual retailer. These can be very successful, but remember to answer these questions first:

(a) How are you going to handle the multiplicity of specials in your inventory system?
(b) How are you going to make sure retailer A does not get retailer B's special custom packs?
(c) Will all other retailers also ask for specials from you? If they do, can you cope?
(d) How much stock will you have to make to meet your production department's minimum? What will you do if the retailer will not, as is likely, take the lot but only a part order?
(e) Will custom packs affect your brand's identity?
(f) Is there an easier way to customize your packs than reprinting labels? Could you use stickers?

8.5 Checklist for tailor-made promotions

Before embarking on a programme of tailor-made promotions, review this checklist[2] to see if you have covered all the other options before committing yourself:

CHECKLIST

Rule 1: Be honest about the precise objective
Is the tailored promotion designed to increase consumer sales, increase the number of branches stocking the product, convert trade bonuses into consumer promotion, keep on the right side of the buyer,

counteract a successful tailored promotion by a competitor, stop the national accounts man nagging about lack of support for his efforts – or what?

Rule 2: Don't even think about tailored promotion if there's a cheaper and quicker way of meeting the objective

Too many discussions about tailored promotions concern themselves with trivial or transient trade problems. Too often, suppliers reach for a promotion as the solution to a problem, when a clear, frank and factual presentation of the problem would stand a very good chance of persuading the trade customer that a different course would make sense. Such a presentation, fully supported with visual aids, is certainly much cheaper and much quicker to prepare. The lead times for tailored promotions – slotted, as they must be, into the customer's own promotion programme – are such that the problem has often gone away by the time the promotion designed to solve it finally appears.

Rule 3: Don't create a tailored promotion from scratch, if an already planned national promotion can be adapted

If there is a big national promotion due to run at about the time a specific push is planned with an individual trade customer, check first to see if the power of this big promotion can be harnessed to the specific customer's resources. It often can be. See Rule 4, however.

Rule 4: Make the tailored promotion reflect the customer's own trading policies

It is not enough just to stick the customer's logo on the print material. Retailers have their own increasingly distinct trading policies and their own advertising and promotional propositions. A supplier's tailored promotion will gain a much more ready acceptance if it supports the nature and style of the customer's business. The creative skill comes in relating this to the promoted brand's objective.

Rule 5: Make each tailored promotion an integral part of the marketing plan for that customer

Major trade customers deserve, and should have, individual marketing plans from their suppliers. There should be numerical budgets, for sales, shelf-facings, feature displays, stocking levels, support expenditure and special terms. And there should be a bottom line profit budget. Tailored promotions, at their most cost-effective, are merely part of this plan, playing a clearly defined role within the total effort the supplier intends to make towards the individual customer. There should be no panic-stricken resort to extra effort to salvage a crumbling situation.

Rule 6: Cost the management time the tailored promotion will require
All sales promotions have irreducible minimum fixed costs. They often include design, artwork and plate-making charges for print material. The costs of personnel time taken up in creating, negotiating and implementing *any* promotion, and in particular a tailored promotion, where so many people are engaged, will be much greater.

In the case of a large budget promotion, to be mounted nationally through all trade outlets, these fixed costs are spread over a large volume of promoted goods. This is not possible to the same extent with the majority of tailored promotions, and these fixed costs are likely to loom large in relation to variable costs. They should not be ignored therefore. If they look too large in relation to the importance of the objective to be achieved, revert to Rule 2.

Rule 7: Leave the John Bull printing set at home!
Do *not* attempt to reduce any of these fixed costs by doing it on the cheap. Too many tailored promotion leaflets and POS displays still look as though they have been printed by the local sales representative on his child's John Bull printing set.

Magic markers are fine, if that is what the outlet uses, but the brand or products promoted surely deserve a printed presentation compatible with the standards achieved on the packs and in classic print media, such as press and posters. Otherwise the trade customer might reasonably conclude that the supplier is giving him third best.

Rule 8: Where possible, relate the promoted brand(s) to other goods or services sold by the customer
The wholesale or retail customer is primarily interested in total outlet sales, not just in the brand or brands promoted by the tailored scheme. Tailored promotions that also help to push related products are therefore of particular interest to many trade customers. If the related products have the customer's own label, so much the better.

Rule 9: Promote the brand and the trade customer, not the Post Office
National, all-outlet promotions commonly require consumers to mail in applications, and to receive back what is on offer through the post. Negotiations about tailored promotions should usually contain a proposal that shoppers should be able to enter the promotion in the customer's store – via 'post-boxes' mounted on displays, for example. This method is cheaper and more convenient for shoppers, and it can result in a higher level of participation and a much more successful promotion. Remember too that with the more modern technologies (like the telephone of course) and even EPOS (see Chapter 6) you may be able to simplify the consumer's task in participation. Give some thought to whether you expect to get consumers participating while

in-store on the first shopping trip or whether you want them to return to that store to enter on a second visit.

Rule 10: Spend whatever is required to achieve the objective
All too often, a brand appropriates a lump sum for tailored promotion, say £100,000 for the year. This amount is then broken down on the basis that Tesco accounts for 18 per cent of the brand's sales, and needs two tailored promotions. The budget for each is therefore £9,000.

It is highly unlikely, however, that this £9,000 is equal to the task to be accomplished by the promotion. It is also very surprising if £18,000 happens, coincidentally, to be precisely the sum of money the supplier's Tesco marketing plan can afford. The size and nature of the objective to be achieved, set in the context of the marketing plan for the customer, should determine the budget for the tailored promotion.

If in doubt, Rule 10a – 'Spend more to be on the safe side' – should be applied. In many classes of trade, retailer time and space are scarce resources. If it is worth going to all the time and expense of creating, negotiating and implementing a tailored promotion, it makes sense to be sure it succeeds. There may be a long wait before there is a second chance, and by then it may be too late.

8.6 Some techniques reviewed

8.6.1 Is it legal?

Sales promotion has had to cope with the vagaries, eccentricities and hard and fast rules of legislation both in the UK and abroad for a long time. Now, the advent of 1992 has thrown into sharp focus the fact that more clients will be considering European markets. Agencies too need to have a thorough and convincing grasp of the likely problems and feasible solutions in order to convince indecisive customers that, with sales promotion, most things are possible. If the initial concept is grand enough, ways will be found to circumvent the obvious problems of differing law, culture and taste in each country, while precisely targeting the various markets. If the 'grand plan' is good enough, it will convince the affiliated or network member offices in each country that a promotion is relevant to their individual needs and aspirations for the brand.

The legislation in the different countries is certainly a minefield, and the more one learns about a particular country's legislation, the more it seems there is to know. There are very different constraints on sales promotion in different countries but that is a poor reason for believing the concept of a pan-European promotion or brands is not possible.

An in-depth study has been made by the sales promotion consultancy IMP, based on research and its own experience in the field, in an attempt to formulate a basic guide to the various countries. Many European member states have codified legal systems which, at first glance, unravel the legal complexities by providing an easily accessible reference source, but interpretation can vary dramatically. In Denmark, for example, Article One of the 1974 Marketing Practices Act bans 'unfair marketing practices' and provides a Consumer Ombudsman. The courts will look closely at the Ombudsman's interpretation of 'unfair'. Ideally, contact the Ombudsman first: our British sense of fair play could be seen as 'unfair' in a more restrictive European context. Occasionally, with luck, the opposite may be true.

IMP has developed a table to show which countries allow which promotions (Table 8.2). The table is intended to give an overview of Europe, providing a quick point of reference and topline starting point for planning an approach to a particular marketing problem. It is not intended to be, nor can it be, comprehensive and definitive, with so many exceptions to the rules. There are three warnings:

- In a number of cases throughout Europe both statute and case laws are unclear, often because the techniques have never been used in a given market. Where the course to take is not clear, or depends on a specific official approval, a subjective judgement on the likely outcome is based on IMP's experience.
- At first glance a technique may clearly appear either legal or illegal, but significant exceptions to the rules do exist. On the grid IMP's view – yes, no, or maybe – relates to the *most likely* use of the particular technique.
- The table is only a *guide*. It focuses on possible legal solutions and is a basic starting point for further investigation. All proposals should be cleared through the usual relevant legal channels before implementation.

Will it be possible to run one campaign across Europe? Broadly speaking, yes, although the range of suitable techniques will be limited. This does not mean of course that a pan-European campaign, no matter how clever, creative or imaginative, will necessarily be desirable to the local organization, acceptable to the retailer, or acceptable to the consumer. Or effective!

Spain, Portugal and Greece are governed by very general legislation, although more detailed legislation is planned. By UK standards these markets are relatively unsophisticated in promotional marketing terms, and many of our popular techniques have never been

Table 8.2 *Which countries allow which promotion?*

	UK	Irish republic	Spain	West Germany	France	Denmark	Belgium	Netherlands	Portugal	Italy	Greece	Luxembourg
On-pack price reductions	•	•	•	•	•	•	•	•	•	•	•	•
Banded offers	•	•	•	•	•	•	•	•	•	•	•	?
In-pack premiums	•	•	•	?	?	?	?	?	•	•	•	?
Multiple purchase offer	•	•	•	?	?	•	?	?	•	•	•	?
Extra product	•	•	•	?	•	•	?	•	•	•	•	•
Free product	•	•	•	•	•	•	•	•	•	•	•	•
Re-usable/alternative use pack	•	•	•	•	•	•	•	•	•	•	•	•
Free mail-ins	•	•	•	?	•	•	•	•	•	•	•	•
With-purchase premiums	•	•	•	○	•	○	?	?	•	•	•	?
Cross-product offers	•	•	•	○	•	?	?	?	•	•	•	○
Collector devices	•	•	•	○	•	?	○	•	•	•	•	?
Competitions	•	•	•	?	•	?	?	•	•	•	•	?
Self-liquidating premiums	•	•	•	•	•	•	•	•	•	•	•	•
Free draws	•	•	•	○	•	○	○	?	•	?	•	•
Share-outs	•	?	•	○	?	○	○	○	•	?	•	○
Sweepstake/lottery	?	?	•	○	?	○	○	?	•	?	•	○
Money-off vouchers	•	•	•	○	•	?	○	○	•	?	•	○
Money-off next purchase	•	•	•	○	•	○	•	•	•	?	•	•
Cash backs	•	•	•	?	•	•	•	•	•	○	•	•
In-store demos	•	•	•	•	•	•	•	•	•	•	•	•

Source: IMP   • Permitted   ○ Not permitted   ? May be permitted

tested. The approach in Table 8.2 has been 'legal until proven otherwise'.

The single European market may call for a highly individualistic approach, with different strategies for each constituent market. Each case has to be reviewed on its merits and each programme checked out. Will promotional marketing end up ruled by the lowest common denominator? Is this the beginning of the end for promotional marketing in Europe? Far from it. The year 1992 is likely to stretch creativity, flexibility and inventiveness to the limits and beyond to new levels.

8.6.2 Where to go for ideas

In Chapter 4 we considered the implementation of below-the-line publicity via an outside consultant. Naturally, if you are using an outside consultant or agency, then that would be a starting point. It may be, however, that you are running your own operation and need to get a feel for what is available, either as a premium item or as an advertising or business gift. A distinction has to be made between premiums and advertising or business gifts. The former two are not usually personalized, and are used in promotional or motivational activities. Examples include such things as competition prizes, say a holiday for two, or bone-china items. Gifts are invariably used to carry a message, branded for a product or carrying a corporate logo.

For a broad overview on below-the-line activities, one of the Incentive Marketing and Sales Promotion exhibitions, held usually in London, Brighton or the National Exhibition Centre, Birmingham, is a good place to start. Understandably, such shows will concentrate on those areas best suited for exhibition, namely premiums, incentive merchandise and advertising gifts. Occasionally you will also find organizations offering incentive travel possibilities and voucher incentive operations. If at the show you attend there are surprisingly few service companies, such as sales-promotion consultancies, then that is probably because it is extremely difficult for them to find anything to put on show. Their stock in trade is really ideas, and even the best ideas make poor exhibits.

Whether any given exhibition can be regarded as an actual barometer of below-the-line activity is difficult to say, because the premiums and advertising gifts business is far from being an industry in its own right. It is, rather, an element within a discipline that is itself only part of the marketing mix. However, the 'industry' is becoming more sophisticated, with the accent much more on timing, service and quality. As advertising gifts become more popular and sophisticated, as a result of market pressure, advertisers, facing limitations in their publicity budgets, are having to seek out new, cheaper ways of communicating their messages without loss of image. Well-designed, carefully selected desk items can convey a message more clearly and more effectively than a glossy four-colour advertisement might have done a few years ago.

Some advertising gift companies – such as Bourne Publicity – frequently publish catalogues of their merchandise, and the catalogues regularly contain over 1000 items. Other companies – such as OK Promotions and Source – prefer not to commit themselves in this way, and concentrate on specific or adapted items. The promotions they put together produce specially sourced premiums, and such companies are constantly on the lookout for new ideas.

As far as novelty value is concerned, recent advances in microchip technology have allowed sales promotions to feature such unusual, almost bizarre, premium offers as musical toilet-roll holders, talking birthday cards, or speaking alarm clocks that wake people up with a torrent of verbal abuse in an Australian accent.

Electronic-based premiums and incentives have come a long way since the simple calculators and light-emitting diode (LED) watches of the late 1970s. Liquid crystal display (LCD) watches and even liquid crystal analogue watches began to appear in the mid-1980s, followed a couple of years later by LCD radio alarm clocks. Today specially adapted versions of standard chips are being used to produce merchandise such as musical coffee mugs, voice-activated alarm clocks, and sales presenters that deliver an 8-second message. Technology is also being used to produce such items as:

1 Kitchen calculators that 'instantly' convert measurements for cookery recipes to match the number of servings.
2 Electronic medical equipment for the home, from pulse meters to digital blood pressure monitors as premiums.
3 Smoke alarms, personal attack alarms, and solar-powered products.

While prices are coming down, the premium business is actually moving further upmarket. Although there is still a demand for the more basic products, there is a growing interest in more sophisticated electronic products, especially those that can be allied to the theme of the promotion itself.

A dealer incentive offered during a Bailey's Irish Cream promotion featured a 'solar-cooled safari hat', which had a mechanical fan at the front, powered by a tiny solar panel. It was amusing for the trade, but it did tie up with the brand message, which was all about staying cool in the summer. However, be warned! It may be that electronic wizardry will detract from the seriousness of a brand's message. People might be so impressed with the technology of the premium that they forget the message. Don't use technology to replace creativity. As stated earlier analyse, plan, *then* find the idea, not the other way round.

Another good source for ideas is the Premiums, Incentives and Prizes price guide (PIP). When PIP reviewed its most popular items, it found that as far as selection of gifts is concerned, the industry was very conservative. Traditional gifts include keyrings, towels, and cameras, all of which have been top-selling items for over a decade. Companies have become aware that the gift can reflect the image of their organizations, so are selecting fewer gifts at better quality. PIP is being inundated currently with requests for high-quality materials such as fine bone china, lambswool and leather. PIP suggests that 'people want to gain more intangible results – i.e. that it communicates more about their main product'.

As movements in the gift selections in the main are slight, it is difficult to spot any major trends. However, those that are 'out' are the socially less acceptable items, such as ashtrays and lighters; 'in' come the 'greeners', i.e. biodegradable carrier bags, wild bird feeders and the like. Because banks and other financial institutions are looking to be more marketing-oriented and are using below-the-line expenditure on promoting their image, there has been some development in goods of better quality and higher perceived value for their image. Premium and gift suppliers have also noticed that they are getting more enquiries from computer firms with a strong business-to-business need that is fulfilled by quality desk items, pens and leather business card-holders.

Curiously this part of the below-the-line publicity sector seems to be weathering the general economic downturn. 'When companies are buoyant they have more money available to spend on promotions, and when there is a downturn they are anxious to preserve their market share and so increase their promotional activity budget' according to Don Wood, MD of Source, one of the UK's leading suppliers of a wide range of incentive and gift items. Lucky for some!

8.6.3 *Couponing/vouchering/ and discounting*

Today there are some blurred lines that make it hard to explain the difference between couponing, vouchering and discounting. In broad terms:

- *Coupons* are cut out of newspapers and magazines or off packets, and entitle us to, say, 5p. off our next purchase.
- *Discounting* means that by taking some form of special identity or a

passbook into a retailer, one may get money off products or services. Companies often produce such means for their employees to use at specific outlets, particularly for company car drivers to get money off new tyres, for example.

- *Vouchers* are invariably beautifully produced forms of pseudo-currency that are redeemable for one type of goods or at one specific retailer. It might be £50 to spend at Harrods or £10 to be spent on a bottle of Moet at any one of a number of off-licences. An extension of this idea – multi-vouchers – provides vouchers that are exchangeable at a mixture of different stores.

Vouchers are popular means of providing incentives for, and rewarding, staff, because, while income tax is due on them, National Insurance is not. Pound for pound, employees are currently 11 per cent better off with vouchers.

The roots of the voucher and coupon industry come from the bottom of the market. There are record and book tokens, redeemable at W.H. Smith, for example. They make a gift seem a little more personal than plain cash, are easy to mail across the country, and ensure that the recipient does not get an unwanted gift. There are also the mighty schemes, such as Green Shield Stamps, recently revived, and luncheon vouchers (legislation is being revised to increase the value of vouchers that can be paid to an employee in any one day from 15p. (3 shillings), where it has been for over 40 years).

Voucher schemes are very attractive from the retailer's point of view. Retailers get paid before the goods are sold, customers are tied in to a shop with vouchers, and even if the customers don't bother to spend the vouchers, the retailers still get their money. The idea is not limited to shops either. Anyone who has a product the public wants to buy can benefit, including hotels, airlines, restaurants, even theme parks.

The 1980s was a boom period for the sales promotion and incentive industries and this has meant that companies are constantly on the lookout for new motivational ideas. There is still a hint of snobbery about paying for goods with vouchers, possibly because there is still confusion between vouchers and coupons. Redemption on coupons is much more prevalent in the North of England than in the generally more prosperous South. Someone buying £100 worth of groceries probably will not bother to reclaim 5p on a promotion, even though they may have clipped the coupon. The trick therefore in using *vouchers* as incentives is to ensure that they are for products or services the recipient would not normally be able to afford. The market, consequently, is continually driven upwards. Harrods and Fortnum & Mason have been doing good business this way for a long time. F&M will even open the store in the evenings for companies to bring their people in for private shopping functions. We shall discuss vouchers again in later sections of this chapter as incentives and alternative currencies are reviewed.

Let us now turn to couponing, which can be an expensive item in any consumer goods marketing campaign. Brand managers, before launching a coupon campaign, are taking more time investigating the cost-effectiveness of alternative media for distributing the coupons, and trying to assess the redemption rates attributable to those media, so essential in budgeting for such a campaign.

Couponing can be defined as a printed price offer made to a target group of customers, using a variety of media – direct-mail leaflets, printed advertisements, or coupons in and on packs. Usually potential customers need to take the printed offer to their chosen retailer for redemption against a named product. Some retailers have been successful with their own coupons, used by customers against, say, their meat bill. When manufacturers issue coupons, the consumer can relate the price reduction to the manufacturer – or more likely the brand – rather than the outlet.

Couponing is one way in which manufacturers persuade retailers to stock or display the product – justification alone for the expense in some cases – and by which substantial, usually short-term sales increases can be stimulated. In 1965 estimates put the number of coupons redeemed in the UK at 55 million. By 1976 the figure was 242 million, by 1981 324 million and by 1983 over 350 million, according to Nielsen Clearing House (NCH) Data Bank. In July 1992 plans were announced in the journal *Marketing* to offer money-off coupons in loose national newspaper inserts (already common in the USA): 'Coupons are expected to reach 9 million shoppers by the end of this year and ultimately more than 50 per cent of UK households'.

Coupons can be distributed through a number of different distribution media: the most commonly used are newspapers, magazines, door-to-door, and both in- and on-packs. Figure 8.2 shows the division of total coupon volume among the principal distributing vehicles during 1981.

Because they offer significant advantages over other methods, *newspapers* are used most widely. Newspapers' sheer volume is one major reason for their popularity, and the fact that the cost of the coupon can be shared with the cost of an advertisement is another. Newspapers' good market selectivity means that targeting the coupon is easy. Newspapers also offer planning and execution flexibility, and pinpoint timing.

Magazine coupons may form part of the advertisement, be stuck to the page or bound in, or appear as loose inserts. Magazines offer fine colour reproduction, which helps bring the coupon to the readers'

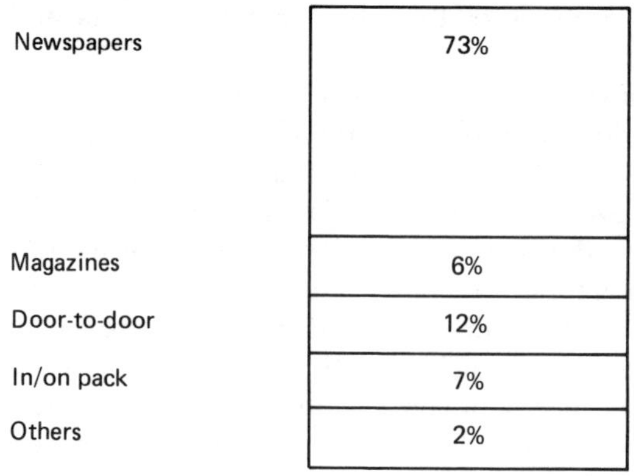

Newspapers	73%
Magazines	6%
Door-to-door	12%
In/on pack	7%
Others	2%

Figure 8.2 *Breakdown of distribution media in 1981 (total 7614m). Source: NCH Data Bank*

attention; at the same time they offer a showcase for the product and information about it. Audience selectivity is good, and each magazine is often retained and read by more than one person.

Door-to-door distribution today does not mean someone goes round inserting coupons specially for you, although some companies do offer this service and it can be quite useful for test-marketing purposes or for joint promotions with retailers in certain areas. Door-to-door today usually means your coupon is included as part of a larger advertising publication, often produced by some of the multiples to attract people to their stores, *which may in turn be mailed out rather than sent by hand.* The redemption rates are higher than with either newspaper or magazine distribution (see Figure 8.3). The impact on the consumer is high, as with many direct-mail promotions, providing the targeting is accurate.

One organization that has been successful in this coordinated approach is Pampers. When someone has a baby, the midwife gives the mother a bounty pack containing a registration card, which notes the date of birth of the baby, and free samples of a selection of products, including a Pampers Nappy. Regular purchasers will appreciate the home delivery service offered for these bulky items. At the appropriate time a short 12-page magazine is mailed out to the mother with articles written with emphasis appropriate to the baby's age; bound on the front is a coupon offering quite a substantial saving (20 per cent) off the next size bulk pack of nappies. (The cost of this magazine has been offset by advertising sold to non-competitive companies, e.g. washing-powder, food and toiletries manufacturers – all of which are delighted to target their products so accurately.

Advertisers always include a coupon in their advertisements.) Mothers are thus encouraged to remain brand loyal, as the larger nappies can be bought from the same home-delivery van, and the coupon redeemed across the mother's front door.

With distribution *in-* or *on-pack*, the coupons offer direct access to the target customer. They serve the vital function of encouraging repeat purchase by existing users (increasing brand loyalty) and may influence new users to buy with the promise of later saving. On- or in-pack distribution has the cheapest distribution costs of any couponing technique, and by far the highest response rate, with 62 per cent of the 324 million coupons redeemed in 1981 having been distributed by this method, which gives a 37.7 per cent redemption rate.

The widely different redemption rates will be borne in mind by the wise marketer in making his choice of method of distribution (see Figure 8.3).

The growth in coupon use is likely to continue, since coupons' flexibility allows them to be successfully incorporated into marketing plans. As a result, they can be used to achieve various objectives, including:

(a) To gain customers and convert them into regular users, particularly for new or improved products, when customers are encouraged to trade up.
(b) To widen the distribution of products.
(c) To redress high, or low, stocks.
(d) To level out sales, peaks and troughs, thus maintaining economic production.
(e) To offset price increases.
(f) To create new interest in an established product and improve results from in-store displays.

But remember, if you are including a coupon in an advertisement in a newspaper, then for every 1 million papers sold you can expect 9300 coupons to be redeemed. Similarly, if you print 100,000 pack labels and get that product on-shelf, you can expect 37,700 coupons to be redeemed. How are you going to handle them?

8.6.4 Handling houses

Handling houses are a crucial, though rarely seen, part of the sales-promotion mix. They must be chosen with care because their performance can make or break a promotion. Known as 'fulfilment

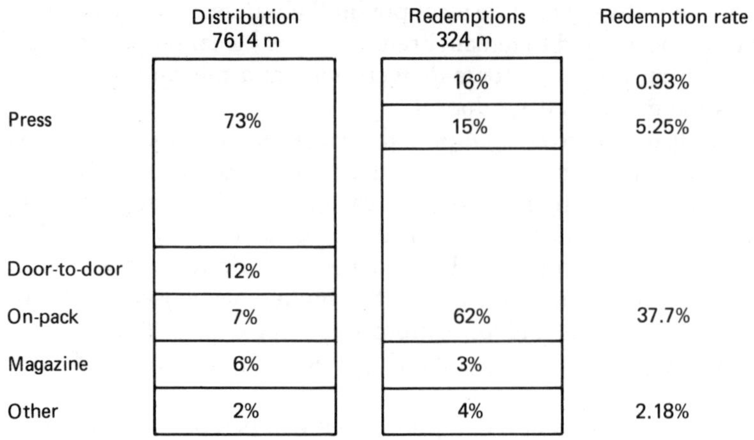

	Distribution 7614 m	Redemptions 324 m	Redemption rate
		16%	0.93%
Press	73%	15%	5.25%
Door-to-door	12%		
On-pack	7%	62%	37.7%
Magazine	6%	3%	
Other	2%	4%	2.18%

Figure 8.3 *Comparison of coupon distribution and redemptions, manufacturer and retailer-generated coupons, 1981. Source: NCH DataBank*

houses' to the trade, handling houses are the specialist companies used to sort coupons, package merchandise of every conceivable size and shape, and distribute it to specified destinations. They are also responsible for checking coupon requests, competition entries, and accounting for payments that are sent in by retailers and consumers. As a first line of contact to customers, handling houses may be quite distant in the advertiser's mind. However, a weakness in this link in the chain can destroy a campaign where millions of pounds have been invested. One handling house 'overlooked' 8000 consumer claims for refunds worth over £3000, producing a lot of unhappy consumers, to say nothing of the effect on cash flow once the problem had been identified.

Beware too the hidden pitfalls. A Hedges & Butler Hirondelle wine promotion became complicated when the offer was changed from twelve bottles for the price of eleven to thirteen bottles for the price of twelve. To cope with this apparently simple concept change, a specialist handling house had to package, label, and distribute 1200 bottles of wine to 110 Linfood cash and carry outlets, after first sorting through the requirements of four different types of table wine. No such problem would have arisen with the original concept, because a case of twelve bottles is standard.

A recent review and buyers guide published by Incentive Marketing and Sales Promotion lists fifty-nine organizations in the handling houses' section. Ease, simplicity, and peace of mind – along with price – are important considerations.

One organization, Nielsen Clearing House, is best known for its expertise in coupon-redemption. Speed in processing has enabled

Nielsen to turn round coupons from Belgium and France to its UK base more quickly than competitors on the Continent, despite the added transportation time. Another strength is that Nielsen has the financial resources to rebate retailers as soon as coupons are handed over: this can prevent a wait of up to 2 months. At any one time, Nielsen estimates, the company could have around 100 different promotions under way. This explains why they need 400 full-time or contract employees.

In March 1985 Nielsen launched a new venture – the Nielsen Shopping Survey. This survey is based on a door-to-door question-naire, which identifies households that do not use a particular grocery brand, so that they can later be sent a package of money-off coupons or samples. The scheme, which has already been used with considerable success in Canada, enables sales-promotion activity to be concentrated where it is most likely to yield new customers.

The larger handling houses have computer-based systems, which are adding a variety of new facets to their service. PHM (Mailings), for instance, has facilities permitting an instant on-line check that requests for one-per-household applications are being observed. The checks can be adjusted to give a refusal once a certain number of applications – three or five, say – have come in from the same surname and address. This is a useful facility if your promotion proves so attractive that it unleashes a flood of multiple applications.

Always think about the fulfilment side of your promotion early enough: consult the handling house as early as the design stage of the promotion. Not only can it describe any new services on offer, it can also examine existing options to improve presentation or save money.

There can be a considerable difference in presentation of packaging. In 1986, for example, the Design House overlooked the need for secure packaging when distributing a special edition plate, and there were so many breakages in transit, it had to commission another limited edition. Remember, it is the packaging that introduces you to the consumers. If they have saved up half a dozen packet tops for your special-offer beer glasses, do not antagonize them by sending them the glasses in poorly thought through packaging that gives no protection from breakages and, worse, looks like it should contain motor parts. A professional handling house may be able to recommend packaging material that not only is functional but looks good too, at little or no extra cost. Remember, 90 per cent of the distribution price is fixed by postal or delivery charges, so do not skimp on the packaging.

Another area worth remembering is that when you design an order form for consumers to use, try to leave enough space, preferably a box for each character, so that you can help eliminate some of the complaints about non-delivery. It would also help prevent the embarrassment caused by the handling house misspelling names on return labels. Keep an eye on such details and you will not spoil a well-considered promotion.

8.6.5   The games people play

In the mid-1980s the sales-promotion industry's interest in promotional games was rekindled by the forecourt promotion war between the major petrol giants, and fuelled by Fleet Street circulation battles and fierce competition in the drink and confectionery markets. However, a few disasters prompted many to consider alternative methods of promotion. By the end of the 1980s petrol companies had almost exclusively gone over to the 'alternative currency' idea of gifts offered in return for a collection of tokens.

If a game goes wrong, the effect can be disastrous. In 1985 Beatrice Foods was forced to end a major promotional game in the USA after it discovered that the game did not contain sufficient variations. The company found itself facing claims amounting to more than £16m only a few days after the game was launched. Around the same time in the UK the Noughts and Crosses game launched by Esso had to be cancelled and all stocks of the game withdrawn from participating outlets because of a printing error. The game was designed to produce only a couple of winners of the £100,000 top cash prize. Instead Esso received more than twenty claims for the top prize in the first few days.

The message is simple. Seek the help of both game experts and legal advisers before launching a game promotion. The design of a game should be the preserve of a game specialist, as should the structuring of the prize fund. Structuring has to establish the ratio of prizes to the game universe, and requires some fairly complex computations. Game specialists consider it to be a minefield for people who don't understand it.

Not surprisingly, however, leading sales-promotion consultancies do not accept that game promotions should be only handled by the specialist game companies. 'The creative execution and the working out of traffic building or loyalty mechanics is very much the preserve of the sales promotion agency', said one consultancy director. He also warned, 'Sales promotion agencies should not dabble in games unless they have a real understanding of how they work, otherwise they could give a client bad advice. Unless they are aware of the risks involved, fundamental errors can be made in the structure or production of a game'. So check your agency's experience in this field first.

The safest route is for sales-promotion consultancies and game specialists to work side by side on a game promotion. The most successful games are those in which the client totally understands what he wants the game to do, the sales-promotion consultancy has the ability to translate that objective into a creative idea, and the game specialist can construct and produce the most suitable game pattern and game design.

Finally, remember to insure yourself against the jackpot being won. For instance, a company put up a motor car from a local garage as a hole-in-one prize on a specific green when it was sponsoring a golf day, and insured itself to the value of the car, against someone winning the prize.

By the end of the 1980s prize draws, which do not require any skill to win, added a new twist to an old tale and began to hit the jackpot with manufacturers. Heinz ran its 'Win a car a day for 100 days' as a multi-brand climax to its centenary celebrations in 1986; and ran it again in the autumn of 1987, a sure sign that the 1986 campaign was a success. Around the end of 1988 Heinz ran it for a third time, but with more prizes to add to their 100 Metro cars, plus 1000 Heinz hampers and 110,000 Heinz vouchers. Heinz concluded that internal boredom arrives before public boredom; also that the public often understands a new promotional concept better second time round.

Why was 'Win a car a day' a breakthrough? Prize draws had been around for a long time and remain the favourite promotional technique of *Readers Digest*. But the Heinz type of competition, where no skill was required to decide the winner, was governed by the Lotteries and Amusements Act 1976. Essentially it is illegal if entrants have to make a purchase. It is easy for *Readers Digest* to send two envelopes: 'Yes, I want to buy the book and enter' and 'No, I do not want the book, but please enter me in the prize draw'. Likewise petrol companies and fast-food outlets can run scratch-card games, for non-customers can walk in off the street and ask to enter. However, if the vehicle for the sales promotion is the back of a cereal packet, meeting the legal requirement can be more tricky. Heinz got round this by supporting the promotion with a significant spend above the line in the free newspapers and on TV, explaining that no purchase was necessary.

Naturally, Heinz took very careful legal advice and followed it to the letter. While the law is unclear, there is now a much more open-minded attitude, particularly on the part of consumers, who believe that this type of promotion is fairer than a skill-based competition that requires entrants to be literate, creative, or numerate. There was, however, a general reluctance by manufacturers to adopt the technique because they were:

- Unsure of the attitude of the retailers.
- Unsure of the effect on trade.
- Unsure of the law.

Today a number of manufacturers have found the technique very attractive. Asda supermarkets used a tailor-made version of a Rowntree promotion to give away 100 bottles of Asda champagne a week. Asda reported it as one of the most successful the store has ever run.

As far as sales are concerned, prize draws are found by many manufacturers to shift the product very effectively. Cadbury's major countlines – 'Crunchie', 'Wispa', 'Flake', 'Double Decker' and 'Go' – shared a major promotion towards the end of 1988. On offer had been seventy-nine pairs of British Airways' tickets to any destination on its route network, plus £1000 spending money. The top prize was four air tickets and £8000. While Cadbury's initial research found holidays a little *passé*, giving prizewinners the choice of exactly where they wanted to go seemed to be a very powerful motivator. A significant number of entries came in on plain paper, which did not bother Cadbury's, because it secured the display it wanted at retail. Cadbury's judge success particularly by whether it achieves its display objectives, because its representatives can easily measure that, and because sales follow it. Naturally, if the product is not on a shelf, it cannot so easily be bought.

As for the legal battle, it shows that the sales-promotion industry is pushing back the barriers. In the summer of 1988 Gordon's Gin ran a promotion where the inside of each bottle cap carried a symbol denoting a prize, ranging from a pair of coasters to an exclusive fragrance. How did this meet the legal requirement that no purchase was necessary? The hurdle was overcome by allowing consumers to send in for bottle caps, and claim the appropriate prizes.

What has emerged post-Heinz is a pattern for prize-draw promotions for packaged goods. Part of what they have in common is dictated by the legal requirements. Thus, they all accept plain paper entries, with a 'no purchase' requirement, and this feature is advertised widely, usually on television, but also in press or on leaflets, as well as on the pack. In addition, such promotions tend to offer a large number of prizes over an extended period. Consumers will keep on trying if they are not restricted to one entry and they know there are many prizes to be won. Each time they enter they are remembering and interacting with the promoted brand.

Heinz admits that its promotions can be expensive. The 1988 promotion offered prizes worth more than £650,000. The *Media Register* calculated the advertising spend on their previous year's similar campaign at £275,000. Since Heinz is selling around 3 million units a day, even a shift of a few percentage points in sales is worth a lot of money. Although this might sound as though the technique is reserved for big spenders only, one could offer, say, 100 record albums a day, which would cost only £350 each day, and with the right target market, one could expect a high response.

For the future it is likely that this type of free draw could spell the death knell for the skill-based contest. Consultants can be expected to go on pushing against the legal barriers with new variations, until someone oversteps the mark, and finds himself, or his client, in court. Prize draws will continue to increase in popularity, perhaps through the 1990s. Inevitably, at some stage, they will peak: consumers/promoters/retailers will get bored with them. Particularly if the public becomes disillusioned, entries and sales levels will fall off, and the returns will not be there to justify the high investment. For now, the prize draw looks well worth considering for some markets.

8.6.6   Clubs

One basic human need is that of belonging, for it confers protection. Belonging to a family, group of friends, workplace, peer group or just people that share a common interest, is important to all people. This sense of belonging applies equally well to groups of people who share a common product. For example, Volkswagen Beetle owners are renowned for flashing lights at an oncoming Beetle to acknowledge that they share a common interest. Motorcycling across Europe in the summer months becomes quite irritating, as one is forever having to acknowledge other riders. If there is a readily quantifiable segment of the market, then forming a 'club' to promote this camaraderie has many benefits, not least the generation of a direct marketing database.

The Ford Motor Company formed a rather loose club when it enrolled company car drivers in a scheme and mailed out a series of magazines titled *Talkback*. This publication formed a forum for drivers to share experiences related to driving, as each issue contained a questionnaire on a variety of topics, with results being published in the next issue. (The Rover group countered and issued a broad-interest magazine titled *Catalyst*. Rather like an inflight magazine in layout and content, it tried to offer a selection of specific interest articles which, again through a questionnaire, could be targeted to the reader in future issues. However, the basic idea was to offer a forum to detail Rover products to a specific target group, sharing common interests. Special offers were included, but these offers were special only in that they were offered to *Catalyst* readers.)

The idea of using a club, where something exclusive is offered to members, is not new by any means. Twenty years ago some garages used the technique to attract account customers. Rather than relying purely on passing trade, offering special deals, discounts or gifts to account customers ensured that, wherever possible, the account customers would return to where they received preferential treatment. In the early 1970s Combined Anglian Newspapers launched SCOPE, a club for women readers. Realizing that they had a large proportion of women readers who, at that time, had been identified as housewives with children, and by and large were not in full-time employment, CAN developed SCOPE membership to enrol those readers in a wide variety of activities and meet other women with similar interests. The club offered exclusive deals and discounts on a variety of female-interest events, from flower-arranging to scuba-diving, from evenings at Norwich's Theatre Royal to ski-ing holidays. Naturally the female readership of the newspapers, particularly the evening papers, was increased as members wanted to have regular updates on local events of their club.

'Focus' was a club launched in 1988 by four companies with a common interest – eye care. Dollond & Aitchison, First Sight, Eyeland House and Theodore Hamblin launched 'Focus Eye Care Assurance'. In practical terms it meant that every enrolled member, wherever they were in the UK, would be near a branch that would guarantee members a welcome, reliable optical service and advice, and a variety of free benefits: an offer of free frames, free servicing and 12 months 'no quibble' guarantee, 'sight-seeing' offers and discounts, and special prices on all purchases. The all-important membership card, the Focus eye-care card, was valid for 2 years, and, rather like a credit card, was used when claiming the scheme's benefits.

If you can identify a specific group of customers who not only have a common interest but in some cases want to share that interest, then there are a number of points to remember:

(a) Create a membership card that opens the way for members to receive privileged offers.
(b) Consider presenting those offers, discounts and so forth as a book of vouchers.
(c) Use the book to illustrate membership advantages.
(d) Create the forum for 'club' members to exchange views if appropriate to market.
(e) Maintain the interest and momentum of the club by keeping the variety of offers and events going, demonstrating always the benefits of remaining within the club. This maintains brand loyalty.

Businesses and industries where clubs have and can be used to good effect include:

- *Airlines, ferry companies* and so forth, where one is trying to keep passengers using the service. British Midland Airways has a 'club' for regular users of its 'Diamond' shuttle service. Members receive a special credit card that can be used for rapid check-in. British Midland also offers a chequebook-style series of tickets, where the passenger can fill one in and sign it at the check-in desk, without having to buy a ticket beforehand. Regular travellers receive points for each journey made, and these points are refundable against diamond-shape-designed lead crystal glasses and decanters, maintaining the 'Diamond' service theme.

- *Hotels*: where regular custom can be attracted to the group.
- *All types of vehicles* for road use, although the technique works best when the vehicle is specialized, like Morgans, MGs, Harley-Davidsons, etc. An enthusiastic collection of Sierra drivers seems unlikely.
- *Media*, especially newspapers and magazines. One such example comes from 'Mirrorcard'. In 1989 *Daily Mirror* and *Sunday Mirror* readers were invited to become personal holders of Mirrorcard. More than 2 million readers accepted and have since received many privileged offers. Mirror Group Newspapers rented out the database so generated to other companies that wanted to reach that special and well-defined target audience. The first mailing package went out in January 1990.

8.6.7 Alternative currencies

Rather than enter into the damaging arena of price-cutting, major petrol companies have gentlemens' agreements over forecourt pricing. Instead of competing on price, they compete by added value. Tiger tokens, Shell stamps, Texaco stars, all are issued as alternative currencies, which petrol-buyers can collect and cash in for a selection of goods. Loyalty to a particular petrol company is created and drivers will make sure they always fill up at their 'brand' of petrol. The schemes had developed by the end of the 1980s into quite sophisticated catalogue-led promotions.

One of the later refinements to the petrol-token idea was Mobil's 'Premier Points' Collecting Card, a scheme linked to Argos Stores and launched in early 1991. Motorists were issued with a free plastic card – like a credit card – which held a magnetic strip. All fuel purchases were translated into points and were loaded electronically on to the card at forecourt cash desks. No tokens to collect, no cards to stick stamps on, and every 10p. of fuel (rather than every £6.00 spent in Esso's scheme) gave a point credit on the card. The Premier Points could be redeemed only at participating Argos stores in full or part payment for any goods illustrated in the then current Argos catalogue, obviously giving a much wider choice than any other specific catalogue could offer.

All schemes relied on a wide network of petrol stations, and those companies with fewer outlets tended to maintain a lower price strategy to keep custom. However, the token schemes had to come, as the 'free glasses idea' had been overplayed.

Many people feel that buying petrol at a lower price is more important than collecting tokens. It depends on who is paying for the petrol, the driver or the driver's employer.

Ring-pulls, packet tops, and other tokens are all forms of alternative currencies that can be collected and spent in varying amounts to buy goods. Their main difference to pure vouchers and coupons is that they do not have a face value of £1.00 or 20p. (and have to be 'spent' on a certain range of goods), but they have a perceived value in the eyes of the consumer. For example, in 1989 John Smiths Bitter launched an on-pack promotion quoting:

> . . . a pint tankard made from finest English pewter and engraved with the finest name in English ale, John Smith's. Simply send a cheque or P.O. for £5.99 made payable to 'John Smith's Tankard Offer', 8 special ring pulls and your name and address to . . . Alternatively you may wish to send no ringpulls and enclose a cheque or P.O. for £11.99.

Each ring-pull is therefore potentially worth 75p. to the collector.

Barclaycard Profiles demonstrate another form of alternative currency. Credit cards, though, present a delicate challenge. However competitive the market, a credit-card company would never want to be accused of irresponsibly trying to increase the amount of a customer's debt liability. Rather it should be trying to establish a relationship with the customer. Barclays recognized this potential problem when it instituted its Barclaycard Profiles scheme at the beginning of 1988.

The concept allows cardholders to build up a 'bank' of points, depending on the amount they spend with their card. One point is awarded for every £10 spent, and a minimum of 175 points is required to qualify for an item from a catalogue of 100 products. At least one of each of these items has been redeemed, says a Barclaycard spokesman, including the top-of-the-line hi-fi, which required a card spend of £75,000.

Barclaycard was anxious in case the scheme would encourage people to overspend, so certain rules were introduced. Profile points cannot be redeemed if the credit limit is exceeded. Points are taken away if the user gets into serious trouble. The scheme was selective too, and not merely handed out *carte blanche*. Barclaycard has not published precise figures for the boost this has generated in membership but admits that 1.5 million of Barclaycard's 9 million holders were signed up in the first 9 months of the scheme. This represented a 'significant increase in turnover'.

Another unusual, yet imaginative, way of creating an 'alternative currency' was launched by the brewing group Ind Coope Taylor Walker in 1989. The scheme was called 'Weekenders'. Taylor Walker issued a leaflet, which it called a passport, and distributed these around the tables in its pubs. All the customers had to do was to make ten visits to any participating Taylor Walker pub with the special Weekender Passport and ask one of the bar staff to sign and date it in one of the spaces in the grid on the back. Once ten signatures had been collected, the passport was sent in with a cheque or PO for £10. In return, the claimant received a brochure and vouchers for free accommodation for two, dinner and breakfast to be taken at one of the hotels chosen. Depending on the quality of the hotel, each signature would have been worth £10 or more.

Air Miles is another form of alternative currency. While discussed in more detail later in this chapter, Air-Miles tokens are collected by registered collectors on a wide variety of products and services. The collector saves up tokens worth 1 mile of flying on (usually) a scheduled British Airways flight. Then the tokens are exchanged for a ticket.

8.7   Incentives for staff

Some companies will fund staff incentives out of their salaries' budgets, and some will use their publicity expenses, since performance rewards are paid out as salary, but if they are related or proportional to sales of a particular brand, then they are coded against the below-the-line expenses for that brand. Further, if the incentive is paid out to reward sales success by a retailer's or merchant's representative, then the costs are true below-the-line expenses.

John Banham, former Director General of the CBI, is quoted as saying, 'Successful businesses are found where ordinary people achieve extraordinary performance. Motivation of people at all levels in the organization is the key'.

To be motivated, we all need a goal and a plan of action – it doesn't matter how 'unimportant' one may feel if the work is within the grand scheme of the company as a whole. The truth is that every single person can contribute to the company's success, and one piece of careless or sub-standard work can affect the whole company. Quite simply, all staff must be encouraged to think positively, and goals attained must be rewarded, though not necessarily in material terms. A personal 'thank you' from the MD or a mention in a company newsletter can be just as effective in building a positive atmosphere. However, if you do decide to offer an incentive with tangible rewards to your employees, or someone else's, there are some important things to consider.

8.7.1   Get advice

If you do not have an in-house specialist, bring in outside help in the form of an incentive and motivation company. Programmes do not have to be costly, but they must be professionally devised and administered, otherwise they can backfire.

8.7.2   Sales objectives

Before bringing in outside help, analyse exactly why you want to run an incentive and what you want to achieve in measurable terms. Incentives can be used to improve flagging sales, to focus efforts on a specific product, or to inspire staff to realize their full potential. However, a programme will not 'mend' low morale due to redundancies, unreasonable targets, under-staffing and so on. Therefore set realistic sales objectives by establishing in what precise areas it is possible to increase sales. There is no point creating incentives for increasing distribution, for example, if your product already enjoys 95 per cent distribution.

8.7.3   Theme

Ensure the theme, prize structure and presentation style of your programme are suitable to the participants. Don't run sporting themes, with activity holidays as prizes, if your target profile is one of ageing retainers.

8.7.4   Broad appeal

Make sure the prizes have a broad appeal, where everyone should win something, in return for above-average performance. Equally, there must be aspirational and valuable rewards for your high-fliers – they are, after all, your most valuable people.

8.7.5   Presentation

Cheap designs and print will indicate to your participants a cheap incentive – even if it is not. If you value your participants – show it. Good presentation can make modest incentive programmes more attractive.

8.7.6   Targeting

Spend time on setting achievement targets and rewards formulae. Too easy – and you'll give money away without generating extra business. Too hard – and most participants will switch off and you'll gain nothing. The right balance is critical to a successful incentive.

8.7.7   Simplicity

If the reward scheme is so complicated that participants cannot easily work out the benefits, it will be binned. Use short words, short sentences, short paragraphs.

8.7.8   Duration

The ideal is 3 months, unless you update the scheme with new graphics, new targets or different criteria for winning. Otherwise most will either have forgotten the programme or be treating it as part of the normal commission/rewards currency.

8.7.9   Communications

Write to, or otherwise communicate with, the participants regularly during the programme to let them know how they are doing against target and compared to their peers. While probably the most time-consuming and least interesting element of the entire administrative programme, it is one of the most vital from the point of view of effectiveness.

8.7.10   Recognition

Make sure your winners, especially your big winners, get the kind of peer group respect they deserve. Publish their success in company newspapers, trade press, company noticeboards. The ambitious often regard recognition as at least as important as the material rewards.

8.7.11 Rewards

Do not undo all your good work by keeping winners waiting for their prizes or by presenting merchandise which disappoints them because of its poor quality or perceived low value.

8.7.12 Novelties

Motivational programmes are *not* novelties. They are a valuable tool in obtaining the best performance from staff, thereby ultimately increasing company profits. They should not, however, be used in isolation, or on a one-off basis to carry the company through a bad patch. Instead they must form a part of the company's sales and marketing strategy.

How do you go about deciding on your rewards? If the budget does not stretch to holidays, or cars, and pure cash is deemed too unexciting, the hard work has to start. Although agencies and sourcing companies advocate a number of different approaches, the keystone of them all is research. You may start with an element of gut feel, instinct and previous experience, but if you are running a major scheme, just as with a major above-the-line advertising campaign, *research* a range of premiums within certain bands with high perceived value compared to actual cost. It is not a question of what you can get, or purely the creative application. Ultimately the rewards should be judged on the likely appeal to the prospective target market. Although research is not quite so important for sales-force incentives as for consumer campaigns, because some reliance is often placed on the hands-on experience of the sales director, one can introduce more science about it in terms of how you go about assessing with those key decision-makers what sort of incentives should be presented.

Most schemes are based around some form of 'alternative currency' or vouchers. At one end of the scale participants are collecting points towards a defined range of gifts, preferably presented in a specialized brochure, which not only sets out the stall of gifts but also clarifies the details of the scheme. Simple to set up and administer, provided a good organization supports the distribution of the goods, such schemes have their limitations, as not everyone wants a coffee percolator! At the other end of the scale there are numerous voucher schemes, from luncheon vouchers to more prestigious and flexible schemes such as capital bonds. The 'bonds' have a cash value and can be used in part payment for a wide selection of goods and services across a broad range of retail stores countrywide. What these schemes gain in flexibility and wide appeal they tend to lack in personalization.

Whatever methods are finally adopted, employees must be convinced that *their* work and *their* achievements are important. Managers who view their organizations only from a profit standpoint will dehumanize the company, risking a backlash that will ultimately affect profits. There is a saying that is relevant to any company, whatever its business: 'The only game in town is the personnel game. The only difference between companies is the people they employ'.

8.8 Air Miles: bridge the sales promotion and incentive gap

Since the start of the 1980 many companies, but not all, see the use of incentives as an effective and vital part of the sales and marketing mix. Incentive travel has become the most-sought-after award and, rather like the American experience 20 years ago, is now fully established in the UK and is thought to be a £300 million a year market. Not only is the value high, but a lot of companies in the travel industry have spent considerable time in developing schemes.

One of the most innovative schemes was launched in November 1988 and called 'Air Miles'. The idea was simple. Thousands of shops and services throughout mainland Britain gave away Air-Miles vouchers when consumers made purchases from them. Consumers collected as they went along, and when sufficient Air Miles had been collected for the chosen destination, they were redeemed for a free ticket on British Airways or other leading airlines. Alternatively, the vouchers could be used for discounts from a selection of leading holiday companies, such as Sunmed, Sovereign and Thompson as a late signing. Over ninety companies participate in the Air Miles scheme. In July 1989 British Airways reduced the number of air miles necessary on many routes, reinforcing the scheme's likely success.

Air Miles was a world first. The key to it all was the empty seats on most scheduled flights, and Air Miles attempted to fill them. Through its association with British Airways, and using the very latest in sophisticated reservation technology, the scheme is able to predict well in advance the seats that would otherwise have been empty. The 'free travel' is only available on flights that are predicted to have empty space. Therefore, at some times during the year, some destinations will not be available. Collectors will also have to be flexible about the time of day or day of the week they travel. Air Miles suggested that there were millions of empty seats throughout the year and, if demand was high, the vouchers could still be redeemed on a wide range of package tours. However, once booked, collectors would receive a *confirmed* ticket for the flight ordered.

Air Miles was offering companies 'exclusivity' in any particular market sector, i.e. once one company in any sector was using the scheme, other companies in that sector were precluded from entering it for the duration of the contract period (at least 12 months). The minimum annual expenditure on vouchers, in order to gain exclusivity, varies with the particular sector. The absolute minimum expenditure was £50,000 over 12 months (in 1989) and no contracts would be considered at any level below this. However, for companies wishing to use the Air-Miles scheme to give incentives to their own staff, exclusivity does not apply. Registering your staff as collectors not only gives them an opportunity to *earn* air miles, they can supplement their earning with retail collecting – reinforcing the incentive scheme.

According to the Air-Miles rate card (April 1989) the cost per Air-Mile voucher for expenditures of £50,000 is 9p. per mile. For expenditures of £3m, vouchers drop to 6p. per mile, but you would have bought 50 million miles' worth of vouchers.

In March 1989 it was announced that Air Miles was giving its scheme a £9 million support package, largely in response to the flood of rivals being launched. Competitive schemes include Action Miles, Miles Better, Holiday Points, Premiere Cheques and even *Today* newspaper's Air Smiles. At launch, Air Miles was praised by promotion veterans, most of whom wished they had thought of the scheme to use empty BA seats. However, even in its early stages the scheme came under heavy fire because of its limitations. This criticism paved the way for other 'save and collect' schemes, leading to a bitter promotional struggle and to consumers becoming increasingly confused.

One of the many competitive schemes in operation is promoted by Action for Business and called 'Action Miles'. While there remains a dispute over 'copycat' practices, Action Miles claims that it is more accessible for collectors than Air Miles, being present in both big and small retail outlets. Further, the Action-Miles scheme is not limited to just air travel; it can also be used for land or sea travel, as well as for voucher contributions to package holidays.

Air Miles' main competitors use available seats on numerous airlines. The obvious advantage of this is that the limitations of BA's scheduled flight seat availability can be avoided. Naturally, Air Miles, with 51 per cent ownership by BA, is confident that it will have more to offer, and still be in business when the other schemes have waned. With an approximate turnover of £50m in the first 12 months, Air Miles has good reason to be confident. Spending £9m on advertising and marketing is planned to snuff competitors out of the market, and to tell consumers that Air Miles is the most effective and easiest scheme to collect. Air Miles hopes this will prevent consumer confusion.

However, if competition in the travel-voucher market continues to escalate, there is the very real likelihood that consumers will become so confused that they will shy away altogether from the whole concept of save and collect travel miles. We shall watch developments through the 1990s with interest.

Beware, however, of overenthusiasm for travel-based promotions without careful planning. The *Financial Times* reported on 3 April 1993: 'Hoover's free flights fiasco . . . culminated in the dismissal of three top managers and a $30m provision by Maytag, its US parent . . ..' The article said: 'Hoover neither did its sums properly nor did it take out insurance.'

8.9 Summary

1 The techniques of sales promotion and direct marketing overlap, but strictly speaking sales promotion consists of: 'An offer that features tangible advantages not inherent in the usual product or service in order to achieve marketing objectives.'
2 Examples of sales promotion techniques are cost incentives, free gifts, coupons and competitions (with prizes to be won).
3 Successful sales promotion is not primarily a matter of selecting a 'bright idea' but of careful analysis and planning to achieve clear objectives. The 'bright idea' is the means by which the objectives are achieved, not an end in itself.
4 Equally important is to ensure that the actual mechanics of the promotion (which can be quite complex) are planned and operated efficiently.
5 Increasingly sales promotion is a cooperative affair managed jointly by manufacturers and retailers.
6 Sales promotion is subject to quite detailed legal and/or voluntary constraints and these vary considerably from one country to another.

References

1 Dakin, Tony (1974), *Sales Promotion Handbook*, Gower Press, p. 127.
2 Toop, Alan (1983), *Marketing*, 3 February.

9 Direct marketing

9.1 Direct marketing and sales promotion

As discussed in the previous chapter, there are many similarities between direct marketing and its stablemate, sales promotion. Sales promotion is used to increase take-off of a product or service by added value, whereas direct marketing is used to achieve the same end by addressing its target audience personally and taking the offer to the customer. Therefore the two disciplines can borrow quite heavily from each other. Direct marketing means there is a direct two-way dialogue between individual customers and a company.

In May 1989 *Marketing* magazine estimated that the direct-marketing industry was worth over £235m. There are a number of reasons why direct marketing has become such a popular technique. Primarily, the cost of computer power has shrunk dramatically, and more sophisticated operations have become possible – notably the development of marketing databases, which seek to develop a long-term relationship with the individual consumer. Cheaper computing also means that the cost trend in direct marketing compares well with that in above-the-line advertising, particularly TV advertising. Naturally the promise of quantifiable results holds a lot of appeal to hard-pressed marketers anxious to justify their budgets.

While *Marketing* was able to put a value on the direct-marketing industry in the UK, it acknowledged that there was a problem with trying to measure the size and the growth of direct marketing. 'Billings' (the amount spent on 'media' such as postage, telephone and, with response off-the-page, some advertising) is an artificial figure and inappropriate; 'turnover' of the direct-marketing agencies was a better guide. Turnover included such items, people among them, bought-in and passed-on to a client. Some agencies prefer 'income' as a guide, because this actually measured monies received from clients and suppliers via fees and/or commissions. However, on the basis of turnover, *Marketing* prefers to quote £235m plus as the likely size of the industry.

Direct marketing is growing rapidly, and many new industries are looking seriously at it for the first time. Many direct-marketing agencies reported a shortage of new business in the first half of 1988, largely owing to the traumas of the financial sector (large users of direct marketing) – traumas following the stock-market collapse and due to the uncertainty of the new legislation around that time. As evidence to the broadening base of direct-marketing usage, new business in 1989 was not all financial. New entrants included retailing, packaged goods, and general services. British Satellite Broadcasting used direct marketing as a central element to its marketing strategy.

Expenditure on direct mail dropped in 1990 but its share of total ad spend increased, according to the Direct Mail Information Service. 1989's £930m dropped to £895m, but the share rose from 10.5% to 10.6%. Total ad spend decreased in 1990 by 4.7%.

By the middle of 1992 it was reported in *Marketing* that the direct marketing support services seemed to have been particularly hard hit by the early 1990s recession. The largest supplier of all, the Colorgraphic Group, reported a turnover drop by 15% to £46.4m in 1991. Their £2 million profits (£4 million in 1989) became a £2.3 million loss. Sales were down, prices were down, and of course interest rates were up.

One industry that would seem to be dragging its feet, although an obvious candidate for direct marketing, is the consumer-durables sector. The reason behind the slowness to adopt the technique may have at its heart a possible confusion on the part of the manufacturers or their retail customers between direct *selling* and direct *marketing*. However, that is not to say that the manufacturers do not use any direct-marketing techniques. They may not be into marketing databases as yet, but they do use direct response advertising to pull in requests for catalogues. These points will be discussed in Section 9.4.

Bryan Halsey, chairman of the direct-marketing agency HLY-Grey Direct, was reported to have said in 1988 that the UK's marketers in fast-moving consumer goods and branded goods manufacturing are wasting half their marketing budgets, primarily on sales promotion. He also suggested the determination of these companies to adhere to a system where the individual brand is king was utterly outmoded. Halsey has researched the past, present, and future of direct marketing in the FMCG and branded goods sectors both in the US and in the UK. He believes that while we started on a par with the US in this area, the UK is now more than 10 years behind. He says:

I'm not trying to be an evangelist and say direct marketing is the answer to every marketeer's prayers. But it is estimated that 90 per cent of sales promotion is wasted, and since 60 per cent of the nation's (the UK's) marketing spend goes on some form of below-the-line activity, mostly towards sales promotion, half of all the money spent on marketing is believed to be wasted.

This is just one man's view. But there have been suggestions that three prime, distinct and overlapping concepts are available to achieve accuracy and selectivity in direct marketing, thereby improving efficiency and profitability.

9.1.1 Multiple branding

One potential problem facing FMCG and branded goods companies is that they are almost invariably structured by brands, with brand managers who have brand loyalties, budgets and rules. Individual brand managers, who feel that their reputation is linked to their brand's success, may try their own direct-marketing campaign. Sadly, many of these prove uneconomic. A company wishing to establish and maintain a dialogue with 1 million of its individual customers will not get much change out of £1m per mail shot.

More and more, however, broad-minded marketers and general managers are transcending the individual brand manager's usual domain and are starting to recommend direct marketing for the company as a whole, i.e. multiple branding. Consider a bank – a brand-owner with many 'products', e.g. current accounts, deposit accounts, mortgages, personal loans, insurances, assurances, pensions, etc. If the bank had a brand manager for each one, it would be wasting its money. If, however, the bank were to look at its clients as potential customers for all its products, and record who is best suited for one and not the other, and who has already bought but could want more, some of the problems of direct marketing would start to disappear. The high costs could be shared across the various products.

This concept may at first appear to be difficult for fast-moving consumer and branded goods companies to accept, especially since many a brand manager, who is rising rapidly by pushing his brand, may find a technique that works and then be asked to share it with all the company's other brands. Halsey suggested that the big FMCG and branded goods companies in the UK should stop thinking in terms of brands and start thinking in terms of customer needs across brands, and even across companies, and this process is starting to happen in sales promotions, e.g. in Rowntrees' confectionery. An on-pack promotion, where tokens have to be collected for a free gift, is copied across four or five brands. Each different wrapper carries the same promotion, and all share in a slice of the sales-promotion cake. Across-company advertising has occurred before, as with milk bottles carrying Kelloggs Cornflake advertisements, so why not direct marketing, providing there is not a clash of interests?

9.1.2 Householding

A company may target its marketing to an entire household rather than individuals, and on a multiple branding basis. A food company may have dessert products for the mother, energy products for the father, and sweets and snacks for the kids and the whole family. Similarly, breakfast cereals could be treated in the same way. But these examples are on narrow brand ranges. If it were for a company with main meal products, the economies would be greater.

If one household responded to a sales promotion for one type of food item by mailing in an order form for an incentive gift, why not send them a money-off voucher with their gift to entice them to sample from across the range. It would be a simple matter to design the order form to ask about the make-up of the household, e.g. ages and sex of any children. If you had products that matched the profile of the people in the household, then your targeting of a promotion could be improved.

9.1.3 Personal marketing

This means important companies affording and conducting a permanent dialogue with customers. In the US General Electric turned its complaints service on its head by transforming it into an answer centre for consumers. That facility now receives 3 million calls a year, only 15 per cent of which are complaints, resulting in a true dialogue with consumers. In the UK only a few companies have reached that level of sophistication, but car companies such as Ford, VW and Citroën are some that are making headway. They know when customers bought cars, approximately how long they'll keep them for, when it is time to replace them, and what they are likely to be replaced with – a true and continuing dialogue with customers. This subject will be discussed at the end of the chapter in Section 9.9.

9.1.4 Problem areas

On a more general level, direct marketing can help FMCG and branded goods manufacturers in the UK overcome hurdles faced in two problem areas – the product that cannot be advertised and the new product that is unable to establish a foothold in the retail market.

Advertising unsuitable
Halsey suggested that there were more products not suited to advertising in the FMCG and branded goods market than in other

sectors. Either the brand cannot stand the cost of TV or press advertising, or a company simply has too many brands to be able to advertise them all. The law is another factor in areas such as tobacco and alcohol, and there are sensitive factors in areas such as incontinence products, condoms and female hygiene goods.

The toy industry has products with advertising problems. It is difficult to have a successful toy that isn't part of a TV series, so the toy manufacturers end up with a couple of big products and dozens they cannot advertise. Using direct marketing and multiple branding, companies could tell children about new toys that are never going to have the luxury of a TV series. And of course the more products a company creates, the bigger the problem.

Retailers not stocking
This usually happens because the competition is too strong, the margins too low, the volumes do not interest the retailers, or they have done a deal with someone else. In a number of cases the direct-marketing approach was shown to get round this problem for FMCG and branded goods companies. They sold direct to the public, created a major awareness, even leading the big brands in some cases, until the retailers were queueing up to stock the products.

1   Georgio perfume in the US started by selling direct and went on to become the best-selling fragrance in its market.
2   In the UK a similar strategy was adopted for Dee Weed, a garden product launched with a single advertisement. Uptake of the product was such that within 2 years the company could afford to spend £1/2 million a year on advertising and had major garden centres knocking at its door.
3   Again in the US, General Foods' Gevalia coffee was considered by its producers to be an upmarket product that would not retail in the conventional way. General Foods opted to sell direct. Within 3 years the product was estimated to have broken even.

Many may say that the method cannot work, since the volumes (of customer buying) are so low as to be of little interest to the larger companies (because of their high minimum production runs). But the method can work for the smaller ones, and even General Foods is prepared to take the long-term view and continue with the experiment. Long before every FMCG and branded goods company is able to use direct marketing to maintain a dialogue with every one of its customers, some companies will go public with the fact that they only want to deal with their customers (and not with retailers), and they are likely to establish a marketing edge. Once they do that, many other companies will follow suit.

9.2 The European picture of direct marketing

The future of direct marketing across Europe is uncertain, given the intricate and complex nature of the many directives in front of the European Parliament. The laws governing sales promotion are different between one country and its neighbour. Furthermore, there are VAT differences, data-protection variances and non-uniform laws governing unsolicited goods, language barriers, cultural problems and different product standards, all complicating the picture still further.

Yet the prospects are that direct marketing will continue to expand across Europe, not least because of the opportunity it offers to target and segment consumer groups, offering them products tailored to their tastes and life-styles. As TV budgets spiral, the measurable results seem less. Companies will turn to direct marketing to test the acceptability of products. Customer databases will be built to support the network of appointed dealers and distributors. Finely honed campaigns, using the mail, telephone marketing (or telemarketing as it is called) and direct response broadcasting (on TV, radio), and direct response advertising will justify the medium's use in Europe.

The most successful companies using direct marketing across Europe are the established US multinationals – *Readers Digest*, *Time/Life* magazine, American Express, IBM, and Xerox – all with world-wide networks, regional production bases, and national fulfilment points. They are united in achieving a single global positioning message for their products, with local versions for their local markets. (It would be of little value having a photocopier with the LCD instructions in a foreign language.) Most of these companies see no reason to change their current mode of operations, and regard '1992' as so much hype!

Readers Digest knows that 'concepts travel'. It has an enormous exchange of ideas as to what has and has not worked in different markets. Each *Digest* company runs autonomously in its own country and chooses suitable material for its own market. These companies use questionnaires frequently, so that customers can tell them what they want. While a cooking, DIY or gardening book may 'translate' well into another market, the whole project – design, idiom and pricing – may have to be changed, a decision made by the local *Digest* company. *Readers Digest* does not promote products internationally by direct mail. Prize draws and offers on the magazine, books, music and insurance products are generated locally.

181

Satellite TV has recently opened mainland Europe to UK companies, and falling rates on Superchannel and Sky in late 1988 made the medium attractive to direct-response advertisers. Towards the end of 1988 the *Financial Times* had just completed a campaign on Superchannel, using TV both as a direct-response medium to raise subscriptions – callers dialled a number in Holland for twelve free issues – and to influence people's attitudes. Two bursts of 90- and 15-second spots ran in both the spring and autumn of 1988. The advertising broke new ground, because tactical advertising was combined with an invitation to respond, and the messages were therefore believed to work harder.

The agency prepared three creative approaches in early 1988, using a telephone operator (who invites viewers to call) at the beginning and end of the advertisements, with the product message sandwiched between. This encouraged a dialogue with the operator similar to those seen on fund-raising spots on US TV. Once responses from each advertisement had been logged, with conversion to sales measured, the agency was able to judge which approach worked best before going 'live' in October 1988.

When we speak about a 'dialogue' between a company and a given customer, we are referring to a two-way exchange of information. Naturally the quickest exchange is achieved over the telephone. Shopping by telephone is beginning to catch on in a big way across Europe. Interactive teleshopping could come in Europe on the lines of the highly successful and innovative French Mintel system. Prestel is the UK equivalent.

Wet weather, and the high cost of sales forces have alerted the Scandinavian countries to telemarketing, with ninety agencies in Sweden, which boasts the highest home ownership of telephones in Europe. Most activity is so-called 'outward bound', business to business, where the 'seller' calls the potential buyer. The Nordic countries have yet to realize the usefulness of the "inbound" Freefone calls so far. Here, the 'buyer' calls the manufacturer or supplier.

In the UK such systems as 'Next Directory', 'Barclaycard Kaleidoscope' and many catalogue companies use the telephone as the communications medium, where callers quote their credit-card number to make a purchase, even if there is not always a Freephone number. This method opens up the opportunity to select at leisure and shop 'out of hours' all from the comfort of the buyer's living room.

The way forward for telemarketing companies in Europe seems to be to coordinate the strategy centrally, then leave it to run under local control. Remember too that, within one country, regional differences apply. Regional accents are well known in the UK, but the Spanish are very regionalized too. They are highly sensitive to dialects, so do not use 'Catalan' to cold-call a 'Gallego', for instance.

9.3 Direct marketing versus other media

Programmes Telephone Marketing ran an advertisement[1] that said: 'In America more money is spent on telephone marketing than on television advertising or direct mail . . .'(see section 9.8). Similarly it was reported that 'In the UK in 1984 £225 million was spent on advertising in free newspapers; in the same period, close to £325 million was spent on direct mail (billings) – with a substantial further expenditure on door-to-door distribution . . .'[2] That there has been a deluge in direct mail across Europe is shown by data researched by Services Postaux Européens (1988) and by the Direct Mail Sales Bureau (1989). Table 9.1 shows the results.

It is interesting to note that the most heavily mailed countries with the European Community have severe data protection restrictions and consequently there are great difficulties in producing tightly targeted lists. So, while the volumes in these areas might be high, the efficacy is reduced.

If we look at more data supplied by the Direct Mail Sales Bureau, direct mail represents over 16 per cent of material posted through UK

Table 9.1 *Addressed direct mail received per head of population and recent trends*

Territory	No. items received		% Increase	Volume in millions
	1982	1987	1981–8	of items mailed
Belgium	35	54	4.3	556
Denmark	26	43	4.4	235
Finland	33	50	9.6	216
France	28	44	5.2	2500
Ireland	2	6	-0.1	20
Netherlands	31	40	14.7	780
Norway	26	52	4.7	225
Portugal	8	8	0.0	85
Sweden	46	62	5.9	541
Switzerland	76	95	2.9	638
UK	20	29	8.6	1766
West Germany	49	55	7.6	3607
Spain	N/A	N/A	N/A	980
Italy	N/A	N/A	N/A	435
	Services Postaux Européens		Direct Mail Sales Bureau	

letterboxes (March 1989). Table 9.2 shows the changes from the first quarter of 1988 to the first quarter of 1989.

The gain is mainly at the expense of unaddressed material, such as coupons, brochures, leaflets and free newspapers, and one possible explanation is the increased use of such targeting tools as computer-controlled customer databases. Since the first quarter of 1988, the proportions of private social mail and all unaddressed material except newspapers have decreased, while other non-advertising addressed mail showed only a 0.1 per cent increase. However, as Table 9.2 shows, direct mail's share of the letterbox grew from 13.7 per cent to 16.4 per cent over the 12-month period.

Table 9.2 *Letterbox profile trend*

	Quarter 1, 1988 (%)	Quarter 1, 1989 (%)
Addressed, non-advertising material	48.6	47.2
Unaddressed	37.7	36.3
Total direct mail	13.7	16.4

Source: DMSB

The DMSB also reported that nearly 96 per cent of AB demographic households received at least one piece of direct mail in the first 12 weeks of 1989, with that 96 per cent receiving an average 28.4 items over the period. While direct-mail receipt tails off by social class to a 78.6 per cent penetration among DEs, giving a UK average penetration of 87.9 per cent, this trend is less marked than for other forms of direct mail. Table 9.3 shows how direct mail is divided between the various sectors of the market.

It is interesting to note that while the first quarter of any year is traditionally the period for advertising holidays, only 3 per cent of direct mail originated from holiday companies and travel agents. Further, it was found that 62 per cent of all mailings used some form of incentive to respond, with discounted goods featuring in more than half of these. Such is the close link between direct marketing and sales promotion.

But what of the link between direct mail and other media? Direct mail's share of total advertising expenditure in 1982 and again in 1987 was estimated and published by Services Postaux Européens in 1988. While the method of calculating the figures changed slightly in 1986, and some estimates have had to be made, Table 9.4 shows some interesting European trends and differences.

Table 9.3 *Percentage share of volume of Direct Mail monitored in Quarter 1, 1989*

Sector	% of volume monitored
Mail order	29
Retailers	17
Charities	12
Utilities	11
Book clubs	10
Manufacturers	9
Financial (banks, building societies)	8
Holiday companies (and travel agents)	3
Others	1

Source: DMSB.

Table 9.4 *Direct mail's share of the total advertising expenditure (%)*

Country	1982	1987
Belgium	17.4	17.9
Denmark	30.0	33.0
Finland	11.5	15.0*
France	9.5	9.6*
Ireland	1.8	4.7
Netherlands	18.4	N/A
Norway	27.9	29.9*
Portugal	15.4	4.6
Sweden	31.0	22.0
Switzerland	35.0	N/A
UK	9.8	7.7
West Germany	11.1	12.0

* Estimate–definition changed in 1986. *Source*: SPE, 1988.

Towards the end of 1988 the Post Office Communications Panel in the UK gave details about television viewing and newspaper readership. The results are summarized in Figure 9.1. For the purposes of this analysis, heavy, medium and light viewers are defined so that there was one-third of the sample in each category. In the case of direct mail, light is five items or less in 12 weeks, medium is six to fourteen items, and heavy is fifteen items or more, per individual in 12 weeks. The heavy receivers of direct mail accounted for 68 per cent of the volume while only 8 per cent of the total volume is sent to light receivers. The index shown in Figure 9.1 indicates the ratio between the share of direct mail and the share of the population. It was derived by dividing the percentage of direct mail volume received by the groups by the percentage of the sample in each weight band by TV viewers.

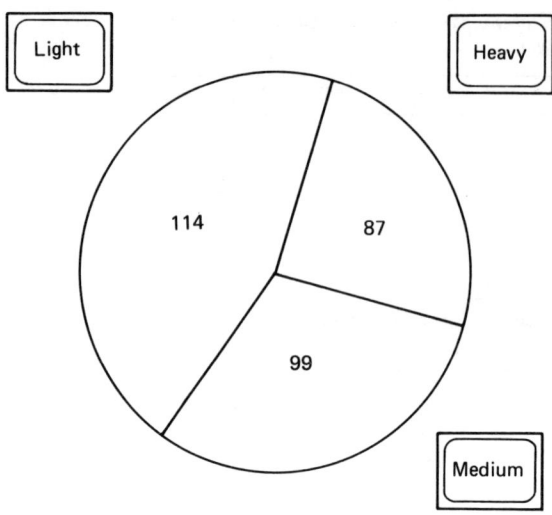

Figure 9.1 *Index weight of direct mail by commercial TV viewing. Source:*
DMSB

Since direct mail is often used by advertisers to reach people least
exposed to TV advertising, it comes as no surprise that the lightest
commercial TV viewers receive the most direct mail. There are only
very small differences between ITV and Channel 4 in this respect, but
there are greater differences if respondents are grouped according to
newspaper readership. See Table 9.5.

Table 9.5 *Index volume of direct mail by newspaper readership*

Day newspaper received	Quality of newspaper	Index
Sunday	Upmarket	129
	Tabloid	94
Daily	Upmarket	144
	Tabloid	90

Source: DMSB.

Upmarket readers receive much more direct mail than others, and of
the upmarket papers, the *Financial Times* has the highest index. The
Direct Mail Sales Bureau made an interesting profile of the person who
was probably a heavy receiver of direct mail:

Age:	under 45.
Sex:	more likely than average to be male.

TV:	light viewer of commercial TV.
Paper:	reads upmarket newspapers.
Financial:	better than average position.
Bank account:	89 per cent likelihood.
Credit card:	60 per cent likelihood.

In 1988 the Post Office handled 1,766,000,000 items of direct mail, 25 per cent more than in 1986. Direct-mail cost increases remained low – although total billings' expenditure rose by 9.7 per cent to £529.84m, the average cost per item increased by only 1 per cent. Production costs were stabilized by the increasingly efficient use of merchandisation and computer technology; however, postage rates did increase by 1p. towards the end of 1988. Although postal rates are ever likely to increase, direct mail will continue to climb in its importance.

But direct marketing is not limited purely to direct mail. The telephone has a vital, and growing, role in the direct-marketing mix, as we shall see later. Direct-response advertising, where a product or service is advertised through one of the standard media (TV, radio and the variety of press) but the consumer is asked to make a direct response by telephoning an order, writing to a given address or, in the case of printed media, clipping a coupon, may be viewed by many as above-the-line. However, because the supplier and customer are in direct dialogue, and a dialogue that exchanges information is building a relationship over time, the subject has been included in this section of direct marketing. It is another example of the grey area between the broad divisions of the publicity mix.

Direct-response advertising, as far as the main printed media are concerned, is not limited to page space. Included in the subject are loose inserts (sheets included within the publication and not fastened in in any way, and sometimes disparagingly referred to as 'dropouts'). Inserts may be bound into the publication, however, or bound in but appearing on the outside of the publication ('outserts'). Finally, one may occasionally find the reply card is stuck on to the appropriate page of the publication – a so-called gummed insert – a favourite technique of MEC phones. Nationwide Market Research has quantified the variety of inserts' popularity according to the expenditure on each form, as shown in Table 9.6 for March 1989.

In the 3-months period January to March 1989, the *Sunday Express Magazine* was top of the league in direct response advertising, when calculated on the basis of page space and inserts, whereas by volume of loose inserts *You Magazine* was top. As far as direct response is concerned, the most advertised brand in the year to March 1989 was Britannia Music Club. Its rate card spend in the first 3 months to March 1989 is shown in Table 9.6. It spent £1.465m, buying around seventy-

Table 9.6 *Inserts by percentage expenditure, Britannia Music Club, March 1989*

Inserts and outserts	% expenditure
Loose	84.8
Bound	7.7
Gummed	7.2
Outserts	0.3

Source: Nationwide Market Research Ltd.

Table 9.7 *Details in 12,110 coupons monitored, March 1989*

Without	% of all space advertisements	% of inserts	% of all couponed direct-response advertisements
Keycode	24.4	14.0	23.7
Mr/Mrs/Miss/Ms request	78.0	37.2	75.1
Postcode request	36.6	10.0	34.7
Telephone ordering facility	50.4	77.7	52.4
Telephone number request	62.8	60.0	62.6
With			
Premium incentives	8.0	31.3	9.7
Limited editions	0.4	1.5	0.5
Payment requested with order	29.1	30.9	29.3

Source: NMR.

one page-space advertisements and 113 loose inserts, reaching a circulation of over 140 million. So obviously there was some duplication of effort; but, with most printed media, audience selection is such that targeting by demographic criteria has much improved over recent years.

Nationwide Market Research Ltd monitored 12,110 coupons in March 1989 and reported on the techniques employed with this direct response mechanism. Their findings are summarized in Table 9.7.

NMR reported that 65.3 per cent of the advertisements with coupons monitored in March 1989 asked for the postcode, which was an improvement on March 1988. Fewer than a quarter of the 12,110 coupons monitored asked for titles (Mr/Mrs, etc.) and only 37.4 per cent asked for the respondents' telephone number, although this was an improvement on 1988.

In March 1989 there were nearly 900 coupons printed back-to-back with another from a different advertisement. While this problem accounted for just over 7 per cent of all couponed space advertisements, it is rarely spotted and brought to the publisher's attention, and compensation sought. On the other hand, poor reproduction of advertisements is often queried, though this was a problem with only 0.8 per cent of all couponed space advertisements.

9.4 Direct marketing in specialized areas

9.4.1 Cosmetics

Above-the-line expenditure on a whole range of male, female and unisex cosmetics and toiletries (apart from hair-care products) was £117.3m, excluding inserts, in 1988. Expenditure on direct response advertising was £6.5m, including inserts, which made up 22 per cent of the advertisements appearing. These statistics would suggest direct marketing is rarely used in the cosmetics business, though there is evidence to suggest that, despite the very traditional approach to marketing by the larger companies, direct marketing is playing a growing part in the beauty products business:

(a) Direct-response mechanisms are beginning to appear in press advertising. Lancome, one whose products are usually a retail markets's preserve, has recently opened a mail-order scheme in cooperation with Harrods.
(b) Scratch 'n' Sniff perfume advertisements often include mail-order coupons.
(c) Telephone numbers are appearing in advertisements, so that customers can phone an order through, quoting a credit-card number. Companies ranging from Schwarzkopf to Regina Royal Jelly use telephone numbers in this way.
(d) The traditional door-to-door and party-plan operators are moving more into direct marketing through the media. Avon (the original 'ding-dong, Avon calling' company) has, on the advice of its US division, introduced a direct-mail arm called Avon Direct, which undertook two test mailings in 1988 and a major pre-Easter campaign in January 1989. While Avon remains successful in its time-honoured approach, it suspects that some of its traditional markets are declining and it is finding it difficult to maintain market share. Direct mail became more attractive because the available direct-mail market is becoming younger, owing to such popular influences as the Body Shop; and the newer expertise behind direct mail means more success with less risk.

However, there was a threat from outside the UK. One competitor, which in 1989 was advertising fairly widely in the Sunday colour supplements, was Yves Rocher – striving to establish itself in the

British market by advertising mail-order cosmetics. Before that, Oriflame International, a Scandinavian – European group, had started up a subsidiary in the UK called Vevay. In 1987 the Vevay Beauty Club was started, and it built up its membership by using a mixture of inserts and off the page advertising. Over 75,000 members (in 1989) each received a bi-monthly newsletter and notification of new products every 6 weeks or so. A club environment was encouraged by using a telephone chat-line, enabling members to phone up for the latest beauty tips. Not surprisingly, 99.9 per cent of members were women, between the ages 16 and 40.

Oriflame began in Sweden as a party-plan operation (where a commissioned salesperson holds a party of local people usually at their own home, and presents the product range, taking a commission off sales – a technique often used by 'Tupperware'). Oriflame has never operated a retail operation, and does not do direct mail. It is happy to reach its target audience and attract new members through advertising in the press, with direct response mechanisms.

9.4.2 Financial services

It would be hard to find two more dissimilar groups of people than financial-service marketers and direct marketing agency executives, and yet the paradox is that these two types of people need each other more than any other two mutually dependent groups. Agencies need financial-service clients because they have bigger direct marketing budgets than any other type of client: financial services companies need agencies because they have the biggest identified customer databases of any type of organization, and hence the largest direct-marketing opportunity that can be found, invariably needing an agency to make things happen.

Nevertheless, there is a paradox. Agencies cannot understand why the simplest decisions take 6 months, and why, even then, everybody has to have a voice. Companies are equally at a loss as to why agencies fail to understand that their cherished logo, the Consumer Credit Act, and the Financial Services Act cannot be flouted. Consider the problems:

- Database development costs millions of pounds, so that transactional work (what the customer really sees) has to take second place.
- If people in a financial-service company have to make a decision, they are sticking their necks out: no one will decide quickly nor alone.

- Lawyers do not make the best copywriters, and copywriters do not make the best lawyers.
- Financial-service companies have had long-term battles with the CCA's and FSA's more obvious absurdities, and require equally long-term commitment from their agencies.

From the companies' point of view there is much the financial marketer can do to improve the relationship with his agency.

1 Start by selecting an agency carefully, and ensure that people who truly understand the market and its problems are chosen.
2 Then continue to work at the company–agency relationship rather than ending it the moment a more attractive looking option comes along.
3 Always 'tell it like it is'. Acknowledge that an agreed marketing plan is really an option to purchase, which must be re-justified at each stage. Further, be honest. If you are not the only person who makes the final decisions, no matter how accountable you might be for results, say so.

Christine Kitchen, Business Development Director of Chapter One Direct, a major agency to the financial-service market, suggested the following moral for both client and agency alike.

Choose your partner carefully: tell him the truth, and only enter into a relationship when you are absolutely sure that you can establish and maintain true mutual empathy; even when things look bleak, stick with him in spite of what may look like more attractive options.

9.4.3 Direct marketing in fast-moving consumer goods (FMCG) markets

In the first part of this chapter, mention was made of the FMCG approach to direct marketing. Many might see this approach as unworkable, because FMCG is essentially a wholesale distributed business. But what is direct marketing's present status with FMCG companies?

Couponing – direct marketing after all but beneath the dignity of many agencies – is widely used, and some companies have considered targeting, by means of the geodemographic market modelling system. In a few product areas, such as disposable nappies, direct mail/home delivery is well established. Lists are readily available and annual purchase values are high. Other companies have dabbled in the techniques but have since withdrawn, possibly owing to the inappropriateness of the chosen projects or bad planning. (Obviously direct marketing is not a cure-all or a panacea, and quite simply does not work every time.)

Interestingly, many larger FMCG companies also have trade/industrial products too, for which direct techniques are readily acceptable and growing in use. Can anything learnt here be transferred to the consumer sector?

Let us first consider four 'other' Ps when looking at the strategic issues for the 1990s:

(a) *Proliferation* – both of products and media. This leads to more pressure on individual brand support and uncertainty in media selection. Here, direct marketing has strong intrinsic appeal, being *ideal* for niche products and, in the future, manufacturers could be well advised to design products for niche segments that can be effectively delivered by direct means.
(b) *Product promiscuity* – finding loyal consumers is difficult, and brand substitution rife. Building stronger customer loyalty is easiest by means of direct marketing techniques.
(c) *Powerful retailers* – and therefore a growing retail concentration – represent a major concern to manufacturers. For a European test-bed, look to Sweden, where three grocery chains dominate and manufacturers are screwed to the floor on price, and many products never even see the light of day on-shelf. A directly controlled consumer base is therefore of great strategic potential to the manufacturer. Couponing is a traditional simple answer, but mal-redemption in the UK makes this a very blunt instrument.
(d) *Pollution concern* – has become a big issue in the 1990s. The 'green' consumer, demanding more information, has become a dramatic reality, and the direct-marketing method offers an obvious way to supply the information.

Direct marketing has strong claims to be able to help with each of the above strategic concerns, but there is another advantage for a FMCG company in working with a direct-marketing agency. The best agencies *eat, sleep* and *breathe* targeting, research data and cost-effectiveness. And to write effectively to their targets, agency copywriters have to *get inside* their heads. Do the same thought processes lie behind much TV and press brand advertising?

So, where can FMCG companies go with direct marketing? One path is via database marketing – where the manufacturer keeps a list of consumers and has a dialogue with them regularly to keep their loyalty. In most cases this would be pure fantasy: for most product groups, product promiscuity means that knowing about today's habits doesn't tell you too much about tomorrow's. Further, for most products, the annual consumer spend at factory-gate prices could not possibly justify the maintenance of a database and the use of direct mail, especially if this is to run in parallel with traditional brand-image advertising above-the-line.

However, database marketing does offer potential to support retail distribution where one or more of the following apply:

1 In product areas where heavy users account for a high proportion of the total market spend.
2 For products where the potential annual consumer spend at factory-gate prices is high enough to absorb database maintenance costs.
3 Where there is high brand loyalty, or potentially high loyalty, which might be built into the brand identity for new products designed to be promoted via databases.
4 Where a significant proportion of the brand spend can be put into database marketing. (Obviously a major rethink for existing brands, not so for new products.) There are clear opportunities for making a consumer club an integral part of a brand's identity.

Using the above criteria, products such as beer, new 'green' products, some older brands at relaunch, and a whole range of new niche and/or added value brands could be marketed through a database. But what of tactical direct marketing?

While the complete solution will not be found by using direct marketing exclusively, the tactical use of direct marketing in a limited way should not be excluded. Examples of tactical techniques that are directed towards consumers from manufacturers or suppliers (so-called tactical 'outbound' communications) include:

(a) Magazine inserts and/or mailings to special-interest groups (greens being a current example).
(b) Mailings to known product *group* users derived from life-style databases. (These are usually no more than 10 per cent of the total market, but, given that they can be strongly influenced, then an extra percentage point on market share is a feasible target.)
(c) Mailings to suitable affinity lists – where the product character-istics make this feasible.
(d) Mailings to electoral roll lists or via household distribution, using the various target group modelling techniques available.

What of the costs? If the product is suitable and the target groups can be effectively reached via direct techniques, one can expect to get between $3\frac{1}{2}$ and 5 million *quality* impacts for a £1m spend; and as rapidly increasing consumer awareness is appearing in the 1990s, direct techniques will be essential to get complex messages across. There is therefore a wealth of unexploited potential for FMCG companies to use tactical outbound direct marketing, without even beginning to consider maintaining a database.

Direct marketing does have a number of roles for the manufacturer strategically concerned with the threat of retailer power, as follows:

1 Using a customer database can deliver customers to the retailer – especially powerful since retailers are likely to be the heaviest users.
2 Specific retailers can be offered the opportunity to benefit from tactical outbound communications, by selecting targets in the catchment areas of their stores.
3 New forms of incentive, ones that do not rely on retailers for redemption, can be developed.
4 Alternative distribution channels can be used.

Strategically the last item can appear unworkable. FMCG companies are traditionally geared up for wholesale distribution, so the most natural way to expand is to find new retail outlets. A good example is petrol stations for bulk packs of paper products, a practice well established in Scandinavia. Party plan also resembles wholesale distribution, but needs managing agents. Last but not least comes direct sale, which works for certain products (remember General Food's conception of Gevalia Coffee as a continuity series) but is very much 'out of the FMCG mould' for many. Each FMCG company will have a different view as to the merits of these strategies. However, in order to decide if any will work for your brands, you would need to undertake a direct marketing audit, to cover the following areas:

(a) Current brand characteristics.
(b) Possible or planned repositioning.
(c) Position of brand in its life-cycle – pre-launch, launch, early life, maturity, decline.
(d) Sales targets to be achieved.
(e) Current distribution pattern.
(f) Reachability of target group (or groups).
(g) Assessment of strategic relevance of database-building (if any).

Only in this way will one be able to maximize the opportunities for direct marketing as part of the future for FMCG marketing.

9.5 Database marketing

Direct marketing is not simply a means of obtaining sales, even though it does so more measurably than advertising and more cost-effectively than salespeople. Direct marketing is not just for short-term gain but for long-term rewards. Companies, more and more, are not using it simply because they want to know which half of their advertising works, or to give a shot in the arm to their sales effort, but because they recognize the advantages of creating a private medium with their customers and developing a prolonged personal relationship with them.

The other name for this strategic capability is database marketing: the science of identifying customers and prospects and placing them on computer to record their details, and the art of communicating with them on a continuing basis. It has the added advantage of providing constantly updated, expanded and instantly accessible market research. Database marketing will become more important than marketing through indirect communications channels for a variety of interrelated reasons.

Markets are becoming more segmented as consumers become more sophisticated. Such selectivity is causing companies to create products for these specific market segments and customer life-styles, making a more selective promotional approach more attractive.

Although indirect media (press, radio, TV, etc.) are segmenting at a phenomenal rate to cater for virtually every consumer interest and life-style that has ever been thought of (and a few more besides), specialist media are too fragmented to provide mass manufacturers with an acceptable communications medium. At the same time, the distinction between brands is becoming ever more subtle and increasingly more difficult to communicate cost-effectively through indirect mass-audience and specialist-audience media. The direct approach, however, enables brand benefits to be described in as much detail as is necessary.

Customers are valuable – obviously. But increasing recognition that a significant proportion of sales each year should come from last year's customers will also favour direct marketing. It is always easier to keep a customer than it is to find new ones.

Cost factors as well as market trends are reducing the gap between private and mass media. In the 9 years to 1984 TV advertising-space costs rose by 332 per cent and press advertising space by 247%.[3]

Although the Post Office is often criticized for putting its rates up, postage only rose 144 per cent over the same period. The cost of computer technology, the engine that drives the database marketing concept, on the other hand, has fallen substantially. While a computer cost the equivalent of twenty people in 1970, by 1990 one person cost the same as twenty computers of the same size.

Building a database takes time, perception, and money. The starting point is obviously existing customer and market information and an analysis of future information needs, because what a company needs to know in 5 years' time has to be based on data it starts to collect now.

If building a database is a science, then marketing to that database is definitely an art. The concept behind database marketing is the building of a continuing relationship – not always selling when a communication is made and not always demanding a response, even though these aspects have traditionally been seen as direct marketing's greatest assets. It means obtaining loyalty through customer service and care, by building a relationship centred around the customer rather than the product.

Companies should primarily be in the business of keeping satisfied customers, rather than in the business of selling products. Whereas companies were once production-oriented, they are now market-oriented, and in future they need to be customer-oriented. This means analysis of the customers:

1 Who they are.
2 What they want.
3 What their attributes are.
4 What characteristics they have.
5 Geographic and demographic data.
6 Purchase habits.
7 Life style information.

Refining and profiling customers will identify discriminators. In short, database marketing is like a wheel, with a database at its hub. To start it in motion, the product and the audience need to be defined: then the audience must be attracted so that it identifies itself. Sources of information include existing customer data, lists from compatible companies, and promotional history. When looking at promotional history, don't just look at success on a global basis, but break down the data and find out whether customers responded, how they paid, which advertisements they responded to, and so on.

All this information, fed into the central database, supplies the information with which to create and maintain a personal dialogue. Then the products or services are sold, the responses analysed, and, on the strength of that analysis, products are redefined or new ones introduced. Thus the cycle continues.

Database marketing can look at customers and determine trading patterns. It can see what type of person buys which products, and whether they tend to buy the same product again and again or to try out new and different ones.

One or two companies in the US are using such data analysis to calculate a lifetime value for each customer. One company bases its marketing strategy on being able to determine, within the first 3 months of dealing with a new customer, precisely what that customer will be worth over the next 10 years. The company allocates its promotional budget on a customer-by-customer basis.

Successful analysis of customer values obviously leads to better targeting and response. Christian Brawn achieved a 200 per cent increase in response in one geographical area simply by comparing the penetration of two products on the basis of postcodes – no ACORN, no demographics, just postcodes! If that response improvement is found by looking at just one variable, imagine what could be achieved by analysing, say, twenty variables.

As more companies use database marketing, so more companies will be chasing the same people with the same products and services. The limitation to database marketing will not be simply wrongly targeted or badly produced material, but unimaginatively and insensitively devised communication programmes. The successful companies will be those that realize people do not like to be sold a product every time they receive a communication, and that customers will only reciprocate with their loyalty if they get something in return – as every *Readers Digest* Condensed Books customer will tell you.

Ultimately, as more companies turn to database marketing – as the technology becomes cheaper, targeting more accurate and customers easier to evaluate – it will be preferred to press advertising. Thus image advertising through the letterbox will appear as well as in the press. Direct marketing will cease to be just an alternative or bolt-on element in the marketing mix, it will become a strategic central core around which other media will be grafted. The sooner companies are able to adopt such philosophy, the sooner they will catch up with their more enlightened rivals, and the sooner they will leave behind competitors that blindly insist 'direct marketing is not for us'.

9.6 The use of premiums to build a database

Database marketing techniques can be used to make a promotional activity more effective and efficient. Carefully selected premiums can be used as response incentives to help build tightly targeted databases. Always *keep* respondents' names and addresses, and analyse details of purchases and any other information your customers are willing to tell you. Companies such as Shell, Texaco and American Express use premium promotions to gather names and life-style information about their customers, or potential customers. This technique is especially important to tobacco manufacturers for the following reasons:

- There is the possibility of a future total ban on *all* cigarette advertising; it was last seen on television in the UK in early October 1991.
- Database building must be highly targeted to existing smokers.
- Activities must be designed to prevent brand switching (or to entice other brands' customers).

Hence more cigarette brands' promotions invite smokers to mail in for premiums. Preprinted entry forms often ask for specific information, such as name, address, marital status, age range, previous brand smoked.

Of course competitions can be used to collect names and addresses but there are two drawbacks: people are sceptical about winning competitions so may not enter; and others will enter virtually any competition on the basis 'you've got to be in it to win it'. Are these necessarily the right people to attract?

By using an appropriate and a worthwhile gift, it is possible to stimulate a response from precisely the target group you want on your database. Since such a file is only valuable if it is clearly defined and can be validated, it is important to avoid attracting people outside the parameters of the intended database. The selection of the gift is crucial; it must be relevant to the intended audience, as well as being appropriate to the image of the product or service being offered. Further, the perceived value of the 'reward' might also have to rise in line with the number of questions the consumers are being asked. However, the premium must not be *too* attractive, otherwise people might respond just to get their hands on the gift, rather than because they are interested in the product or service.

Give a thought to the choice of medium through which the incentive offer is communicated to the target group. It can also play an important part in determining the validity of the database. On-pack is usually the best medium, because this will attract actual users of the product, but keep an eye on the number of proofs of purchase you are asking for. Just a couple of proofs could attract the occasional 'gift-seeker' who is not too committed to the brand, but a dozen proofs and you'll only attract the regular user, who probably does not need too much convincing about your brand in the first place. Naturally the actual value of the product and type of product will have a bearing too.

One agency has recently been building a database for Wagon Wheels by using responses from consumer promotions. Additional questions are built into entry forms in order to obtain extra information about respondents. However, the agency admits it is much more difficult to build the database when the unit cost of the product is low.

Makers of electric power tools used in the home employ the simple device of the registration of the guarantee as the way to build their databases. (A series of tick-boxes are used, so that the manufacturers can identify opportunities in any given household. Running up to Christmas, direct mail is used to offer suggestions for the most appropriate gift; the recipients can then add it to their Christmas list.)

Creativity could, alternatively, be applied in other ways to get a good response to build the database. For example, you could offer people part of a premium – a pen cap or one half of a pair of bookends, maybe an item from a set. Then you ask them to do something, such as complete a questionnaire or test drive a car, in order to get the rest of the premium. Premiums can be used as action-achievers – things that make people want to respond. However, you will have to create a feeling of excitement in order to generate action.

9.7 Direct mail

Junk mail is not necessarily mail that is of dubious artistic merit; it is more often irrelevant mail. To be fair, there can also be junk leafleting, junk press and junk television. However, because direct mail is so personal, since it arrives in our homes or in our offices, we can feel offended if it is irrelevant – or poorly addressed, or poorly presented. There lies the problem. We all have fairly strong feelings about the mass of junk mail we receive, and we throw most of it away. The reaction from a prospective user could be, 'Well, I put all direct mail I receive straight in the bin so I guess my customers do the same. No, direct mail is not for me'.

The real problem, however, lies with a preoccupation on the part of companies with volume. Mailing 250,000 can demand no more management effort than mailing 25,000, so it can seem logical to mail to the larger audience. In many markets, particularly financial services, a small response percentage can reap rewards, often without regard for the majority who do not respond, and who have been mailed several times already. Tough luck if you happen to be in the 220,000 who regard the mailing as irrelevant, as junk. No wonder direct mail has got such a bad name.

The professional approach should not be a case of creating a mailing, then deciding a quantity to mail and scratching around to find names. The way is to practise the fundamentals and consider our data as a first stage in a strategic approach. Ask yourself some straightforward questions:

(a) What are your objectives?
(b) Whom do you want to communicate with?
(c) Where are they?
(d) What do they want to know?
(e) What have you to offer?
(f) What do you want them to do?
(g) What is the benefit to them?

Write down your answers to these questions and then decide if writing a letter, or sending them some written information through the post, will actually achieve those objectives. Would another medium carry that message for you? Can you target that message to the people on your list or is it rather a matter of hit or miss? Maybe direct-response advertising would work better first time round: then you can reconsider your message to those who respond, your database will improve and you will not add to the volume of junk mail being distributed. That will be better for everyone – companies and customers alike.

9.7.1 Writing a direct-mail letter

So you have decided that yes, direct mail is the right way for you to go, and you have a pretty good list of people who you believe are ready to hear your message. So how do you go from here?

In 1973, a young copywriter called Bill Trembath sat down and wrote the beginning to a letter: 'The American Express card is not for everyone . . .'. That letter has since persuaded millions to become American Express cardholders. While many a humble scribe has tried to write a better one, that letter consistently outperforms any other in most languages and markets around the world.

A good direct-mail letter can be extraordinarily potent and versatile. Apart from American Express cards, it has helped to get rid of obsolescent Mercedes diesels and sell £40,000 cruises. It can even help to sell new telephone systems, mainframe computers, pharmaceuticals and new factory developments. Sadly, however, the direct-mail letter remains underrated. Since most businessmen write letters every day, they imagine any fool can write a sales letter. However, it is a noble art, and like most art forms it is not easy to learn or develop the flair required to turn the mediocre into the remarkable. Nonetheless, one can learn a few techniques to improve the impact of your campaign.

In 1985 the Post Office discovered that 90 per cent of direct mail is opened and 75 per cent is read, at least in part. The challenge is not whether your mail shot will be opened but whether, once opened, it grabs the attention of the reader in those precious first few seconds.

Let us start with the envelope. Professional copywriters put messages on the envelope, not so much to get them opened, but to get them opened in the right frame of mind – to ensure they are singled out from the mass and opened with a pleasurable feeling of anticipation. Good mailing-list management should mean that the look of the envelope will be of some interest to the recipient. Your company should have an image to be proud of, so put your logo or name and address on the outside – possibly the back edge near the opening is best. Thus, for a cookery book Time/Life showed the beginning of a recipe on the envelope – it has to be opened to get the rest. For *Psychology Today*, 'Do you lock the bathroom door behind you, even when there's no one else in the house?', and for a travel and leisure magazine, 'How much should you tip when you're planning to steal the ashtray?', are some notable examples. Other techniques include the use of coloured envelopes, textured paper, or windows to display the free offer, a free gift, or the chance to win a competition.

Once inside the envelope, follow a formula. A salesman can adapt a message accordingly, but direct mail is salesmanship in print. A constant, logical, and flowing message applies through the piece from envelope to sign-off on the letter. A formula also keep the writer on track and ensures nothing gets left out. One of the most widely accepted formulas is WISCDA: an acronym for:

W – Wavelength.
I – Interest.
S – Sell (the benefits).
C – Conviction.
D – Desire.
A – Action.

Thus, show the reader that you *understand* him and have something of *interest* to tell him. Then sell the benefits of your product to him, the reader. Support that with some conviction, e.g. third-party endorsement. Create some desire in the reader that can be fulfilled by him taking some action. As a guide, here are twenty golden rules to use as a checklist to help you make your direct mail more successful and solicit that response you are after:

1 Have you thought sufficiently about your readers – their likes and dislikes, their needs and wants, hopes and fears?

2 Define your product or service's benefits properly:
  (a) Is it more attractive than alternatives?
  (b) Is there one benefit or a combination?
  (c) Develop the USP (Unique Selling Proposition).
  (d) Is there any *news* to offer?

3 Make the best possible offer. Will it motivate you?

4 Is your opening too indirect or too clever?
  (a) Don't let your reader work too hard.
  (b) Make it clear what you are offering.

5 Be precise. Don't say nearly £5.00, say £4.99.

6 Beware hype. Superlatives such as amazing/fabulous/fantastic are to be thrown out.

7 Write in a conventional way:
  (a) Tell it like it is.
  (b) Don't use too much jargon, don't be pompous.
  (c) 'Talk' to the reader.

8 Build conviction. Use testimonials, research figures, clear scientific proof.

9 Do a complete selling job:
  (a) Lazy writers only do half the job.
  (b) If there are good reasons, give them all.

10 Have you overcome every single objection to replying? If there are disadvantages, it is usually best to mention them early, then explain them away.

11 If your letter is long, use subheadings to break it up.

12 Is your copy easy to read?
  (a) Tabloid journalism is to be avoided (if only to preserve the national heritage of our beautiful language).
  (b) Use short words, short sentences (sixteen words maximum) and keep one idea to each paragraph.

13 Does your copy flow?
 (a) One sentence or paragraph leading logically to the next.
 (b) Try ending paragraphs with questions to be answered in the next.
 (c) Use 'carrying expressions' like 'and', 'moreover', 'what is more', 'this is why' at paragraph beginnings to maintain the flow.

14 Talk about the reader and his needs, not yourself and your product:
 (a) Make your copy 'you'-oriented
 (b) Not 'me'-oriented.
 If you continue to write 'XYZ Company Ltd is delighted to announce the launch of . . .', perhaps you should pursue some other career.

15 What about length?
 (a) Eliciting an enquiry may only need short copy.
 (b) Purely informing could be brief too.
 (c) One-shot selling demands longer copy.

16 Work hard at your copy:
 (a) Write down every idea you have, good or bad, then select.
 (b) Overwrite, then edit.
 (c) Don't spend hours polishing one indifferent idea; there may be a better idea around the corner.

17 Restate the benefits – you'll lose nothing, especially when rounding off the letter:
 (a) Repeat good news, people like good news.
 (b) If what you have is bad news, say something else.

18 What are you doing to overcome indifference?
 (a) What incentive have you given to reply?
 (b) A gift/a contest/a free report/a discount?
 (c) What about replying promptly?
 (d) A limited offer open only until the closing date?

19 Do your readers understand you as well as you do?
 (a) Test your draft with *several* people unconnected with the job.
 (b) They may spot things you missed.

20 Postscript:
 (a) Always use a PS.

(b) People look at the end of the letter to see who is writing to them.

(c) Summarize important points in the postscript.

(d) Try using handscript printed at the end.

Of course, there is never any substitute for knowing your customers and knowing how they respond. Don't use bright polkadots on your mailing if you are selling to solicitors!

9.7.2   The all-important response element

The prime objective of most business-to-business direct mail is to generate leads, these to be followed up by the salesmen and sales increased. However, if the quality of the leads is low, then salesmen's time is wasted and morale diminishes. The solution is to give the salesmen as much information as possible beforehand about the potential customer by providing them with qualified leads.

Accurate targeting through the right mailing list helps ensure a quality response. However, many industrial markets are fragmented, making potential customers difficult to define accurately. Where new or wider applications are being sought for an existing product, then the task of providing good leads is harder still. Fortunately, there is a solution with any mailing: the reply-paid card or RPC. This can be used to qualify the lead so the true potential of an enquiry can be assessed. Therefore, do not make the RPC an afterthought; start designing the mailing around it. After all, if your mailing is designed to get sales leads, make them good leads. These three following examples demonstrate the potential of a well-considered RPC.

3M Griddle Cleaning System

This product was sold through distributors whose salesmen were not controlled by the 3M company. It had therefore to receive significant sales attention. The mailing had to provide good qualified leads.

The 3M System was a low-cost, purpose-made product for cleaning griddles in catering establishments of all kinds. Unfortunately, no data existed on potential customers and their type of equipment, on which the 3M System might be used. Fast-food outlets were an obvious target but precluded other sectors. It was therefore decided to test-mail a list of fast-food outlets that also included traditional catering establishments, such as pubs, restaurants, canteens and cafeterias.

A free sample of the product was offered in return for a completed RPC, with tick-box sections, which would both qualify the sales leads for the distributors' salesmen as well as give 3M the data to position the product in the right markets. A 12.62 per cent response rate with all cards completed in full was achieved. Analysis of the reply cards gave 3M a great deal of valuable information:

- Griddles were more prevalent in non-fast-food outlets than expected, thus widening the potential market.
- Griddles were mainly being cleaned with scrapers or stones, which could damage the surface – a major selling point for 3M.
- Many suppliers named by respondents were already 3M distributors, so making lead conversion easier.

The 3M company was able to strengthen the position of the product with distributors by increasing the distributors' awareness of the market and by providing qualified leads for their salesman to follow up.

Elanco Products
A similar success was achieved by Elanco with its fungicide Rubigan, a spray to protect apples from mildew and scab, which had been successful for a number of years. However, Rubigan's disease control had been extended to cover other fruits. Elanco needed to give its sales force and its merchants' sales teams new leads as well as market information. While fruit growers were known, no details were available on the types of fruit being grown. Elanco mailed growers with details promoting Rubigan's increased effectiveness and asked for details on the grower's business. A free spray-record chart was offered – a useful item to the grower – in return for a completed card. The RPC was clear and easy to complete, tick-boxes being used wherever possible to reduce the amount of writing expected of the recipient of the mailshot. The package yielded both a high response rate and valuable information, producing qualified leads with a high conversion ratio – making the exercise very cost-effective.

Bowater-Scott
This company wanted a much wider scope of information and thought this could lead to a lower number of replies. They put this to the test when they used an RPC to gather information as part of a mailing for WypAll disposable industrial wipes. The primary objective was to put a sample of the product into the hands of

potential customers; the two secondary objectives to generate qualified leads for the sales force and to provide the marketing department with additional data on product usage. The mailshot was therefore designed around samples, the recipient being asked to use the product and record his views on a reply card/questionnaire. In return, each respondent was offered a full WypAll benchtop dispenser, plus the chance to win a luxury holiday.

Collaboration between sales and marketing departments at an early stage identified the information that would be most useful. Provision was made to ensure the mailshot design could incorporate the reply card as a central component, well-placed, attractive and easy to use. (The company started with the RPC and designed the rest of the package around it.) Tick-boxes were used to enable the card to be completed with the minimum of writing.

Response topped 14 per cent. Salespeople got the leads they wanted; knowing that a free dispenser was already in place, they then had only to sell the refills. Moreover, the potential of each lead was qualified so the salesmen could grade their leads to make the most economical use of their selling time. This ploy increased the leads-to-sales conversion ratio, and WypeAll increased its market share.

For the marketing department, analysis of the data provided important market information, which could otherwise have been obtained only through market research. Quite possibly it would have cost more to get the same amount of data from research than from RPC and the benchtop dispensers would not have been in place.

In each of the above examples, success was achieved because:

(a) The mailshots presented the recipient with a reply card as the next logical step to take to find out more about the product, and encouraged relevant response.
(b) The RPC was the starting point in the mailing design.
(c) Only information that was relevant to *both* the product and the recipient was requested. (Respondents' goodwill can be lost if they feel they are being interrogated too deeply.)
(d) Finally, the information was asked for politely: 'Please help us to help you'.

Asking for information does not reduce response rates, provided it is handled properly. On the contrary, business people like suppliers that are genuinely interested in their affairs – it shows they mean business. Equally, asking for more than just a name and an address on an information-gathering reply card discourages leaflet collectors and encourages responses from people who are genuinely interested in the products, and who are therefore more likely to purchase. Direct mail can thus provide much more than simple response. The reply card can be a valuable source of information and significantly improve the leads-to-sales conversion ratio, without costing a penny more.

9.8 Telephone marketing

Telephone marketing, linked to computer technology, is the start of a relationship with your database. In short, it is the finger on the pulse of your customers' needs, wants and perceptions. More than any other medium, telephone marketing puts you in touch with your public. It is, in direct-marketing terms, a relatively small market, valued at approximately £60m a year for agencies and bureaux – according to a survey by the British Direct Marketing Association conducted in 1988.

In the US the telephone is the single biggest marketing medium. The American Telephone Marketing Association believes that its market is worth at least $34bn, including in-house activity. That figure is bigger than all the US above-the-line expenditure. If the UK grew at the same rate, we would have had a £5bn market by mid-1990.

Telephoning is the closest you can get to existing and prospective clients without actually being there. The emphasis of any telephone-marketing programme must be firmly placed on the word 'marketing', and not simply on 'sales'. Campaigns should be undertaken as a series of tactical exercises, each one strategically planned as part of the company's marketing mix; campaigns can thus generate a storehouse of valuable information. There is of course a strong degree of flexibility demanded of telephone marketing; responses can sometimes be entirely unpredictable, leading to new opportunities for cross-selling products or services. Used tactically, the telephone will:

1 Encourage seminar attendance.
2 Arrange appointments.
3 Generate and qualify leads.
4 Develop cross-selling opportunities.
5 Promote and close sales.
6 Research new markets.
7 Reveal customer opinion.
8 Source media response.
9 Handle fulfilment.
10 Answer queries.

Telephone marketing can be defined as any measurable activity that creates and exploits a direct relationship between supplier and consumer/customer by the interactive use of the telephone. In some respects the telephone is like the other direct-marketing media – mail, press and broadcast – but in many ways it is different. *Understanding* these differences is crucial to any *understanding* of what it can achieve, as opposed to just realizing its potential.

Many would feel there is no mystery to telephone marketing, because virtually all know how to use the phone. However, most people cannot remember when they first learned to use it, any more than they can remember when they first learned to tell good food from mediocre food. Most people can make a phone call, most have at least one phone at home and another at work. Most people have a TV at home, and they also know how to use it. But the television viewing population is not expert in the use of broadcast media for marketing and advertising. (Even if they hold strong opinions about it!). Why then do so many people believe that they have an automatic level of expertise when it comes to telephone marketing?

Have they been conditioned into such a belief because the telephone is a relatively simple tool to use, and is comfortable because of its familiarity? One should no more expect to master golf without coaching than to master telephone marketing without some specialist training: not doing so means that a major business opportunity is being missed. Remember too that handling advertising response or generating sales leads and appointments can prove both time-consuming and costly when they tie up your own staff and business resources. It may be better therefore in some circumstances to employ specialist help to take on the extra workload.

So how does the telephone differ from other direct marketing media?

9.8.1 'Outbound' and 'inbound'

The telephone works in two directions: 'outbound', where you call the customers, and 'inbound', where they call you. Both are just as important and both need as much attention. If a customer has plucked up courage, made that emotional step to phone you, and dialled the number, only to find he is talking to a machine or to find the line continually engaged, how do you think he feels? Inbound calls are all driven, all stimulated by other media. The outbound call differs: it is the stimulus, it is the message.

9.8.2 *Problems of sight, touch and smell*

On the telephone speakers cannot see or touch each other, and the telephone cannot convey smells. A clothing catalogue mailed out can contain a swatch of material, as Next Directory occasionally offers; fragrance companies mail samples or occasionally use 'scratch-and-sniff' areas on direct-response advertising; and mailshots can be printed on 120 gram antique wove stock paper to give them a quality feel. Telephone marketing, however, depends on the ear, and, unfortunately, detailed product descriptions do not lend themselves naturally to the telephone.

9.8.3 *Time limits*

Direct mail is usually limited by weight, and press advertising by space; telephone marketing, on the other hand, is limited by time – the time for which attention can be attracted and maintained. But unlike other media, the telephone does not have to fight so hard to achieve levels of attention. It is invasive. The phone will interrupt meetings: in some office environments people will use the phone to butt into a meeting when they themselves will not interrupt. And when did you last run downstairs to open a direct mail shot?

9.8.3 *Cost and commitment*

A telephone seller can ask for commitment, much as face-to-face salespeople do, but the phone call is much cheaper than the salesman's visit. Selling over the phone means decisions taken by the market are taken as a result of a very short conversation. This does mean the commitment may be low, and can fall away quickly, yet the telephone offers an advantage despite low commitment. If the customer says 'No', the caller can ask 'Why?', thus providing the opportunity not only to interpret the market's reaction to an offer but also to do something about it. People who say 'No' to direct mail or an advertisement don't usually say why. To change a telephone approach is easy; to change a direct mail message once 100,000 of them are with the Post Office is impossible.

9.8.4 Integrating telephone marketing

So how can telephone marketing be integrated into the marketing mix? There are many different approaches, and the one selected depends largely on the company's objectives and of course on its existing work ethic. There are three main criteria upon which a choice is made.

Incremental contribution per order
How much can you afford to spend to acquire a new customer? Knowledge of cost per order goes hand in hand with an understanding of allowable cost per new customer acquired. Book clubs and catalogue marketers understand this, because they deal constantly in a return over a period of time, i.e. they know how much can be allowed off four books as an offer to the first-time member of a book club as compared to the average purchases by that new customer; equally, catalogue marketers know what value of free gifts can be offered with a new customer's first order.

The income derived from a customer may be spread over a 2- to 3-year period, provided the customer can be kept. In the magazine subscription business calculations can be based on the number of subscribers who will renew after the first year, the second year, and so on. It is possible to forecast the income from a subscriber over a 3- to 4-year period, and the cost of retaining that subscriber.

Volume or market-share considerations
These considerations are important for new-product launches or major pushes for existing products, and maybe more important than contribution per se. A good example is the competitive automotive industry, which is interested in market share and in shifting product just to keep the production line moving. Companies in this industry are also keen to use the phone to isolate and attack well-defined individual market segments and geographical areas. And any company facing a new source of competition can protect its market share the next day by phoning its existing customer base in order to isolate the new competitor when it is at its weakest – at launch. The phone is immediate, and, unlike other media, can be invisible: competitors do not see it, although they may hear about it when it is too late.

Gut feel
This last criterion has been the basis of some very successful campaigns. Bright individuals can buck all the rules and make the telephone work. Gut feel makes a company's marketing campaign very difficult for the competition to predict. But unless marketers really know what they are doing, have considerable breadth of experience, or

can afford to take risks, they should stick to the more traditional and proven methods of analysis, plan, implementation and evaluation of all components of their marketing mix where the phone can readily be integrated. Do not be the person who jumps on a horse and runs off all over the place. Plan first. Remember the British Telecom's early advertising message in your planning: 'If it can be said . . . phone instead.'

9.9 Personal marketing

This form of marketing can be defined as: 'The practice of selling direct to customers identified not only by geodemographic, psychographic and lifestyle data, but also by their willingness to communicate future buying plans and needs.'

As we have already seen, direct marketing is all about that two-way dialogue between suppliers and consumers. Personal marketing refers to the communication between suppliers and consumers where the consumer is actually willing to stand up and be counted. Let us consider the evidence establishing that there is a sizeable market of direct shoppers who welcome the opportunity to inform marketers of their current needs and future buying plans, so that they can be targeted more effectively with what they want to know about products and offers.

The evidence comes from one of the foremost direct marketing agencies, HLY-Grey Direct. American colleagues at Grey-Direct in New York identified the interactive consumer, a high value, long-life direct shopper; they found that half the US population who were direct shoppers were 'direct marketing involved'. When researching the UK market, they discovered that 47 per cent were willing, to some extent, to provide personal information in at least one of three circumstances. The data are summarized in Figure 9.2.

The three circumstances when customers were willing to interact and provide information were:

- When ordering products.
- When requesting information.
- When a frequent user of direct shopping

The preferences for these circumstances vary according to the type of product the customer is buying, and how it relates to travel is shown in Figure 9.3.

Personal marketing is one-to-one marketing, the ultimate segmentation in database usage that so many marketers have been talking about

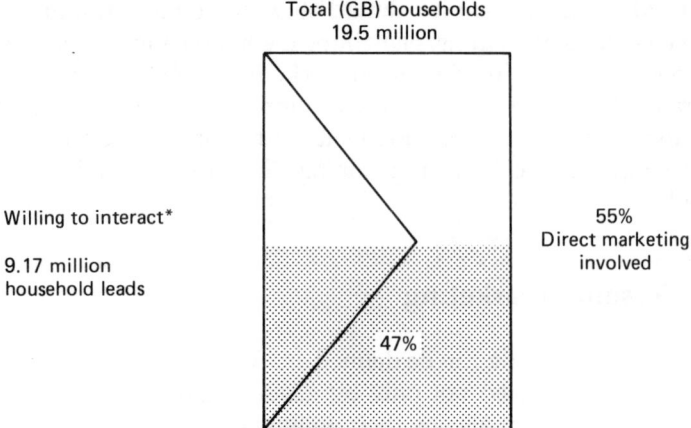

Total (GB) households
19.5 million

Willing to interact*

9.17 million
household leads

55%
Direct marketing
involved

47%

*Very/somewhat willing to provide personal information
in at least one of three circumstances.

Figure 9.2 *Nearly five out of ten UK households may be ready to interact. Source: HLY-Grey Direct*

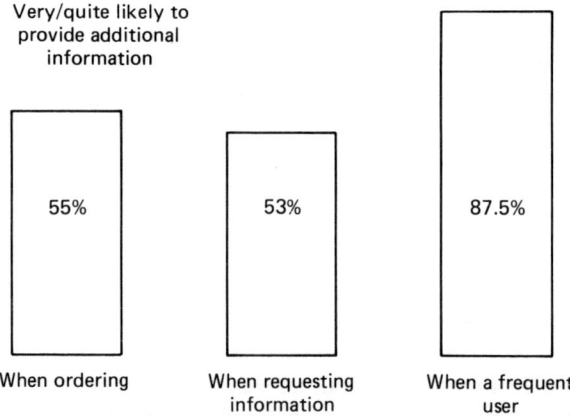

Very/quite likely to
provide additional
information

55%

53%

87.5%

When ordering

When requesting
information

When a frequent
user

Figure 9.3 *There is a willingness to interact in at least one of three circumstances and especially in relation to travel. Source: HLY-Grey Direct*

recently. The interactive database accesses more customer information than has ever been asked for before – with inevitable bearing on consumer attitudes to data protection. It results in direct mail that, by definition, is relevant, wanted, and welcome – a strong case against junk-mail accusations. This explains why people who receive and use direct mail are happy to interact by providing information about themselves – they realize that they will get mail that is more relevant to them.

The essential requirement for these potentially interactive customers is that marketers should be forthright and honest with them, from the outset. Not only should marketers be candid about the uses to which their personal data may be put, but marketers should treat them as mature individuals intent on making their own decisions about purchasing, based on full information. Personal marketing is an organic relationship between seller and buyer, and marketing hype has no place in such a relationship. While this two-way openness may sound alarm bells in the 'old school' of marketing, the qualitative findings of this new research point the way for the 1990s to a more aware, confident and sophisticated direct buyer in the market place.

Honesty and candour raise response to questionnaires – and there is every reason to believe that raised response will be the first commercial advantage to companies making a start on personal marketing. It is possible to segment your direct-mail list by interactives and non-interactives, picking out the most responsive direct-shopping audience and targeting them with mailings based on their own personal input.

The philosophy of personal marketing will change perceptions of direct transactions and increase the market as a whole. That will benefit companies and customers alike.

9.10 Summary

1 Direct marketing uses the mail, direct response broadcasting, telephone selling or direct response press advertising to deal direct with the customers, rather than through retailers.

2 Increasingly, direct marketing relies on electronic databases of customers and their known preferences.

3 Like sales promotion, direct marketing (and especially data bases) is subject to very strict controls.

4 Also, like sales promotion, direct marketing is a very rapidly growing area of activity (because of its high success rate).

5 Apparently simple, direct marketing (including the writing of direct mail letters) is a highly skilled range of activities, calling for a highly professional approach.

References

1 In *Precision Marketing* (1986), June. *Source*: the American Telephone Marketing Association.
2 *Newstime* (1986)
3 *Marketing* (1986) 2 October, p. 41.

10 Sales literature

10.1 Introduction

Many people believe that others outside their company know far more about it and its products than they actually do. They also expect customers and potential investors to have a well-balanced and well-informed view of their company's business as a matter of course. Sadly this is not the case. But a well-prepared publication or sales literature strategy can do much to redress the balance, providing full information about every important aspect of a company's operations, its products and its services is provided.

It is an unfortunate fact that the publication of company literature is often unplanned, hurried, ill-conceived and sometimes quite inappropriate. To be effective and efficient, literature must be part of marketing and corporate strategy.

Thus every single piece of literature must stem from a defined objective, starting with an outline of the target audience. What do they need or want to know? This may not be quite what *you* would like to tell them. Consider too the method of distributing the information. Is it going to be a loose insert in a magazine, mailed, handed out by sales representatives at sales interviews, or available for customers to pick up at point of sale? Or maybe a combination of any of these? The target audience and the method of distribution employed will affect the basic message the piece is required to deliver.

Given this start, it would be wrong to suppose that the production of a well-conceived range of literature will solve the communication problem. It is well recognized from page traffic studies, which estimate how much of which pages in a magazine or newspaper are read, that less than 25 per cent of literature, however efficiently distributed, is ever read at all. With these discouraging statistics, more and more importance centres on what is produced and its quality. Your literature will really have to do its job for you when it is read. All the more important to analyse what you need to say and to whom. No matter how much you spend on the actual print and production, little can be done to undo the wrong created by ill-conceived copy and poorly targeted information.

10.2 Planning and scheduling print production

The preparation of sales literature often runs late, and even when a production schedule exists, it is gradually compressed so that the final printing stage – that part that makes that all important first impression, and certainly the most expensive – is rushed so much that quality suffers and errors creep in. This is invariably due to bad planning, or planning that has lost direction.

The first stage in effective planning of sales-literature production is to ensure that it is carried out in exactly the right sequence. Whatever piece is being prepared, the production sequence is largely as follows:

1	Analysis	– Why is the literature being produced?
		– Who is it being produced for?
		– What do you or they want/need to know?
		– Why do they need to know it?
		– How many people need to be informed?
2	Objectives	– Written down and agreed.
		– Clearly stating the end results of what is to be achieved.
		– This is the basis of evaluation later on.
3	Copywriting	– A written brief is essential.
		– This synopsis or outline should still be written, even if you are doing your own writing.
		– Approve every single word of copy before passing the job to the next stage.
4	Design	– The designer is best employed when introduced to the project at the outset.
		– He/she should work with writer and executive in close cooperation.
		– A design layout, however, does not start until writing is both complete and fully agreed with all concerned.
5	Artwork	– This is matter, strictly other than text, prepared for reproduction, such as illustrations, diagrams and photographs.
		– Often, for convenience, also used as a term to include the 'words', which have been assembled by hand, machine, or by photographic techniques, ready

for printing (this process is
typesetting by a typographer).
- Artwork needs careful checking,
  rather like an engineer's blueprint,
  before production.

6 Proofs
- An impression obtained from an inked
  plate, stone, screen, block or type
  in order to check the progress and
  accuracy of the work.
- This is not a substitute for checking
  errors in artwork, but is essentially
  a stage to ensure that nothing has
  'fallen' off the artwork when the
  plates were made before a commitment
  to printing is made.
- Colours, if used in printing, are
  checked at this stage, particularly
  to ensure that the registration of one
  colour relative to another is accurate.

7 Print production
- This is the final stage when the job
  is completed and delivered.
- There are often further stages where
  the printed literature is folded,
  collated, stapled (stitched) together.
  There may be some special cut-outs or
  assembly required.

Each stage in the sequence must be satisfactorily completed and approved before the next stage can begin. It is false economy, for example, to decide that you want to prepare a certain design of literature before starting to write the copy. If you decide on an A5 (20.5cm × 15cm) four-page leaflet first, then start to write the copy, you may end with too much or too little space. Equally, if you start a subsequent stage before the former is approved by *everyone* who needs to see the work, you will start to run up a large bill for the cost of all the changes, as Table 10.1 explains.

Remember that planning a piece thoroughly at the outset means that you can control the budget on your literature production. Similarly the most appropriate printing process will tend to come out of the original definition of objectives, or, if not here, from the visual treatment. Independent of this will be the kind of paper to be used, number of colours, degree of finish, and method of presentation. A more difficult matter is the choice of a printer.

Table 10.1 *Preparation of literature and costs*

Stage	Costs	Cost of one word change
Copywriting	If your are writing the copy yourself, the costs are only of your time, and that of a typist. Word-processors have speeded up the time taken, and therefore the cost of making small changes are small.	Negligible
Design	While small textual changes probably have no bearing on the design, it is important to get the copy right at the outset. That means getting everyone to agree, and sign to indicate their approval.	Negligible
Artwork	Depending on your sources, the specialized skills of artwork and typography can cost upwards of £50 an hour. (You may also be charged for some materials over and above this cost; possibly for some typographical processes, most certainly photography.)	If the word has not been already set in the typeface chosen and to the right size, you could be charged a £50 minimum typography charge. You may get a charge of £10 minimum for artwork too.
Plates	The artwork, photographs and so forth are scanned and plates made. Full-colour photographs are made up of four coloured inks, each needing a separate plate. Depending on the complexity of the job, plates could cost £200 or more – each.	Sometimes a word can be 'stripped off' a plate and, rarely, another substituted, but the results are poor. One word change may mean £200 plus for a new plate. If the word is 'white out' of a full coloured background you will need four new plates.
Proofing	A sheet of paper is taken out of the early print run, the printing machine is stopped, and the job awaits approval of this proof. Down time could be £100 or more for the proof.	This is not the time to look for text corrections! A proof is to check the colours are correct. Any changes sum the above costs and add to down time.
Printing	Printing is costly; good printing more so. Once you have made the investment in the plates, unit costs decline as you increase the print run. Nonetheless, any changes mean you have to start again.	About the only possible way to change printing is to overstick a label. This is only just acceptable for your telephone or address changing. For anything else – forget it!

The variations that occur between one supplier and another in quality and delivery make price alone an unsatisfactory and incomplete basis on which to select a printer. The soundest basis is to build up a relationship with a few printers with whom the majority of business is placed, establishing from the outset that certain standards of quality, service and, most important, integrity, must be maintained and that any serious defects will result in a termination of the relationship. Even so, it will be necessary to put an occasional print job out to tender in order that cost comparisons can be made.

The second stage in effective planning is to establish from the outset a realistic time schedule. Moreover, take steps to enforce it. While easy to say, it is sometimes difficult to enforce; nevertheless it must be done. If the schedule is not adhered to, then, given that the date the literature is required is invariably fixed (for a sales meeting, product launch, store opening and so forth), the later stages of the schedule are condensed. In this way the proof stage may be missed or the printing rushed. This may mean that you end up asking for 'fifty made up proofs' for the field force – at a very high cost – or the printing is not given time to dry thoroughly and you get a 'shadow' on the opposite sheets or reverse of one piece; worse still, you may not get quite the right shade of colour you wanted – to match the rest of your literature – when the job is delivered.

So, do you go with it or not? Good planning and adherence to that plan will limit such horror stories. However if, from past experience, your managing director is likely to require a complete rewrite at a certain stage, the possibility must be included in the schedule, and to do so is probably the surest way of bringing home to him just what effect a change of mind can have on a project.

Table 10.2 Print schedule and critical timings

Actions	Time period (days)
1 Write objectives and gain approval	1–7
2 Brief writer, obtain synopsis and get approval by all interested parties	7–21
3 Write copy	1–14
4 Obtain complete approval	1–14
5 Design	7–14
6 Approval	1–14
7 Artwork* – including type mark-up and typesetting	7–21
8 Approval	1–7
9 Proofs	7–14
10 Printing and make-up	7–21

* No provision has been made for the commissioning of special photography, illustrations or technical drawings.

Table 10.2 shows the likely timings that a print schedule would need to accommodate. Obviously, if you are preparing a postcard, the stages will be that much shorter, and much less complicated than if you were preparing a 32-page, full-colour corporate publication. However, the same principles apply. There may be occasions when print is required within a week or even less, but work to high standards will need adequate time to develop, especially for a publication that could, after all, last for perhaps a year and sometimes considerably longer.

One can see from Table 10.2 that a good 5 1/2 weeks should be allowed as the minimum time required to do a good print job for any given piece of sales literature. For complicated publications, however, one should allow up to 20 weeks – that's 5 months almost.

10.3 Distribution

Experience shows that a considerable amount of sales literature is produced at considerable expense, then left substantially unused for a few years before being repulped as wastepaper. This underlines the need for considerable thought being given to:

(a) The audience for the sales literature.
(b) The number of copies required.
(c) The built-in obsolescence of the piece.
    (Will it be replaced at some stage? Has this been planned?)
(d) How the target audience is expected to receive the literature.
(e) How heavy will the piece be, especially if you plan to mail it out?

From the answers to these analytical questions you will be able to build a clear strategy, one that has planned its audiences and methods of distribution.

There will no doubt be a primary audience. For example, a leaflet about a new electronic device may be aimed primarily at all design engineers within certain defined industries. Secondary audiences may be the technical buyers and production engineers in the same factories; other audiences to consider include the press, your own staff, distributors and retailers, as well as other end-users. A prestige brochure, on the other hand, may be directed towards the senior management of customers and prospects, again to employees, and perhaps also to shareholders and suppliers.

Remember, it is only literature in the hands of the intended target audience that is of any value. Anywhere else, including your storeroom, and all you have is capital underemployed, or, worse, capital down the drain.

As far as your storeroom is concerned, it is necessary for efficient distribution to maintain adequate stocks to meet demand. Here it is useful to install an efficient system of inventory, coupled with an adequate system of maximum/minimum stock control, and a procedure which ensures that before re-ordering takes place, the full 'pass-for-press' procedure is used to ensure that the reprint is completely up to date.

For any given product there is likely to be a distribution chain from manufacturers through to consumers. All parties in the chain interact with the same product in some way and therefore need to know different things about that product. While all parties will require some common information, certain players in the distribution chain will need to have specialist knowledge: on occasions you may need to address those information needs quite separately with specific, dedicated literature. However, it may be that you could prepare one basic information source, containing everything anyone would need to know about the product; from this central core specific information could be withdrawn, reproduced in an appropriate fashion and distributed to a finite target group. One fine example of how these layers of literature can be developed comes from the animal feedstuffs industry.

10.3.1 Medicinal feed additives

About £20m a year is spent on medicinal feed additives.[1] These are products added to animal feeds to treat specific clinical or subclinical diseases, such as coccidiosis or salmonellosis. They are essential products, used to maintain the health of farm animals, to protect them from disease, and to help towards the attainment of optimal food production and food quality. Medicinal feed additives do not include hormonal growth promoters; by limiting the ravages of disease, an animal can make optimal use of the food it gets and grow stronger and healthier than if it were suffering such diseases.

As one can see, there are important issues in this subject for consumers as well as certain pressure groups. There is a need to provide consumers with clear, informed details of the products in question to help educate them and allay fears about the products' usage in the food chain. Many would echo the thoughts of a car sticker seen recently which said 'Don't criticize farmers with your mouth full!', but much can be done by all people using these products to educate and inform. This process naturally has many aspects, and many below-the-line publicity techniques are used in the dissemination of this type of information. Various layers of literature are used to publish facts and data about medicinal feed additives, including literature produced by the additive manufacturers.

Consider first the distribution chain between manufacturer and farmer, and their information needs.

The manufacturer

The original research and development experts within a company that first discovers an active compound that can be used as a medicinal feed additive will have generated a considerable amount of data, compiled into a registration dossier, for the Ministry of Agriculture to review, before a licence to manufacture and market the product is granted. The manufacturer needs this information, not only to market the product, but also to distribute such details as required by health and safety executives, production workers, packaging people, warehouse and transport people. All will need some angle on the basic product details.

Feed compounders

Medicinal feed additive manufacturers supply the large feed compounders, which blend the additives in precisely the right amount to make intermediate or finished feeds. These major compounders employ animal nutritionists who select the appropriate raw materials and design production formulae for the feed mill to blend the right mixture of ingredients to make a feed for the various classes of livestock. Within these finished feeds will be incorporated small amounts of the medicinal feed additives as required.

The nutritionists will need thorough technical training and information, enabling them to make appropriate decisions about the use of the various products. The mill manager and his health and safety people will require other specific details on the use of the product – what it may or may not be mixed with, and what hazards or warnings need be addressed in the production, if any. The mill may employ salesmen to sell its finished product to farmers; alternatively, the mill may make intermediate products that smaller feed compound companies may use in their manufacture of finished feeds. In each case the salesman will also need product literature to support his sales pitch.

Regional feed compounders

These companies have similar needs to the larger feed mills. However, their raw materials may not be quite the same as those of the bigger mills, and their information needs whilst being similar may not need to be to the same depth. Again, the regional compounders may have a sales team calling on farms. Much of the literature used here establishes productivity data on the use of the medicinal feed additives on livestock.

Farmers

Farmers themselves will need to have specific product information; some may be 'home mixers', making their own finished feeds. It is likely that they will also need to know about the diseases the products are designed to counter. They will need to know about how much product to feed and for how long, and when to withdraw the product before sending the livestock to slaughter.

Consumers

Consumers are the end of the distribution chain in that they buy the final product. While this part of the chain is important and their needs must be addressed, not only by the manufacturers but by compounders and farmers, they do not fall into the category of medicinal feed additive *users*, and literature distribution would not be the best method of informing this massive section of people. Editorial publicity is probably the best method (see Chapter 13).

Numbers of people needing information

So how can various layers of literature be used to the best advantage to educate, inform, and allay any fears of any of the first four groups described above? Let us first consider the number of people in each of the four groups; this is summarized in Table 10.3.

Table 10.3 *Approximate number and type of people engaged in the distribution of UK medicinal feed activities from manufacturer to farmer*

Producers, distributors and users	Numbers of people
(a) A manufacturer of feed additives	10 health and safety people/manufacturing staff principally concerned with production.
(b) National feed compounders	50 nutritionists, production managers. Each compounder will also have people particularly concerned for health and safety issues.
(c) Regional compounders	300 manufacturers mixing smaller batches, 2000 representatives, calling on farms.
(d) Farmers producing livestock	10,000 principally concerned with animal production.

As we move down the pyramid, the number of people gets larger but the amount of detailed information required by each individual gets smaller. The dissemination of information to all these groups is best handled by literature that each can keep and refer back to as required.

In this structure, the problem of publication is most effectively handled in the following ways.

Compendium of medicinal feed additives.
The manufacturer has, say, five products, and will be able to compile a file for each product, maybe running to 100 pages, covering all the relevant detail on the product – its manufacture, its usage in feed compounding, and in disease control. The five such sections can be brought together to form the five sections of the company's compendium. Less than 100 final copies would be required to satisfy the needs, not only of the manufacturer's employees, but also of the national feed compounder's nutritionists.

Booklets for regional compounders
At the end of each of the above five sections, one could imagine a four- or eight-page summary of the section, which would distill the important points as appropriate to the smaller regional compounders; 2500 × 5 booklets would need to be printed to distribute to these compounders' staff; either direct from the feed-additive manufacturer or via the larger compounder. The series of five booklets would form an interesting and valuable set for the regional compounders' representatives calling on farms. Successive booklets could be mailed out bi-monthly to named representatives.

Each booklet could have a simple multiple choice questionnaire on the product included with a reply envelope within the mailing. Satisfactory completion of the questionnaire would ensure that the educative process is being enhanced, as well as improving literature readership, and success could be rewarded by a £1 voucher (or other appropriate incentive) included with the next booklet in the series.

Leaflets for farmers
Finally, up to 15,000 × 5 farmer leaflets could be produced, again as a distillation of the earlier booklet. Each leaflet would need to be no longer probably than a few hundred words, supported by facts, figures and simple diagrams to explain the product's benefits, particularly in terms of productivity.

The layers of literature produced in this way are illustrated in Figure 10.1. It is much easier to produce the literature in this way from the top downwards, rather than the reverse. Only when all the information has been gathered to write the compendium can one assess the data in its entirety and decide on what can be included in the next, subordinate stage, and what can be excluded. Naturally, as each layer of literature has a slightly different target audience, it will be important to define at the outset of the project the precise needs of the target group and the objective that the literature is to fulfil.

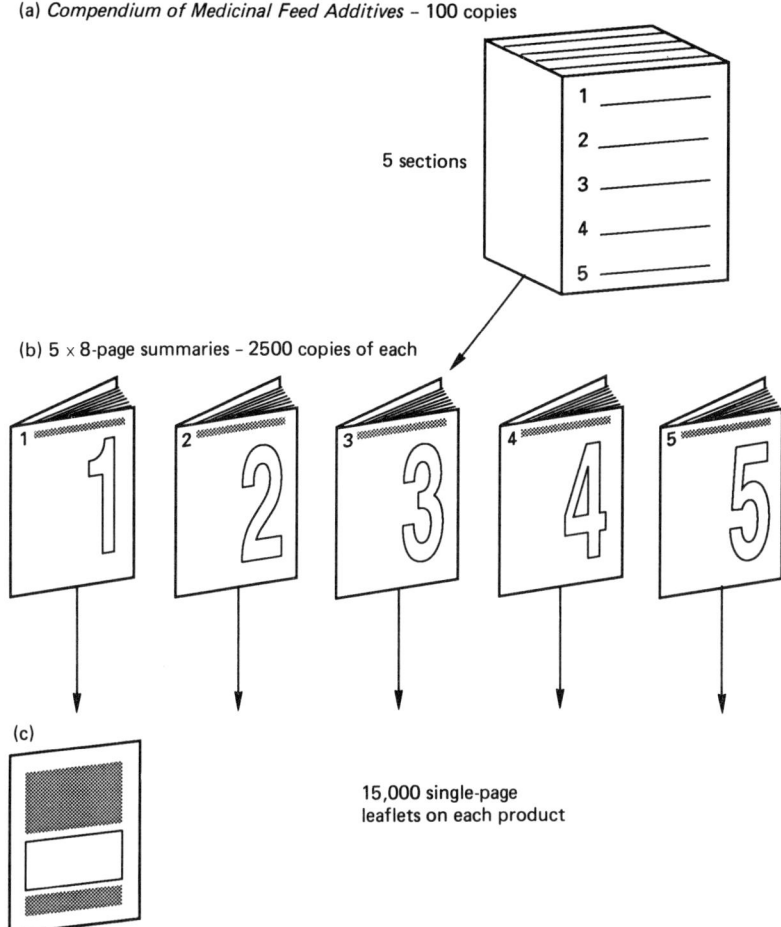

(a) *Compendium of Medicinal Feed Additives* – 100 copies

5 sections

1 ————
2 ————
3 ————
4 ————
5 ————

(b) 5 × 8-page summaries – 2500 copies of each

(c)

15,000 single-page
leaflets on each product

Figure 10.1 *Layers of literature of decreasing complexity but increasing numbers to address the needs of the medicinal feed additive industry*

10.4 Enhancement of company image through literature

The following copy was used in a press advertisement for McGraw-Hill magazines. It has not been bettered as an argument for business-to-business advertising:

I don't know who you are.
I don't know your company.
I don't know your company's products.

I don't know what your company stands for.
I don't know your company's customers.
I don't know your company's record.
I don't know your company's reputation.
Now – what was it you wanted to sell me?

Moral: sales start *before* your salesman calls
  – with business publication advertising.

The flaw to this argument, however, is that there are rather a lot of points in the advertisement to be answered, and it could take a long time and a number of advertisements to put across the whole story about a company. Yet it is possible to produce literature which, if read, will help to create the kind of image that a company hopes for, and answer the points raised. This of course presupposes that a plan defining the company image exists. If it does, the publications that can be produced will have a sound business basis, rather than just a general feeling that they are things a company ought to publish.

Company brochures, for instance, can cover all the activities of a company, its subsidiaries and overseas operations, and express them in terms the defined key audience can recognize as valuable. Such a publication may be preceded by research to establish the level of knowledge about the company and where gaps exist. It is important to avoid being introspective and writing about the company just for the sake of it; but if the capability of top management or the existence of modern company facilities are exceptional, they are worth publicizing. The first step in such a publication is an objective analysis of a company's strengths in relation to competitors and the nature of the audience.

Company histories are often published – but 'Who cares?' If the history is outstanding, relevant, or includes particular personalities, or maybe there have been a number of innovations that people in general do not know about, then there may be justification for such a book. Personnel departments often use them to attract new staff. However, a company may be in a fast-developing industry where little regard is paid to the past and in which the future – long- and short-term – is all that seems to matter. Perhaps the criterion to be adopted is to try and demonstrate the need and value of such a publication, and if this cannot be done, don't publish.

Industry publications are useful if a company is in an industry that has a wide consumer interest, or maybe as a topic in educational programmes. Certain industries producing basic materials such as paper and steel come into this category, along with, for example, textiles, soap, aircraft, electronics, railways and so on. Food companies are increasingly entering the educational field, particularly Kelloggs breakfast cereals. Not only is the company keen to help in school education programmes but it is also keen to address dietitians and nutritionists as a target group. (For Christmas 1989 Kelloggs sent every practising dietitian in the UK – about 2500 of them – a free Filofax. While not a 'prestige publication' it did reflect well on Kelloggs' company image.)

As far as this chapter is concerned, it is enough to ask 'Will an industry publication help to achieve our defined objective?' Providing the answer is a qualified yes, then the job is worth doing. But it should never be done purely to make the management feel good (sometimes referred to as a 'brag and boast' exercise).

The annual report poses a dilemma for both financial directors and art directors. This dilemma is best summed up by the jaundiced comment of a shareholder in a research report commissioned by financial literature design specialist Wolff Olins Hall, compiled in conjunction with the London Business School: 'The more they spend on it, the less there is for my dividend'. Quite simply, if the annual report is perceived to be too slick and glossy, shareholders point angrily to money wasting. Yet if it is too dull, the company is accused of being slow-moving, stodgy and behind the times. Getting the balance right is becoming harder and harder. When the Arts Council updated its 1988 annual report to create a lively 120-page document, *The Times* thundered against a public body producing 'coffee table reading'.

Markets in both the public and private sectors are now more complex and sophisticated. Competition is tougher, and patterns of funding, marketing and recruitment are changing. The need for organisations to communicate internally and externally is putting demands on the annual report to do more than plainly relate the facts and figures of the year's performance. In the late 1980s British annual reports followed the American approach and communicated a broader picture of corporate activities and personality. Designers played a major role in this new style, replacing rows of figures in tiny type by magazine-style productions with glossy colour photographs, tricks with origami and elaborate diagrams. It appeared that the more bullish the message for the City, the more brilliant and exuberant the visual design.

The idea for the 1990s, born out of the unstable economy in the late 1980s, is to make the annual report work harder as a strategic element in an integrated corporate communications programme, rather than let it stand alone as a one-off piece of bravado publishing. The design of the annual report might even be a political issue.

Take, for example, the 1988–9 report for Thames Water. The concept of water privatization was not popular – even if the shares were oversubscribed five-fold! There had been many accusations of hype, particularly advertising hype, so the annual report could not be too lavish. The result was, in fact, low key, the cover of the Thames Water report being likened to a school textbook's. Eurotunnel's bilingual 1988 group accounts were presented with a similar dilemma. The subject was less unpopular, unless you lived in Kent, but at the time it was being prepared the true cost of building the link had just been revealed. With the overriding aim to reassure investors, the design avoided anything that might hint of extravagance.

In an annual report it is essential to make the financial data – the primary function of the report – as accessible as possible, though this is often a neglected aspect of annual report design. One can in fact regard the annual report as just one of a series of visual assets, such as brands or identity, belonging to the company. Visual assets should be protected and developed in the same way as capital, human, or financial assets. Work on the 1989 Hambro's annual report revealed how this approach works. Common design characteristics are intended to build up a sense of corporate personality for a financial company trading in what is essentially an invisible product.

Many describe this new design activity, whether visual asset management or corporate communications programming, as being part of the 'Americanization' of British annual reports. Corporate America grasped the concept of the annual report as a marketing tool long before Europe did. However, the idea has, in turn, been influential in Britain. This is not surprising, given the trading links between the two nations and that there have been a dozen acquisitions of US design firms by British consultants in recent years, more than £70m having changed hands. Some of the most progressive American exponents of the annual report art are now British-owned. Traditional British design produced 'beautiful books without too much direction as to content', explained one design-agency president. 'Americans on the other hand are expert at "theming" annual reports. A theme-orientated approach might focus on the quality of management or the human face of employees.'

Some analysts find it hard to get to grips with the real results amid a welter of colourful theme editorials. Writing in *The Wall Street Journal*, one analyst said: 'To some financial analysts the annual report is nothing more than an exercise in corporate duplicity – gripping graphics can hide bad news buried in obscure footnotes.' Few companies had more bad news to impart than British retailers in the end of the 1980s, and their annual reports necessitated carefully constructed statement and sentiment. Sir Terence Conran used his own designers in Conran Design Group to communicate the 'difficult' year in a clear, undemonstrative style. The calmness played down the rising panic within the company.

Asda, meanwhile, felt it was being unfairly treated by financial institutions so it aimed its 1989 annual report at them. The report, entitled 'The Facts, the Figures, the Future', was large in shape, which made it awkward to file, and used bold headlines, which were hard to ignore. Asda felt that many reports were rather bland because they had so many audiences. It wanted a special annual report to make the institutions, specifically, sit up, take notice and reassess its performance.

The message is that, although individual, one-off flashes of visual brilliance are now out of vogue, annual reports will continue to be highly designed documents. However, the design will be different – careful, structured and strategic rather than casually applied by the stylists' brush. There is no substitute for analysing the target audience first, defining your objectives clearly and planning your publication carefully to meet those objectives.

10.5 Technical publications

In the field of industrial publicity there is almost always the need for technical publications, which range from specification and data sheets to servicing and operating manuals. Some such materials will naturally have to conform to industry standards. (Pharmaceutical data sheets have a regular format and each drug's product licence defines the precise wording of the piece.) To have technical validity and authority most other technical publications must be written by engineers, technicians or scientists, who frequently do not wish to undertake the task, and anyway are not always able to express themselves clearly. The result is often a compromise, and the job is not as good as it might be.

There are of course technical writers, but the good ones are few and it is not a profession that attracts many talented specialists. One could sub-contract the writing to an outside organization specializing in the production of technical publications, and this can be satisfactory, particularly for the smaller firm, which may not have a constant demand to maintain a regular workload for its own technical writers.

As pointed out in Chapter 4, exercise caution in using an outside organization, as quality and capability vary considerably. There may be a high staff turnover too in any one given agency, which naturally affects continuity. However, if the product warrants first-class materials, it also warrants first-class literature, and the rate for the job – which can vary between £30 per 1000 words to, say, £50 per hour – must be paid to the few good technical writers available.

10.6 Catalogues

Where a company has a wide range of complementary products it is usually necessary to provide a catalogue, with all the concomitant difficulties. Catalogues are expensive to produce, impossible to keep up to date, and never meet the requirements of everyone. Nevertheless, with many technical products they are so essential a part of the marketing operation that they are used by the customer's design department to specify a certain type number, and this predetermines the brand of product ultimately to be purchased.

Interesting catalogue developments have been taking place over the last few years, particularly in the development of microfilm storage units and computerized information retrieval; this, added to desk-top publishing packages, has revolutionized catalogue production. There are also specialist distributors that arrange to send out staff to a given market on behalf of a number of clients and actually place the latest materials in customers' catalogue files. This scheme, while having a limited application, works quite successfully in some fields.

When the various subsidiaries (Carrs Farm Foods, Carrs Fertilisers Ltd, Oliver Snowdon Ltd, James Reive Sons, and Thos Edmondson Ltd) were organized into a single company – Carrs Agriculture Ltd – in 1989, they produced a catalogue listing all the diverse items sold by the new group of companies. The catalogue was comprehensive and circulated in early 1990 to a wide farmer audience in Cumbria, Northumberland and South West Scotland, and was expected to be in frequent use by around 20,000 people. In order to offset the cost of its production and circulation, advertising space was offered to a wide variety of manufacturers that wanted to reach the defined audience. Some may have found the catalogue an attractive medium, since it would remain an active reference and source of business for a whole year. Carrying non-competitive advertising could be considered an easy source of revenue to help fund a catalogue.

It should be remembered that catalogues can also form the backbone of a direct-mail order business. In these situations the catalogue is the shop window for the company, and considerable investment goes into its production. Many retail organizations also offer catalogues, either for a parallel mail-order business – like Next Directory – or the catalogue is offered to shoppers to give them the opportunity to browse at home. Two notable examples are Habitat and Laura Ashley.

Laura Ashley also offers a mail-order facility, the catalogue being principally designed to allow customers to select at home; moreover it is also the vehicle for idea generation, as it carries a wide selection of indoor scenes built around various pattern themes. Customers can sit in their own homes and adapt ideas for decorating their rooms from the wallpapers and soft furnishings handsomely illustrated in the catalogue. In any one catalogue there can be dozens of 'model' rooms, far more than could ever be built into a retail display.

10.7 Sales literature and benefits

'Customers don't buy products: they seek to acquire benefits.' This is the guiding principle of the marketing director of one of Britain's more innovative companies in the hair-care business. Behind that statement lies a basic principle of successful marketing. When people purchase products, they are not motivated in the first instance by the physical features or objective attributes of the product but by the benefit that those attributes bring with them. A simple formula therefore to ensure that this customer-oriented approach is adopted when writing sales literature is always to use the phrase 'which means that' to link a feature to the benefit it brings:

- 'Maintenance time has been reduced from 4 to 3 hours, *which means that* most costs are reduced by . . .'
- 'Homepride flour is made from graded grains, *which means that* graded grains make finer flour; and, in turn, Homepride has finer flour, *which means that* baking is lighter.'

By translating product features into consumer benefits, less work is required on the part of the consumer to recognize the benefits of product ownership. In this way the literature will serve to complement the sales effort, whether it be selling 'off-the-page' or to support the salesman's efforts.

Benefits should be reviewed at two levels:

(a) Benefits that can be obtained by purchase of a particular product.
(b) Benefits that can be obtained by purchasing that product from a particular supplier.

For example, Rotary lawnmower sales people need to consider the benefits of a rotary lawnmower over a cylinder mower, as well as the benefits that their company's rotary mowers have over competitors' models. The company's sales literature may have to address these two issues together or separately. Naturally the product literature will only form part of the total marketing-communication mix, but it should follow the appropriate company-communication strategy.

If the sales literature for the lawnmower example used above considers the benefits at the two levels described, then the salesman has maximum flexibility to meet the various sales situations that may be found in the field.

When developing literature to support the sales team, give considerable thought to how the piece will be used. One standard sheet could reasonably be used in a variety of ways:

1 *As a selling aid*. Here the product might be featured by means of a photograph and a brand name, surrounded by feature/benefit statements that the salesman can use to remind him about the product. The detail aid may be presented to the prospective buyers by the salesman, and can be used as a focus for the sales interview. Visual elements are important in such interviews to reinforce the information that the buyer is hearing from the salesman.
2 *As a 'leave-behind'*. At the end of the interview the salesman might leave a copy of the selling aid as a reminder of the interview. On the reverse of the piece, for example, a technical specification may be written, giving precise details of the product. Such literature can be valuable in ensuring that the customer gets it right when he tries to pass on to colleagues the enthusiasm generated by an effective sales call.
3 *As a loose insert*. In many instances the same leave-behind piece can be used as a loose insert in a journal that has a readership directly comparable to the defined target audience the salesman is trying to see. Although there is no face-to-face selling, which the product might demand, at least the majority of the target market will receive selling-copy (the feature/benefit headings) and the technical specification. When the salesman does make his call, the prospects have been 'softened' a little in that they are more aware of the product, and the discussion can start further towards matching the prospective needs.
4 *Direct mail*. Loose inserts have the advantage of immediacy, but direct mail has flexibility and can be personalized. If a salesman works purely on appointments or maybe works an area, only some of his calls being fixed, he may decide that mailing known individuals or customers in specific geographical areas, say 2 weeks before this visit, would improve his call-to-order ratio. With the right database, this support could be given him. Again, the information derived originally from his detail aid can be used. Indeed one can sometimes use the same piece of literature in every method described above.

The contents of any piece of literature used to support the salesman should not be based solely on what a buyer wants to know. This is only the starting point. The contents must be planned deliberately to provide a prospect with what the selling company wishes him to know, no less and no more. Always leave the prospect wanting more; the salesman can provide it and take the order.

Various other items of print can come under the heading of sales literature. Some of these have been covered under direct marketing, and others will be under point-of-sale. Two that are not used as much as they might be are reprints of advertisements and of editorial mentions or articles. It seems likely that if a printed advertisement is worthwhile, it is wasteful to rely simply on it being seen in a magazine. From readership data, it can be reliably forecast that perhaps only a third of a potential market will ever notice it, let alone read it. The exposure must be increased if it is mailed out to the prospect list, and the cost of doing so is very low compared to the media space cost. Similarly a salesman leaving a copy of the advertisement further reinforces the brand/company image.

In industrial markets, where product-buying decisions are frequently based on the technical merits of a product, third-party endorsements carry significant weight. Similarly, in some consumer markets, especially when considering 'white goods' (i.e. kitchen appliances – washing machines, refrigerators) or home-entertainment products (TVs, videos, hi-fis), the Consumers' Association magazine, *Which?* can make a substantial impact on buyers' choice of product. All such technical articles, whether scientific research papers, journalists' reviews, or other written third-party comments, may be copied for salesmen to use as 'proof statements'. (Remember to respect copyright laws, however.)

Customers with previous experience of the use of a product who are satisfied with it and are willing to have their positive views recorded, are worth their weight in gold, particularly if their product endorsement is seen to be independent of the manufacturer. It is possible for salesmen to use the recorded experiences of customers, or opinion leaders, who have already bought/used the product (early adapters) to influence the group of customers who are next most likely to purchase (early majority). See Section 11.10 on reacting to the product life cycle, for fuller description of the effect of fuelling the 'diffusion of innovation' process.

If any customer happens to say something good about your products or company, make sure other customers share the experience.

10.8 Specialist product-support literature

One device occasionally used by pharmaceutical drug manufacturers is called the sample catch-cover, whose purpose is to enclose tablets or capsuled products. Manufacturers need to receive a written or signed request from a General Practitioner to supply a small quantity of free samples. (This is a legislative requirement instituted to stop the heavy sampling techniques favoured by the less 'ethical' pharmaceutical companies in the 1970s.) Rather than simply provide a small standard pack of the product, manufacturers would develop a special pack that had an extended print area to carry further benefit information. Now that many oral pharmaceuticals are packed in blister strips – a small strip of plastic with wells for the tablets or capsules sealed with foil – it is a simple matter to sandwich the strip in a card envelope that can be folded over to give the product some protection. The card flap can be used to carry the sales message and, if perforated, it can be removed from the drug before dispensing. Holes in the reverse of the flap permit tablets to be pushed out from the other side. Sales representatives often used the sample catch-covers (illegally) as simple 'leave-behinds' when a product was on a low priority detail behind some more important products.

Another specialist area for sales literature concerns after-sales support literature. Included among these items would be, for example, user guides and operating manuals, pack inserts for specialist foods and medicines, and guarantee registration forms.

There is little that is more frustrating for consumers than, having got their multi-function hi-fi stereo system home, realizing that they need a degree in electronics to follow the connecting instructions. In this situation a clear picture or simple diagram saves a thousand words.

Proud owners of gleaming new Honda 750cc motorcycles were congratulated in the opening lines of the riders' manual with the words 'Thank you for having the wisdom to buy a Honda motorcycle . . .' Although it was required to absolve them from any liability Honda had a momentary 'loss of wisdom' when telling new owners in the first instruction not to ride the motorcycle away with the steering locked (at 45° to straight) or a serious accident could result. As the steering lock had to be released before the ignition would turn on, the 'warning' was superfluous. While the majority of motorcyclists are not judged on their Intelligence Quotient, such instructions are derogatory, and mean that the rest of the manual is thrown away, even though it contains some sound advice that the most experienced can overlook from time to time, resulting in serious product failure.

Attention to the detail in over-the-counter (OTC) medicines' pack inserts can also affect consumer satisfaction and product performance. Many such products carry pack inserts that have a considerable amount of close-typed information, written at too high a level for the average person. As many OTC medicines are taken by the elderly, who may have trouble reading the small print, they often take the products incorrectly, being unable to follow the manufacturer's instructions. Again, pictures speak volumes and are more readily understood than close-typed copy. And a simple illustration has no language barrier either.

10.9 Literature checklist

1 Have you written a plan for literature into your marketing plan?
2 Does this plan fit the marketing strategy?
3 In the preparation of a new piece of literature:

  (a) Has the objective been defined?
  (b) Is the potential audience agreed?
  (c) What do they need to know?
  (d) How do you plan to distribute your literature?
  (e) Has a production schedule been produced?
  (f) Does the schedule make provision for:

     (i) Briefing?
     (ii) Writing?
     (iii) Visual treatment?
     (iv) Quotation?
     (v) Finished artwork?
     (vi) Photography?
     (vii) Proofing?
     (viii) Printing?
     (ix) The MD changing his mind!?

4 In briefing a designer has guidance been given on:

  (a) Number and size of pages?
  (b) Choice of card or paper?
  (c) Illustrations?
  (d) Style of design?
  (e) Number of colours?
  (f) Typefaces and sizes?
  (g) Expensive budget?
  (h) Printing process?
  (i) Quantity?

5 Has provision been made for (i) storage and (ii) stock control?

10.10   Summary

1   Sales literature must be targeted at clearly defined audiences, to convey specific information and to achieve a specific purpose. Proper briefing is vital.
2   A very strict schedule from conception to printing must be worked out and adhered to.
3   The chapter refers to a number of specific types of literature, including:

   (a) Company image brochures.
   (b) Technical publications.
   (c) Catalogues.
   (d) Sales aids.
   (e) Specialist product-support literature.

4   A checklist indicates the vital matters to be considered when producing literature.

Reference

1   From National Office of Animal Health, NOAH (1991).

11 Sales aids and sales-support material

11.1 How the sales force operates

A sales force is one of the most effective marketing tools that a company can use to create and keep customers, particularly in industrial marketing.

As the cost of keeping the sales force on the road is high – probably the highest cost in the marketing mix – marketing management must first ask 'What cost-effective role does the sales force play in achieving the company's marketing objectives?' Behind this question lies the unspoken one, 'If we did not have a sales force, would we have invented one?' For most companies the answer has been to recognize three stark facts of economic life:

- A sales force is an expensive marketing tool that must be directed selectively towards very specific objectives, markets and customers.
- Salespeople must produce profitable, not just voluminous, results to justify the financial investment.
- In the fight for markets and for sales revenues, the role of the sales force is of crucial importance.

Throughout the world thousands of men and women are employed in selling products, services or ideas. In the highly competitive environment in which the majority of firms have to sell their products today, salespeople are often the spearhead of a company's total marketing efforts. They carry the main responsibility for getting through to the customer and securing the order. Vast financial assumptions depend on the efforts of salespeople succeeding.

The managing director of an important manufacturer, summing up the challenge facing his company at the end of a national sales conference, said:

After our clever marketing men and women have put their plans to bed, after production has made what our marketing researchers have told us people want and will buy, we are not in business until you (the salespeople) have sold these products again and again to our existing customers and to new ones. That is the importance of the sales force.

Of course the role of face-to-face discussion with the customer may be carried out by people not directly employed by the supplier, e.g. in the case of insurance they may be employed by brokers. In other cases the sales team is employed by retailers or distributors. In such cases the main supplier will need a sales team to sell to those retailers, distributors or brokers.

In most companies more money is spent on the sales force than on advertising and below-the-line publicity combined, which is not surprising, since companies depend to a large extent on personal selling. For example, insurance companies need to discuss the details of individual policies with their customers, and this can be done best through personal representation; so personal selling is a vital and expensive element in the marketing mix, and has to be planned as carefully as any other element. So how do we go about it? First, the selling company must identify the major influences in the buying company on any purchasing decision. Then it must try to find out what each decision-maker needs to know at the various stages of the buying process.

It will also need to know if the customer is buying for the first time or whether it is a repeat order. It is then possible to decide what part personal selling (and above- and below-the-line publicity) must play in all this.

Personal selling has five principal advantages:

(a) It is a two-way form of communication: the purchaser gets a chance to ask about a product or service, specific to his needs.
(b) The sales message can be made very flexible, and therefore more suited to the needs of particular customers.
(c) The salesman can use the depth of his knowledge of the product to relate his product's *benefit* to the perceived needs of the customer, and the *benefit* of buying the product from his company.
(d) The salesman can *ask for an order* and perhaps negotiate, within limits, on price, delivery or any other special requirements.
(e) When the sale has been made, the salesman's task becomes one of reinforcement, underlining the wisdom of the purchase and encouraging the customer to consider other products or services in the range.

A salesman is a person who, to the customer, personifies the company making the sale. So personal selling is an essential part of any marketing plan. Its value varies from market to market, but it must always be present. The salesman's role must be carefully considered in the sales plan, and salesmen must be given the right tools to do their job.

11.2 The structure of a sales interview

Let us leap over sales analysis, management, planning, organization and targeting, and assume the salesperson has made an appointment with a potential buyer. For simplicity, we have taken this step to concentrate on the important role that the salesperson must play in the scheme of business life, and that is to take an order for the product. Again, for simplicity, the sales interview can be broken down into its component parts.

11.2.1 Preparation

Thought must be given to, and answers provided for the following questions:

(a) What are the objectives of the call?
(b) What are the opening words going to be?
(c) What benefits are going to be important?
(d) How will these be demonstrated?
(e) What objections are likely to be raised?
(f) How will these be answered?
(g) How will the interview be closed:

    (i) With an order?
    (ii) With a commitment to purchase?
    (iii) With a commitment to trial?

(h) How will this call be followed up:

    (i) A visit after a defined period of time?
    (ii) A telephone call? When?

11.2.2 *Opening*

First impressions can be crucial. Sales interviews are unnatural, and both salesperson and customer can feel ill at ease. Planning will help the salespeople. Openings should put customers at ease, and four objectives should be achieved:

(a) A good impression.
(b) The customer's full attention.
(c) An exploration of the customer's needs.
(d) Getting the customer to talk about them.

11.2.3 *Presentation*

The most important part of any sales interview, the presentation, follows the establishment of customers' needs or the identification of their problems. Customers will be interested but they want to know whether the salespeople's propositions will produce *benefits* that satisfy their needs and solve their problems.

Remember, benefits are the desirable results from the customer's point of view and, in business terms, from the points of view of all the other people the customer is concerned with – consumers, staff, and their families. Benefits do not include any of the following:

(a) The technical features of a product or proposition.
(b) The way a product is packed.
(c) The price of a product or service.
(d) The method of operation.

Benefits are the desirable results produced by these various features for any person who uses the product. Their effectiveness and their appeal depend on the extent to which they satisfy a customer's needs or problems. People buy products, services and ideas, for what they *do* for them, not for what they are. All materials prepared to support a salesperson's presentations must reflect this.

11.2.4 *Handling objections*

Sooner or later in most sales interviews, objections will be raised. Objection is the term applied to the situation when the customer says 'That is very interesting, but . . .' ('It seems very expensive', 'I don't like that colour', 'It won't fit in my kitchen', etc.). Obviously salespeople must know the answers. But knowing them and putting them across to the customer's satisfaction are two different things. Support materials can reinforce an argument and minimize or negate drawbacks.

11.2.5   Negotiation

A salesperson may be given some latitude to negotiate the terms of sale, (i.e. price within limits, credit terms, any trade-ins, delivery schedules, etc.). Success in negotiating comes from preparation beforehand, and the application of negotiating skills.
  Preparation comprises four factors:

(a) *Assessment of the balance of power*. The less options the buyer has, the better solution provided by the salesperson's product over the competition, and the more important the buyer's problem, then the stronger the seller's position is. The assessment of the seller's position is an important planning process, permitting clear objectives to be set and any concessions determined.
(b) *Setting objectives*. There are two types of objective: 'must have' objectives are the minimum criteria that must be met for the deal (e.g. price/volume relationship), and 'would like' objectives are the maximum a negotiator may realistically achieve. Seller and buyers' opening positions might be defined in this way.
(c) *Concession analysis*. From the assessment of the balance of power comes an analysis of what might be traded to reach a mutually satisfactory position for both parties.
(d) *Proposal analysis*. If the likely demands of the buyer can be anticipated and met satisfactorily by the salesman's counter-proposals prepared beforehand, the errors that arise in the heat of the moment can be avoided.

  The application of negotiating skills rests on two principles: first, start high but be realistic, and second, trade concession for concession. Starting high means that the buyer might agree to it, and the salesman would not have given something away for nothing, and it gives room for negotiation. As buyers are often under pressure to achieve some concession, and indeed some may expect it, the salesman has left room to move towards agreement. The salesman must ensure that any proposal to give the buyer something (say extended credit) is matched by a concession in return (say a higher volume of product).

241

11.2.6   Closing

Closing the sale by asking for a buying decision is often one of the weakest areas of sales techniques. It needs to be the strongest. There are two main problems: salespeople naturally fear social rejection; and salespeople believe that their presentation will be sufficiently beguiling for the customer to buy without being asked, which rarely happens. The close converts acceptance of the idea, plan or product into action.

This is the six-point structure around which salespeople should build the flesh of their interviews, so that the problems of tension, nervousness, lack of appeal to customer needs, and woolly talk are reduced. An example of a structured format for planning a sales interview is the following:

Objectives	*Methods*

(a) The specific objective of the sale is . . . .

(b) The person who has authority to make
    the buying decision is . . . .

(c) The opening will be designed to . . . .

(d) The presentation will aim to . . . .

(e) The following likely objections are . . . .

(f) The following buyer's decisions are required. . . . .

(g) The support materials to the presentation are . . . .

(h) What concessions can I give? . . . .

(i) What concession must I get in return?. . . . .

Salespeople sometimes argue that because one cannot foresee what the customer will do or say, planning and preparation are pointless. This is making perfection the enemy of the good, because to some salespeople such planning implies a muzzle at the mouth. But salespeople cannot be permitted to play sales interviews off the cuff when the company's turnover depends on the way they communicate with, and how they present to, customers who are always short of time, and when, in a free market, competitors are also after the business?

11.2.7   The need for sales support

Because the sales-force role is so vital but also so costly, we need to squeeze the maximum value out of every sales interview. For this reason salespeople are usually provided with 'sales aids', which give additional impact to their verbal presentations. These can range from a simple leaflet or more elaborate, printed 'sales presenter' (which presents in dramatic graphic form the key points of the sales story) to a much more costly full-scale cine-film or video.

11.3   Visual imagery in support of the spoken word

Imagery is an experience in the mind without an actual 'real' corresponding situation. For example, if you were asked to describe what you had for breakfast this morning, you are likely, assuming you actually had something first thing, to conjure up a mental picture of your breakfast table. There is a wide variation among people in the clarity of their visual image, but studies have suggested that everybody does possess a considerable degree of imagery, whether they are aware of it or not. As long ago as 1965, in a study of 500 people, everyone reported having images of some kind; 97 per cent reported visual images and 92 per cent auditory.[1]

Most people use imagery in memory quite naturally, often starting very early on in life. Some have various images associated with number, often involving a spatial arrangement of the numbers. They may be strung out in a line, the line weaving its way through space, perhaps receding from the observer the higher the number. The individual numbers may vary in size, important points like 10, 100, 500, 1000 appearing bigger than others. Or they may be in colour, each number or group of numbers being in a different colour. It has been estimated some 80 per cent of the population has some such 'number form'. Many people have similar forms for the alphabet, for the days of the week, the months of the year, etc.

To investigate the power of imagery in memory, students were given twelve pairs of unrelated nouns, such as 'dog' and 'bicycle', and told to associate the two by imagining a visual scene in which the two objects interacted in some way.[2] Thus a person might imagine the dog riding the bicycle. The students were also given twelve pairs of words that they simply repeated about three times. In both conditions the time allowed for each pair was the same – 8 seconds. Immediate recall tests showed that 80 per cent of the imaged pairs were remembered correctly, whereas only 33 per cent of the repeated pairs were remembered. Thus, by creating strong associative images the subjects had increased their recall two and a half times. When the images were 'seen' vividly and distinctly, as if they were real, recall was around 95 per cent. Other experiments on verbal memory have shown that words that evoke a strong mental image are the most easily remembered. The more vivid the imagery, it seems, the more stable is the memory.

Imagery is valuable in memory because it strengthens associations and links. If the imagery does not actually link the ideas, it is of little value. This was shown by giving lists of word pairs, such as dog – bicycle, to two groups of people. The first group was told to create a strong visual image in which the two objects interacted in some way. The second group was also told to create a strong visual image but with the objects separated, e.g. example, the objects could be pictured as being on opposite walls of a room. Recall tests showed that those who had produced strong interactive images recalled 71 per cent of the words, whereas those who had formed separated images recalled only 46 per cent of the words, only a little better than the 33 per cent scored by rote repetition.

Imagery is most effective therefore when it is as vivid as possible and as interactive as possible. The results of these tests are summarized in Figure 11.1.

Even when people claim to be poor visualizers, imagery can still be very valuable in helping memory. In fact, poor visualizers and good visualizers show the same improvement in memory when instructed to use imagery. The only difference is that the good visualizers tend to be more confident of their memory than poor visualizers. Even if people are poor visualizers, they can be given the pictoral basis upon which to build their own mental picture. In the dog–bicycle example, even if one could not actually visualize an association, being shown an illustration

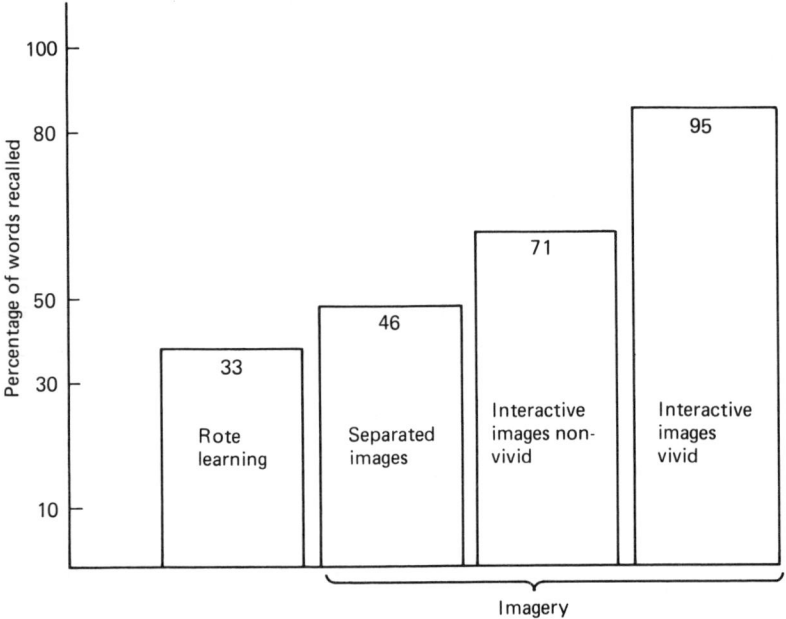

Figure 11.1 *Effectiveness of imagery over rote learning of word pairs, and the value of interactive and vivid images*

or sketch of a dog riding a bicycle will reinforce the link and help in the memory process.

It is this particular feature of the mental processes of memory that is easily exploited in the development of sales aids for representatives, where pictures are used to reinforce the spoken word. It is well recognized that visual images are generally much better remembered than words – so much so that visual recognition is practically perfect.

This bold statement is supported by the results of a study designed to assess the potential of visual memory. In this study subjects were shown a series of 2560 photographic slides at the rate of one every 10 seconds.[3] These 7 hours of viewing were split over several consecutive days. One hour after the last slide had been shown, the subjects were tested for recognition by showing them 280 pairs of slides in which one member of each pair was a picture from the original series, while the other was from a similar set but had never been shown to the subject. They recognised 85 to 95 per cent of the original slides correctly. These high scores were maintained even when the presentation rate was speeded up to one every second, and even when the pictures were shown as a mirror image, so that the right-hand side became the left-hand side. The experimenter commented that these experiments with pictoral stimuli suggest that recognition of pictures is essentially perfect. The results would probably have been the same if we had used 25,000 pictures instead of 2500.

So how can this information be used to develop sales aids? Let us consider the hypothetical example of a product called 'Porcinex'. Let us suppose that Porcinex is a medicinal feed additive which, when included in the diet of fattening pigs, will stimulate the flow of their digestive juices, and maximize their development. (This example is for illustrative purposes and is not based on scientific fact.)

The sales story to a pig farmer might be expected to flow as follows:

By adding 2kg of Porcinex to each tonne of finished feed, you will stimulate the flow of digestive juices in your fattening pigs. This has the effect of encouraging a more complete digestion of the feed. With a more complete digestion there follows a more complete absorption of essential nutrients, leading to an enhanced food conversion ratio (the ratio of the weight of food eaten to the weight gained by the pig). The daily live weight gain can be improved by as much as 12.5 per cent.

This story so far has described the *features* of Porcinex: what it does, how it does it, and a measure of its performance. Pig producers understand the *advantages* of enhancing food-conversion ratios and elevating daily live weight gains. But where are the *benefits?* We need to apply the formula introduced in the last chapter as follows: 'The enhanced food-conversion ratio leads to an improvement in daily live weight gain *which means that* you make more money per pig at market, increased profit more than compensating for the cost of Porcinex'.

This story is comprehensible enough on the printed page, but if a salesman had presented it in a busy feed-compounder's office, say, it would have given you a better idea of what Porcinex would do for your pig-farming business if he had used some simple visual to reinforce what he was saying. Figure 11.2 is just one suggested way in which the financial benefit of using Porcinex might be reinforced in the

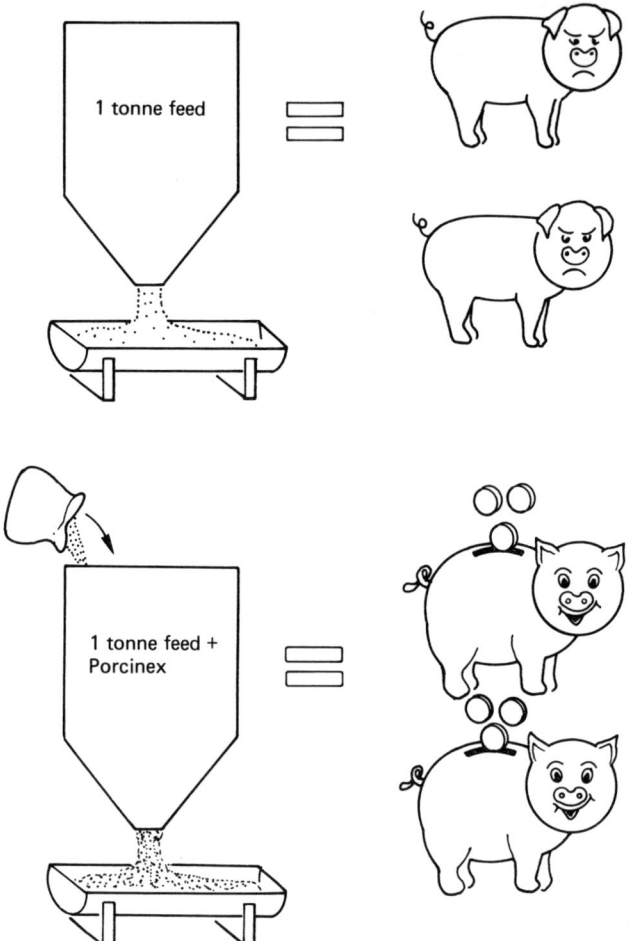

Figure 11.2 *Visual representation of benefit of adding one bag of Porcinex to a tonne of pig feed. Larger pigs and £1 coins representing extra profit put the benefits across much more clearly than words alone*

246

farmer's mind. The pictures virtually tell the whole story and hardly need explaining. However, the spoken word and visual support work together to put across a strong message.

It must be remembered too that many people are more likely to believe the printed word than the spoken word. Therefore, giving the sales force such a simple printed piece will not only reinforce the spoken message but also lend some endorsement to the story. In addition, the literature will have created a vivid interactive image (money in the piggy bank), which means the sales message for Porcinex has a good chance of sticking in the memory of the buyer. While this is a very simplistic example it does show what can easily be achieved.

In the case of the pig-farming market the association of money into the piggy bank has been rather overplayed, but the example serves to illustrate the technique. In order to differentiate the Porcinex message from the mass, using similar visual imagery, one could use simple illustrations of chubby pigs with Porcinex tee-shirts standing out proudly from smaller pigs, or perhaps a pair of seesaws where the Porcinex-fed pigs are the heavier. So long as the visual image is vivid and relevant – not too clever or obscure – then the spoken sales message will be that much more readily remembered.

11.4 Films and video

A film, whether produced on celluloid or on video tape, is sometimes the most expensive single item in a publicity budget and yet, once produced, is often the least used, because it has few or no preplanned objectives. As with all other marketing activities, one has to start with the fundamentals of analysis: determine the need for a film or video at the outset. It is easy to think of good reasons to justify a film, once you have decided to make one, but this sequence of thinking often leads to the film being the end in itself rather than simply the beginning of a promotional process. So what is the objective? This is the essential question. Note too that it is in the singular: *objective*. This is deliberate in order to avoid the other common failing of film-making, that of trying to satisfy the interests of several different audiences with one and the same film. The result is generally a film of no special interest to anyone.

The objective, for instance, may be to demonstrate to dentists the versatility of a new piece of equipment and its range of attachments to help a salesperson to put across their selling proposition. While dentists would naturally want to handle the instrument to gauge the all-important feel of the product, they may be reluctant to start using it on a patient until they have seen its practical application. In this instance, a film or video is a natural choice of medium to communicate the benefits with 'live' action, supported by informed commentary, i.e. by a recognized hospital dental consultant.

From the definition of the potential market in the original marketing strategy, the precise nature of the audience will be known – say the larger urban dental practices with the resources to finance the purchase of the equipment and the larger volume of patients to justify the expenditure, compared to the smaller, possibly rural, practice – and this will help determine the method of film distribution and display. There may also be a case for examining secondary audiences, but this must not cloud the principal objective.

In the above example there may be an overseas potential (the narrative being provided by a local, recognized dental consultant); dental schools and hospitals are other likely outlets too. However, these ought to be regarded as ancillaries and of secondary importance to those defined in the original strategy.

Having set a specific objective, you must next restate it in quantitative terms, fixing not only a measurement against which performance can be judged, but also an assessment of value for money *before* production begins. Suppose the total potential market is 10,000 people, can a realistic target audience be set at 2,000 a year? If that seems practical, when the method of distribution available and the estimated life of the film have been taken into account, is the expenditure justified? The answer is often that given planned distribution, the cost per viewer is very low.

In the above example, for instance, a film costing £15,000 would obtain an exposure in the first year at a cost of £7.50 per viewer. Compared to the cost of getting a salesman in front of a dentist, or of getting as many dentists as were contacted by salesmen to visit an exhibition, this may be quite reasonable. If the distribution continued at the same rate for 3 or 4 years, the cost would come down to no more than a few pounds per viewer. At the other extreme, there are films that have been so little used that the cost per viewer has reached tens, if not hundreds, of pounds.

A film can be regarded as one of a number of channels of persuasion to publicize a company, product or service, and it is useful to consider the merits of a film in relation to other media by looking at a number of facets:

1   *Impact.* Clearly of a high order – probably more so than a salesman's visit, owing to the (usual) absence of other distractions – provided the viewing is well organised. Prerecorded films don't forget key points, either! However, it must be remembered that it may not be able to vary the argument to suit the circumstances, or to counter an objection. Obviously, however, a

film has much higher impact than press advertising.

2   *Costs.* Initial costs may be high, maybe between £10,000 and £50,000, depending on the film. A useful yardstick is £1000 to £1500 a minute of filming if you are planning a 10 minute plus film. Of course costs vary considerably, depending on what goes into the film, e.g. it is much more expensive to film your offices from a helicopter than it is from across the road outside. Organizational and distribution costs must be included too. However, cost per viewer may be low.

3   *Coverage of potential market.* Coverage depends very much on how precisely the purchasing influences can be defined and how willing they are likely to be to view the film. These are probably the biggest challenges.

4   *Depth of sales message.* In press advertising, for example, the sales message is subject to severe limitation. In a film there is virtually no limit and, moreover, the sales argument is presented both visually and audibly – simultaneously.

5   *Speed.* Films can be produced very quickly, but it is usually unwise to do so. A year might be needed for production alone. Distribution might have to be spread over a number of years.

6   *Intrusion.* With a direct-mail campaign, for example, the buyer may feel a sense of intrusion that can build up a resistance. With a film he is likely to have gone to a showing, or have invited someone to bring the film to him, and will probably at least start with a favorable attitude of mind. Even if the video has been mailed to him, he is likely to be receptive to your message if he watches it.

Furthermore, films have a relaxing, 'entertainment' connotation.

Once the pros and cons of film have been balanced, the target audience defined, and the decision to make a film reached, there are a number of stages required in logical sequence to ensure an effective result. In the previous chapter the need for logical progression was stressed; in film-making it becomes even more important, since changes made, particularly towards the end of production, can not only be very expensive, but can lead to the film's quality being poor. It is assumed that the objective, audience and distribution procedure will have already been put down in writing and that the budget, type and length have been given some consideration. Plans for distribution and for securing adequate publicity to attract an audience will run concurrently with the following sequence.

11.4.1   Outline synopsis

Either the publicity department or the advertising agency will need to set down in detail the points that need to be made verbally and visually in order to communicate the essential sales message. A factual outline will be more important than a creative treatment at this stage; the ideal creative sequence can be formed later. This written piece will form the basis for briefing and can be prepared while selection and negotiations are being undertaken with the short-list of film units already made. Top management's active support is vital, right from the start, and top managers must be made aware of the stages that need their considered approval, and are unlikely to be changed. Approval of the outline synopsis is one first critical stage.

11.4.2   Choice of film unit

Filming is one area of below-the-line publicity that must be left to the experts. Choose a film unit that has gained a reputation in a particular field of activity, technique, or price range. View their recent productions, judging them from the entertainment point of view as well as their audio-visual interpretation of the client's objectives. Having chosen one or two units that appear to meet your requirements, give them data upon which they can make a quotation; also find out whether the personal chemistry between the unit and your team is satisfactory, and whether the unit is capable of understanding and interpreting what is required. Only rough quotes can be expected at this stage.

11.4.3   Briefing

One good way of operating is to commission the chosen unit to prepare a treatment and maybe a script for a nominal fee, with a full quotation to follow. Just as a printer will be unable to provide a firm quotation for printing a leaflet until you had defined certain parameters, one could not ask a film unit to quote on a film until a full treatment had been agreed.

   The outline synopsis is now the basis for briefing the film unit, which in turn must be allowed to ask questions about the brief and visit locations. Good cooperation leads to the best possible creative contribution. Technical films require assigned senior technical advisers at the outset. Don't film a factory unless the factory manager is present for consultation. Remember, the brief is the client company's most serious contribution to the subject. Thereafter the matter moves progressively out of its hands.

11.4.4 Treatment

This document is the brief feedback to the client. It is a detailed synopsis, with a written description of both visual and sound effects added. A story board – a series of cameo sketches of principal scenes – may be produced, and it will define the usage of locations, music, narrative, direct speech, animation, film stock or video, and 'rostrum' work. (Rostrum work is that part of a film where, for example, various graphics are formed, i.e. bar charts developed, and captions added. This work is usually done at editing but needs to be defined at the outset, because the development of graphics can be very expensive. It has been said that the lead-in sequence to the *News at 10* cost over £100,000.)

The story board is the film's blueprint and full specification. Everyone engaged on the film should read and agree the treatment; it is a good idea to get the film producer to speak directly to all concerned to ensure they fully understand what is proposed. Alterations here are relatively inexpensive and can be done quickly.

11.4.5 Quotation

Treatments can be accurately costed and should not differ greatly from the original estimate. The creative treatment can be altered if necessary to bring down the costs, provided the producer feels the film's objective will still be reached. Remember too to formalize the film contract, e.g. agree progress payments beforehand and make provisions for contingencies such as bad weather and lack of access to specific locations owing to plant closedown.

11.4.6 Script

Good writers are rare and it's worth paying for the best. The writer needs a good brief, and the script needs careful studying, along with the visual and timing schedule, so that everything is seen to fit properly. Any subsequent alteration can have the most undesirable consequences.

11.4.7 *Organization and shooting schedule*

Many people within the company will need to be co-opted in order to ensure the smooth running of the film; management support has been stressed but other departments and employees may have to be lined up alongside the film crew. Someone with executive authority over the whole internal operation needs to plan the event and to organize the detail. Equally, especially if you are going to include interviews with your industry's opinion leaders, you will need to ensure that they are not antagonized or disrupted too much – an experienced producer who knows the market is essential.

11.4.8 *Rushes*

As the shooting of the film progresses, each sequence will become available as uncut pieces of film ready for viewing. It is at this stage that technical advisers should be consulted to ensure there is nothing pictorially inaccurate. If you are shooting in video format rather than on to celluloid film, it is possible to have a video monitor available so that one can view the filming 'as it happens'. Depending on the system, instant playback may not be available, but at least one can see if the recording looks acceptable on the small screen.

11.4.9 *Editing and recording*

Work such as this is best left to the experts, although the client company may want to hear the soundtrack to ensure that the right emphasis has been placed on certain passages or that technical words have been pronounced correctly.

11.4.10 *Viewing*

An audience composed of all who have been concerned with the film should view the finished effort to ensure that the result matches the objective, and as a final check that everything is technically and factually correct. From this stage a film will go to processing, and production is complete. Naturally copies will be made, as it is best not to let the original leave the security of the film company. If the copy is damaged, all is not lost. If you had been filming on video you are likely to have had an original 'one-inch master' or similar, and have run off

VHS copies as usual cassettes. Again, the master rarely leaves the film company.

11.5   Video technology

11.5.1   Introduction

Video technology has fast become a vital part of business communication – both of the corporate body and the product message. Salesmen carry playback units to show clients and prospects video presentations of new and upcoming products. Companies are using them for internal PR purposes, replacing the corporate newsletter with regular video news circulated among all employees, particularly those away from main sites.

Conferences, product-launches and so forth make increasing use of video technology, alongside more traditional media such as film and slides, and the video revolution is only a part of the larger revolution in information technology where computers offer the key to dissemination of data. More of computers later (Section 11.9).

The choice of video equipment grows ever wider; competing products from different manufacturers create new standards of quality and performance. Video is a dynamic, ever-changing medium, which means that expert, totally reliable advice is essential. The Audio Visual and Video Presentation Advisory Service[4] exists to give that advice, and its local dealers are there to help.

11.5.2   What's the choice?

Source equipment
Modern domestic hi-fi systems are designed to cope with programme material on cassette tape, vinyl disc (EP and LP records) and compact discs (CD). A similar range of sources exist for video, including:

(a) Video tape (in a variety of formats and standards), still the major source of programme and display material.
(b) Video disc (again in different formats) – rare, but usually used in combination with a computer for technology-based training packages, particularly in new-product usage.
(c) Computers – often used to display up-to-the-minute information, e.g. at staff training meetings or major conferences for product launches. The new graphics packages present computer-based data

exceptionally attractively. There are a number of different standards for computer displays.

Display equipment
The choice widens continuously, so that it is more important than ever before to pick the right tools for the job. Video-display equipment can be broadly divided into four main areas:

(a) Portable presenters combine a video-tape player with a screen and a small built-in speaker. These units are comparatively lightweight and very resilient.
(b) Monitors and receivers look like professional versions of top-of-the-range domestic TVs. Receivers, as the name suggests, incorporate tuners, so they can receive broadcast programmes. Monitors operate directly from a source such as a video-tape player, and have no integral tuner.
(c) Video projectors, which can produce larger single images from 5 to 22 feet wide.
(d) Video walls, consisting of multiple monitors (or a combination of monitors and projectors), providing multiple images under computer control.

Remember, not all display equipment can cope with the full range of video sources; computers in particular will sometimes require special or additional circuitry to be fitted to monitors, receivers and projectors. Always make sure you match your source with the display equipment.

A word about sound
Sound was always the poor relation to video, and to some extent it still is. Many receivers, monitors and projectors feature small, built-in speakers; however, for high quality sound you will need an external sound system. Unless you are connecting to an existing public address (or PA) system, you will need an amplifier, loudspeakers, and good quality cable. Once again, since your own hi-fi is not up to the task, get a professional set-up.

11.5.3 *Video-tape players*

These are invariably easy to operate, particularly if you are familiar with domestic machines. Professional machines offer many more features, can be connected properly to receivers, monitors and sound equipment, and are vital for serious presentations.

Choice of player

Generally your tape format governs what video player you need. ('Format' refers to the physical dimensions of the tape cassette and the way the signal is recorded on it.) There are five formats in general use:

(a) Video 8 uses 8mm-wide tape, the smallest and most compact format currently available. While ideal for in-house presentations, it is not really suitable for large-scale presentations. However, professional Video 8 machines offer great flexibility.
(b) VHS (Video Home System) is the commonest domestic format, but more robust professional players and player/recorders should always be used for serious presentations. VHS uses cassettes of 1/2-inch wide tape.
(c) S-VHS (Super VHS) is a development on VHS using the latest technology, giving nearly double the picture sharpness. S-VHS players can play VHS tapes, but VHS players cannot show S-VHS tapes. However, to get the best from a S-VHS player, always use the correct high-quality tape stock and get the right connections to designated display equipment.
(d) Low-band U-matic, the original industrial format introduced in 1972, is still available, giving good quality sound and pictures from its 3/4 inch tape cassettes.
(e) High band U-matic uses the same size cassettes as low band, but the signals are recorded in a different way, so that the two systems are not compatible. High band SP (Superior Performance) is a further development of the High band U-matic format, improving picture quality still further. As not all U-matic format machines can replay all types of tapes, your dealer's advice is essential.

Although other formats exist, they are either high-quality broadcast formats or domestic formats that are no longer serious contenders in the professional market place.

Sound on video tape

On U-matic and VHS formats sound is recorded on a narrow strip at the edge of the tape, but more advanced VHS, S-VHS and Video 8 models feature hi-fi sound, which is achieved by 'layer recording' the sound under the picture, and gives excellent results. Machines with this facility switch automatically between hi-fi and conventional sound as required, since not all programme tapes will have hi-fi sound.

Connections

All professional video-tape players offer separate connections for the video and audio parts of the signal. Video is normally on a 'BNC' connector, audio on a phono or 'XLR' plug. Always seek your dealer's advice to ensure you are properly connected.

11.5.4 Portable presenters

A growing range of units now combines a simple video player with a small monitor and loudspeaker on a single, comparatively lightweight chassis. These portable presenters are ideal for anyone who needs to take a video 'on the road', although they have many other uses as well.

Choice of presenter
Video presenters are available for the VHS format (with 11-inch and 14-inch screen sizes) and Video-8 (with 3-, 5-, 9- and 14-inch screens). For what they are, they are not expensive, so do not be tempted to use a domestic unit; they are not designed to be truly portable, neither will they stand up to the stresses of commercial use.

Hints and tips
(a) Always read the manual first; it's much cheaper than a repair bill.
(b) As it is portable, the presenter probably requires no other connections than the appropriate mains plug. Certain smaller machines can use rechargeable batteries, some of which can even be recharged in a car's cigarette lighter.
(c) If the presenter or tape has been stored in a cold room (or a cold car-boot), always allow it to warm up before use. Any condensation may cause serious damage. Some machines have a 'DEW' warning light. Similarly, if the unit is illuminated, don't use it until the light goes out.
(d) The controls are usually very simple. Volume (for the built-in speaker) and tape controls are usually on the front of the unit and will be familiar to home-video users. There may also be an extra key labelled 'AUTO REPEAT'. This is used when the presenter is left unattended, for instance in a window display or at an exhibition, and ensures that the tape will automatically rewind and play again until it is stopped. Remember that:

  (i) Once pressed, it is likely to disable all other keys.
  (ii) Repeating your presentation many times on a long-play tape will improve the effect.
  (iii) The early part of the tape before your first run of your presentation may have to be cut professionally to limit any unnecessary footage being displayed.

(e) Some machines switch directly into PLAY when a tape is inserted, particularly if the 'record tab' has been removed from the cassette body. Check your machine *and* the tape you plan to use beforehand.

(f) Remember that when you 'stop' some machines, part of the video tape may be rewound back into the cassette, so that it starts at a slightly different spot to where you stopped it. Practise with your machine and tape so that you can judge the correct place to stop the tape for a crisp start to the presentation.

Using the equipment

Portable presenters are surprisingly versatile, being used in many different situations:

(a) One-to-one presentations, for instance, by a salesperson to a prospect. The use of prerecorded programmes ensures an expert presentation, where no sales points are missed, while items of special interest can be seen again.

(b) Small group presentations, especially within a company. The presenter can be set up virtually anywhere, and is perfectly adequate for a group of two or three people.

(c) Display, particularly in shop windows, in customer areas of showrooms and on exhibition stands, where particular products or services are being shown to one or two visitors.

11.5.5 Monitors and receivers

A monitor is like a TV set without the tuner. This means that video and audio signals, e.g. from a video-tape player, a video-disc player, or a computer, have to be fed in separately. This has the advantage that much of the circuitry used in the domestic TV is left out and the resultant picture quality is improved.

Receiver monitors are also available; these take direct signals but can also receive programmes off-air. However, you will need a TV licence to use one, and some of your staff may find it distracting, especially when a test match is on!

Choice of monitors and receivers

Many sizes are available, from 4-inch to gigantic (and heavy) 37-inch monitors. Choosing the right design for your needs is important, especially for data display, where different computer-graphic boards are likely to require different features on the monitor.

Using monitors and receivers

Many are not fitted with high-quality speakers, so you may need to use a separate sound or PA system. To get the best from S-VHS equipment you will need the proper connections and a designated monitor. For U-matic, proper connections are also needed, but it may be possible to adapt or upgrade older equipment.

Occasionally you may want to 'chain' a series of monitors together so that all are fed from a single video source: very useful at large conferences, where it offers an alternative – or a supplement – to projection video. Not all monitors offer this facility, but it is quite common. Good-quality cable is essential, and long runs may need the signal boosting with an amplifier.

11.5.6 Video projectors

For conferences, or any application where even a 37-inch screen is simply not big enough, video projectors are the obvious answer. Like film projectors, these throw a video picture on to a screen, but unlike film, that picture consists of separate red, green and blue images produced by three cathode-ray tubes that must be lined up with absolute precision.

Choice of projector

Smaller video projectors are combined with a special screen and a good quality sound system in a custom-built cabinet. Once installed, the unit should not need to be lined up again, except during normal servicing. Screen sizes range from 36 to 100 inches. Larger projectors can be mounted on the floor or on the ceiling, behind the screen or in front of it, but they must always be set up by a qualified technician. A separate sound system is vital.

The biggest projectors, using light valves, are intended for major presentations in theatres, conference centres, stadiums, etc. Maximum screen width for a projected picture is about 22 feet. Once again, a separate sound system is necessary. Three types of lens are available. In order of cost, weight and quality they are:

- *Plastic.* The lower weight advantage of these lenses is offset by poorer image quality, especially at the edges.
- *Hybrid.* The most common alternative, where a mixture of glass and plastic lenses are used to improve image quality. This is especially important in data presentation.
- *Glass.* All-glass lens combinations are unusual, but offer the best possible image quality.

Projecting data
Video projectors, like monitors, cannot always cope with the variety of signals from computers. If you need to project a computer display, always consult your AVVPAS dealer to ensure you have a match between source and projector, and let a trained technician carry out the necessary internal switching before your presentation. Switching between data and ordinary video presentation can also present difficulties – so, again, seek professional advice.

Hints and tips
Video projectors are designed for use by experienced professionals. There are few controls, and anyone can operate them safely, but always read the manual first. Moreover, during set-up, only a technician should attempt to line up, focus, and adjust the equipment.

11.5.7 Video standards

History often appears to be a series of mistakes, false starts and boundary disputes. The history of video is no different, and as a result three different colour-television standards cover most TV viewing:

- PAL (Phase Alternation Line) is used in Britain, Western Europe and former British colonies.
- NTSC (National Television Standards Committee) is used in North America and Japan.
- SECAM (Sequential Colour with Memory) is used in France, the former French colonies and Russia.

Some countries in South America use unusual standards of their own. It will be essential to discuss the matter with your dealer before using tapes from this area or sending tapes to be used there.

As a general point, as many more companies are becoming more and more global in their marketing, thought must be given to the video standards in current use in the various territories if you are planning an international product launch with a video presentation as part of your communications mix. Your overseas agent simply may bin your carefully thought out and expensive presentation purely because you have sent out a format that may be difficult to use locally. Your agent may not take the trouble to convert your video tape to the local standard.

Presenting SECAM and NTSC tapes
It may be that you are on the receiving end of a tape standard that you are not familiar with, so what do you do? In practice, presenting SECAM and NTSC tapes is less of a problem than it seems. You have two options:

(a) Playing back the tape on a professional multi-standard tape player and a suitable monitor (which must also be multi-standard). This combination will cope with any of the three main standards. Ensure that the tape player is suitable for use in the UK – most domestic multi-standard machines are not.
(b) Using standard conversion, which gives an inexpensive copy tape in PAL format suitable for standard PAL equipment.

Modified NTSC
This rather confusing term is sometimes found on professional multi-standard tape players and monitors distributed in the UK. It does not refer to another version of the American NTSC standard, but to the way in which the player outputs signals from ordinary American NTSC tapes so that they produce full colour and sound on modified PAL monitors.

Tape speeds
Occasionally NTSC VHS format tapes are recorded at half-speed (EP: extended play) in the USA, just as some domestic video recorders with extended-play facilities will record. However, many professional multi-standard machines available in the UK cannot operate at this speed. Always check that your video film can be played on your chosen video-tape player before the presentation!

11.5.8 What should I use?

The answer may not be as simple as it seems. Even so, by following a few simple rules you can be sure of a successful presentation that everyone in the audience will see and hear with absolute clarity. The secret is to pick the right display equipment for your audience and for the location. In this way you will have the best chance of getting your promotional message across.

Small audiences
For one to three people, the obvious choice is a portable presenter, which combines a video player and a monitor in a single lightweight unit. This is especially useful where you need to show a programme on

someone else's premises – the sort of thing salespeople do virtually every working day. However, even a 'lightweight' model gets heavy by the end of a day, and an important client is unlikely to be impressed by the small screen. In this case you would be well advised to choose a good-sized monitor (less portable perhaps) or even a video projector, and to arrange a showing either on your premises or at a suitable venue, such as a hotel or conference centre where such equipment is available on hire.

Larger groups

Monitors or small video projectors are more appropriate here, although think about the size and shape of the room. If it is long and narrow, a video projector (or additional monitors on either side) will make it easier for people at the back to see the picture. If it is wide and shallow, you could use two or three monitors side by side. Remember, the screens in cabinet-mounted video projectors have quite a narrow viewing angle – they are best suited for smaller groups, and in longer, narrow rooms.

Conferences

Video projection on to screens up to 22 feet wide are the preferred option, but results may not be equally good in all parts of the hall, especially if you are using a high-grain screen surface. If so, try repeating the image on large monitors placed along the sides of the hall. Another possibility is to use two video projectors placed on opposite diagonals.

Video walls offer a dynamic, attention-grabbing alternative to straightforward display. They are particularly appropriate for product or promotion launch events or for high powered conferences. With suitable professional help, it is possible to arrange a satellite relay of live or recorded video and data material to one or more conference centres – ideal for that pan-European product launch (see Section 11.6). This technique is increasingly used by major companies who need to put across information very quickly, or those who wish to avoid the cost and time wasted in sending senior executives to other operational sites.

Exhibitions

These are ideally suited for video presentations. Portable presenters are perfect for small, specialist displays. Single or multiple monitors can be placed around the stand for continuous display of one or more sources. Video projectors can be used in on-stand theatres to show prerecorded programmes or live computer-based demonstrations, and video walls are an ideal way to catch and hold the fickle attention of passing visitors.

11.5.9 *Video walls*

A video wall is an array of video monitors with associated control equipment. It allows one or more video sources, e.g. live camera, video tape, video disc, etc., to be 'split' across the whole display. Some video walls are used simply to produce a big image, but in many display applications they are 'programmed' by a computer that allows the image arrangement to be continually changed. Each monitor can show part of the same image, all can show the same, or all different; the combinations are endless. In such cases the video wall becomes a creative medium in its own right.

Shows made especially for video wall presentation can be very effective indeed. Even if your production budget is limited or you have only a very short time to pull a presentation together, a video wall creatively programmed can bring a series of 35mm slides to life, way beyond what can be achieved with pure projection. However, it is a specialist task and you will need many slides for the production team to work with.

What are video walls used for?
As a dynamic display medium, video walls are best suited to trade exhibitions and retail displays, where the programme material should be short and sharp. Video walls are also widely used in discos for the dynamic presentation of pop videos (to boost retail record sales); in conferences for big image sales presentations; as elements in theatre and TV sets; and in museums, visitor centres, and theme parks, where they are effective for short video programmes presented to groups. Video walls can be used in areas where there is high ambient light, but not in direct sunlight or outdoors in the daytime.

Monitors or projectors?
Video walls can be made up of monitors (usually 28-inch) or back-projection modules. The latter use special high gain screens, usually with diagonals 35 and 45 inches, and have the advantage that the division between image sectors is minimal. This means they are best suited for conference or other 'big single image' applications, although continuous projection of the same image divided among all screens is not making best use of the creative options that the video wall can offer. Walls using monitors give a big, bright image and occupy a

minimum of space – the picture division actually giving the monitor wall a look and a dynamic of its own.

How big?

Video walls can be any size or shape; walls using up to 400 monitors and more have been built. Most applications call for arrays such as 3 × 3, 4 × 4, 8 × 8 etc., in which cases the display has the same proportions as a single TV image – obviously convenient for production.

'Wide screen' walls such as 4 × 8 and 6 × 12, or walls with unconventional shapes, such as triangles, can be very attractive. But they usually need multiple sources and special programme production.

11.6   Satellite technology

11.6.1   Why use a satellite?

Your staff can only be in one place at a time – and senior staff can ill afford the time it takes to address half a dozen large meetings in different parts of the country, let alone different parts of the world. Satellite technology provides a solution. It allows you to hold just one meeting at a convenient venue, and then relay its proceedings – including up-to-the-minute data displays – to any number of other venues worldwide.

11.6.2   How it works

Your video material is relayed to an 'uplink', e.g. London's Telecom Tower, which beams it up to the satellite. If necessary, other satellites relay these signals to the areas you need to cover. A 'downlink', e.g. a satellite dish, will pick up the signal and pass it to your chosen venues via landlines or microwave links. At present European law makes you dependent on PTTs such as British Telecom for uplinks and downlinks, even if you have booked satellite time through a private company.

Time can be your enemy. Satellites are becoming ever more busy, and booking early is the only way to secure your spot at the time you will need it. If there is a major problem, one alternative is to record your conference on tape and transmit it later, when time is available on the satellite. However, this does lose the immediacy that satellite offers. You may as well take duplicates of the conference tape and mail it out to the other venues!

11.6.3   And the future

Satellite broadcasts of single events are increasingly common, and the advent of a single European market should make them even more popular. But in the USA several corporations have gone even further: they have set up their own satellite-based corporate video networks.

The principle, once again, is very simple. A single, permanent studio facility at a convenient location prepares the programme material and sends it up to the satellite. Downlinks at main offices throughout the United States receive the transmission, which is recorded on tape. The employees can watch tapes during coffee and lunch breaks, or even take them home. Ideal for internal PR.

Users say that this system need not cost much more than broadcasting a single important event via a satellite link. Clearly, the same thing could happen across Europe in a few years' time, but not until costs begin to come down to a level comparable with those in the States. Currently British Telecom, for example, is keeping them nearly four times as high – a situation that is unlikely to be allowed to continue.

11.7   Film or video?

The choice between film and video depends on a number of factors. For example, it is much cheaper to film a sequence using a video camera, and of course you have opportunity to monitor or quickly review the recording. However, the best criteria to use to choose between film and video is one of distribution and likely audience.

If you expect to invite large groups of people to one auditorium to show them your film, then it is far better to work to 16 mm or even 32 mm film, because the quality of the image on a large screen is that much better than if you are using 'Super 8' cine film or video projection. This format is acceptable for home movies but the projected image is very poor for larger screens. The ultimate is 64 mm, but unless you are planning *Star Wars*-type epics – which used 64 mm – then do not even consider it!

If you plan to produce a film but prefer to run-off many copies so that the sales force can take them in to see a customer or small groups of people, then maybe video is much better. Once a video film has been produced, extra copies can cost between £3 and £1, depending on the quantity ordered at one time. In this way it is quite possible to use them as the basis of a direct-marketing campaign. However, it will be important to ensure that the distribution of the cassettes is closely followed by a salesman's visit.

More usually, a salesman will use the basis of a video-film showing as a way of getting the whole buying group in an industrial or business-to-business environment together. In this case the buyer may be able to produce a video cassette player and television for the salesman to use – if so, make sure you have ample opportunity to become familiar with its operation *before* the audience assembles. However, it is better to equip the salesman with an all-in-one monitor/ video cassette player that can be used in all circumstances: at least one can be familiar with its functions and assured that it is working. But, once again, set it up and make sure the tape is ready to go well ahead of the audience assembling.

11.8 Tape/slide presentations and overhead projectors

The oldest technique here is film strips, which go back almost to the beginning of film itself. The process comprises a series of individual frames, usually on 35mm stock, each of which portrays part of a story sequence. Alternatively, each of those frames can be individually mounted in 35 mm slides, placed in a rotating carousel and a tape/ slide presentation prepared. The fixed audio sequence contains special pulses which activate the slide mechanism so that the next slide is projected; this is very useful, as an operator has only to start the programme running and it plays itself. Remember, however, that the sequence of events may not suit every audience, and special equipment is required for a tape/slide projector.

A better alternative may be to provide the sales team with the 35 mm colour transparencies in a carousel projector and train them in its use; include of course the preferred script. This then gives the presentation much more flexibility because the salesmen can alter the emphasis of certain points to suit the needs and interests of any particular audience. Moreover, slides can be changed, updated, omitted or used in a different sequence to suit the circumstances.

One word of caution. It is possible to buy a 35mm film of 36 transparencies, which includes the cost of developing and mounting the slides, for around £5. Professionally produced 35 mm slides are not as cheap. Suppose you wanted to project a 35 mm slide of a simple sales graph, histogram or bar chart. In order to make it interesting and more easy to understand, you probably would want to use some colours, especially for the background. Now, depending on the complexity of the graph, you may have to pay over £50 for just that one slide. Why? Well, you will need to produce artwork and typesetting for the graph, just as if you were going to print the graph in a brochure. The photographer would then lay screens of colour over the artwork to produce the desired effect. Even computer-generated graphics, while much faster, can be as expensive. (Data projection from computers is possible, avoiding the need for working in slides at all. See Section 11.9.) Remember that even producing a crisp clear 35 mm slide of your company logo could cost £10. If you had got your planning wrong and asked for rush rates, that cost could double.

If you are producing a slide of your logo, then why not produce half a dozen and use them to start and end your presentation, or to divide up a long presentation into manageable pieces. Your logo is much better than a glaring white screen illuminated by strong light, which invariably projects around the screen on to the wall behind.

As an example of how expensive 35 mm slides can become, a pharmaceutical company based near Maidenhead, Berkshire, took its whole sales and marketing team (some sixty people) to L'Hotel l'Horizon in Jersey for a 4-day, 3-night sales conference. The total cost of all flights, accommodation, meals and entertainment was less than the total bill for the 35 mm slides prepared solely for that conference!

Specialists in audio-visual programmes have developed techniques that use multi-projector images, coupled with integrated sound tracks, which provide an impressive show, coming close to one on cine-film. As with still photography, it is important not to fall into the trap of expecting such a programme to be produced for a few pounds, or even a couple of hundred. Top quality photography is essential and, if sound is to be used, a thoroughly professional recording too. Even so, there is no doubt that if the subject is suitable for this form of treatment, it can be produced for considerably less than a film.

Overhead projection of a series of transparent images is becoming a very useful tool for salesmen explaining something to a large audience. Transparent 'acetates' are used, and the subject matter can be written in full colour if required. Some types of acetate can be fed through a photocopier in place of the standard paper, so that anything printed can be transferred to an acetate and projected; colour photocopiers can be used for added impact. Flexibility is enhanced because any given acetate can be written on while it is being projected, by means of special felt-tip pens, so that the salesmen can build up a picture or diagram as they develop their sales story.

While the projected image may not have quite the same quality as 35mm slides, the advantages are such that portable overhead projectors are becoming standard field-force issue. The projection may not always be on to a special screen – a handy clear white wall often proving adequate – but the fact that there is a large illuminated area to watch will hold the audience's attention often better than a smaller sales presenter.

If an acetate is likely to be used for more than one presentation, it is always preferable to use a card frame to hold it. Apart from holding the image square and in the right place on the projector, the card surround can carry key points to help the salesman remember the whole story. If you are using a stout card frame, it is possible to use overlays to screen off part of the acetate, the overlay easily being folded away as the presentation progresses, revealing the image on the acetate beneath. Alternatively, it is possible to hinge another acetate to the frame so that a superimposed image can be developed.

Technology in this area is moving ahead so rapidly that it is worth visiting one of the many sales and marketing exhibitions held at the principal conference venues in the major cities. Many companies are demonstrating their wares, and it is possible to see the wide variety of equipment now available to enhance a salesman's presentation. Make sure that expensive equipment and impressive presentations are not substituted for well-thought-out and well-researched campaign strategies. All the glossy pictures in the world will not help if you are trying to sell the wrong product to the wrong person.

11.9 IT is it!

The decreasing cost of computer technology has allowed more and more companies to use the benefits of information technology as sales aids for representatives. Computers available today can have massive memories, equal to those of their larger office-based cousins, yet be built small enough to be as portable as a briefcase. Portable personal computers need only a three-pin 240 V standard wall socket to be up and running, and, with ever-improved screen quality, are becoming an integral part of a salesman's kit. Smaller machines with mains adapters that can run on integral rechargeable battery power-packs are available – the so-called laptop computers. The applications are numerous and varied and include the following.

11.9.1 Data back-up for salesmen

Rather than carry loose-leaf files crammed with product details, competitor information, call-reporting data, customer records and call histories, representatives can have such information filed within their computers, all data being recalled at the touch of a button. But more than this, the technology is such that the computers can also carry quite extensive product-usage data, ordering patterns, and market-research data, as well as hold interactive training programmes.

11.9.2 Communication packages

By adding a telephone modem to the computer – some machines come with one already installed – one opens a whole new world of communications. Suppose a representative makes five sales calls in 1 day. At the end of the day the computer can be set to dial the head-office computer and send the five updated customer records. If all representatives are doing the same at the end of the day, the head-office machine will carry the very latest customer data base.

If a customer telephoned head office and spoke, say, to a customer-services department or to a technical services person, one could immediately record the basis of that enquiry on the same customer database. Then, at the beginning of the next day, as the representatives 'signed on', they could collect all updated customer files. Imagine then the situation when a representative is making his calls on day 2 and visits someone who telephoned head office the day before and says 'Good morning, Mrs Errington, I hear you spoke to our Mrs Payne yesterday afternoon about the availability of product X; I trust everything is okay now?' That customer will recognise that she is dealing with a truly coordinated company. Such is the power of electronic-mail and database management, properly used.

11.9.3 Interactive training programmes

Simply by sending the salesman a new piece of software, you equip them to take interactive training programmes to their customers to help them learn about the preferred application of a given product. Interactive training programmes are used, for example, in the medical world. Suppose you were marketing a new heart drug to general practitioners. One could imagine a computer program that GPs needed only take a few minutes to work through. The representative could load the appropriate software into their computer, personalize the information appearing on screen appropriately, and present it to the GPs during a sales call. The program would be such as to guide the GPs through the various stages in a straightforward fashion using simple key controls.

A typical case history could be presented, describing a patient and his symptoms as any GP might be expected to encounter them in his surgery. Then there would be a multiple choice series of, say, five alternative therapies, A to E. By pressing the appropriate key, the GP could signal his choice. Now, in medicine, as in so many other situations, there is often a spectrum of possible solutions, ranging from those that would not be considered the best course of action to those the majority would agree with. A GP, having made a choice, would then be shown (on the computer screen) how his action compared with his peer group's or with a noted opinion leader, such as a well known hospital consultant.

Such schemes are a very useful way of helping GPs understand the use of new products in real-life situations. The graphics available make the presentations, as well as the learning progress, very interesting and memorable. By recording a GP's responses to each of the questions asked as the case unfolds, the manufacturer can monitor the level of awareness and understanding of the target market and of the product's application. This can be the basis for researching the need to amend the communication plan as necessary. What is more, the representative can go home and print out that GP's interaction, and answers can be mailed back to the practice to reinforce the sales message.

Each time a representative makes a return visit to that customer, a different program can be used, perhaps more advanced or designed to explore other product features and to highlight their benefit to the GP. While the technique must not be overplayed, as with any other technique, the company providing the software will be recognized as making an innovative contribution to a GP's postgraduate education. Pharmaceutical companies can also adopt the programs for use in hospitals or pharmacies, if the product has application in these areas too.

Interactive training programmes go beyond the simple one-to-one new product detail. Major pharmaceutical companies dealing with GPs are very aware of the changing face of group practices. All GPs are having to manage their health-care budgets much more carefully now, and therefore those companies that are able to help them manage their affairs are going to be viewed favourably. Programs on computer are available to help practitioners learn about managing a practice, deal with personnel problems and run profitable drug dispensaries. In other industries too, such programs have application and are being used not only for product promotion but also to strengthen a corporate image (see also Section 14.7).

11.10 Reacting to the product life-cycle

When we talk about the features of a product, we apply the formula 'which means that' to translate those features into benefits for the consumer. There is, however, a very important characteristic of products, and it applies to services too: 'nothing offers benefits that last for ever'. All products have life-cycles (Figure 11.3). The sales performance of any product rises from nothing when the product is

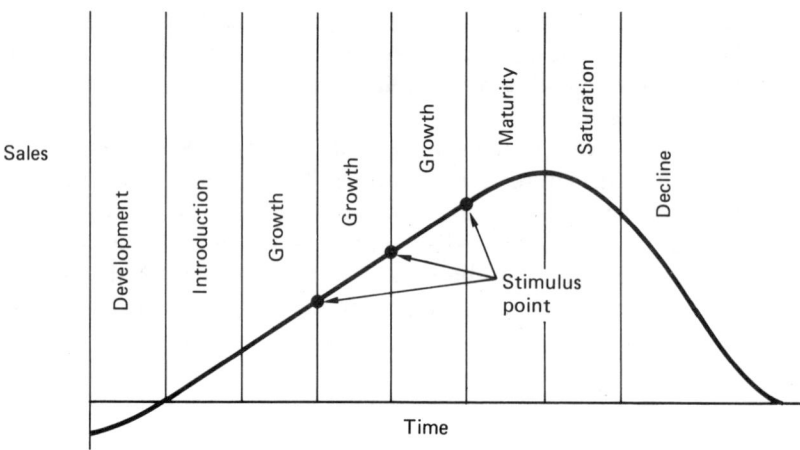

Figure 11.3 *The product life-cycle*

introduced into the market, reaches a peak and then declines to nothing again.

The product life-cycle affects the marketing mix, and each of the four elements of the mix responds in its own way. For instance, the product itself might have to change during its lifetime, the price will need to change as competition moves, and the pricing policy will need to be flexible to maintain market share – a crucial factor when the market declines. The distribution strategy could radically change between the introductory phase and the end of the growth phase. Likewise, promotion will change: during the introductory phase it is important to create awareness of the existence of the product, whereas during the growth phase it may be necessary to point out the advantages of the company's product over its competitors'. Publicity objectives, using both above- and below-the-line techniques, may also change, as shown in Figure 11.4, throughout the product's life-cycle.

There is, however, another factor that has a profound effect on the chain of publicity objectives. That is diffusion of innovation.

Diffusion is the adoption of new products or services over time by consumers within social systems as encouraged by marketing activities. Diffusion refers to the cumulative percentage of potential adopters of a new product or service over time. In some classic marketing research, Everett Rogers[5] examined some of the social forces that explain the product life-cycle. It was found that the actual rate of diffusion of a product is a function of the following:

(a) Relative advantage (over existing products).
(b) Compatibility (with life-styles, values, etc.).

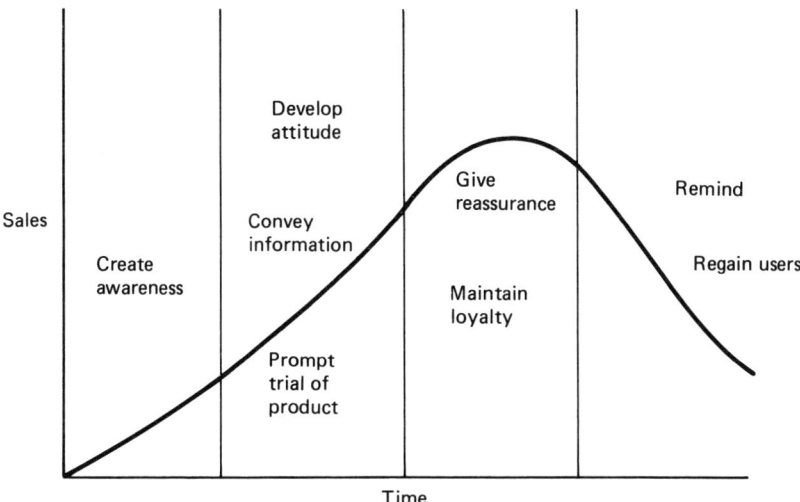

Figure 11.4 *Publicity objectives varying over a product's life-cycle*

(c) Communicability (Is it easy to communicate?).
(d) Complexity (Is it complicated?).
(e) Divisibility (Can it be tried out on a small scale before commitment?).

Diffusion is also a function of the newness of a product itself, which can be classified broadly under three headings:

(a) Continuous innovation, e.g. the new miracle ingredient.
(b) Dynamically continuous innovation, e.g. disposable lighter.
(c) Discontinuous, e.g. microwave ovens.

Rogers found that not everyone adopts new products at the same time – in fact a universal pattern emerged (Figure 11.5). In general, the innovators think for themselves and try new things (where relevant), sometimes just because they are new; the early adopters, who have status in their particular segment of society as opinion leaders, make new products acceptable and respectable. (These are the people to keep up with – Joneses.) The early majority are more deliberate and only adopt products that have social approbation. They are the so-called upmarket Smiths, or 'Smythes'. The late majority, who are below average status and more sceptical, adopt products much later. (They are the Smiths, the laggards, with low status, income, etc., who view life through the rear mirror and are the last to adopt products – the Smiffs!) This pattern demonstrates the need for different kinds of

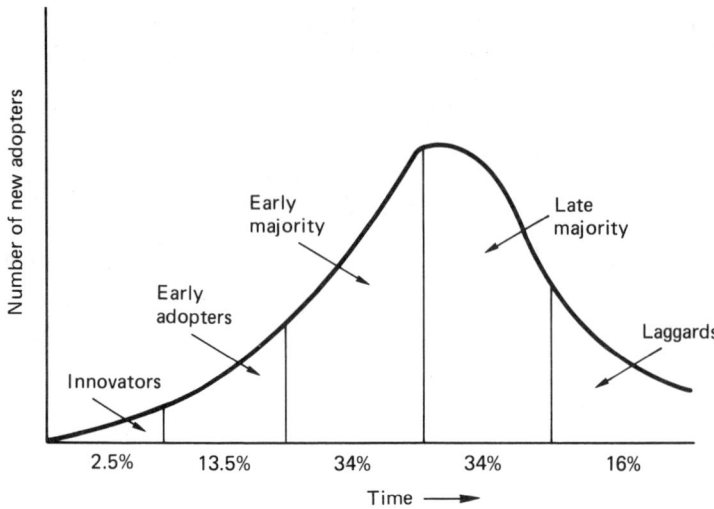

Figure 11.5 *Percentage of potential adopters over time*

publicity for each category of customer, and points to the need to consider a different set of promotional objectives for different stages in a product's life-cycle.

This diffusion model was used by a veterinary pharmaceutical company when assessing its publicity plans for its range of dog and cat vaccines in 1989, 2 years after launch to UK veterinary surgeons. It was recognized early in the development phase pre-launch that the products themselves were not particularly innovative and would be entering a crowded, highly competitive market, essentially satisfied by existing products. However, the dog and cat vaccination market was growing rapidly, not only in value but also in volume terms. The reason was that, although the need for primary vaccination of puppies and kittens was well-known and understood by owners, and this market sector was fairly flat, the need to boost those primary vaccinations every year was only gradually being realized (by owners). The booster vaccination market was therefore the rapidly growing sector, particularly in volume terms, and this was where the company positioned its range.

To support this positioning, the company devised a unique direct marketing package for veterinary surgeons, providing personalized printed materials to help the vets promote their practices and individual services to their known customers. When any dog or cat was due for a booster vaccination, on the yearly anniversary of the primary vaccination course, the owners were sent an invitation to make an appointment to see the vet, a 'Why you need to vaccinate leaflet', and a discount voucher redeemable if the appointment was made within the next 2 weeks. Included in the package was a personalized summary of what that practice could also offer clients when they came in for the annual booster vaccination.

Such value-added items as free annual health check, free dental examination, free wormers, free dietary advice, were among the offers. The literature also carried information about the other services and facilities offered by the practice, from 24-hour emergency services to tattooing (for identification purposes) and, for example, private cremation services.

On the basis that it is cheaper to keep a customer than it is to find a new one, this scheme was very popular. Only veterinary practices that signed an annual contract for the supply of the vaccinations received the package as 'free added value'. The scheme was very successful. Not only did it help the veterinary pharmaceutical company build up contracts with a significant number of veterinary practices – an approximate market penetration of 10 per cent was achieved within 2 years post-launch – but the number of booster vaccinations that each contract veterinary practice achieved also grew. So both manufacturer and veterinary surgeons were happy? Not quite.

After 2 years of success, growth slowed down. It became harder and harder to achieve new contracts. Business with existing customers was growing, but something had to be done to improve the penetration of the products. The diffusion of innovation model showed that the veterinary company had persuaded most early adopters to take the products and the scheme. But how could it convince the early majority – those more conservative veterinary practices – that the scheme could work for them?

The veterinary market is served by a monthly video magazine called *Practice*, which is circulated as VHS copies to virtually all veterinary practices in the UK, and contains a selection of veterinary interest topics from the purely academic through to the practical. The interest in the video magazine has been widened by including subjects of interest to veterinary nurses as well as those concerned with practice management and finance, even to the point of giving the occasional car road tests.

The veterinary pharmaceutical company marketing the dog and cat vaccines contacted *Practice* and agreed to sponsor the filming of a modern, well-run veterinary practice that had had great success with the direct-marketing package. The profile included an interview the company's practice manager, who described the various marketing programmes and gave a thorough appraisal of the vaccine suppliers' direct-marketing package. While the film unit were on site, the marketing manager was also filmed giving a 90-second introduction.

In late September 1989 *Practice* (issue No. 26) as a VHS copy was circulated to nearly 2000 veterinary practices in the UK. Contained within the programme was the 10-minute film, including a strong third-party endorsement for the direct marketing package. At the same time, as the veterinary pharmaceutical company posted its October price-list to veterinary practices, all veterinary surgeons were asked to look out for the programme on issue No. 26 of *Practice*. If they did not regularly see a copy, then they were invited to telephone for an excerpt that contained the interview.

The excerpt was prefixed by the marketing manager's brief introduction. Further copies of the video were sent out to the sales representatives to show to those selected practices that had been identified as so-called 'early majority' practices i.e. the practices were considered to be most likely to follow the example of the more innovative practice shown in the video. Within a month of the video being circulated, the excerpt publicized, and the representatives showing key prospects, the value of contracts signed in that time indicated that the cost of the film sponsorship and video production was more than covered by the increased business. Using a video recording of third-party endorsement of the scheme was shown in this example to be the most effective means of publicity. The film would have application for a reasonable period of time, probably a year. Ultimately, veterinary practices will need to be given assurances that their long-term commitment to the scheme is still paying dividends – thus the publicity objectives will change.

11.11 Summary

1 In most companies more money is spent on the sales force than on advertising and below-the-line publicity combined. It is thus vital to get maximum return on this investment in the sales force.
2 This means that material to support the sales team and help them to do a better job is itself a good investment.
3 In particular, supporting material can add a crucial visual element to the salesperson's words (tests have shown that people remember a far higher proportion of the 'words' when they are associated with 'images').
4 Visual support material can range from films and videos at one end of the scale to simple printed leaflets or 'presenters' at the other (see Chapter 10).

References

1   Mc Kellar, P., (1965), 'The Investigation of Mental Images' in S. A. Barnett and A. Mc Laren (eds), *Penguin Science Survey*, Penguin.
2   Bower, Gordon (1972), 'Mental Imagery and Associative Learning', in L. W. (ed) Gregg, *Cognition in Learning and Memory*, John Wiley, pp. 67 – 69.
3   Haber, Ralph N. (1970), 'How we remember what we see'. *Scientific American*, May, p. 105.
4   AVVPAS, Unit 4, Riverway Industrial Park, Trowbridge, Wilts.
5   Rogers, E. M. (1962), *Diffusion of Innovation*, The Free Press, p. 162.

12 Merchandising and point of sale

12.1 An overview

In many marketing situations the contact between the manufacturer of a product or supplier of a service and the people who use it is indirect. A typical pattern is:

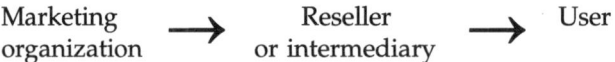

| Marketing organization | → | Reseller or intermediary | → | User |

In this situation decisions have to be made about the kind of promotional activity that is necessary and the weight of promotion to be applied at each stage. Different promotional techniques can be used to persuade wholesalers, retailers, distributors, etc. to take the product into stock (a selling-in or push strategy). Similarly they can also be applied to the user end of the chain to persuade or encourage the users to demand the product (a selling-out or pull strategy). What happens at the point of purchase (or point of sale, POS) can also be vitally important, and is described by the term merchandising, which demands close attention to all activities that take place in-store designed to actively sell goods at maximum profitability. It includes:

- The selection of products to be stocked.
- Stock control i.e. making sure there are the right quantities of each item.
- Store layout, lighting and decor.
- Space allocation and merchandise location.
- Traffic flow.
- Display.
- Promotional activity.
- Pricing policy.

While merchandising is obviously vital to retailers and other resellers, it is also an important link in the chain for manufacturers and other marketing organizations. To some extent their interests are the same. 'How can we sell maximum volume at maximum profit?' But there is also a conflict. The manufacturer is concerned to move his products rather than those of his competitors. The retailer is interested only in achieving maximum turnover and/or profit and is not too concerned about whose products he uses to achieve it. Thus the manufacturer's viewpoint is likely to be that merchandising is vital because:

(a) His whole marketing activity only begins to take effect when customers actually buy the product.
(b) He can achieve a higher sell-in rate if he helps the retailer to sell-out.

On the other hand, the retailer's approach will concentrate on identifying his most profitable lines and giving them appropriate emphasis, and identifying less profitable lines so as to eliminate them from his stocking list or to take steps to improve their profitability. Because of this difference in emphasis, the manufacturer's view of merchandising is likely to be a narrower one, concentrating on ensuring that his products are in stock, well-displayed and (when appropriate) priced and promoted as planned. However, manufacturers need to be aware of the much wider spectrum within which these activities must take their place.

An important part of the manufacturer's end of this merchandising aspect is to ensure that he provides what is necessary to make his products stand out at point of sale. This will not only include designing packaging so that products will be dramatic and easily recognizable, but also include the provision of point-of-sale material such as:

1 Racks or bins for the display of material (where necessary, designed to assist in self-selection).
2 Stickers, posters, labels and 'shelf-talkers' – which carry a message on a mobile – to act as reminders and tie in with above-the-line advertising (although in many modern self-service stores the scope for this may be very limited). However, as we shall see, modern technology is altering the picture somewhat.
3 Identification, on the pack and/or elsewhere, of current sales promotional activity.
4 Provision of any necessary leaflets, catalogues, etc. to assist customers' decisions to buy.

However, the dealer often finds himself in the situation of being overwhelmed with the amount of display material offered to him by his suppliers. The more sophisticated he is, the more conscious he is that he needs to get maximum turnover from each square metre of shelf-space, the more selective he will be. Concerned more with profits than which brand actually sells best, manufacturers need to convince retailers that their display will increase profits. Using POS material to feature a national promotion (especially if it is to be heavily advertised) is one way of doing this, but its apt design is crucial if it is to be used and not discarded.

In some cases POS promotion is used to persuade people to shop at one particular point of sale rather than another. The petrol promotions are intended to encourage people to buy their petrol or oil from one company's site (or sites) rather than another. Trading stamps are another way of building such brand or company loyalty. So are the so-called 'loss leaders' that many retail outlets feature, when one or more items are heavily marked down in price and featured in advertising, or put on posters in the window, etc. to tempt people into that outlet in preference to a competitor's. Naturally the hope is that, once in, they will buy other items besides the featured 'loss leader'.

12.2 So how and why do shoppers buy?

This is a perplexing question. Most grocery marketers, from time to time, watch consumers in action in-store. What do they see?

Some shoppers push their trolleys around at speed and shop like Billy Whizz; others walk round in a daydream and examine products and displays in a leisurely way. Why do they behave so differently?

Marketers know much about buying habits in their particular markets, but little was known about the shopping process into which the purchase of individual brands fitted until *Marketing* commissioned a study into this area to answer the fundamental question: 'How and why do shoppers buy?' Conducted by the Q-Search division of the Schlackman Group in the early 1980s, the research covered the total shopping cycle from preparation before leaving for the store, to finally putting away shopping in cupboards at home. The research technique included a qualitative stage, in which shoppers were individually accompanied to the store by a research executive, and interviewed in depth at home afterwards. There was also a quantitative stage, based on self-completion questionnaires. The technique is summarized thus:

1 Researchers selected thirty representative housewives who normally did one main shop weekly at a supermarket.
2 Interviewer met housewife at home, accompanied her to the supermarket, and observed a few feet behind – in most cases, the housewife soon became unaware of being observed.
3 Interviewer accompanied housewife home and watched unpacking.
4 In-depth interview lasting 45 minutes.

5 Self-completion questionnaire, mailed to 450 housewives on home-testing panel.
6 325 questionnaires returned and analysed – sample representative by age, class, North/South and family structure.

During the qualitative stage three different shopper types were identified: relaxed, controlled, and rigid. This last group could be sub-divided into two distinct groups: those rigid by personality and those rigid by situation. The results of the larger scale follow-up research confirmed that these types exist, and allowed a rough estimate of the extent of each type. Shoppers fell into one or other types of category according to their degree of pre-planning, willingness to experiment and try new products, attitude to price and budgeting, and flexibility in accommodating to different tastes of individual family members. These findings are summarized in Table 12.1.

The total shopping process is quite complex, as can be seen in Figure 12.1. It has been suggested that the use of a computer would greatly ease the planning task for the housewife. The important point to note is that housewives buy 'meals' not products. Housewives shop by starting to consider whole meals, including snack meals, before

Table 12.1 *The different types of shopper and how they behave*

Type	Relaxed	Controlled	Rigid (a) Personality	(b) Situation
Rough %	20	60	10	10
Demography	Young Non-working 45+ years old Work part-time	–	–	C2D
Uses list	No	Partial	Yes	Yes
Experiments	Yes	Little	No	No
Meets individual family preferences	Yes	Yes	No	No
Budget control	Lax	±£2	Rigid	Rigid
Notes	Looks carefully at displays, takes time. Tends to enjoy shopping.	Looks for variety, uses list for basics but decides rest in store.	Operates with military precision. Decides on list at home. Menus planned.	Behaves as (a) but for economic reasons. Also shops quickly.

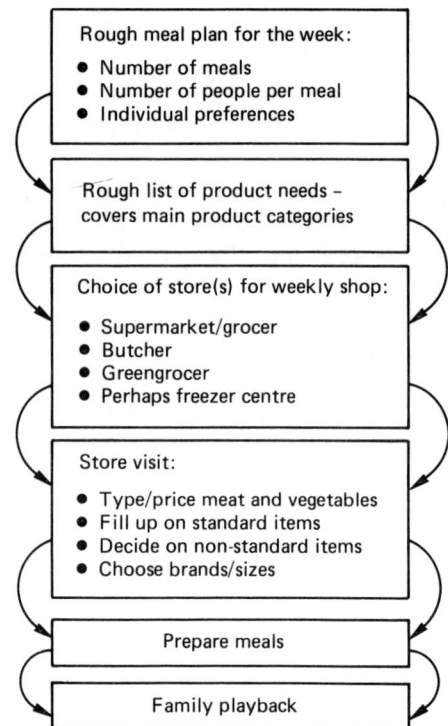

Figure 12.1 *How the typical weekly shopper makes his/her decisions*

translating these ideas into product needs. The degree of pre-planning, however, varies, with 38 per cent making no list before they shop.

The following categories coincide broadly with the different types of shopper.

(a) Usually make a list of everything, to avoid forgetting	23 per cent
(b) Usually list some things/decide rest in shop	36 per cent
(c) Usually make list, so buy nothing else	3 per cent
(d) Don't make list – usually know exactly what they want	26 per cent
(e) Don't make list – decide in shop	12 per cent

Like much background research, it is too broad in its scope to make any definitive statements about changing one's tactics overnight, but it does illustrate that while many shoppers do undertake some pre-planning, virtually half the shoppers questioned in this study (48 per cent) decide on what to buy once they are in their chosen shop. So, though not as glamorous as a multi million pound TV advertising campaign, a well-planned and carefully managed in-store sales merchandising operation can make a sizeable contribution to company profitability.

12.3 The basics of point-of-sale merchandising

Point-of-sale (POS) merchandising can either direct customers to a specific product from a generic idea or switch them from one brand to another. Consider the sequence shown in Figure 12.2, where a customer goes on a shopping trip. That customer will have had a variety of messages directed at him or her from a number of sources, making recommendations about what product to buy (1). Customers also have specific needs, which the purchase of a product is planned to satisfy (2). So that customer decides to go on a shopping trip with two fundamental objectives: either to obtain a generic product, e.g. to buy toothpaste (3) or to buy a specific branded product (4). Once in a store, the POS material may attract the shopper with the generic idea to Maclean's toothpaste, product A, away from the generic (possibly own label) toothpaste (5). Alternatively, the POS material may attract the shopper away from the specific (product 4) and *switch* them to Gibbs SR, product B (6). There is a third way in which POS can work; the

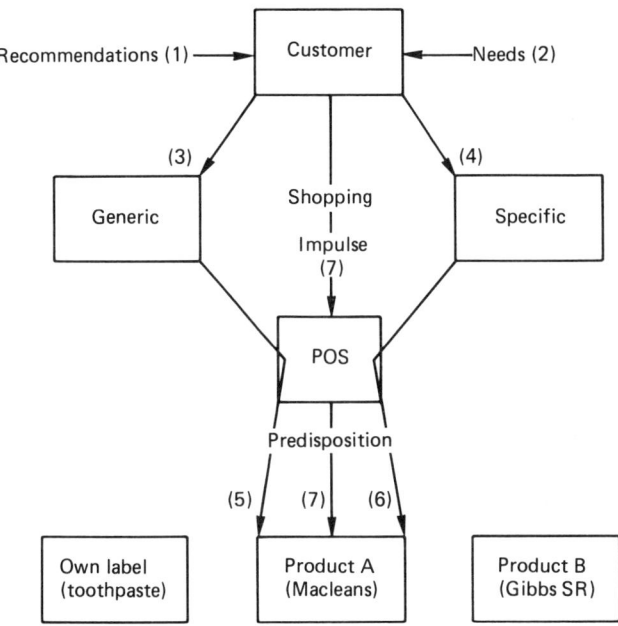

Figure 12.2 *How POS can influence a shopper's predisposition to a particular product*

customer in store may be on a regular shopping trip and be attracted, by the POS material, to product A, and make an impulse purchase (7). So, in summary, POS can:

- *Direct* a generic need (5).
- *Switch* a specific need (6).
- *Activate* a latent need (7).

One can see from this that above-the-line advertising and POS can work well in harmony. The advertising is addressing the customers' attitudes to a product by educating them, persuading them and motivating them, creating needs and desires in them that the product is proposing to fulfil. POS can work as a reminder of that advertising, especially to subconscious ideas, and can translate those ideas into action. Obviously therefore the activities of sales promotion are also closely linked to the objectives of POS merchandising.

The wide variety of types of POS materials can be broadly classified into two groups: static displays and moving or active displays. The types of POS are summarized thus.

12.3.1 Static materials

(a) *Packaging*. This is of the highest importance, and relates closely to sales promotions on-pack. However, to be effective, on-pack 'attention getters' need to be on shelf first.
(b) *Decals*. These are small designs, usually of the pack or brand's logo often attached to windows, doors or counter fronts, and serve as useful brand reminders elsewhere in store in addition to the pack on-shelf.
(c) *Posters*. These may reinforce the brand's advertising or pack design, and are usually attention-getting. Their main limitation is their size, and not all stores will carry them. Included here are pavement signs.
(d) *Displays*. The variety of displays is considerable. As merchandising units, they are attention-getting in-store and need to be convenient for the retailer to display the product. The outer packaging or case of a product is important in this respect.
(e) *Dispensers*. Again, the dispensing units vary considerably but are used either to dispense smaller packs of the product or to dispense product leaflets.
(f) *Dumpbins*. Large bins, often found at or near to check-outs, carry a random selection of a product where impulse purchases are encouraged. It is important that the product is not too neatly

stacked in the bins, otherwise shoppers are discouraged from 'upsetting the display'. (On-shelf, however, the converse applies. Product badly stacked can look old and unkempt, unlikely to attract custom.)

12.3.2   Mobile or active materials

(a) *Shelf talkers*. Decals reproduced on card and suspended from a base card attached to the shelf where a product is stacked are a popular approach, although not all stores will permit their use. Naturally they can be placed elsewhere in-store, not just on the shelf.
(b) *Motorized displays*. Attractive attention-getters, although they are expensive to produce. They are often best placed in a shop window to attract passers-by.
(c) *Hi-tech*. The use of new technology is flourishing in the world of POS, particularly the use of flashing signs, message screens, holograms, interactive videos, and computers.

12.4   A manufacturer's in-store merchandising operation

As the multiples reinforce their dominance in most retail markets, the traditional sales representative's ability to influence the order at the point of sale decreases day by day. Yet it is still vital for a supplier to have a regular physical presence in-store – to maintain agreed fixture layouts, for example. Above-the-line media costs continue to escalate. Between 1975 and 1984, TV advertising space rose by 33 per cent, press advertising space by 24 per cent. Manufacturers are therefore showing a renewed interest in the basics of selling and display in store. A well-trained, well-managed and highly motivated team of sales merchandisers can improve a manufacturer's presence where it counts – in-store. If only 20 per cent[1] of all purchasing decisions are made by housewives in the shop, right at the point of sale (as the research at the beginning of this chapter would suggest) then, in the grocery business, that proportion would account for over £1 billion worth of sales.

Once a manufacturer has decided to mount an in-store merchandising operation, some fundamental questions need to be answered to set clear objectives:

1 How many outlets need to be visited, and how often?
2 Should the operation be aimed at retailers only, or should wholesalers and cash-and-carry outlets be targeted too?
3 What are the operational objectives of display and distribution?

4 What type of person would be best suited to such a team? A basic requirement would be for an articulate, outgoing owner/driver.
5 Do you need an in-house team or to contract out the scheme to a specialized organization? If you go 'out', two types of merchandising coverage are available: the shared service, where personnel work for a number of manufacturers in the same store, or the solus method, where personnel work for only one manufacturer. Shared merchandising lowers the operation cost, whereas the solus route encourages loyalty to the manufacturer as opposed to an individual retail outlet. The style of the operation will depend on whether what is required is a tactical campaign, say to exploit seasonal bursts of activity, or a long-term presence in store.

Whichever operation is chosen, pre-call planning must be meticulous:

(a) Refer to all records made on previous store visits.
(b) Check all supporting equipment, such as visual aids, point-of-sale material and samples.
(c) Check essential information on pricing, products, and current or future promotions.

Retailers that continue to raise their standards of professionalism expect no less from the sales merchandiser.

It is also vital for merchandisers to build up a good relationship with the store manager. On the first visit to a store merchandisers should introduce themselves to the retailer and explain their presence, and outline what they have been asked to do and by what authority they are acting. (The retailer might want to check the background of a complete stranger who has asked to rummage through the store and stockroom.) Only then can the full cooperation of the staff be achieved. A merchandiser's activities will then include:

1 Running an outlet check:

(a) Focusing on stock levels.
(b) Assessing POS materials – particularly window dressing, if applicable.
(c) Inspecting product displays.

2 Undertaking a thorough brand spring clean:

(a) Restocking empty shelves.
(b) Cleaning dusty or dirty fixtures.

(c) Renewing faded or old POS materials.

3 Completing the on-pack branding exercise:

   (a) Packs arranged to face the front of the display.
   (b) New stock priced correctly.
   (c) Stock rotated with regard to shelf-life.

Weetabix, for example, generally introduces a new on-pack promotion every 2 months. Once the promotion has changed, the old pack immediately becomes obsolete. Part of the merchandiser's brief will be to ensure that the older packs are positioned at the front of the display, so that they sell out as quickly as possible.

4 (Occasionally) building a feature display:

   (a) Most effectively sited at the end of fixture (or gondola) to create maximum impact.
   (b) Occasionally other 'hotspots' to highlight a particular product or promotion can be identified.
   (c) Good retailer rapport will enable a good merchandiser to make the most of the opportunity.

A good merchandiser will not only ensure that the correct amount of space has been allocated to the brand, but will actively encourage the store manager to increase the facings for the fastest selling lines; it is possible to boost sales dramatically in this way. In addition, merchandisers can be the manufacturer's mouthpiece to the trade, fulfilling a valuable communication role. They are in an ideal position to talk to the retailer about new products, line extensions, promotions and other new developments.

Finally, the merchandising operation can provide a valuable and immediate research opportunity. Careful record-keeping and well-planned methods of assessment will ensure that the cost, coverage and operational objectives are measurable against budget and in-store performance targets.

What is sometimes overlooked is the added value to the manufacturer of the market information provided by the merchandiser on product turnover, pricing, stock, distribution and facing levels, of both its own and its competitors' products. If the manufacturer is to get maximum value from what has become an increasingly sophisticated activity, great care must be exercised in the recruitment, training, control, and motivation of a highly professional and powerful human resource.

Companies use a merchandising force in quite different ways:

- Heinz and Weetabix generally limit them to shelf-filling and pricing operations, particularly those linked to specific sales promotions.
- H. P. Bulmer will use cider bottles and the outer packaging to build attractive displays at POS to encourage off-take at key periods such as Christmas.
- Walls (ice cream) mounts an annual merchandising campaign through its appointed agency to re-dress the nation's freezers in 20,000 plus retail outlets, replacing old POS materials in time for the peak summer season.
- Dairy Crest Foods' merchandisers will make weekly stock and order calls on cash-and-carry outlets, and telephone the orders taken direct to Dairy Crest, obviously generating useful market-research data.
- Mars uses its network of merchandisers to sell, in the summer, the in-store concept of its 'Cool-em' promotion, which recommends retailers to keep Mars confectionery in the refrigerator.
- Thomson Holidays employs a regional network of merchandisers to inform, educate, and motivate counter staff in the travel industry. A visit to a travel agent might comprise providing information on new promotions and programmes, taking staff through the Thomson brochure and promoting trade competitions to encourage retail staff to study the literature.

12.5 Retailers' domination of the POS market

The point-of-sale is gradually changing, not overnight but as a continuing evolution that shows little sign of being reversed. It does not mean that the market for point-of-sale merchandising material is decreasing. Far from it. What is happening is that the purchasing power is shifting away from the manufacturers of consumer goods and settling increasingly with the retailer. Point of sale, particularly in the non-food sector of the market, is no longer a mish-mash of separate items thrown together at whim. Retailers are increasingly exercising control over the images their stores present to consumers, with the aim of creating a selling environment in which the consumer's experience is, say, 'buying a pen at Smiths' rather than 'buying a Papermate'.

The word 'retailer' must, however, be widely interpreted to include the high-street operations of banks and building societies, which now form an important sector of the high-volume point-of-sale market. That, and the power of the retail chains, are probably the most important changes that have taken place in point of sale in the last decade. However, these changes are slight compared to the radical changes foreseen in the next decade, as electronics comes of age in the world of point of sale.

Currently retailers are becoming the dominant force in the POS market, and are trying to ensure that all aspects of in-store presentation and design contribute to a unified shopping experience. A good example is Habitat. Terence Conran, who set up Habitat, has proved the effectiveness of design, offering a total image from the product to the store. While one cannot necessarily see the store's image in any given item, the total design concept is evident.

Even small retailers are more aware now of the need to develop their own identities. In the toy market, for instance, a manufacturer-supplied merchandising unit does nothing to enhance the retail outlet. Many agencies working the POS area have now moved into total shop design, working closely with the retailer. Some agencies operate a computerized system to provide advice on layout and even shopfitting. 'The Early Learning Centre' and 'TOYS-R-US' are two contrasting examples of the designer's work in the toy market. There is still some tailor-made POS hardware for shop-in-shop installations in prestige stores such as Hamleys. (Such tailor made POS materials are *de rigueur* in the fine bone-china market.)

POS merchandising can be used as an integral part of sales promotion and good design is essential. These points are well recognized by the relative newcomers to POS – the banks and building societies.

12.6   Point-of-sale in car showrooms

Most car manufacturers appear to believe in the strength of point-of-sale material, to judge by the amount of it about, but they have almost all chosen to concentrate their messages on one aspect of the transaction and the one that is potentially the most self-destructive, namely price. By the mid-1980s the POS message had become a message of distress, echoing the disastrous price war that was raging within the motor industry – a message still reverberating through the showrooms in the 1990s.

Rather than highlight the superiority of the brand or the benefits of a given model, the manufacturers continue, with few exceptions, to focus the buyer on price. By making the point-of-sale message so price-orientated that the surprised consumer may be offered an instant cash discount, even before he has asked for one, the manufacturers are robbing the car salesmen of a chance of doing their jobs properly. Customer dissatisfaction is being in-built: the cars are not holding a good resale value, the low price reflecting the initial discount. If the point-of-sale material is not shouting how low the price of the car is, it is telling customers how cheap the finance deals on offer are – again pushing price ahead of product benefits.

Well-conceived POS material, which points out or underlines customer benefits, can be of enormous assistance to buyer and seller alike. Traditionally a vehicle was presented in a 'multi-point features pitch', in which a salesman would walk around the car indicating its features and explaining how each one could benefit a buyer. Point-of-sale material can be used effectively here to prompt the salesman and grab the customer's attention. For example, a boot sticker reading 'Cavernous boot – × cubic feet capacity' is a natural conversation point. In a *Marketing Week* pilot study of fifty-seven dealerships covering eight franchises and conducted pre-August 1985 to discover what assistance potential consumers were being given, it was revealed that, in virtually every case, price was the first 'benefit' that the salesman sold, and credit terms came a close second.

Even today, take a test drive and you'll be lucky to find someone to take you through the car's features, let alone its benefits. A severe lack of good point-of-sale material, and the damage that can cause, was shown by Vauxhall at the launch of its new Cavalier in 1988–9. The brochure on the new model continued to be such a rarity 18 months post-launch that some had commented that it would be easier to get one from a Sotheby's auction than a Vauxhall dealer. A severe lack of demonstration models compounded the problem. As a result, Vauxhall lost many sales, particularly in the fleet-car market.

Marketing Week's pilot study showed that the price message blazened across the showroom window was always referred to early in the salesman's conversation. In other words, the selling techniques extolled by car industry training departments had effectively been erased from the salesman's minds by the point-of-sale message. In one case an immediate discount of £950 was offered when a shopper taking part in the survey enquired about a car priced about £6000. That's nearly 16 per cent discount off the gross income, so what is left for the dealer's margin? Pity the poor customer who finds a fault in his new, cut-price car, because the dealer cannot have made enough to offer much of an after-sales service.

Professor Krish Bhasker of the University of East Anglia Motor Industry Research Unit believes it is still possible to use the traditional virtues of selling the benefits of a car, rather than cutting its price and the dealer's margin, and still achieve the manufacturers' quantity targets. In a report on the future of car retailing in the UK, he says:

Concentrating on quality rather than quantity may pay off. Dealers should aim to make the maximum out of each sale by using it as an opportunity to sell optional extras, accessories, extra dealer warranties, special finance deals . . . and to retain as many customers as possible.

Dealers should look at their image and reputation, rather than price, as a means of beating the opposition. This could be achieved by concentrating on offering a distinctive level of service; offering something extra to customers which cannot be found elsewhere.

Increased attention will need to be paid to marketing and public relations, to ensure that the dealer has a positive image and a high profile in the local area. The object will be to convince customers that they are getting value for money, which is not the same as getting a cheap deal.

Based on this premise, a point-of-sale campaign can provide a promotion medium that is simple and bold, and which highlights the product features, showing them as benefits to the customer. It should also echo the national selling proposition of the above-the-line publicity, as Austin Rover has done with its 'Now we're motoring!!' sales material. This makes the potential customer stop, look and consider buying for the right reasons.

12.6.1 Audi/VW Case Study 1985

Audi/VW prefers not to use window displays at POS, believing it distracts people's attention from the models on display. However, inside the showroom the POS material concentrates on features as benefits. There is no reference to price-cuts or deals, but, over the 3 years that Audi/VW adhered to this policy (1982–5) its share of the market increased from 4 per cent to 6 per cent. What is more, sales increased without destroying dealer profitability!

12.7 The view from the USA

Information emerging from the eighth annual study of consumer-buying habits carried out by the Point-of-purchase Advertising Association in association with Du Pont showed that US expenditure on POS in 1983 amounted to an estimated \$6.2bn and that the average annual increase during the preceding 15 years had been 12 per cent. While this may not be evidence that all the money is wisely spent, it does show that a lot of people attach a great deal of importance to it – not surprising when the same study reported that two-thirds of every dollar spent in American supermarkets is decided upon in the store. (Compare this figure to that found in UK supermarkets in Section 12.2, p. 278.)

With the cost of TV advertising escalating and its coverage fragmenting, the advantages of POS will increase. POS units in the US already surpass all other media in delivering the lowest cost per 1000 exposures. For example, in the US around the mid-1980s a 30-second spot on TV would cost between $4.05 and $7.75 per 1000, whereas an in-store temporary product merchandiser or sign that costs from $2.50 to $10 delivers a cost per 1000 ranging from $0.18 to $3 – and that assumes a lifespan of only 2 weeks. One can reasonably assume that the POS message is targeted at a more relevant audience than TV too – after all, the customers are actually in the shop where the product is readily available. Further, there are no problems about recall with POS, its message being delivered where it counts.

In the Dayton Hudson flagship department store in Minneapolis POS is applied in such a way as to make the place an entertainment, an education, and a perfect example of the extent to which POS – in department stores, at least – has been described by some to be way ahead of the UK. Dayton is the company that transferred the overlooked business of selling bridal gifts into a touch-screen computer registry, accessed by thousands of grateful customers, for whom it solves a tiresome problem with the minimum of effort. Harrods adopted the system in the UK in the mid-1980s, apparently with equal success. By the end of the 1980s Debenhams had installed similar touch-screen systems in selected stores, and some of them were being used by a 1000 people a day.

Dayton Hudson is using another technique right where it counts – where the merchandise is sold. The store group has installed a media wall, and is also using media cubes. The media wall is about the size of a 48 sheet poster site but consists of six adjoining video screens, back projected to create a wall of sound and vision that has a massive impact. The media cube is a stack of 3 foot square boxed screens, similarly back projected, to create a mobile version of the wall. The mechanism used is tape-slide, because it gives a much better picture quality than video. This medium, which can be used in a variety of numbers of screens and configurations, has three very powerful plus points:

1 By lending a degree of theatre and entertainment to the sales environment, it enhances customer appreciation of the store.

2   It does what no mannequin, cardboard sign or poster can do (and indeed what few salespeople can do) it demonstrates on a grand scale the selling points of the merchandise or groups of merchandise, in a way that grabs attention.
3   It boosts sales. Tracking studies on specific store areas have shown definite increases in sales where the cube has been employed. In one shoe department, for instance, a 60 per cent increase was recorded.

Dayton-Hudson's vice-president, John Pellegrine, describes the system as:

> Not so much POS as electronic marketing, which plays an important role in the total marketing mix, and as such its task at point-of-sale is to instruct the customer with the degree of credibility the store deserves; to instil confidence; to invite a response; to impress with a sense of post-sale satisfaction - and then to sell!

12.8   High tech at POS

Until a couple of years ago most developments in POS display were design-led. But now, in a new decade, the application of new technology has been moving on apace and looks set to become a major growth area. In the process we hope that the importance of design will not be lost.

Recent innovations in the market range from large format holograms, visually more stunning than anything seen before, to computer-driven systems that serve a proactive role in POS marketing. Here are six examples of high-tech already operating at POS in selected markets:

12.8.1   Electronic Point of Sale (EPOS)

In the EPOS system a scanner emitting a beam of laser light can recognize patterns and bar codes. These codes are simply numbers printed in digital form, containing information on such things as the nature of the product and the name of the manufacturer. When the bar-coded goods pass over the scanner, it sends the coded information to the computer, which assigns the goods a name and a price, and transmits a running total of the transactions to its own file. Customer and retailer both get a record of the sale, including information on date and time, items bought, prices charged and method of payment. But the store gets something else: a full record of its sales and a stock inventory, since the digitized sales records can be matched instantly against delivery records. Scanners mean that the retailer will actually know what he has sold minute by minute, line by line, branch by branch. For the first time retailers will know accurately not only how many units are sold but also the profit made on each line.

The rate by which grocery stores have adopted this system is remarkable. International Computers Ltd (ICL) suggested that in 1984 21,000 EPOS terminals had been installed, and predicted that by 1990 244,000 would be in operation and scanning will be the norm. Saturation will be reached around 1995. By then about one-third of all British stores will be using some form of EPOS, but because most will be multiples; they will account for 70–80 per cent of packaged-goods sales and as much as 50 per cent of retail turnover. It was reported in *Retail Automation* in March 1992 that Sainsbury is currently the leading scanning retailer with 257 scanning stores and almost 90 per cent of its turnover recorded through scanning lanes. In second place is Euromache – only forty-nine scanning stores, but almost 80 per cent of sales now scanned while Asda is in third place with 126 scanning stores covering 60 per cent of turnover.

As the 1990s progress, the following scenario is developing:

(a) Over half the largest retail branches in the grocery sector will use scanners.
(b) The big six – Sainsbury, Tesco, Asda, the Co-op, Safeway and Dee – will have done a product-by-product analysis of turnover and reappraised their stocking policies accordingly.
(c) Only the fastest-growing product sectors will have a wide range of brands. The rest will be cut back to two or three leading brands – a high-quality product, own-label product and a 'cheapo'.
(d) Shelf allocation and filling will be calculated on an arithmetical basis: manufacturers' staff and merchandisers will not be allowed near the shelves or the stockroom.
(e) All branch deliveries will be ordered by computer through head office.

Manufacturers will have to realize that retailers are changing their basic strategy away from low-price-low-margin trading to providing a different kind of value for money. Retailers are looking at the range of goods they stock – moving into more fresh foods, fish, fruit, greengrocery and some kinds of non-food products. Retailers will be also developing new products for changing life-styles and will plough back some of the savings from efficiency into new ways of serving the consumer. Manufacturers will therefore have to be negotiating on something other than just price and start finding out what sort of thing will justify the retailer giving the manufacturer a bigger order.

12.8.2 Computer-based information services

In 1988 Thorn EMI Business Communications (TEBC) was approached by Selfridge's, in London's West End, with a simple brief to raise customer awareness of the wide range of products and services available in the store. In common with many large department stores – Selfridge's has over 450,000 sq. feet of selling space on six floors – customers tended not to move freely from the entrance floor. TEBC responded with a computer-based information service for use at POS; it provided up-to-the-minute information through a network of 28-inch television monitors around the store. Called 'Network in View in Store', it delivers a combination of teletext, high-resolution graphics and video footage initially to twenty-seven monitors but expanded to 200 in 1989.

Programmes can be targeted to individual monitors, zones, or all monitors, and pre-programmed to allow unattended operation. Teletext and the graphic systems allow the programmes to be updated quickly, and even videos can be produced quickly too. For example, on one occasion, a fashion show was filmed in the morning, edited and replayed later to advertise the afternoon show. Although the system cost approximately £400,000 and requires two staff, it is largely self-financing, since advertising space is being sold to manufacturers, usually those who already have TV advertisements ready-made. Alliance and Leicester Building Society, however, produced an advertisement specifically for the system. Research has shown that the advertisements, which occupy about 25 per cent maximum of the 20 to 30- minute programmes, can increase sales of specific products by as much as 50 per cent.

12.8.3 Computers in POS

Although the application of computer technology to POS is still in its infancy, there is already a range of successful applications. The cosmetics company Elizabeth Arden developed 'Elizabeth' – the friendly computer. As early as 1986 'Elizabeth' was visiting British cities, showing clients a 'new them'.

At £10 for a 15-minute session the £50,000 software package reveals on a computer screen a selection of new looks, made up of changing hairstyles, hair dyes, make-up and dress colours, etc. The session begins with the client's picture being taken and projected on to the computer, which 'strips' the face of make-up to determine skin colour and other characteristics. 'Elizabeth' then makes suggestions, while a make-up artist takes her advice, adding the changes with an electronic stylus. The client sits back and watches herself changing. The company claims that 'Elizabeth' can duplicate the full range of make-up, from foundations to eight different brush strokes. Various hairstyles, clothing and jewellery can also be shown.

Since mid-1988 Boots (Chemists) has scored a major success with its '2000 skin-care range', which offers a 'made-to-measure 'service to meet customers' needs. An integral part of the brand merchandising is a computer that asks a series of questions to elicit comparatively intimate information without embarrassing the consumer. The computer is straightforward to operate, with no more than five keys – no more complicated than a bank's cash dispenser. A built-in screen presents the questions with a range of possible replies. The '2000 range' is effective because it backs up the brand image. The hardware at POS has been designed to harmonize both with the brand image and other merchandising.

12.8.4   Data broadcasting

Another new area of technical innovation that is emerging in POS is data broadcasting, a means of transmitting information by means of spare capacity in the TV signal (via the BBC). Bishopgate Systems has already supplied a system to Coral Racing, and won a £3m contract to provide the Halifax Building Society with a national presentation system. This will be the first true example of the application of data broadcasting technology to POS. It will display high-quality, full-colour graphics and laser disc video sequences in the customer service areas of branches, and will be used initially for communicating promotional information on Halifax's financial services.

12.8.5   Holograms

A new German product launched in the UK in early 1989 by Blakecare was 'Panorama – The Talking Mirror'. This consists of a mirror concealing a central product box surrounded by promotional images, and from a distance looks like a normal mirror. However, as a customer nears, photo-sensors activate the unit to give a presentation, illuminating the product and images in a pre-programmed sequence synchronized with a stereo soundtrack. The unit's cost is about £1500.

The know-how to produce holograms has existed for some time, but technical limitations have largely restricted their application to areas such as product authentication and packaging. But in May 1989 the UK's first promotional campaign featuring a new generation of holograms, called stereograms, was launched. Promotion for the new Stevie Nicks album, released by EMI, included a full-colour stereogram of the singer packaged with the music and utilized in store at POS. In addition, major outlets featured a window display of a stereogram measuring 1 metre square.

The three-dimensional animated colour photograph is considered to be an extremely unusual and intriguing display medium, which can be offered at reasonable prices. Many see it as the first major breakthrough in POS display materials for a long, long time. Once designers become familiar with holographic images, each of which can provide a series of changing views of a product, the range of applications will become wide and varied. One specialist in POS and retail design is already considering the possibility of using holograms with a high-street jeweller. Used for high-value items, such displays would allow retailers to create dramatic window displays of small items, improving security by reducing the value of stock the jeweller needs for a window display, while not restricting viewing.

12.8.6   Interactive video (IV)

Although popular in the US, interactive video has yet to find much success in the UK retail environment. The way it works is best demonstrated by an IV programme developed for Austin Rover to display its range of cars. Rather than detail every car and model, from the smallest Metro to the 8-series Rover Vanden Plas, to every potential customer, viewers were asked a series of straightforward questions about their needs when selecting a new car. After they answered the first question, the hardware selected an appropriate piece of film from a video disc to explain what was available within the range to satisfy those needs. By answering each question in turn the viewer was taken through the sequence of film, building to a picture of their ideal car available from the range. Further, the final question identified those extras of likely interest that could also be demonstrated in a colourful, attractive and impactful way.

A schematic representation of the pathway a prospective new-car buyer might follow when viewing the Austin Rover interactive video sequence is the following:

Question 1   What is your price band?
    to £14, 000   £20,000+

Question 2   What is your preferred fuel system?
    Petrol   Diesel

Question 3   What type of car do you need?
    Saloon   Hatchback   Estate

Question 4   Do you want to limit your engine capacity?
    1.11   1.61   2.01   2.31+

Question 5 What extras are you interested in?

Sunroof ....

Electric mirrors ....

In-car entertainment ....

Metallic paint ....

Alloy wheels ....

Car trim ....

Obviously a key benefit is that customers' needs can be determined quickly by their responses to simple questions or menus. Appropriate products can then be shown or demonstrated, while delivering a full and consistent sales message. Date and time of user decisions, and routes taken through the programme can also be recorded for later analysis.

A new concept in combined IV and information systems was launched in April 1989 by Quadrant Network. Called the Video Booth, the system had a telephone-kiosk-like design aimed at providing users with a familiar and private environment. What was unusual about the system was that it could record user responses on audio or video tape. Naturally, seeing a person's face and how he or she was responding was a very powerful method of market research. The tapes could be used for internal promotions or for discussion on topics such as customer relations. It was a powerful way for a company to demonstrate that it cared enough to want to hear directly what consumers had to say.

Retailers recognize that IV has potential in that it can blend in with the store, and yet it has a segregated identity that arouses interest and encourages the consumer to become involved. However, while IV has a value, it is often overstated, and it also has some difficulties. Retailers generally need to remain flexible and change their messages quickly in response to a volatile environment. Having to shoot the video and cut the disc makes IV an expensive and relatively inflexible medium.

IV may score more highly with manufacturers. For example, Zanussi uses IV as product guides in Rumbelow's stores. Manufacturers generally need to change their marketing messages less often and can also gain a competitive edge over the store's other suppliers. However, IV must be implemented as an integral part of the general marketing or merchandising plan if its potential is to be utilized.

It is possible to integrate data from IV and EPOS. The days of an electronic, integrated in-store marketing environment may not be far off.

12.9 Summary

1 The retail outlet in which a customer buys the product is an important link in the sales/purchase sequence.
2 What happens at the point of sale is therefore of crucial importance and manufacturers and retailers need to get this crucial area working hard for them.
3 Point-of-sale activity is of two types. The first – called merchandising – means ensuring that the type, number and disposition of merchandise are designed to generate maximum sales. A crucial factor is the 25 per cent or more of purchasing decisions that are made in the store.
4 The second type of activity – point-of-sale material or POS – is the provision of various types of display materials.
5 Studies of shoppers show three main types – relaxed, controlled and rigid – who have different approaches to the shopping process and who therefore may need different treatment.
6 A relatively new development is the increasing use of high-tech POS material, including interactive videos, holograms, media walls and Electronic Point of Sale (EPOS).

Reference

1 Research conducted by the Market Research Society in 1986 suggested that 20 per cent would be a reasonable figure to represent those purchasing decisions made by housewives at the point of sale.

13   Editorial publicity

13.1   Introduction

In this chapter the subject of editorial publicity is considered only in so far as it contributes ultimately to the promotion of sales and is strictly within the confines of marketing strategy. Editorial publicity is both a whole professional activity in its own right and also a series of specific techniques. It runs parallel to above-the-line advertising in supporting the same objectives, e.g. new cars are publicized through appraisals by newspaper motoring correspondents as well as by advertising. On the other hand, much advertising is used to achieve the same objectives as editorial publicity, especially if used as part of a corporate image-building programme, e.g. BP uses TV advertising to project the contribution it makes to the British economy, and ICI projects its 'world solutions – world class' image.

These examples sound like good PR. But what is PR? The letters PR are used to mean both 'public relations' and 'press relations', and these two are not the same:

- *Press relations* (more accurately media relations) is the process and technique of providing information to the press, radio and television.
- *Public relations* is the much wider activity of communicating with the many groups of people who constitute an organization's 'public' – the carefully defined groups of people with whom the organization needs to have good relations.

The Institute of Public Relations defines public relations as 'the deliberate, planned and sustained effort to institute and maintain mutual understanding between a company and its publics'. Public relations is not a haphazard business; it is not merely the use of gimmicks or the razzmatazz of a launching party. It comprises conscious decisions and plans for a future that is accurately charted; a constant monitoring of a sustained programme of two-way communications (hence the use of the word 'mutual' in the definition) that gives a company or a product a good feeling in the minds and hearts of its customers. This good feeling must be constantly reinforced to ensure that a company will have a score of bonus points for the occasion when a problem arises.

Marks & Spencer, which is reputed to spend 90 per cent of its below-the-line publicity on public relations, and has done so for years, was able to recover from poor publicity on the purchasing and renting of its directors' houses because it had had 50 years' good communications with shareholders and the City, and a record of good dealing with all its customers that sustained it through this slight hiccup. In the year to 31 March 1989 M & S purchased £4.2bn worth of British-made goods, £400 million more than 1987–8.

However, much PR activity (including 'corporate advertising') is aimed at the many other groups, apart from customers, who have an influence on a company's successful operations. It is for this reason that we talk about a company's publics in the plural as a reminder that there is more than one influential group. Remember too, that ideally PR should always be two-way. As well as talking to our publics (plural) we should listen to what they think of our product and how they see our company.

A look at Marks & Spencer's company principles will suggest some of the publics that need to be considered. The principles are:

1 Selling clothing for the family, fashion for the home, and a range of fine foods – all representing high standards of quality and value.
2 Creating an attractive, efficient shopping environment for customers.
3 Providing a friendly, helpful service from well-trained staff.
4 Sharing mutually beneficial, long-term partnerships with suppliers, encouraging them to use modern and efficient production techniques.
5 Supporting British industry and buying abroad only when new ideas, technology, quality and value are not available in the UK.
6 Ensuring staff and shareholders share in the success of the company.
7 Constantly seeking to improve quality standards in all areas of the company's operations.
8 Fostering good human relations with customers, staff, suppliers and the community.

13.2 The PR universe

The term 'publics' (plural) has been used in the preferred definition of public relations in recognition that each group that a company needs to communicate with may need such special treatment that they are best dealt with separately. Figure 13.1 is a diagram of the PR universe; note that the arrows of communication are two-way. Not only should information pass from the company out to the various publics but their reactions and opinions should be noted too. It is worth noting that each of the groups shown in Figure 13.1 sub-divides further, depending on the market. How important each of the publics is to any given company will depend not only on the industry but also on what is currently happening in that market.

Opinion-formers are an important part of PR. They are the out-front people in a community – the chairman of the parent–teacher association, the mayor, the vicar. They may be the various minority groups or leaders of the principal industry associations.

The local community can form an important group of people. A new superstore may be of benefit to many in the local community, but those people living next door to the site may not think of it in quite the same way. Consider their thoughts, feelings, and allay their fears early, and you should avoid a local picket on your opening day. That would be the wrong story to read about in the local press!

Central and local government will be considered later in this chapter as we review a specialist area of public relations – the work of the lobbyist. See Section 13.6.

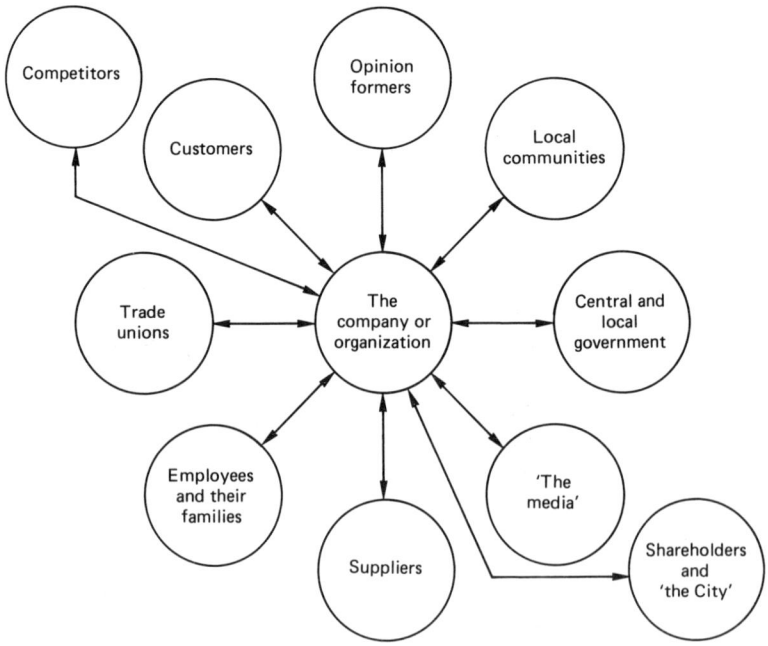

Figure 13.1 *The PR universe*

'The Media' does not just mean newspapers, TV, and radio, although these form the backbone of the routes of communication used by public relations. Virtually all other means of communicating with particular groups of people will fall under this heading. Included will be direct personal contact, audio-visual and films, special events (conferences, seminars, visits, open days), as well as a whole range of printed matter produced by the company, from the annual report through to a regular in-house newsletter. All have a role to play in the public relations communication mix.

Shareholders and the City will need to be addressed, particularly if funding of a new venture is planned, or assistance in difficult trading conditions is to be achieved. The annual report, while of considerable importance, is not the only way of influencing this group. Favourable editorial coverage in the 'serious' newspapers, particularly the *Financial Times*, is one way; a shareholders' meeting is another. As large and small shareholders are equally important, direct mail is going to be a valuable communication medium.

In order to get your suppliers 'on your side' it will be important that they understand your objectives and plans. This becomes particularly important, as so often happens nowadays, when a major multinational has a number of subsidiaries, maybe sharing the same administration or production facilities, perhaps even operating in the same broad industry sector. In this situation the 'supplier' may be the parent company. The exchange of ideas and information will help limit any prejudices that may otherwise develop.

It is said that good public relations is only achieved when there is good publicity, good performance and good management working together. One of the important tasks of management is internal communications. So, does the fork-lift driver understand why he is being asked to work extra overtime, or does the mailroom appreciate why it is having to handle a few thousand reply-paid cards from your last direct-mail campaign? But it is not just the company's staff that need to know what is going on – their families are important too. If you are running a sales-force incentive scheme, consider the partners: a holiday for two in the Caribbean is a goal for two people – salesperson and spouse.

Companies that ensure their affiliated trade unions are kept fully informed about the various projects and plans for the company develop the team spirit required for success. All employees can then work together.

Competitors are included in the PR universe because the 'don't tell 'em nuffin' approach will rebound on a company, whereas a friendly and communicative approach to competitors will facilitate under-standing within an industry and the mutual tackling of problems within that industry. Membership of Trade Associations within an industry is particularly important in this respect.

Last, but naturally by no means least, there are customers. It goes without saying that the defined target market for a product or service will also need to be addressed. While direct publicity from a supplier to a customer is designed to be a powerful sale-influencing force, the power of third-party endorsement should not be underestimated.

13.3 The planning and control of a public-relations campaign

Like all forms of promotion, PR must be conducted on a planned systematic basis. A fully efficient PR campaign consists of the following seven stages:

13.3.1 State the problem or aim

Obvious? Maybe, yet it is a sad fact that managements may be coerced into sponsoring a gymkhana or supporting a Christmas bazaar with no planned idea about what PR they should be aiming for. Is it to generate the feeling among the local community that the company is generous, caring, or committed to the social welfare of the neighbourhood? One needs to be quite clear about the aims, and define them in writing at the outset. Unless the objectives are clear at the start, how can one judge the effectiveness of the PR effort at the end?

A company must be sensitive to how it is viewed, and PR should always endeavour to be two-way – speaking to its public and listening to what its public has to say. Only in this way can any potential problems be identified ahead of them becoming serious. There will always be the unforeseen problem, say a hazardous spillage from a production site, and you will need to react fast. However, you will be in a better position to respond if you know where you stand with respect to the publics. This brings us on to the second stage of PR – research.

13.3.2 Do the research

One can undertake a full programme of qualitative and quantitative research, but there is much to commend informal research. When you are next out of the office, telephone your own sales office and find out how your customers and potential customers are dealt with; a word with the police will often illuminate a transport manager on how his drivers are regarded on the road. Listening and reading, internally and externally, are important sources of information in the PR universe. For example, listen to sales staff and office staff – talk to people. Review press cuttings, which, while only 70 per cent reliable, will give you a fair outsiders' view of your company. In addition, monitor feedback from any of the publics by noting what is said either over the phone or by letter.

13.3.3 Identifying the publics

When a company has established its PR aim and done the research, then it will need to identify the people to whom it wishes to speak. It is a useful exercise to review Figure 13.1 and draw your own diagram of the PR universe. By defining your publics in this way, you will not only find out whom you wish to speak to but also begin to build a picture of what they will need to know from you. Once you begin to clarify what you want to say, you will begin to have a good idea of the most appropriate media to carry that message.

13.3.4 Choose the appropriate media

The choice can range from TV to newsletters, conferences to films, depending on the objective and the public concerned. The types of PR media that can be used include the following:

Direct contact
Briefings
Education
Professional recommendations
Research papers, White papers
Social responsibility programmes
Badging (tee-shirts, car stickers)
Print (brochures, annual report)
Direct mail
Competitions
Events (conferences, exhibition, seminars, visits, open days)
Audio/visual films

The media
– Press
– Broadcasting on
　TV
　Satellite
　Cable TV
　Radio
Advertising
Lobbying
Sponsorship
Newsletters
Databanks (Prestel, Teletext)

Advertising is included because it can be part of a PR campaign. Advertising carries messages, paid for and controlled by the company. Most PR, on the other hand, is not controlled directly by the company but is intended to generate evoked responses by persuasion. However, paid-for advertising can be used to carry general messages as part of the PR activity, rather than directly to promote products.

There is a constant change of emphasis in the different media used and the new technologies coming to hand now (cable and satellite television, video discs) are creating new opportunities for PR. All the time, though, one must give due thought to what message is being communicated and to whom before the appropriate media can be decided.

13.3.5   Monitor the effects

Public relations is never cheap. It is highly labour-intensive, with very skilled labour at that, so constant monitoring must be maintained to make sure the message is being received and understood in the way intended, and to ensure that the declared aim is being achieved at an acceptable cost.

The finite measurement of the cost-effectiveness of public relations in general and of editorial publicity in particular is not easy. Every release to the press must be analysed in terms of each and every publication's needs. Assuming a press release was written for a given publication, then one might assume that that publication would carry the story. One method of measurement therefore is to determine the percentage of publications using a story, expressed on a base of the total number of releases circularized. One hundred per cent response is sometimes attained, but 50 per cent can be regarded as a good achievement, and 20 per cent or lower implies that the release was sent to too many publications or was wrongly written. At any rate it points to the need for enquiry. If a publication consistently fails to use a company's material, there should be an adequate record system to indicate this fact, and the editor should be contacted diplomatically to find out why.

Measuring results in terms of sales leads can be misleading. One might deliberately leave out certain key data in technical articles, forcing readers to write in for it. While this will bring in sales leads measured in tens, there could be thousands of dissatisfied readers cursing the omission.

Measurement by column centimetres is used extensively, but has been subject to a good deal of criticism. One could no more add the number of centimetres in a national newspaper to that in an industry journal than add apples and pears. Nevertheless, for a given company or campaign, the results can be sufficiently homogeneous to be assessed in this way. One could express the column centimetres in terms of equivalent advertising space, and this may well provide useful information on value for money spent. The same technique could also be applied to other media, where the cost of equivalent advertisements as air time could be assessed.

13.3.6 Look to the future

Vigilance must be maintained to ensure that the declared aim is being achieved. But the aim may well change. PR is never 'finished', but always part of an ever changing situation. One needs to be aware of the future objectives of the corporation – over the months and over the years ahead. Furthermore, by monitoring the feedback from customers and from the activities of competitors, the PR aims will need to change too. We also need to watch for development and changes in media opportunities – an increase in local newspapers may be an opportunity for us to get more coverage, for example.

13.3.7 Maintain financial checks

It is difficult to quantify the effects of PR, but unless this is undertaken seriously, much money can be wasted, e.g. on a stand at an inappropriate exhibition or trade fair, on a misguided sponsorship scheme or a costly seminar. Constant vigilance is the only way to ensure that the operation is cost-effective.

13.4 Press (media) relations

The process and technique of providing information to the press and also to radio and television relies on two approaches. You either meet the journalists and reporters face to face or you write to them. If you are planning to meet journalists on a one-to-one basis, then it is best to visit them at their offices or perhaps their favourite restaurant. Alternatively, you may call a press conference, where you can brief a large number of people at one time. If you have a new building or factory to show off, then obviously you will need to organize a reception on the premises. If you are putting pen to paper, it is usual to write a press release. Let us first consider press conferences.

13.4.1 Press conferences

Do you need one?

Press conferences are expensive; they use up both time and money – fast. Would a press release work better? Perhaps individual editorial visits or lunches would suffice? If you still feel you need a press conference consider:

(a) You must have something new or important to say, to warrant journalists' time.
(b) You must have something to show or demonstrate (or someone they can gain information from) that they could not have gained by telephone or post.
(c) The story's importance to *you* must warrant the great expense and time invested.

Timing

This all depends on who you are trying to attract. For the time of day, remember:

(a) Evening papers close by 12 noon.
(b) Dailies can accept material up to around 4pm for the following day.
(c) TV stations start around 10am for evening news features.
(d) Local radio can take 'soft news' recordings at virtually any time, but early morning is best.

As far as day of week and time in month, note:

(a) Mondays and Fridays are bad for most publications. But sometimes Monday is a good time to place a well-researched article, because there is little business or parliamentary news.
(b) Early Monday is acceptable to dailies (it's a low newsday), and weekly trade press, which goes to press Tuesday evening.
(c) Wednesday is a bad day for virtually everyone.
(d) Mid-month is a bad time for the monthly magazines, which usually make up their pages at this time.

The ideal compromise is often a Thursday in the first or last 10 days of a month, especially if you are seeking a wide spectrum audience.

It is important to check that there will not be any conflicting events. A music publisher once tried to launch a new product on the same day that the Ideal Home Exhibition opened, and only a single freeloading, freelance journalist turned up. Call the *Daily Telegraph* information office or chat to a friendly news editor to find out what might attract national journalists away from your event.

Venue and catering

Chapter 7 on corporate publicity will give you some ideas on choosing an interesting venue and some appropriate catering. Consider seriously a breakfast reception: 9 for 9.30am is a good time for working journalists, as they can return to their offices to start the day.

Most people will be interested in going to a novel venue. One company launched cat vaccines and invited the press to the London Theatre, then home to the hit musical *Cats*. Complimentary tickets for the matinee provided the icing on the cake. If you want to get the women's press to attend, remember that few will come too far from the great triangle of IPC at Kings Reach Tower, SE1; Paul Street, EC2; Elm Street, WC1; and National Magazine House, W1. No wonder the London Press Centre, Shoe Lane, EC4, is so well patronized. More people will attend a venue that is easy to get to.

Consider offering unusual sundry other services appropriate to your product. For example, Wilkinsons Sword hired manicurists to attend guests when it launched its manicure scissors.

Make arrangements work

As is so often the case, attention to detail pays dividends. It can also mean the difference between success and failure. For example:

(a) Is there power for TV cameras?
(b) Is there a quiet place for radio interviews?
(c) Avoid doors that open behind speakers.
(d) Is there ample parking?
(e) Do you need costly decor, or will fresh flowers and a photographic blow-up of your picture suffice?
(f) Do you really need a VIP? Your chairman may not be the best speaker, and so rarely do the press really want to hear from him.
(g) Celebrities are costly, e.g. £5000 upwards, and can still fall flat. Don't pay them cash in hand to reduce costs – it could backfire on you if they are caught tax-dodging!
(h) Take spare bulbs for the projector. The bulb may have been working 10 minutes before the presentation, but it can still blow as the room lights are dimmed. Make sure you have a couple of the right size replacements to hand, and someone with a clean handkerchief who knows how to change a hot bulb quickly standing by, in case the bulb blows in mid-presentation. (You only need this to happen to you once to know that you cannot take anything for granted!).

(i) Have you catered for any vegetarian journalists? *Animal Pharm*, a journal reporting on the world animal health and veterinary pharmaceuticals markets, had one who attended the launch of pet foods recently. Roast meats were carved at the table!

Demonstrations

Organize a dramatic visualization for your product. A computer company trained a German Shepherd dog (Alsatian) to operate a computer terminal, to show how simple the controls were. It is virtually impossible to launch a vehicle without a demo ride. At worst, show a film.

Press kits

Some companies prefer to hand them out at the beginning, but more often it is better to hand them out at the end of the presentations or as the journalists leave. This way, they will not be shuffling through the kit during the presentation, and you will not dilute the impact as the presentation uncovers the new product. The contents of a press kit will be described later (p. 314). Make each one relevant to a specific journal in a *named* kit (so you can identify the different releases), with one relevant photograph, and possibly a free sample.

Invitations

Perhaps the most important part of the reception, invitations will allow you to demonstrate your ability at direct-mail selling and also to gauge the impact of what you have to say to journalists. The essential criteria are:

(a) Personalize your invitation.
(b) Include a programme, as some editors may want to slip in/out at the end or halfway through. A few days after mailing, phone a few up to test their interest level and uncover conflicting dates.
(c) Enclose a map, include parking, railway stations, underground routes, etc.
(d) A reply-paid card is essential. Personalize it to the addressee too, if possible, to limit the amount of effort required in replying.
(e) Invite fifty, to get thirty-five acceptances and twenty-five actual arrivals.
(f) You may cheat, by keeping five or six freelances up your sleeve, to fill an over-large room. It is better, however, to send invitations in two batches – priorities, then second priorities if response to the first is poor.
(g) Be a pessimist. Put out chairs for only half the number you expect. (It looks better to carry chairs in than to carry them out). Assume

the nationals will not turn up, nor, despite their promises, your most important acceptances.

(h) Telephone them again the *day before*.

(i) Ensure the invitation at least hints at a story, why should they come?

(j) Make the invitation impactful. One company sent out a free, BT-approved telephone to named journalists, and on the phone was the number to call to make a reservation at the press conference (the phone had a modern jack-plug attached). A company launching pet foods in cans, where the cans had a unique ring-pull device, sent out invitations sealed in otherwise empty cans. On the outside was a special label mimicking the brand's image and design without actually stating the product name or the type of product. (Obviously recipients had to be told to open the can!)

Exploit the event

Discuss longer-term feature opportunities and other special articles with journalists; write them all a *personal* thank-you note; and send a press kit and a *personal* letter to all those who did not attend. Then chase them to see if a story will emerge, or if you can interest them in another story.

Speeches and presentations

Do not allow the speech-making to last more than 30 minutes in total. As for speakers themselves, field your best speakers, not the highest management. Perhaps let the MD welcome everyone and introduce the first speaker – 60 seconds at most! Keep all presentations relevant, entertaining and informative, especially to editors. Don't mount a trade sales pitch or a back-slapping occasion.

Questions

Leave plenty of time for questions, both formal 'from the floor' and informal (probably best around a buffet). Remember to circulate freely. Try not to eat too much – it is difficult to remain fully at ease while balancing a slice of quiche and a drumstick. No one likes to shake a greasy hand either. Lay off the booze too – you'll need a clear head until the last journalist has left, then have a well-earned drink!

13.4.2 Press releases

The cornerstone of much media relations is the written press release, itself part of a composite press kit. Before beginning to write a press release, define the audience to whom it is addressed. Start by compiling a list of all publications, people and other media that can conceivably be interested in news from the company, and use it as the checklist for each proposed press release. Over time the list can expand by the inclusion of contacts such as freelance journalists, trade organizations, specialist news agencies, house-magazine editors, named journalists with a special interest, as well as overseas publishers and agencies as appropriate. The list will be added to, or names will be deleted from it, as the publications change or the business is modified. The list, like any other database, should be reviewed regularly and updated frequently.

When circulating a press release, always make sure you:

(a) State where the information comes from.
(b) State where it is to go – so always try to personalize the release.
(c) Give a clear release date.
(d) Give a clear headline showing what the release is about.
(e) Provide a telephone number for day and night contact, and always give names and addresses for further information.
(f) Remember within the body of the release to include the five Ws and How (Who/When/What/Where/Why and How).

There are no hard and fast rules about how a press release should be laid out, but a model that many press releases are based on is shown in Figure 13.2.

Writing
Writing a press release is easy. Writing one that gets published just where and when you wanted is not. Most people think they have writing ability, but, sadly, very few have. Writing is difficult to do well. It comes from instinctive flair, an original mind, and experience. George Bernard Shaw wrote a long letter to a friend; at the end he wrote: 'I'm sorry, I didn't have time to write it shorter'. Be concise. Business people are busy people and editors are busier than most. So do not fling a scatter of phrases on to a page and hope they will do. Do not be satisfied with the first draft, especially if the copy is dull, long and fails to inform. Good writing is a rare blend of imagination and planning.

The key to writing a good press release is being able to write like a journalist. Therefore follow basic reporting rules in writing the release (the five Ws and H). Once you have determined the purpose of your release, summarize your story in the first paragraph. (Some editors will only use that paragraph.) This is 'the grabber' – a short sharp statement that grabs the editor's attention. For example, do not start with 'Accuracy is very important when stocktaking'. Instead, bring it alive: 'How *do* you count 5 million photocopier parts by hand in just 36

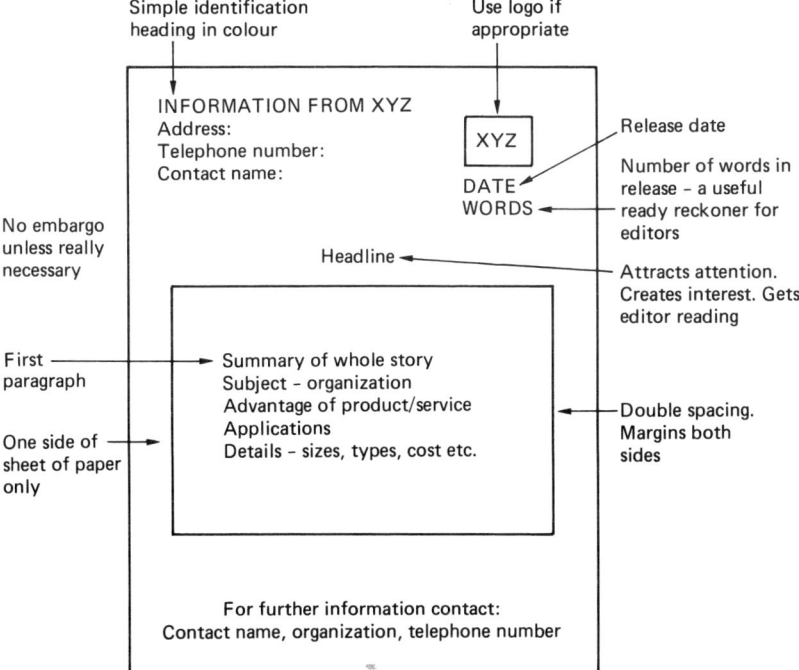

Figure 13.2 *Press release layout*

hours, and stocktake throughout a 100,000 square foot warehouse – without disturbing customer service?' Make the reader want to read on. Be certain the product/service is specifically and correctly named here and that its function is clear.

After the summary, add paragraphs in order of importance – the editor will probably cut from the last paragraph upwards. Give pertinent facts and enough detail to tell the full story in as few words as possible. What are the guidelines?

1 The time is never right to write. There is always a reason not to. Don't succumb. Get on with it. Rather like going swimming in the sea, it's OK once you are in. There is an old Greek proverb that says: 'Once you've started, you're half-way there'. Even if you throw the first page away, at least you have started.

2 Study the message you want to convey. Consider the reader, as with writing direct-mail copy. What does he want to hear? Agree the length and fix the deadline. Start thinking.

3 Write down the ideas on a note pad as they come to you. Quickly. Inspirations or just ordinary ideas come in a moment and are gone as swiftly.

4   Try to keep to plain English. Don't use long words when short ones will do. Seek to touch a common chord or emotion. Avoid jargon, clichés and hackneyed phrases. They indicate a lazy or pretentious mind. 'Tabloideze' indicates a sick mind!

5   Work at being lively. Use humour with care: get it right and humour can be a powerful asset; wrong and it hurts! Always entertain in the proper sense of the word.

6   Use people. Ask others what they think about what you have written. Don't be proud. Be willing to learn from people whose abilities you respect. Have they understood your message completely? Watch their faces. A frown and you've failed.

7   Don't believe all you learnt at school. As with other copywriting use 'but' and 'moreover' to start sentences, even paragraphs, to encourage the reader to carry on. As you will not be able to control the ultimate printing, unlike direct-mail writing, you cannot rely on underlining, italics, colours, bold letters or even block capitals to influence the ultimate audience, only the editor – and he might not be impressed. You will only have the words on the page in black and white, so make them all work for you.

8   Not all good writers can spell. But the final draft must be without errors. A clever idea is ruined by a simple mistake. It erodes the respect of the reader. So check, check, and check again. Then get someone else to check again. Beware 'Spellcheck' on word processors. The word might be spelt correctly but it might be the wrong word.

9   Beware tautology. You know what that means of course, because you have a good dictionary beside you. So don't use two words together when they mean the same thing, such as 'completely unique' and 'a new innovation'. It continues to remain a common error! Will these suggestions be adequate enough!

10 Think about language. Study words. What does 'very' really mean? Surprise yourself about how often 'the' can be chopped without loss of meaning. Avoid 'hopefully'. If someone or something is well-known, there is no need to say so unless you qualify within what limits it is known. Promise to never split an infinitive too!

11 When you think you have finished – you haven't. Polish, edit, refine, reject, rework, rewrite. Work towards a perfect blend of words.

12 Develop your versatility. Study how others write for different markets. Be as critical of them as you are of yourself.

13 Clause thirteen. Once you have done all that, you must be satisfied. Don't be. All writing could be improved. Read it again tomorrow, a week hence, and you will know how it can be

improved. Complacency is the enemy of a growing ability to write. This is why it is so important to start writing early in the campaign to give yourself time to reach a higher standard than before and still hit the copy deadline.

Format

Press releases should be kept to a standard layout. Figure 13.2 was one model. Editors always prefer to receive material to a standard format: typewritten on A4, double-spaced, text on one side of the page only, two or more pages stapled together (anything over two pages can probably be shortened).

If you want your release held to some future date, clearly mark an embargo date on the front page. 'For immediate release' is as important as it is obvious. Always give an *available* contact for the editor if additional information is needed. Include an address and telephone number.

Photographs

Unless otherwise specified by the publication, send only 8in × 10in black and white glossy prints. Always attach a caption, either with rubber cement or with staples (away from the main elements of the photograph). The caption must include:

(a) Exactly what the picture is about.
(b) Where it was taken,
(c) The date it was taken.
(d) The name and address of the sender.
(e) If small groups of a few people are shown, their full names to be given from left to right.
(f) Any further useful information.

Some publications will not accept photographs that do not have attached captions. The caption will also ensure your photographs do not get mixed up with the hundreds, maybe thousands, of other photographs at the journal.

Never list

As much as rules are disliked, no set of guidelines would be complete without a list of don'ts:

(a) Don't send old press releases – they are never newsworthy.
(b) Don't send copies of previously published articles – this turns editors right off.

(c) Don't make exaggerated claims – editors generally will not touch them.

(d) Don't make one release do the job of two. If a short headline will not summarize the release, you are probably trying to cover too much.

(e) Don't miss an opportunity for free publicity. Now that you have the basics of when, where, and how to get publicity, make it a priority.

Summary

To ensure consistent acceptance of your news releases, you must know (research) the interests of the editors and readers; and you must prepare newsworthy releases in the format that facilitates their use. You cannot expect every release to be used every time, but if a release is prepared properly, if the information is timely, and if the mailing database is correct, a high percentage of acceptance is likely.

13.4.3   Press kits

All press kits contain the press release and illustrations. As mentioned previously, it is better to personalize these, not only on the outside of the folder but also in terms of the content. Furthermore, press kits may include some of the following:

1   Personal background of those making the news.
2   History of the company.
3   Type of product.
4   Parts of the world to which the product is marketed.
5   Reasons for the choice of venue.
6   Relevant photographs and captions, etc.
7   Examples of product, if practicable.
8   Writing materials.
9   Company accounts, chairman's statements, etc.
10   Small, branded, promotional gift.

13.4.4   News interviews and features on broadcast media

One spin-off of good press relations is often found when the local radio or TV picks up the story. One Essex company managed to get 15 column centimetres in the *Daily Mail* on the Monday morning of its product launch in late 1989. At 9.30am Essex radio telephoned the company and asked for a live interview with someone to do with the product. The interviewer telephoned at 12.15pm and conducted a

10-minute live interview with the company spokesman. Later that same afternoon, TVS called the company and arranged for a filmed 'on location' interview with that person the following Tuesday morning. This interview was broadcast that evening, just the second day of the launch. Had the Chancellor of the Exchequer not resigned, Breakfast TV would have had that person in for another interview that same week. So be prepared. Public relations can snowball quite fast. In preparation for news interviews on radio and TV, whether they are in person or over the telephone:

(a) Anticipate and have the information ready.
(b) If the interviewer is coming to you or is telephoning, have a quiet spot set aside with 'Don't Disturb' notices available.
(c) Remove obtrusive external noise. Ask and explain politely why the noise has to be stopped and for how long.
(d) When being interviewed over the phone, remove extraneous noise and never switch on the radio.
(e) Jot down the points to be covered but answer spontaneously – and never flap papers.
(f) Avoid statistics and bare facts – put your enthusiasm in and describe vividly what you want the audience to see and feel.

You may choose to record your own interviews and features on audio cassette or video film. While this is usually best handled by the professional agencies, remember that you will need to prepare about a dozen copies for the national media so that they can be circularized to any department that might use them. Always research your market thoroughly and listen to programmes that carry your sort of feature. Be clear whether your feature is to amuse, inform, instruct and so forth, and, as always, get the length right.

13.5 By Royal Appointment

The presence of a Member of the Royal Family at your event can virtually guarantee press coverage. First level Royals are covered meticulously by the press, and occasionally by other media too. Even quite distant members of the Royal Family can enhance the chances of good coverage. So how do you go about securing a Royal to attend?

The procedure is formal and consistent. Proposals are submitted twice a year in May and November to the preferred Royal's secretary for engagements in the following 6 months. The proposal should be short and concise, covering one or two paragraphs about the proposed event, where it is to be held, what the Royal would be expected to do, and for how long his/her presence is requested. Secretary (or lady-in-waiting) and Royal then confer on the merits of each proposal, drawing up the engagement diary. The chances of success are greatly improved if the event is organized by or in conjunction with one of the charities actively supported by that particular Royal, or lies in an area where their participation or interest has been made evident.

When an invitation is accepted by the member of the Royal Family, the company or charity concerned will be notified and any further details of the day's proceedings will be requested. Correspondence, advance meetings or 'recces' will then establish the press arrangements on the day and beforehand. Such meetings will be attended by a member of Buckingham Palace Press Office or a representative from the regional Central Office of Information on its behalf. Discussions will cover numbers of guests – the Royal will generally have an entourage of two or three – whether the event will be televised, the required press coverage and arrangements for the press at the function, as well as the information to be given out in any press release.

The Press Office is obviously interested in what is being said about the Royal and the implications of his/her connection with the company concerned and with the event. It will want to establish that the Royal is not being used or manipulated in any way for publicity. Always therefore let the Buckingham Palace Press Office see any press releases before they are sent out.

The Royal Family's particular interests are the following:

The Queen represents the United Kingdom, both in this country and abroad.

Duke of Edinburgh
Duke of Edinburgh's Award Scheme, World Wide Fund for Nature, Central Council for Physical Recreation, Royal National Institute for the Deaf.

British food and farming, sports, design, engineering, scientific and technological research and development, conservation and state of the environment.

Prince of Wales
Prince's Youth Business Trust, Prince's Trust, Royal Society for Nature Conservation, Business in the Community, Times/Royal Institute of British Architects, Community Enterprise Scheme.

Inner cities regeneration, architectural design, natural environment, horticulture.

Maritime, the naval forces.

Musical and cinematic arts.

Princess of Wales
British Lung Foundation, Birthright, Barnardo's, London City Ballet,

Royal Academy of Music.

AIDS Research, medical research and related social issues, infants.

Princess Royal

Scottish Rugby Union, Save the Children Fund, Royal Yachting Association, Council for National Academic Awards, Intensive Care Society, British Knitting and Clothing Export Council, Home Farm Trust, College of Occupational Therapists, University of London, Riding for the Disabled Association. Equestrian events, hospital facilities, international development, education, services for women, agriculture.

The Duke of York has a full-time career in the Royal Navy, and therefore his engagements are restricted.

Contemporary Dance Trust, Opera North, York Minster Trust.

Prince Edward

National Youth Theatre, National Youth Orchestra of Scotland.

The attendance of a Royal is likely to increase the publicity and administration costs, but no payment. Each proposal submitted is judged on its merits of importance and applicability, and not on financial weighting. Public money, in line with the Civil List income structure, pays for a Royal's engagements. The decision of a Royal to attend an event depends on the suitability of the event to his/her activities, the date, and the particular location of the event. As certain events, such as Royal Ascot, are always attended by the Royal Family, the individual Royal's diary is worked around these.

If one were to take a snapshot of the Royal Family's appointments for 1 month, one would see a tremendous difference in the number of engagements each member undertakes. Of all the Royal Family, the Princess Royal has the fullest diary throughout the year for both national business and charity events. Provided you have the right sort of occasion and product, the presence of a Royal can greatly enhance the event. It does not present any great problems other than the usual one of security. To attract a Royal to the event, remember it has to be of interest to the Royal or of significant general appeal for it not to be overtly commercial in order not to cause embarrassment to the Royal. The approach needs to be made well in advance, though.

13.6 Lobby for results

When Edwina Currie withdrew as Junior Health Minister, it was quickly recognized that the National Farmer's Union parliamentary lobbyists were behind the move. While lobbyists, in popular myth, exercise murky influence in the corridors of power, pulling secret strings behind the scenes of Parliament, Warren Newman, director of PR at the NFU was reported to have said that the key to its campaign was not the NFU's private influence, but the force of its arguments. It did, however, keep the story in the news, and deliberately adopted a strategy that made the public and MPs aware of the effect of Edwina Currie's remarks, to show the damage they had caused. Three cheers for the free society!

The ability of a group such as the NFU to put its case effectively - to react quickly to a political crisis and persuade MPs and ministers to listen - explains why many businesses are becoming increasingly interested in lobbying work. In consequence, PR companies have been moving into this area.

The NFU, which is largely a lobbying body, concentrates on the universally agreed aims of lobby work: building contacts between MPs and constituents (in this case farmers), monitoring developments in Parliament, and providing high-grade specialist information to interested civil servants and politicians.

The NFU ensures that as far as possible MPs are approached by farmers in their constituencies who have been briefed by the NFU; the briefings concentrate on arguments, rather than emotions and supply the essential facts in a case. The same applies to ministers and civil servants trying to assess the repercussions of Government or EC policies. The NFU has a team of economists to supply those answers, and that is why the government often wants to talk to the NFU.

There is a distinction between the work of the NFU, which is continuous and dedicated to the interests of one group, and the work of independent lobbyists who conduct campaigns. However, many of the more sophisticated lobby companies agree that the best lobby work is that which is maintained over a long time. This is where some draw a distinction between the work of the lobbyist and traditional PR.

PR is normally trying to sell a company, product or service, but lobbyists are more akin to lawyers or accountants, only grappling with real problems when they exist, rather than trying to project a corporate image. Lobbyists are trying to spot problems in advance to influence the powers that be, or inform them of potential consequences of their measures on the commercial world. Where pure PR is concerned with putting across a message to the publics of a company, in lobbying there might be no reason to put out a message, especially if things are going well or if there are communications only with civil servants and Whitehall.

A basic activity of the lobbyist is monitoring – running an early warning system on anything that might happen in the EC or Westminster. It entails following debates (through *Hansard*), and studying parliamentary questions (they are tabled in advance) and adjournment debates, which allow MPs to raise any questions and to gain publicity. It is also concerned with identifying MPs who have views that may affect a client's company. Lobbyists also are sensitive to the rhythms of Parliament. For example:

- Early January in any year, the Chancellor is formulating the Budget. So companies will be preparing budget representations. As one lobbyist commented,'If you get an argument right, the Treasury is open to rational debate'.
- Midsummer finds lobbyists concentrating on the Queen's Speech. Once a proposed piece of legislation has been mentioned in the Queen's Speech, it becomes a 'tablet of stone'. Therefore the important lobbying effort comes while the speech is taking shape.

Lobbyists' key expertise lies in targeting MPs and civil servants who have an interest in a subject; and, in order to keep everything open and above board, lobbyists try to make sure the client is seen to do all the running. Lobbyists simply ensure that their clients are talking to people who are relevant. Lobbyists also have to learn parliamentary procedure: when is the right moment to put an amendment in, whether to start a private members Bill in the Lords or Commons, what it means when a certain number of people have signed an early-day motion, for example.

Lobbyists give several reasons for the recent growing awareness and interest in their role. One is, paradoxically, the tide of legislation and regulation unleashed by the supposedly *laissez-faire* Conservative government spanning the 1980s. The pro-business government meant that different business interests needed to be represented by their own lobbyists rather than by a monolith like the CBI. Another reason is the growing power of the European Commission and the EC Parliament. In this situation a parochial approach will not work: the European Commission and Parliament will not be interested if a brief just affects British industry – it must be Europe-wide.

The parliamentary lobbyists may occasionally find themselves in the public gaze when they are engaged in a high-profile piece of issue management like the eggs furore, or, before that, the Rowntree–Nestlé–Suchard and BA–BCal takeover battles. But in general they work quietly.

Building bridges between clients and politicians, and analysing the entrails of parliamentary business to try and foresee the future, may be low-key and unspectacular compared to the glitzy realm of a great deal of PR. However, it does seem to deliver results where it matters: in influencing, if only to a very small degree, government policies and the laws and regulations they create.

But buyers beware: lobbyists aren't cheap!

13.7 House journals

When communicating through public relations techniques and media, one must remember that not only are we considering the 'external' publics of a company, such as customers, politicians and so on, but also the 'internal' publics. Depending on where you are in the company hierarchy, a company's internal publics run up to the board of directors and down to the humble word-processor operative (typist) or fork-lift driver. All employees, whatever their station, work for the same organization, and have a greater sense of belonging if they know what the company and its other employees are doing and are achieving. There is nothing better for the sales representative, possibly relatively isolated from head office and the production facilities, than to hear his team being congratulated for its contribution to the whole, especially since he knows that acknowledgement is being communicated to his peers in other parts of the company. House journals are important 'internal' PR tools.

There are around 18,000 house journals in the UK, with a total circulation of over 20 million readers. They appear mainly in either magazine or newspaper (tabloid) format, with magazine formats predominating 7:3, and their popularity is gradually increasing. Many companies produce regular newsletters, which keep staff/customers informed of company news, policy and developments. Some companies, usually those with a large sales force or multinational concerns with many overseas staff, use non-print media, such as cassettes or video tape, to keep staff informed.

House journals are used to communicate either internally to staff or externally to customers, prospects or opinion-formers, or sometimes to both categories. Within that broad definition, house journals vary from the quasi direct-mail/sales-promotion type to those whose *raison d'être* appears to be corporate-image building or public-opinion forming of the most long-term and indirect kind. Occasionally there seems to be no defined or consistent policy, the house journal merely being an end in itself. An objective assessment of their value is then impossible.

Rarely is a house journal the only form of contact with a particular audience; staff see notices/memos and receive verbal messages; customers and external contacts may see advertising literature – in all its many forms – and editorial references. All these media should be used as part of an integrated communication policy, and the function of each selected according to its merits.

In this way the communication objectives of the house magazine will be clearly defined, and a *written* editorial policy by which to judge both success *and* cost-effectiveness will be available. The two are not synonymous: a publication may be successful in transmitting a desired message to a given audience, but at much greater cost than would be required by another medium, such as press advertising or personal contact.

Once editorial policy and the required audience have been defined, the physical format may be largely decided by cost and reproduction possibilities. There is no need to produce a full-colour glossy magazine to satisfy management ego if the audience is a few hundred, usually tabloid readers. Publication frequency imposes constraints too – 3-month-old stories are probably less obviously dated in a magazine as opposed to a newsletter format. Similarly format will be influenced by such factors as:

(a) The number and type of pictures.
(b) The picture/copy ratio.
(c) The need for foreign-language editions.
(d) Total circulation.
(e) Postage costs.

Whether a house journal is printed, audio or visual in format, its communication objectives must be defined before it can be evaluated to see if it achieves those objectives cost-effectively. Such value analysis of house journals may be difficult, depending on the complexity of the objectives. If readership response is the measurement criteria, then simple key cards for readers to request additional information is one way of judging satisfaction levels. Similarly, the effect of format changes or altering the level of expenditure on the publication can be assessed. Remember, the winning of design awards rarely equates to audience readership (as opposed to that from competitors, print designers, or a panel of judges), but readership levels and response are better than no measurement at all.

In most cases the objective is rather more subtle than that of merely collecting readers. Usually some change of attitude or improvement in climate of opinion regarding the organization is desired. In this case only a survey, or better still two comparable surveys at a reasonable time interval, will indicate the effect achieved. These may be based on a sample derived by statistically valid methods or, if numbers are small, of the whole audience. Either way, it is best to put the research into the hands of a professional market-research agency, including the development of the research method – questionnaires or personal interviews – even if the house journal is used as a research vehicle. Only in this way will the results seem to be unbiased.

Such surveys are expensive, especially if the message/objective is complicated or the audience/sample large, but in relation to the annual cost of production and distribution of the house journal, and, given that the results are valid for two or three years, the expenditure may be quite modest. Remember, it is better to spend money to ascertain what message (if any) is actually being received, than to continue year after year perpetuating an ineffective or perhaps even damaging message.

This last point is particularly relevant to staff-oriented publications. There has been a surge of staff newspapers and magazines in the past decade to mirror the growing awareness among management of the necessity to improve communications with the shop floor. Many publications are criticized by recipients for being too management-oriented and for carrying too little information about company policy, prospects and plans that would be of interest to staff. To ensure a staff journal that justifies production costs, it is essential to find out what workers really think of the company performance on such topics as salaries, promotion, commercial competitiveness, etc.

In summary:

1 Define objectives for the house journal within a total corporate communications framework
2 Evaluate effectiveness of the house journal in achieving those objectives by analysing information obtained from the prospective audience.
3 Test cost-effectiveness by comparing with actual/estimated costs for achieving the same objectives via alternative media.

13.8   Value analysis

As stated before, in order to measure how effective any of your below-the-line publicity activities have been, you need to start with a clear objective of what you wanted to achieve. For example, are you, with your editorial publicity, promoting a product or providing financial information? Are you trying to improve the image of your company, or reassure workers or shareholders?

There are a number of reasons why the evaluation of editorial activities is difficult. Among these can be listed:

(a) Difficulty in collecting data: a good press-cutting agency may 'catch' 60 per cent of press release publications in the UK. How valuable is the 40 per cent that got away? If it got away, it can't be any good, can it? Or can it? Collecting cuttings overseas is several times more difficult and expensive.
(b) How does one evaluate an appearance in one particular publication compared to another? Is readership data, usually based on advertising research, equally valid for editorial?

(c) How far is publication of a story affected by competing events? Would a universally ignored release on an improved type of nuclear fuel be condemned as badly handled if it coincided with the Chernobyl disaster?

(d) If a story goes 'badly', is it because of bad writing, inept distribution, unfortunate timing, boring subject, or another press release from an office with a reputation for too many non-stories in the past? How does one tell?

(e) Alternatively, does a wide acceptance reflect brilliant material or shrewd distribution among the growing number of scissors and paste media which will print anything that does not offend the obscenity laws?

(f) Are you selling a product or a reputation? Is your subject one that would be reflected by enquiries or simply by increasing approval of your organization?

(g) How many 'trade and technical' mentions equals one profile in the *Sunday Times* colour supplement? For that matter, how much work is necessary in either?

While this may sound discouraging, remember it is vital to appreciate that, in any work demanding creative skill and experience, many of the judgements remain qualitative. Always employ the best press-cutting service you can afford; you learn a good deal from the results. For example, if certain media consistently ignore your stories, you will want to know whether it is because your targeting is way off, or your style is not right for that sector. In each case, the remedy is obvious: improve your relationship with, and understanding of, the editor.

Demonstrable results are useful, provided their interpretation is honestly qualified, and the weekly circulation of clippings can be a helpful internal-communication exercise. However, it is much more valuable to study which editors come back for further information, or perhaps for an inclusive supplementary story. You can then judge the most productive areas on which to concentrate your attention in the future.

You can also make useful, if gross, comparisons between general sections of the press, e.g. the specialist trade or technical sections, and local or national newspapers. From this you can either reinforce success or strengthen weak areas, as appropriate.

Thus far we have only been considering the general run of press releases. What about special events, press conferences and facility visits, where you have more control of the media? Here the same general rules apply. Study of the results will soon show which journalists are interested in your activities and which are only there for the lunch. Perhaps more important, especially if you are entering a new area, are those who, reading the story in another publication, say 'Why wasn't I asked?'

Whatever the type of public relations activity, remember that it is always vital to ask yourself 'What is the basis of measurement effectiveness?' The marketing or sales departments' measurement systems may or may not be more quantitative than those used in public relations. But if PR has, as the objective, to promote goods or services, you will quickly learn where the best results are coming from, how well informed the enquiries are, and possibly what new areas you might well address yourself to.

If it is an image or a reputation you are concerned with, it is more difficult. Sixty successive 'mentions' in a national newspaper or in the *Farmer's Weekly* may or may not improve your standing. No one is going to write and say 'I saw your story in the *Blankshire Gazette* and I think you are wonderful'. Attitude surveys, before and after a campaign, can be useful, but how do you separate the effect of press activities, the work of the rest of the publicity mix above and below-the-line, the fortuitous £60m order from China and the appearance of your chairman on TV last Tuesday?

Again, overseas activities compound the difficulty. In one actual case a manufacturer of very specialized products embarked on a public-relations campaign with the objective of arousing interest on mainland Europe. An agency was engaged to generate feature articles – few, but in some technical depth – in selected media. Enquiries came in at an embarrassing rate, but the pressure on management and senior technical staff to clear the stories, as well as process the enquiries, led to the termination of the programme. The client was in fact frightened off by the success. Clearly the exercise produced results but how cost-effective was it? Could it have been more efficient with less effort? Were the selected media the best possible? No one will ever know. This example is not unique, for many an excellent campaign has foundered on rocks beyond the navigational range of the press office.

It is evident that one must monitor what one does as far as is reasonable, learn from mistakes, build on success. Keep the closest possible contact, on a personal basis, with the media. If they approve, you are almost certainly doing a good job. If not, you should not be doing it at all. Experience is, in this area, often a more accurate measure than a slide-rule. Take comfort from the knowledge that this is probably the last area where a computer can take over.

13.9   Case studies

13.9.1   British Bakeries Ltd

The objective of this company's public-relations campaign was to stimulate volume and reinforce its Mothers Pride Champion's market position. The strategy was to publicize a new advertising campaign featuring the children of sporting champions through trade and consumer media. The appointed PR agency (Leslie Bishop Company Ltd) worked in close liaison with the advertising agency (J. Walter Thompson) to establish precise details of the campaign and the commercial. The PR agency prepared photographic stills for supply to the media and identified key journalists in the media. All information was supplied under an embargo as a 'Sunday for Monday' story. The PR agency was also used to field national and regional media enquiries. The results of the campaign were impressive: there was mass coverage in target media (*The Sun*, *The Daily Mirror/Mail/Star* and *Express*), with stories featuring, among others, Frank Bruno's daughter, and the 'Champion' positioning of the brand was reinforced. J. Walter Thompson put a value of £1 million on the PR coverage!

13.9.2   The Nestlé Company Ltd

In a PR campaign for Nescafé, the objective was to build authority for the coffee with trade buyers and retailers. The strategy revolved around the production of an annual detailed review of the hot-beverages market. An edited version was created for independent retailers – even being translated into Gujarati for Asian retailers. This was publicized through trade and consumer media.

Mintel, market researchers, were contacted to conduct trade research into the hot-beverages market. The report was prepared to a 'user-friendly' design – with emphasis on fast access of facts for buyers. Copy was prepared by the PR agency and all production of the report was coordinated by it. Pre-written heavyweight features were negotiated with trade media, and the Gujarati version of the report was inserted in *Asian Trader* magazine. All information distributed was given a consumer slant and publicized through national and regional media.

Subsequent research of trade buyers and retailers confirmed that Nestlé was positioned as an authority on the coffee market. Furthermore, all company sales personnel were supplied with a valuable presentation tool. In this way consumers were encouraged to see coffee as the anytime, anywhere drink.

13.9.3   LRC Products

For their Durex brand of condoms, LRC Products wanted to create a campaign that communicated the quality and reliability of Durex in a modern context to young people, particularly young men, to encourage them to use condoms to prevent the spread of AIDS and unwanted pregnancies. The strategy was to devise two sponsorships that would reach a broad spectrum of younger customers, creating opportunities for face-to-face contact with potential customers, as well as achieving substantial media coverage. The first of the two sponsorship initiatives was the Durex/Suzuki Motor Cycle Racing Team.

Here, young riders who were excellent brand spokesmen were chosen to race at fifteen meetings throughout the year. There was a huge following among the relevant target audience at race meetings. The PR agency developed a whole range of merchandising items and provided a full media service at each of the fifteen race meetings.

The second of the sponsorship initiatives was the Durex Hot Air Balloon, which was designed in Durex livery, and a flying team was organized. The balloon first appeared at Cerne Abbas, Dorset, home of the Bronze Age hill drawing of a man who rose to fame when unwanted pregnancy and the AIDS risk were not headline material. The balloon was subsequently flown at major balloon meets, motorcycle races – where the Durex/Suzuki team were competing – and exhibitions. Again, the PR agency provided a full media service for each flight.

The results were impressive. Millions of people are estimated to have seen the Durex brand in a modern, exciting context. Safer sex education information had been provided in a non-dictatorial fashion. The national media coverage was impressive, with over 100 million opportunities to see/hear/view brand mentions as Durex was presented as a modern prestigious brand.

13.10   Summary

1   Editorial publicity consists of getting a company or its products featured in the media – newspapers, magazines, radio or TV.

2   Successful use of this approach involves:

   (a) Identifying the various 'publics' which need to be communicated with.
   (b) Compiling information which will be of interest to them.
   (c) Providing that information to the media in the most appropriate manner.

3   One useful pattern is the following seven-step process:

(a) State the problem or aim.
(b) Do the research.
(c) Identify the publics.
(d) Choose the appropriate media.
(e) Monitor the effects.
(f) Look to the future.
(g) Maintain financial checks.

4   Press releases, press conferences, etc. need professional manage-
    ment and the chapter discusses the best approaches.

14 Open the doors to the customers – showrooms, factory units, educational activities

14.1 An important part of below-the-line activities

As an extension of public-relations activities, inviting customers, current and prospective, to your company premises can have its own rewards. Getting customers to come to your showroom, for example, is a very good way of demonstrating a particular product or service to them first hand. A showroom is particularly relevant if the product (or products) is too bulky, impractical or the range too wide to demonstrate by other means. A car showroom is a classic example. However, one can think of a variety of other examples, from conservatories and garden furniture to domestic appliances and electronic equipment for home or business use. Here we are dealing with the essential link in the continuum between manufacturer and consumer.

A variety of above and below-the-line techniques can be employed to attract people to the showroom, from advertising, through the whole spectrum of media, to direct marketing and below-the-line sales promotion and publicity. Once the consumer is in the showroom, then, again, a whole variety of publicity techniques can be used to get him/her to make a purchase. Point-of-sale material is particularly important, although staff training and motivation as well as the dissemination of the appropriate information to customers can make the difference between success and failure.

Remember too that a showroom need not necessarily always be there to sell a product or service. It may have a key function in selling a corporate image. With environmental issues becoming more and more important as we approach the end of the twentieth century, many businesses and industries have set up their showrooms to allay fears of local people that the planned building project is not going to damage the total environment or the local area.

A shop window is the retailer's 'showroom', and this too needs to be made attractive to welcome people from the outside to the inside.

Banks, building societies, insurance offices, even estate agents, are realizing that the showroom concept is applicable not only to attract people in but also to create the environment and ambience where personal business can be discussed.

In the ever-changing face of the financial institutions, some banks are opening their doors for longer and longer periods to attract custom – from people who are in full-time employment, often away from their immediate neighbourhood, and unable to visit the high-street 'shop' during normal working hours Monday to Friday. While all cash transactions are now being computerized, and one can get cash, order a cheque book, get a statement, pay money into an account, and order other services, all while standing in the pouring rain, it is rewarding to be able to sit and discuss the range of financial services available in the relative comfort of the high-street showroom – and a showroom it is indeed! The 'product' is on display with a variety of 'life style' people, photographed and illustrated, enjoying the benefits of credit alongside appealing graphs and tables of financial rewards for investments and savings.

Building a showroom, in all its variety of guises, is not the only way of opening the doors to customers. Organizing groups of people to visit the factory can also bring valuable rewards, not only in building a corporate image but also in changing people's attitudes to a product. While not having the same mass audience as advertising, the message received by people visiting a factory can be stronger and longer lasting, and have strong influences on buyer behaviour. Those people who *do* come have been carefully selected.

Factory visits can accommodate only a finite number of visitors at any one time. It may be that rather than get a given group of people to visit your premises, especially if you have no premises worth showing, it is better that you go to visit them. Such visits are commonly centred around some form of educational activity at schools, colleges and universities, depending on the subject. In the business-to-business environment, face-to-face contact can be made at technical workshops and seminars, and often be centred around collective exhibitions, e.g. the Personal Computer show in Earls Court in 1988, where IBM ran some highly effective workshops and study days. Such educational events can of course also be run on a regular basis at one's own premises – again as IBM have done successfully for a number of years.

14.2 It has all to be paid for, then justified

Showrooms, factory visits, open days and many educational activities bring together customer and supplier, face-to-face, in a convivial environment where business can be conducted and product and service can be displayed, be seen being manufactured or presented, and studied in detail appropriate to the audience. As with any other publicity exercise, one must analyse the precise needs of a business to define the clear objectives of the venture.

It may be all very pleasant to have a group of industrial buyers visit your factory, but ask yourself beforehand why are you doing it? Would not some form of corporate hospitality event achieve those objectives more cheaply, more quickly, more meaningfully? Once you know what objectives you want to achieve, not only will you be able to look back afterwards to measure whether or not you have achieved them and say whether the open-day was a quantifiable success, you will also be able to formulate a plan directed towards a defined goal. Implementation is the key to the event but meticulous attention to detail always pays dividends; hence the need for carefully planning the event beforehand.

Value analysis of showrooms is much easier than value analysis of factory visits, open days and, especially, educational events. One can measure, for example, the sales from any particular showroom as an absolute financial yardstick, if the showroom actually takes orders for a product. Some showrooms are only there to demonstrate the product and direct order-taking occurs through other means. This is particularly true in industrial markets, where engineers may be required to visit a buyer's own premises to facilitate a full analysis of his needs, so that a specification can be written, and an order placed. The showroom is only used as the first point of contact, where the prospective buyer can see the product set up and operating.

Showrooms projecting a corporate image require evaluation on different criteria. The number of visitors is one measure, but is a rather abstract tool to measure the effectiveness of actually projecting the company's image. Number attending is only a function of the ability of the publicity methods employed to attract visitors. A properly conducted attitudinal survey in the hands of professional research workers is the only reliable way of ensuring that the right message has been put across, and then only if carried out both before and after the visit.

Factory visits and open days are more difficult to evaluate. If they are designed for specific customers, one can estimate the lifetime value of a visitor, rather as one can do in direct marketing terms. If you are running a factory visit for a group of people, and spending a certain amount on corporate hospitality around the visit, then it is fairly easy to define how much you are spending on each named customer, and you can compare that amount with the business done with that person over a defined period. In this way it is easy to evaluate whether or not the event is worth repeating on another group of people.

However, factory visits and open days, and even in some circumstances educational activities, have one thing in common that makes their total contribution to a business difficult to quantify: that is the knock-on effect of the event on other people the visitor meets. This goes back to the basics of all public-relations exercises, where one is trying to generate a favourable opinion among the publics of a given organization. Each event is likely to have repercussions outside the defined publics. If that knock-on effect is favourable, all well and good, but the impact of the effect, both on individuals and in the spread of the impact, in terms of the wider audience influenced is very difficult to measure. For this reason, if it is decided that factory visits or open days are appropriate to meet defined objectives, then it is likely that the best results will be seen in their broadest terms over a long period of time. One-off events only have a place if you are dealing with a defined audience of just a few people.

Thus in some cases showrooms, but more usually open days and factory visits, should be viewed and evaluated as part of the public-relations exercise, and not treated purely in isolation from the rest of the publicity of an organization.

14.3 Showrooms and shopfronts

14.3.1 Showrooms

In Chapter 12, on point of sale, we saw a good example of how various below-the-line publicity techniques came together to attract people to the car showroom when Audi/Volkswagen launched the 'Golf'. But car showrooms are only one type of showroom. British Nuclear Fuels (BNFL) use 'showrooms' as an integral part of its campaign to build public confidence in nuclear fuels as an essential energy source.

BNFL is pumping millions of pounds into its Sellafield public-relations campaign in a bid to win back support for controversial nuclear plant, particularly since 1983, when Sellafield had a radioactive leak. Since 1986 BNFL's efforts to turn around Sellafield's poor corporate image have attracted a number of awards and drawn an increasing number of visitors to the plant. The Visitors' Centre is Sellafield's showroom, because the nuclear plant itself could not take people inside quite as easily.

BNFL recognized that the 1983 leak at Sellafield highlighted the need for a more open corporate approach. Research had shown that there was a great deal of public misunderstanding, suspicion and concern at that time. BNFL realized that if it did not make efforts to win a significant degree of public acceptance, the whole future of its operation as a commercial and profit-making business would be at risk.

BNFL's campaign promoted Sellafield as a tourist attraction through national advertisements. Around £2 million a year is now spent on advertising, mostly through television, not only putting across a corporate message but also inviting people to the showroom. The advertising has created a general belief that Sellafield is not as remote as might have been imagined, not a barbed-wire fortress with people walking around in asbestos suits waving Geiger counters. BNFL wants people to see Sellafield as a place where any member of the public can happily visit with his/her family, to judge the acceptability and the safety of the operation.

Rather than run its own research into the success of its showroom operation, where results can, with the best of intentions, be interpreted to support preconceived BNFL ideas, it commissioned an independent exit poll at Sellafield specifically to test the Centre's effectiveness in changing public opinion. Initial results showed that 59 per cent of the people entering the Centre said they were well-disposed towards the nuclear industry, and, on leaving, this figure rose to 79 per cent.

14.3.2 Shopfronts

A shopfront is an important way to publicize a business, right in front of those people who are most likely to have the most direct influence on the success or otherwise of a retail business venture – the shoppers in the street. Initially customers will judge retailers and their businesses by what they see first – the shopfront and the window display. One only has to look into Harrods' or Selfridge's shop windows to see the contribution the shopfront can make to the corporate image of the retailer and to see how inviting the shop-window dressers make the merchandise. Compare them to your local gents' outfitters to see the stark contrast. The shopfront, by speaking volumes about a business, will either invite or discourage business.

The more retailers can enhance their business, the greater the rewards, naturally enough. The potential to increase business can start from day 1; some consider an investment in an improved shopfront the best single investment a retail company can make.

Some shopfitters are able to replace the old shopfront in 1 day, limiting closure, if any, and maintaining stock security at the same time. In most cases the shop will not have to close during installation, and trade can continue normally; experience shows that the inquisitive tend to 'call in' during alterations to find out what is going on.

'The cost of a new shopfront can be self-liquidating', says a brochure from one shopfitters. 'Through our finance schemes you can spread your investment over up to 5 years and thus you only pay out of increased business, not out of current cashflow'. In reply to the question 'What will it cost?' the brochure continues: 'The answer is nothing! If you study the examples below (Table 14.1) you will see how the shopfront is paid for out of increased business. Our designers will cost accurately your investment so you get the best return possible.'

This all sounds very plausible. Success is dependent on two things, ensuring that the gain in business is 10 per cent every week from the day the shopfront is fitted, and ensuring that you have a fixed interest loan at 7.5 per cent at the outset. These calculations will certainly need to be altered to accommodate the high interest rates of the early 1990s. As always, buyer beware!

Table 14.1 *Possible cash-flow contribution per week (pw) from installing a new shopfront.*

Turnover scale	Outlet A	Outlet B	Outlet C
Per week T/O	£1000	£2000	£4000
Gross profit	25%	35%	18%
Profit per week	£250	£700	£720
10% increase	£25	£70	£72
Cost of shopfront	£3500	£3500	£3500
Payback	33 mths	12 mths	12 mths
Profit on return	37.1%	104%	105%
Bank/building society interest	7.5%	7.5%	7.5%
Finance over 3 yrs	£24pw	£24pw	£24pw
Cashflow contribution	+£1pw	+£46pw	+£48pw

14.4 Factory openings

The building of a new factory or a major extension provides the opportunity to generate enthusiasm and goodwill both among staff and externally among customers, as well as generate interest in the press and on radio and television. As for any large-scale operation affecting many people from different departments and also different walks of life, it is essential to produce comprehensive plans well in advance, and 6 months is not an overestimate, particularly if there is a VIP or Royal as opener.

Arrangements in a large factory are complex, and the cooperation of a great number of people is essential. It is important to include on the planning board of a factory opening the most senior executives in each department. The apportioning of personal responsibility is essential for the efficient running of the operation. Key executives must be allocated to such matters as transport, security, catering, cleaning and painting, press, unveiling, public-address system, signboards, first aid, publications, gifts or mementoes, special arrangements for VIPs, protocol and precedence, trade-union relations, technical explanations, tour parties and even lavatories!

The following may serve as a checklist:

1. Establish clearly what is the purpose of the open day and who is to be invited. Is it for the local residents, the press, employees' families, or who?

2. Issue tickets/invitations in advance, so that you can stick to the optimum number of visitors, and circulate them well ahead of the day.

3. Issue programmes of events and maps as necessary, not only to visitors but also to the organizing team.

4. Brief all guides.

5. Check with appropriate departments what work will be in progress; check also on first-aid facilities and insurances, etc.

6. Select an opening time appropriate to the guests. Saturday is ideal for families but not for journalists.

7. Catering must match the guests, time of day and quality of event. Warn the caterers or canteen well ahead of the day. Make it clear whether refreshments are free or not, and watch licensing laws if alcohol is sold.

8. Ensure that the car parks are clearly signposted and adequate. Is there a need for attendants?

9. Invitations to the media must be sent well in advance and chased up closer to the event. Assign people to be specifically responsible for entertaining the media.

10. Anticipate the need for special clothing and/or protective headgear, glasses, shoe covers, etc. if applicable.

11. Entertaining may include children's amusements and, for older children who are inquisitive, sufficient sample information to satisfy them.

12. Finally, rehearse:

(a) Can the signposts be followed? Check they are in place *the* morning of the open day too.
(b) Where do people assemble?
(c) Can they hear the speakers?
(d) Is there adequate seating, lavatories, and so on?

A rehearsal is particularly important, and must simulate as realistically as possible the conditions that will apply on the day.

The results of factory openings are hard to measure, but that 100 or so of a company's most important customers and outside contacts should think and talk a company for a whole day has clearly very great potential. But what of the costs? Table 14.2 presents a checklist to help you budget.

14.5 Factory tours

One need not have a full blown open day to justify taking a group of people round a factory. Quite apart from the opening of a factory, there are often valuable opportunities in organizing a regular programme of visits and tours. If done at all, they must be done well: planning and execution must be immaculate, and visits must not interfere with production. Care is necessary to ensure that tours are not too much about the company and its processes, but rather tailored to the interests of a particular group. People are impressed by a programme that avoids delays or too much walking. They also require an adequate number of guides to ensure they receive personal attention.

Pharmaceutical companies often arrange factory visits for specific groups of key customers – doctors, pharmacists and veterinary surgeons. Pharmaceutical manufacturers may develop a unique compound that they patent, license, take to market and continue marketing under a particular brand name until their exclusive patent on their manufacturing technique expires. While the original patent may be for a period of 25 years, the sand starts to run out of the timer when it is granted at the early stage of discovery. A pharmaceutical compound may take 15 years to bring to market. This period represents a massive investment in time, money and resources and may not necessarily produce a marketable drug. The pharmaceutical companies have only maybe 10 years in the market with a particular compound to recoup their high research and development costs on all compounds, successful or otherwise, before their patent expires.

Although the National Health Service medicine bill is only 10 per cent of its total costs, every effort is made by the NHS to reduce

Table 14.2 *Open-day budget checklist*

Item	£	Item	£
Refreshments		Invitation cards	
		Advance publicity	
Prizes		Posters	
Marquees		Outside caterers	
Photography		Employees' overtime and loss of work	
Signs, notices, maps		Postage, telephone	
Product samples		Brochures and programmes	
Children's entertainment		Product demonstrations	
Hire of special clothing		Public-address-system hire	
VIP entertainment		Celebrity expenses	
VIP expenses: hotel, travel		Additional insurance	
Crockery hire, glasses, etc.		Extra transport costs	
Hire of toilets		Mementoes, car stickers, leaflets	

expenditure on medicines. This means that the pharmaceutical manufacturers are hard-pressed to recoup their investment. Once the patent expires, other manufacturers may 'jump on the bandwagon' and produce a generic equivalent of the branded original compound. Quite naturally the generic manufacturer does not have such high developmental costs and so can afford to undercut the branded product's price. Moreover, the market for any given drug will spiral down in price as cheaper 'parallel imports' come in from overseas territories, where possibly the manufacturing standards are not as rigorous as in the UK, and labour may quite possibly be cheaper.

So how does the original branded manufacturer supply the original compound at a realistic price and still claim added value? Among the many techniques available is for the manufacturer to provide a level of service far beyond that provided by the generic manufacturer or the parallel importer. Within the framework of added value comes that massive R & D facility still working away on novel compounds against the diseases of tomorrow and also that considerable manufacturing plant producing products combating today's diseases around the world. A well-organized and interesting site visit is one way the company can put across the simple, yet so often unrealized, message that if you buy branded products, you pay a little more, but it is your investment into the solutions of tomorrow's problems; buying generics and parallel imports only feeds the scavengers of the pharmaceutical industry, which are not investing in original research.

Most medical or veterinary practitioners have no real appreciation of what goes into the research and development of a compound, through the sterile production processes in the massive vats and retorts, to the sterile packing and filling before distribution across to the world's markets. No presentation, photograph or film can take the place of actually going through a complete change of clothing, sterile scrub, and then into a protective 'environment suit' with its own air supply, before going into the specially controlled production units. Such events are truly memorable and make the message stick.

For important groups, a great deal of benefit can be obtained by arranging for some unusual feature, such as the change of clothing mentioned. People visiting a factory must be made to feel they are really important, which of course they are.

14.6 Corporate hospitality in front of and behind the factory gate

A number of other ways in which people visiting a factory can be made to feel especially important all relate to transport. Each is worthy of special mention.

14.6.1 Special coaches

Firms are now operating coach and bus services with full conference and meeting facilities on board. So even if your factory is in some far-flung part of the British Isles, you can still arrange for visitors to meet in a central place, collect them on the special coach and convey them to the factory. On board you have facilities to entertain them as well as present films and videos as appropriate, all designed to make the otherwise rather arduous journey to your factory or other venue that little bit more memorable and useful. Naturally, if the coach should be delayed in traffic, you can phone ahead while your guests relax around the table.

14.6.2 British Rail Pullman coaches

As with the road coaches and buses, British Rail offers special rolling stock that can be hired for the journey or the week. This allows similar facilities to the road vehicles, except you can carry more people in one 'room'. Furthermore, it is possible to organize overnight accommodation on board too, especially if you want to take your visitors to more than one site, each separated by some distance most conveniently covered by rail. If and when the Channel Tunnel is completed, this form of *en route* presentation/entertainment/accommodation will become continental.

British Rail hired out its Pullman coaches in the summer of 1989 to form a travelling school. For 2 weeks the pupils were given classes on board, while the train journeyed between places of particular geographical or historical interest. Similar schemes are possible for business use, if such schemes are of value and a route can be agreed. (Trust House Forte used the scheme to reward certain executives by taking them and their spouses on a 10-day 'adventure' tour, taking in West End theatres and salmon-fishing in Invernesshire, travelling between venues on the Pullman coaches.)

14.6.3 Overseas trips

With so many regional airports developing and airfares becoming so competitive, it is possible to take parties to see other major factory sites, particularly in Europe. With the local expenses picked up by the parent company, UK subsidiaries are able to finance travel to the parent-company's factories, the expense per person being accommodated by the 'lifetime value' of the selected delegate.

Chartering one's own aircraft can also be considered, provided the numbers are high enough and all are prepared to travel to the particular airfield that operates the charter. Airport taxes are too high at Heathrow and Gatwick to bring chartering within most company's budget, but other airports, such as Southend, run 'short hop' charters to mainland Europe at rates competitive to scheduled airfares, providing you can guarantee filling the aircraft.

14.7 Educational activities

14.7.1 Schools

Many organizations will welcome visits from schools as part of a long-term publicity exercise. In early years of schooling children may take on a variety of projects and write to various businesses and organizations in search of information. For example, a traditional project is to write about 'The Story of Chocolate', following the cocoa plantations, shipping, and production to the finished confectionery. Children are encouraged to write to Mars, Cadbury and Rowntree for information. Local schools are encouraged to form an annual trip to the chocolate factories at, for example, York, Bournville, Norwich, etc., and see the end product being manufactured. Naturally such public-relations exercises are useful in building brand loyalty at an early age.

Other local businesses may run visits for local schools and colleges as part of a recruitment drive. Norwich Union, for example, organises visits for sixth-formers and gives them a presentation on insurance and assurance. This is not only because Norwich Union recruits a number of school-leavers with good 'A' levels each year, but also because it recognizes that when these sixth-formers eventually gain full-time employment, they will be considering insurance, mortgage endowments, life assurance etc., and therefore will be well-disposed towards the company they know.

Non-profit organizations, such as the police, road-safety organizations, etc., recognize the value of interacting with schools. They too take the opportunity of arranging school trips to see their organization operative. In the case of the police much can be done at this early age to help foster a good understanding and respect for the police service with schoolchildren. This goes some way towards breaking down the prejudices built out of ignorance. Again, such work also has a useful role to play in recruitment of school-leavers. Road-safety messages are particularly important and many groups, like the Cycling Proficiency Association, regularly run courses for schoolchildren.

14.7.2 Technical colleges, universities

Many local businesses and industries work in close liaison with colleges and universities, not only as part of the education process, but also as part of their own recruitment drive. For example, students studying agricultural sciences at colleges and universities would make visits to a whole variety of businesses and organizations, for example:

(a) Local artificial-insemination centres.
(b) Veterinary investigation centres.
(c) Ministry of Agriculture, Fisheries and Food research centres.
(d) Agricultural development and advisory service centres.
(e) Special laboratories.
(f) Industrial factories and research centres.
(g) Food marketing boards, e.g. Milk Marketing Board's dairies.

As with schools, the visits may be 'both ways', students visiting the organization to see the facilities, and, in return, guest speakers being invited to lecture at the colleges and university.

14.7.3   Business education

As we discussed when we looked at incentives for sales staff and for retailers' staff, there are many ways in which reward-linked learning can be used to help people learn about a company's products. In the business-to-business environment such educational activities are very important in some areas. Postgraduate education for health-care professionals is financed principally by the pharmaceutical companies, which are keen to be recognized not only for providing pure-product training but also for providing broader educational material in other areas.

Seminars, workshops, and study days are many and varied, particularly in the area of information technology. Attendance may be by specific or general invitation and, following the example of IBM at its massive annual UK exhibition each year, are free. In a more general respect some companies in the business-to-business environment are supplying some fairly straightforward products and, rather than spend all their below-the-line publicity monies on the 'traditional' techniques, are prepared to take a fairly bold step and pool their resources and run educational seminars for their business customers. Rather than use the forum of the seminar to provide product knowledge, the company may run seminars covering other business matters, i.e. accounting, finance, personnel management.

Suppliers servicing business clients stand to gain from such exercises in a variety of ways. The supplier will be seen as not merely content to supply a product but also to be committed to the business success of that client. Put simply, if that client's business succeeds, then so does the supplier's. Such seminars can therefore pay considerable dividends in terms of corporate image building.

Case study: BET
International services company BET underwent a period of rapid change after 1985, buying and shedding companies at a rapid rate. As a result, it needed to raise its profile among its private shareholders, many of whom held shares in companies bought out by BET and were unfamiliar with the extent of BET's empire, which included Initial, Anglian Windows, United Transport, Drinkmaster and Boulton & Paul (Joinery). Rather than hold an AGM, where the shareholders would be expected to come to BET, the company initiated a 5-year programme in which it would go to its private shareholders. Through a series of shareholders' roadshows, called the BET Experience, it aimed to have covered every region of the UK by 1991. Rather than choosing more traditional venues – such as hotels and conference centres – for these events, the company has leaned towards the more unusual locations.

The first BET Experience in 1986 was held in an old Leeds tramshed; subsequent venues included a London Docklands warehouse (before its demolition) and the twenty-fifth floor of a new office building in the US. Using such venues had a dual purpose for BET: to lure curious shareholders and to personalize BET's image as a pioneering company with an 'air of ability, experience and slight quirkiness', to quote a spokesman. BET accepted that it had been hard to quantify the success of the BET Experience, but research showed that in the areas visited, BET maintained, if not increased its level of shareholders.

BET maximized the return on its events by using the same venue or location for as many different meetings as possible. For example, the biggest BET Experience of the 1980s was held in Bristol at a cost of £250,000, but it included:

(a) A shareholders' day.
(b) A customers' day.
(c) A sales-management conference for 200 delegates.
(d) A conference for BET's top 200 managers worldwide.
(e) A city analysts' briefing.
(f) A financial directors' meeting.

With the 1989 annual turnover of £2.2bn, such events are affordable. While the BET Experience budget was minute compared with the amount spent on above-the-line advertising, BET realised that emotionally it played a very important role and was an integral part of their communication programme.

14.8 Summary

1   Bringing customers and others to our showrooms, factories, etc. creates special opportunities for communicating with them.
2   As with all publicity, defining the objectives, meticulous planning and tight control of budgets (see checklist on p. 336) are essential.
3   Bringing visitors by special transport such as executive coaches, Pullman Coach or jet aircraft adds another dimension and encourages attendance.
4   Measurement of results can be difficult, but, as always, is vital.

15 Exhibitions, shows and travelling displays

15.1 High exhibition spending in UK

In 1986 the Incorporated Society of British Advertisers (ISBA) published the *Exhibition Expenditure Survey 1985*. This showed that by 1985 companies were spending £192m on taking space and constructing stands at exhibitions – 25 per cent more than in 1983. The expenditures made in 1985 were reported to be a consolidation of gains made in 1984, when Britain hosted a number of international exhibitions. These figures do not include companies spending at overseas exhibitions, neither are expenditures on agricultural shows and private exhibitions included.

According to *The Exhibitor UK Show Comparison Survey* published in 1989, the figure for expenditure on exhibition stands and space alone had reached £300m (see Figure 15.1). The rapid gains over previous years is due to the inclusion of agricultural shows such as 'the Royal Show', as well as such major animal industry events as the Pig Fare, The Poultry Fare (which, incidentally,was an even larger Pig & Poultry Fare in 1992), and so on.

The ISBA report said that the increase in total expenditure on exhibitions was accompanied by increased selectivity by individual companies in how they spent their money. Traditionally accepted attitudes towards stand costs appear to be hardening. Despite an increase in the number of companies exhibiting, the proportionally lower increase in individual spending indicates a reduction in the size and spending on each stand. The use of larger exhibition centres is increasing, with some groups of exhibitions not enjoying the growth they had perhaps expected.

The ISBA report also looked at private exhibitions, including specialized in-store and 'in-precinct' events, as well as hotel venues. This sector showed a modest 2 per cent growth in 1985 over 1984. If one included agricultural shows and private exhibitions with all other events, the ISBA report claimed that British companies spent more than £350m in 1985 on all kinds of exhibitions against a *total* advertising expenditure of more than £5bn. The society said that more was being spent on exhibitions than on advertising in magazines, trade and technical journals, directories, posters or radio.

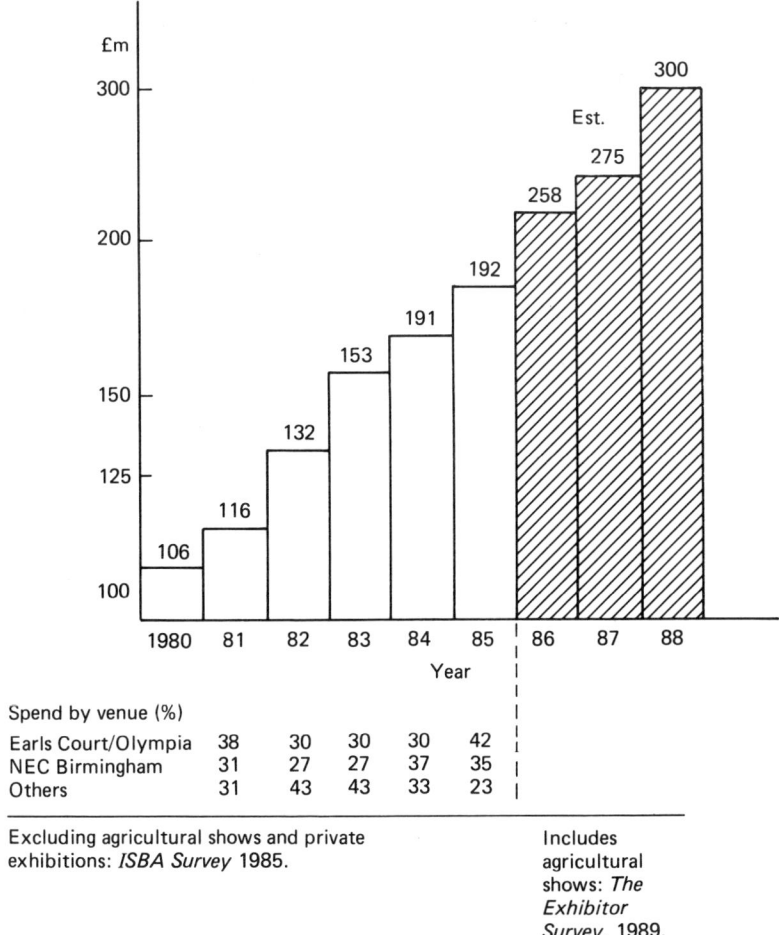

Figure 15.1 *Total expenditure on exhibitions and shows in the UK. Data combined from ISBA Survey, 1985 and The Exhibitor Survey, 1989. Note the growing popularity of Earls Court/Olympia and the NEC, Birmingham*

Exhibitors were becoming more cost-conscious, with increased use of modular stand construction and less use of a high design content. Stand construction, for instance, rose by just 25 per cent in the 4 years to 1985, whereas historically a growth nearer 40 per cent would have been anticipated, taking rises in labour costs into account over the same period. Furthermore, exhibitors themselves appeared to be altering the traditional purchasing procedures in many shows – not making early bookings, but waiting to negotiate rates nearer closing dates.

15.2 Why exhibit – and at which exhibition?

Answers may vary from a detailed exposition of the market place and target-audience profile, to the lame 'because our competitors will be there'. Not that there is anything wrong with a flag-waving exercise, provided this objective is established initially. One example of a strong presence was provided by the Lawson Marden Group's stand at 'Pakex', (LMG has a regular position at the tri-annual NEC packaging industry show). The plan was to promote its position in the market place as the leading packaging innovator; the answer was a show stopping wall 20m (over 65 feet) wide by 6m (around 20 ft) high of industry awards collected by the group.

How closely should an exhibition stand reflect a corporate image? Can it do so creatively and still be entirely practical? And how effective is a stand when constructed entirely of the company's own product, like Pilkington's glass stand, in actual marketing terms? While an innovative and exciting stand design can catch the eye, it is more important that a coherent message is projected – and an organization's corporate identity starts, from the audience's point of view, with its graphics. From a technical point of view it is important that if a company's logo type is to be reproduced, it is done so correctly. What is true for a letterhead must be true for a three-dimensional structure; many companies such as Jaguar, Mitsubishi and Textron, issue their exhibition design consultants with style manuals to keep everything in harmony.

Flag-waving, and thereby projecting a certain company image, is only the first in a list of a dozen reasons why companies exhibit. Let us consider the full list of benefits of exhibitions:

1 Publicizing the company image – a long-term benefit.
2 Meeting existing customers and raising their interest in the products. This is often the best source of new business for a company.
3 Meeting potential customers; identifying new sales areas/outlets.
4 Introducing new products/services.
5 Preparing the ground for future sales by inviting the appropriate authorities, associations, ministries to the stand for talks.
6 Supporting local agents, evaluating their effectiveness, possibly appointing new agents.
7 Giving lectures/meeting top technicians.
8 Aiding market research and long-range planning.
9 Assessing performance of competitors in terms of product, service and presentation.
10 To take orders.

11 Products can actually be seen and sometimes even demonstrated.
12 Many of the prospective customers are in a buying mood, and may often be people the exhibitor's sales force might not normally meet.

Remember, there are many publications listing the various types of exhibition and how to exhibit, but it cannot be stressed too strongly that exhibitions (and trade receptions for that matter) are only one facet of the publicity channels available, and as such must not be thought of in isolation but as the focus of a total marketing plan. For example, it may be that a press-advertising and direct-mail campaign will be used during the build-up to an exhibition, with direct personal calls as the follow-up. The publicity scheme must be planned at the same time as the exhibition (or reception), as the latter play a significant part in the final results that have to be evaluated.

Analysing the plan in the light of the results obtained may well reveal weaknesses in unexpected publicity areas, which will need amendment in the future. Every time you exhibit, the results must be evaluated to ensure that the exhibition you believe to be the best one for your specific product or service is in fact the best, and that your presentation encourages the visitor to stop and ask questions. The fact that your competitors always support a certain exhibition is not a good reason for exhibiting, except possibly on prestige grounds or to prevent, in some sensitive areas, your competitors insinuating that you are no longer interested in these fields of business.

So, which exhibition? This is often the hardest question of all to answer. Shows proliferate in most industries, and new venues mushroom. Successful shows grow with success, taking in a wider scope (and often becoming less and less useful as they do so to any but the multi-product giants). The *UK Show Comparison Survey*, published by *The Exhibitor*, September 1989, was more than just a listing; it compared shows within a given business sector, and gave a complete analysis of all the shows available within one volume. The 1989–90 issue was extended to cover every industry. One can choose the exhibitions in which to participate from reliable, impartial market data. The *Survey* will answer key questions about the massive variety of UK shows and exhibitions, for example:

1 How many visitors from the UK?
2 How many visitors from overseas?
3 How many exhibitors?
4 Cost per square metre?
5 Type of visitors?
6 Type of show?

7 Duration of show?

In practice there are no better pointers (in order of importance) than:

- Previous participation in an earlier show in the series.
- Previous attendance as a visitor.
- Advice by agents, distributors, local regional offices.
- Media and organizers' reviews of previous shows in the series.
- Organizers' promotion for the next event.

New exhibitions obviously demand an act of faith, though the calibre of the organizer and the venue will help you decide, plus, perhaps, a 'feel' for the occasion.

15.3 How much should you spend?

Setting outline budgets comes down largely to experience, and if it is not available from your archives, then it ought to come from a consultant having broad (and current, given the rapid rate of change in the industry) experience of the total exhibitions scene. Rule of thumb solutions can be dangerously misleading, with costs ranging widely with style of presentation and nature or remoteness of venue. Floor area may not even be the overriding parameter, since the cost of a display relying mainly on graphics is more closely related to size and nature of the graphic panels.

In exhibition design, like anything else, you get what you pay for; and exhibiting, unless you settle for poorly printed posters stuck onto otherwise bare walls, is not cheap. Furthermore, with such a highly visible end product, cutting corners is not to be recommended, as an under-budgeted stand is instantly recognizable. Generally a small stand, well done, can be extremely effective. A bigger stand is better, but a bigger stand, badly done, can be counter-productive, especially if all the space boasts is a solitary literature rack and a couple of chairs in an empty area of carpet.

There is not such a thing as an average-priced stand. A set of smart graphic panels on a shell-scheme, costing just a few hundred pounds, can be just as effective in the right context as a multi-million, multi-storey, custom-built showpiece – there are no hard and fast rules.

If it is decided to separate the design and construction functions, it will make a difference to costs. With a design and build contractor, the construction costs are fixed as part of the package – and the company's overheads. Exhibition-design consultants have a free hand to advise the client impartially, and to sub-contract the construction according to the needs of the client. If you choose to go it alone, design your own stand and negotiate direct with a contractor. You are likely to find that contractors' estimates vary as much as the proverbial length of string.

When it comes to costing a stand, an experienced designer will have his own yardstick. Unfortunately it is rarely as simple as X square metres equalling Y hundred pounds in costs. Although it is possible to get a rough estimate once the services and fittings (such as electrical and network cabling, floors, ceilings and lights) have been specified, any 'special requirements' can distort the picture out of all proportion. For example, Mitsubishi once specified glassfibre in the construction, but it turned out to be so expensive, even when sourced through professional marine suppliers, that wood was substituted to bring the project back on budget.

With a long-term (say 3-year) 'rolling' programme, it is still necessary to firm up the exhibition plan and budget for each forthcoming financial year. It is wise to set aside a contingency fund since, even in a long-timescale business, unexpected and worthwhile opportunities do arise at short notice. Selecting an exhibition to shortlist, with an outline budget, implies a decision on style of stand, in which context the nature of an exhibition is as important in setting the level of participation as is your company's standing in the industry or the impact you seek. A 'big' show implies greater effort by the competition and a larger, more expensive stand to avoid your being overwhelmed; whereas a modest budget can make real impact if some of the exhibitors are likely to be seen behind green baize-covered tables.

Apart from the stand space and the exhibition material that goes on it, there may be further publicity back-up to consider. For example:

(a) The exhibition-catalogue advertising.
(b) Press advertising.
(c) Special literature.
(d) Direct marketing: mail and telephone.
(e) Public relations.
(f) Specific audio-visual material.
(g) Interactive computer programmes.
(h) Holograms.
(i) New photography.
(j) Uniforms for hostesses.
(k) Promotional gifts/giveaways.
(l) Car parking.
(m)Tickets, invitations to customers.

All these, and many more, which form no part of the stand itself, must be considered as likely commitments that had better be thought through and their budgets accepted or rejected at the time of deciding on participation. If not, they may be overlooked, remembered too late, or skimped, because no budget exists to do them justice.

Picture the scene. You've booked space at an important trade exhibition, and designed an eye-catching stand, which looks stunning on paper. Your people arrive at the exhibition venue and proceed to erect the stand, only to find some unforeseen problems. Someone has either erred on the generous side when giving stand measurements, or not realized that there's a heating outlet or pillar intruding into your space, and there is no way of trimming any inches off your bulging stand to squeeze it into the allocated area without compromising the visual image.

If you think that is an unlikely scenario, think again. Purpose-built stands all too often fail to fit the space available. So, unless, your stand is sufficiently flexible to allow for sections to be removed or rearranged, consider using modular, easily adjustable exhibition systems.

Apart from the £300m or so spent on stand space, it has been estimated that UK exhibitors spent a further £301m[1] in 1988 displaying their wares. Big business indeed! Since it can cost anything from a few tens of pounds to £1000 per square metre just to hire the space, no one can afford to get it wrong. So how do you go about designing and building an efficient exhibition stand that will be sufficiently versatile for multi-site use, simple to erect in a short space of time, and made to a tight budget? As the overriding aim is to create a display stand that will entice people to visit it, you must first define:

- Accurate stand dimensions, as the earlier example illustrated.
- The organizer's terms and conditions on displays: restrictions may cover not only dimensions but also the types of exhibit permitted, e.g. noise restrictions.
- Whether your stand is an island site, i.e. in the middle of the exhibition hall, or a shell site (with one, two or three fixed walls), as design alters accordingly.

For system selection the main criteria are price, appearance and function. For those who want to exhibit on a regular basis and get good value for money, the modular system route is the one to follow. With little time to put up your stand, simplicity of construction and erection are key issues. By going the modular route you may be able to get more for your money, the 'kit' being adaptable to a variety of exhibitions, and you can mix and match from event to event.

15.4   Site selection

Your company may have one of the most stunningly designed – and expensive – exhibition stands ever seen. But it is a mistake to believe that these factors alone can achieve the required impact among visitors. Stand design, publicity, and on-stand promotions all make essential contributions to the 'pull' of a stand. A recent survey among exhibitors by the National Exhibitors Association, however, identified site selection as the single most important factor affecting the success of an exhibition stand. From this survey it has been possible to draw a number of conclusions:

15.4.1   *The frontage factor*

Organizers plan exhibition spaces to maximize the profit from the area available for hire. Secure as elongated a site, with as wide a frontage, as you can afford: the longer it takes for a visitor to walk by the stand, the greater the chance of attracting attention. The wide, shallow stand places the graphics on the back wall closer to the visitors, making it psychologically less threatening for them to walk on the stand.

15.4.2   *Confluence considerations*

Increase frontage by selecting a corner, end, or island site. These give, respectively, two, three and four times the frontage, usually for no extra cost. If these sites are also at the confluence of two or more walkways, they act as natural meeting points and so benefit from increased traffic flow. Note that island sites need to impact from four directions; small numbers of sales staff also find the barrage of visitors particularly tiring.

15.4.3   *Proximity philosophy*

Proximity to competitors needs careful consideration. The NEA survey showed that 80 per cent of exhibitors picked their sites in the general area of competitors, 12 per cent liked to be 'very close', but 8 per cent wanted to be as far away as possible.

Logically the leading companies are likely to draw high-quality visitor traffic wherever they site themselves. Smaller companies might gain by 'piggy-backing', but being too close can rebound badly if the leader constantly steals the limelight. Further, some customers may be coy about being seen talking to one supplier in full view of another. For the leading company the strategy is more complex: locating far away from competitors denies one the advantages of the follow-my-leader philosophy, though some of the larger companies have taken this one step further and have left conventional shows, setting up their own private events.

15.4.4   Peripheral clustering

Exhibitors selling goods and services peripheral to the main thrust of the show will benefit by clustering in one area. Increased traffic flow is an advantage, and the show of strength may force buyers to take the sector more seriously and allot time to visit it.

15.4.5   Affinity grouping

Many exhibitors display products or services that have a natural affinity to others on show, without necessarily being directly competitive. For example, the supplier of car-seat covers might find it useful to be next to the producer of car seats at a motor show.

15.4.6   Pilgrim's progress

Some exhibitors, such as IBM, run seminars in an attempt to entice more senior and committed buyers to the show. The aisles leading to the seminar or conference rooms may therefore have an above-average quality visitor traffic, thus offering premium sites.

15.4.7   Perimeter points

Less than 10 per cent of visitors to a show will be professional buyers. Most visitors walk round a show once to see who is there, and then return to find the stand that caught their eye. Most will not record the stands on their show map, and therefore may only bother to find those exhibitors in easy-to-find spots. The easiest to find are in fact on the perimeter of the show. But book early, these are usually the first to be sold.

15.4.8 Gratification positions

In the NEA survey nearly 45 per cent of exhibitors said they would like a site near a restaurant. However, only 23 per cent voted to be near a bar. What of the toilets? Perhaps the ideal is to be close to such services as the restaurant/bar but not too close.

15.4.9 Front of house fallacy

If your stand is close to the entrance, visitors will see it first, and organizers cash in on such supposedly dominant positions, especially to industry leaders that are taken in by fanciful notions of prestige, awareness, and high profile. The fact is that the front of show stands probably get fewer interested visitors than almost any other position. Visitors do not want to be stopped as soon as they arrive; they are keen to get inside and have a look around. Equally, having made a decision to leave, the visitor's mind is already on a train, boat or plane, and it will be very difficult for any stands near the entrance/exit to change this attitude.

15.5 Attracting people to the stand

It really is not difficult to attract crowds of people to an exhibition stand, but do you really want to? One shower manufacturer used two Amazonian girls in tiny bikinis to run out on stage every hour, on the hour, take a shower to music and run off. The audience blocked the aisles but the majority of the visitors had very little interest in plumbing, and all the promotion did was to lower the quality of the audience.

Similarly exhibitions offering free glasses of wine to visitors indiscriminately, or running a 'leave your business card for a free champagne draw', have only themselves to blame if all they get is a bunch of alcoholics on their mailing list. Serious buyers do not generally part with their previous business cards just for the chance of a free bottle of bubbly, whatever the vintage. They're too busy buying from someone else. It all depends on the objectives.

Too many exhibitors approach an exhibition in the spirit of 'have to' rather than 'want to', and do not give enough thought to whom they really want to attract. There may be occasions where an indiscriminate attraction is justified, but this is generally where *every* visitor is a potential customer. Very few exhibitors are in that position, and very few shows deliver that quality of audience. Over-attraction at most trade events is expensive, pointless, and self-defeating.

One exhibition organizer estimated that the average visitor to an exhibition spent 4 hours and 20 minutes or so at an event, including taking in some lunch or refreshment. If there are 1000 stands, how can the visitor fit them all in? It is well recognized that people are curious, but the curiosity factor has to be skilfully managed at exhibitions, whether by using competitions, personalities signing autographs, or the stand design itself.

Creating a good stand is perhaps the most difficult design job there is, because of all the restrictions there are. Yet a good stand has a definite impact on the sales staff – they do perform better. Many companies hire professionals of one sort or another to attract crowds rather than attend to the design elements of their stand. Moreover, the biggest mistake many companies make is to expect the professional attraction to do all the selling for the sales force. The attraction should be the first stage in a logical progression aimed at drawing visitors *to* the stand, separating out those with a real need for the product or service on offer, and then drawing on to the stand those of interest.

Sadly, many companies employ expensive entertainers who are largely wasted. An example is the top magician who is paid a large sum of money to perform a stage act every hour. Like the girls in the shower, 'The Great Maroo' pulled in the crowds, including neighbouring exhibitors, who drifted away shaking their heads in disbelief and wonderment.

Entertaining the masses, however, is not cost-effective marketing, and the better use of a magician would hinge around some close-up magic linked to the product or service being offered, and which actually leaves the buyer wanting more information. Another clever use of magicians is to include a simple product demonstration into their repertoire of tricks, thus ensuring that the all-important benefit of actually buying the product or service is reinforced, rather than hidden, by the magic. Alternatively, the benefits can be built into the tricks: for example, rising and falling pom-poms mirroring the ups and downs of market forces and being used to show how a company's products or services can keep profits high and costs low.

But you do not have to use a magician. For example, at the 1983 home entertainment show, Memorex audio-cassette tapes were cashing in on a very successful commercial, which featured Ella Fitzgerald breaking a glass as she hit a top note. Memorex held demonstrations every 2 hours, shattering a few glasses, and it attracted people. So successful was the attraction that they increased the frequency of the demonstration to every half hour; the glasses smashed were not costly compared to the impact.

Similarly British Gypsum once had a great success by simply taking along some craftsmen to demonstrate the use of a new plasterboard, making sure there were enough TV monitors to enable a wide audience to see other people at work. It has been said that demonstrations rank as an exhibition's unique selling proposition, and no other publicity medium gives companies such an opportunity. Use it wisely.

When professionals have been employed as attention-getters, they should always be used in conjunction with, and not to replace, the sales force. Magicians can get sales staff into the act to complete the trick and thereby forge the link between sellers and buyers. On a different level, but using the same strategy, is the use of a professional presenter on a stage to capture the attention of passing visitors and to give a short presentation of benefits. Visitors that might stop for girls, booze or a free magic show, will not waste time stopping to listen to a serious sales message. Serious buyers will, however, and a proportion of these can then be persuaded to step on to the stand for a hands-on demonstration or for more detailed information.

Robots of various kinds are a well-used feature at many trade and public shows. Again, one needs to be careful to ensure that a serious product is not trivialized or overshadowed by a 'Metal Mickey'. Some buyers are self-conscious about being seen talking to an android, especially to a furry talking muppet on a bike, a talking cartoon character on a screen, or a moving hologram, popular at some events. (Nowadays, people are fairly comfortable using simple interactive computers with simplified keyboards, rather like high-street cash dispensers, but these are generally one-to-one attractions. Few will wait too long to 'have a go'.)

If, however, the strategy is simply to attract indiscriminately, then the above, as well as a wide range of professionals, can be hired to good effect. One growth area is the use of look-alikes, and convincing 'doubles' of Margaret Thatcher, James Dean, Elvis Presley, and most of the Royal Family can be hired by the day. Remember, some look-alikes can cost more than the 'real thing', especially if the latter are given an opportunity to plug their new book/radio show/TV programme. Again, set clear objectives at the outset and ensure the entertainer knows them beforehand and contributes to them.

Finally, animals can be just as much a draw as human beings, and, as yet, have not become unionized, so prices may be lower. The 3M company used the colourful parakeet, featured in all its advertising, as a stand attraction, and even hard-bitten buyers called for an opportunity to meet the star. Similarly Arthur the cat, Toucans, Penguins, and White Horses are possibilities. Younger birds were used successfully by another exhibitor at an educational event, where an incubator full of hatching chicks drew crowds of mothers with children, the precise target audience required. Remember, though, that animals are not generally house-trained; and if you do not have a competent handler, apply the maxim 'Never work with children or animals'.

15.6 Prepare an exhibition schedule

After all the careful considerations and briefs written about where to exhibit, when, and with what objectives in mind, the project will have to be set in motion. The start should be at least 3 months ahead of opening day, 6 months for anything complicated, and a year for really big commitments, especially overseas. No one needs this time to design and build, but consider transport time, waiting time, customs clearance, packing and unpacking; consider contingencies needed to bridge the gap between promises and performance.

The problem here is not usually contractors – their reputation depends on acting professionally, delivering on time. The problem is often the company's own staff. Delivering or developing an exhibit or caption, fixing a meeting to discuss a brief or approve a design – all these are low on their own priority lists, because they are outside their mainstream activity. Happy the exhibition organizer who has all his colleagues tamed or who needs no references back to others; but exhibitions are one promotional activity likely to get everyone into the act, from engineers (glumly discovering that a stand is quite unlike their own test laboratory, so how can they put up a realistic demonstration?) to members of the board concerned about the VIP lounge.

All questions asked at preliminary budgeting time must be asked again when the job begins. Then the organizer can only hope that the different answers will not pose a cost problem.

Exhibition projects vary widely in scale, scope and complication, but one thing remains common: a basic sequence of actions. This can be developed into critical paths for the sophisticated, but a simple chronological list goes a long way to establish order. For a small exhibition there are many items that can be struck out or timescales reduced. For larger exhibitions, particularly those in other countries, there may be further items to add, such as translations, shipping arrangements, customs documentation and hotel accommodation.

The important thing is that every possible item should be fitted into a logical position in the time sequence and that a conscious decision is made *and recorded* about each item, even if it is 'No'. Consider the following schedule:

DUMMY EXHIBITION SCHEDULE

T – 52 weeks
- Obtain booking forms and regulations.
- Compare costs with previous experience.
- Consider results at previous exhibitions.
- Decide on budget, take advantage of early booking discount.

T – 26 weeks
- Start project, raise documentation, confirm budget, start to assemble briefing information.

T – 25 weeks
- In-company meeting to decide on policy.
- Allocate responsibility for stand management, catering publicity, etc.

T – 24 weeks
- Complete assembly of briefing information, prepare exhibit lists with dimensions and weights. Indicate exhibits requiring electric power/gas/water, etc.
- Specify any special services required on stand. Do they infringe exhibition rules? Call for copy, captions and pictures to be made available.

T – 23 weeks
- Brief designer, obtain initial idea sketches and layouts, consider in terms of likely cost, check against budget and modify brief as necessary.

T – 20 weeks
- Complete design to a stage suitable for estimating, submit to at least three suitable contractors and submit electrical drawings to electrical contractors. Prepare creative brief for presentation of copy, captions and photographs.

T – 18 weeks
- Receive and judge estimates from main and electrical contractors – especially with regard to budget. Accept one estimate or call for meetings between selected contractor, designer and own management to negotiate simplification and cost reduction.

T – 16 weeks
- Place main contract and electrical contract, approve estimate, etc. and agree details as appropriate. Order furniture, carpets and book floral displays, plus other exhibits or models, for assembly of specified parts of stand on contractor's shop floor.

T – 30 days
- Deliver specified exhibits to contractor for mounting, deliver graphic panels and photoprints to contractor.

T – 10 days
- Have contractor move into exhibition hall.

T – 9 days	•	Supervise laying out of stand in space allocated, check availability of services ordered.
T – 7 days	•	Supervise construction.
T – 6 days	•	Deliver large exhibits to stand.
T – 5 days	•	Supervise installation of large exhibits, test out all working equipment.
T – 3 days	•	Complete check and clean up.
T – 2 days	•	Hand over to stand manager, brief exhibition staff.
T – 1 day	•	Press day – 100 per cent ready!

This is the sort of list you might use, with maybe several dozen other entries in the middle and timings varied to match the event. Estimates, where practicable from multiple sources, orders, timescales, coordination between suppliers, checking, monitoring and approving, all move to an increasing tempo as E–day approaches. Further, real dates need to be matched by a performance column. Approval points have to be emphasized (approval by whom, and will he be in the country that vital week?). Critical paths must be identified and, all the time, budgeting controls maintained.

There is a lot of administration, a lot of detail, with the added constraint that these had better not be allowed to cramp the designer's style, or it could turn out to be the most economic, best-organized stand that anyone ever ignored! In fact, like most publicity activity, it demands the inevitable compromise between creative and mundane factors, only more so. Producing an exhibition stand generally poses more problems than does any other single activity in promotional work, simply because so many different factors need to be organized to work in harmony over the run-up to the exhibition.

15.7 Exhibitors' misconceptions – a round dozen

It has been estimated that 80 per cent of companies exhibiting at trade shows repeat the same old mistakes every 4 or 5 years, because a new man has been appointed. There is a lack of continuity, and practically nothing on the files about evaluating exhibition effectiveness, which means that anyone taking over the task has nothing to build on. The waste is repeated cyclically *ad infinitum*. Yet, if a company spends £50,000 on trade shows, it probably has to sell an extra £500,000 worth of goods or services to pay for it.

Given the possibility of a vast waste of effort, it is worth doing something about it. Sadly, many may feel there is little they can do to get more value from their trade shows. This is particularly surprising, because, regardless of whether a company's exhibition expenditure is £10,000 or £1m, the trade show budget is often a major part of the entire promotional budget, especially for companies engaged in business-to-business marketing. This 'we-take-our-exhibitions-for-granted' attitude has been fostered out of a variety of misconceptions found to be held by managers in a wide range of companies.[2]

15.7.1   First Misconception

'From years of experience we know that the only real way to increase impact at an exhibition is to spend more money on bigger and better stands.'

Research, however, has shown that companies can spend less and still achieve practically the same impact. Companies ought to know when they are overspending, so that the money can be put to better use.

At the 1979 Geneva International Telecom Exhibition a major manufacturer spent £500,000 on an excellent exhibition, but, even for a market leader this was a classic case of overspending, not warranted by the exhibition's potential. Four years later, at the next exhibition, the manufacturer reduced its spend by nearly a third to £350,000. Useful contacts were only 4 per cent down on 1979, but visitors' recall of the company was demonstrably higher. Achievement was practically the same but £150,000 was saved.

In the UK, in the plastics machinery business, a British manufacturer did almost the same and saved £30,000. Overspending can be avoided if you have the facts available to support the decision.

15.7.2   Second misconception

'Anyone at all interested in our products simply must visit our stand because we are the brand leader with the most advanced products at the best prices.'

The brand leaders are often the last exhibitors visited, because everyone knows all about them. Or do they? Are visitors spending time on other, lesser known stands? Research can provide the answers.

15.7.3   Third Misconception

'Because we can only afford a tiny stand, the extra cost of research does not make sense.'

Small stands may mean small numbers of good contacts, so the cost per contact is higher than that of the bigger spenders. For every exhibitor there is an optimum stand size. A larger stand may mean a lower cost per contact, this can be defined by research, and could lead to lower selling costs.

The reason for spending a little on an exhibition is not always lack of funds but rather the perceived high possibility of wasting money. So should you even go at all?

At the 1989 British Veterinary Association Congress held in Glasgow one of the top five animal-health companies spent £14,204 on attending the 4-day trade exhibition. This figure included £2640 on hotels, £900 on travel, and £1200 on entertainment. There were 1608 delegates, of which only 420 were practising veterinary surgeons. The average cost of each of the target audience (veterinary surgeons) attending the Congress was £33.82; the average cost of veterinary surgeons *visiting* the stand was £118. In this case, if non-attendance could be considered damaging, the company would have to think very carefully about the costs of the peripherals to the exhibition as well as giving due consideration to the quality and number of its stand visitors. Having the right information would lessen the risk of wasting promotional funds.

15.7.4 Fourth misconception

'We already produce the most cost-effective stands possible. Research couldn't possibly help us to improve this further.'

Research monitors how cost-effectively a stand works at a specific show, and makes it possible to compare the cost-effectiveness of other stands at the same show. This might reveal that one company's cost per interested visitor was six times that of its competitors, indicating that fundamental mistakes were being made.

At the construction industry show 'Interbuild', for example, four roughly equal-spending companies reached respectively 60, 100, 240 and 580 useful contacts. The expectations of the first three companies were based on similar experience at earlier shows, each being satisfied with past and present achievement. Based on research, the fourth company tried a different approach, gaining 580 useful contacts at a cost of only 10 per cent of that of the exhibitor with a mere 60. The successful know who to aim for and how to get them on to the stand by research. The others set their sights too low, were low achievers and simply had no idea they were wasting the exhibition's potential.

While the cost per useful contact may not be the best or only method of judging an exhibition, an exhibition manager's principal task is usually to provide his company with qualified leads at an acceptable cost.

15.7.5 Fifth misconception

'We already monitor and analyse all the people who visit our stand, and follow up carefully after the show. There is nothing else to be done.'

Analysing visitors is important, but what of the ones the company did not attract – how important were these? Why didn't they come? If a competitor took three times as many good contacts at the same show, then urgent action is needed.

At the packaging industry exhibition 'Pakex', for example, two important manufacturers of labelling machines both attracted about 300 visitors. Company A reported two out of three visitors planned to buy its products, whereas Company B was happy with one in twenty. Company B soon shifted its marketing approach next time round!

15.7.6 Sixth misconception

'Measuring how well we communicate to visitors is impossible or too expensive. There is no point trying.'

Measurement of how well or how badly a company communicates with its target audience is a fundamental need, irrespective of the medium employed, exhibitions or not. It can be costly to 'make do' without the right information.

After a computer exhibition a PC manufacturer discovered that business users in its target market identified its products with a competitor even after the target visitors had all received hospitality on visiting its stand, and collected information from its sales staff. This was due to ineptitude at handling an exhibition, despite being market sector leader, having a large expensive stand, and years of experience at the annual show. Research highlighted the problem and the company was able to put it right.

15.7.7 Seventh misconception

'Everyone knows our advertising slogan.'

As with the sixth misconception, everyone may know the slogan but not know the company. Your slogan may be selling your competitor's products. Research will not only identify the other companies and products that visitors associate with a particular slogan, but may also help you get yours right.

Sometimes industrial advertising slogans and logos are mainly associated with consumer products. At 'Interbuild', exhibition value analysis revealed that the logo of a manufacturer of insulating materials had a strong association with a certain confectionery manufacturer. The consumer-goods advertising proved far more powerful than the company's industrial equivalent. Similarly, in the farming environment of the Royal Show and the Smithfield Show, an oil company's advertising message was associated by potential customers with an advertising campaign by the Milk Marketing Board. Without a conscious effort to study feedback from the target market, this sort of confusion may remain undetected.

15.7.8   Eighth misconception

'It is not possible to learn much about our own sales staff's performance that we don't already know; research cannot help.'

Sales staff should indoctrinate every visitor they meet on the stand. When those visitors think of the types of product shown, they should think of the exhibitor. At the close of a show this can be monitored to establish how effectively the stand staff communicated. If it is not 100 per cent, then it can be put right only if it is known. Such research effectively gets visitors to rate individual staff, because their comments can be linked back to the stand record of contacts.

At the International Business Show, held at the NEC, Birmingham, one photographic-equipment manufacturer regularly researches its exhibition performance, its staff always being rated as excellent by stand visitors. On one occasion the rating was poor, well below average for the show. The two salesmen responsible were identified and it transpired that they were both new to the company and being trained at the exhibition; using inexperienced people at an exhibition is not a good idea. If salesmen are being trained at an exhibition, they need to be supervised.

An exhibitor clearly needs to know how the market rates its staff and how they compare with the rest of the industry.

15.7.9   Ninth misconception

'We know how many sales enquiries we received, therefore, we know how well we did at the exhibition.'

A company may know how many visitors it saw, but not know what the number of potential visitors was. Research can show how many of the visitors were interested in, or planned to buy, the company's type of products. If the company only reached 10 per cent of the potential, it might revise its opinion of how well it did.

15.7.10   Tenth misconception

'We know exactly who we must meet at the show; all our objectives are achieved when we meet them.'

Although twelve key people may be planned as the target for a company, an exhibition may have the potential for many more equally good, but yet unknown, contacts. Research can highlight the real potential and help refine an approach that exploits it to the full.

At the Farnborough Air Show three competitive manufacturers of aerospace equipment were each – unknown to the others – planning to meet about eighty key decision-makers. All three companies knew the market well, had exhibited at Farnborough for years, and yet were unaware that about 450 suitable contacts were regular visitors, of whom 250 could reasonably be expected to be attracted on to the stand. But the three companies were not looking. Then one opened its eyes, saw the potential, and stole a march on the other two.

15.7.11   Eleventh misconception

'The design of our stand, and the techniques we employ, are so stunningly effective they will attract more visitors than any other exhibitor.'

As we have seen earlier in this chapter, it is quality not quantity that matters most. If too many visitors are attracted for the wrong reasons, you need to plan to have a large enough team of professional sales staff to filter the visitors to identify the good contacts.

15.7.12   Twelfth misconception

'We cannot afford to have more than one or two staff on the stand at an exhibition.'

Having invested in actually getting to the show and presenting a display, do not waste the money by having tired sales staff slumped on a chair at the corner of the exhibition. The visitor who arrives at 4.30pm on the third day can be just as important as the one that arrived at

10am on the first day. Remember too that if you have got your planning right, you are at the right exhibition, you have put up an attractive and inviting exhibit and you have relevant products to talk about, you may have, say, 100 possible buyers visit your company each day. How many face-to-face contacts can your best sales representative make each day?

Remember the following:

1 Look to your company's files for evidence of the effectiveness of earlier exhibiting budgets.
2 If there are no data, then every few years your company could be wasting a large part of its promotional budget on ineffective exhibitions.
3 Wasted opportunities can never be recovered.
4 Do something about it, now!

15.8 Measurement of performance

Evaluating an exhibition is not easy, because, as we have seen, there are so many variable factors, but it is impossible unless one has a clear set of objectives against which to measure the results obtained. Thus, having determined your reasons for participating, and your objectives, you must make arrangements to measure the results. Immediate forms of measurement include:

(a) Boxes for visiting cards.
(b) Enquiry pads with room for literature/sample requests.

(i) Make sure literature gets sent out immediately while visitor interest is high.
(ii) Include a reply-paid card for further information requests.

(c) Order pads.
(d) Noting of general enquiries – possibly for market-research purposes.
(e) Noting names and numbers of delegates attending lectures or film shows as part of the exhibition.
(f) Sales from the exhibition, if you are running an over-the-counter operation, can give an immediate answer to the measurement question.

(g) Compare total exhibition visitors with former years. One can usually get a profile of exhibition visitors from the organizers. How many in your target market visited you?

Always remember when checking results that you measure what your objectives were set out to achieve: absolute number or quality buyers. Note how your competitors are faring. Are there traffic hold-ups leading to the show to account for a general low attendance? Is your stand badly placed? Are your products right for the show? Are you in the right section of the show? Are your products in their current format too well-known, and a new twist or repackaging would stimulate renewed interest? These are a few of the questions that will help you afterwards to analyse the results, decide to what extent you met your objectives, and what alterations you would recommend for the future.

When costing out the exhibition, remember to include with the space and construction costs those for literature, hotels, travel and entertainment (although it is not suggested that these last three should be part of the publicity budget). In this way one can compare the cost of a representative visiting a buyer with the total number of valued visitors seen on the exhibition.

Suppose your field-force costs equate to £45 per buyer visited in the usual working day. (This is a representative's annual salary, pension, car, travel and accommodation, plus expenses, divided by the total number of sales calls made each year). Would it be worthwhile paying a total of £12,000 on an exhibition when 250 known buyers were seen by your representatives in a 3-day period?

Well, 250 buyers at £45 per usual visit = £11,250. So, on the face of it, it would not be worth attending the exhibition if the objective was solely to attract 250 already known buyers. However, if you were also attracting buyers that you didn't know, or if you were launching a new product and wanted to tell a lot of buyers quickly, or were able to demonstrate a range of equipment that buyers might otherwise have difficulty seeing operative, then the £12,000 total exhibition costs might be justified.

The methods outlined above might be termed 'do-it-yourself' measurements. They have the disadvantage of taking up your stand personnel's time, and in many cases, as we have seen, the results are subject to subjective analysis and, not unnaturally, can be biased, as self-criticism is exceedingly difficult. Ideally one should supplement one's own measurement techniques with those of a third party to obtain a really subjective assessment.

There are several specialist firms that, for a fee, will conduct a survey and give an audience profile. The cheapest is the 'omnibus' survey sold *pro rata* to exhibitors who can, by paying extra, add questions of their own. Alternatively, separately commissioned surveys on, say, a 10 per cent sample of the visitors can be made, the questions all geared specifically to the company concerned. The audience profiles are normally based on buying influence, buying plans, interest factors, and the ability/influence of stand personnel; and on time spent, where from, density, and the reaction of a percentage of visitors you recorded on your stand.

These research firms can also provide what is termed 'corporate evaluation of exhibitions'. Given the details of your product/service and the potential specifiers or buyers, they will, from existing data, recommend those exhibitions that are most likely to prove effective in meeting your objectives.

15.9 Travelling exhibitions

There may be advantages in moving away from the idea of attaching a private exhibition to a public one, and simply setting up an exhibition in its own right. It might be in one location or, more likely, it would be staged in a number of places near the major potential sources of business (the 'travelling circus' approach).

The operation can be efficient, since, once the exhibition equipment has been assembled, it is a relatively easy matter to move on to another location. Modular designs are extremely useful in this respect, being easy to erect and dismantle and often extremely light. Hotels are generally cooperative in accommodating such ventures and provincial rates can be very competitive. A disadvantage is that a good deal of sales-force time, and management, is tied down by these events, and this time must be justified by an adequate level of visitors of worthwhile calibre. Once again it is necessary to set targets, compare costs, and as soon as an operation begins to fail, either take corrective action or end it.

The British Equestrian Trade Association (BETA) started a company called BETA Trade Fairs Ltd in the early 1980s. Their members were the major suppliers to the equestrian trade – saddlers – and shared the same problem: how to get to all the many and varied saddlery shops across the country with what could be, for some, a wide range of clothes, or heavy leather goods (saddles, tack, harness, etc.). The group also included manufacturers of linament, food supplements, etc. The potential was seen for the major companies to group together and run a travelling trade fair, initially in the UK, but also in mainland Europe.

The first UK event was staged at eight different venues across the country, each chosen to be at a centre within a 50-mile radius of the majority of saddlers in a given area. The first venue was at a hotel in Edinburgh, and exhibitors, limited for this pilot venture to sixteen companies, got together on a Sunday evening to build their exhibits. At 10am the following Monday morning, doors opened on the awaiting saddlery owners. The exhibition remained open until early evening to allow time for some saddlers to shut up shop and still make the trade fair. After closing, the exhibitors dismantled the exhibition, loaded their cars, trucks and so forth, and journeyed down to Scotch Corner that evening to the next venue. Early Tuesday morning saw them busy erecting their stands for the 10am opening. This process continued for 4 days in each of two successive weeks until the country had been covered.

The whole event was a testimony to the planning and organization of the then chairman, Anthony Wakeham. The success of this event lay in the fact that, for the first time, the trade could come to visit sixteen potential suppliers in one place. The second BETA Trade Fair had thirty-two exhibitors. Such a 'road show', composed of different exhibitors, also travelled to the Benelux countries one year.

Trailers and caravans can provide an alternative or sometimes a supplement to the staging of round-the-country exhibitions, although the BETA Trade Fairs were all held under cover, inside hotels and halls. However, in some circumstances, e.g. agricultural shows and markets, or perhaps for export promotions, the simplicity and manoeuvreability of the caravan or trailer have advantages.

Many specialized firms can build exhibitions to a company's specification, in caravans that can be towed behind a car. Such modules are ideal when a virtually instant hospitality suite is required. Weatherproof display material can be put outside and the whole area made attractive by tubs of plants and window boxes. The major financial institutions use some quite prestigious caravans, which need to be towed by articulated lorries, at many of the country fairs around the country. The use of attractive floral displays outside the caravan creates the impression that they are permanent sites.

There is still a good deal of scope for initiative in the field of travelling exhibitions, and the use of railways, barges, ships and aeroplanes has not been yet exploited to the full. The sheer novelty of such ventures can do much to ensure the success of the operation.

15.10 Summary

1 Exhibitions are big business – £300 million was spent on space and stands alone in 1989.
2 Exhibitors must be very sure that they get value for money for

what is always a big commitment, in staffing as well as direct expenditure. Section 15.2 lists the possible benefits.

3 Sections 15.3 and 15.4 deal with cost and how best to set up an exhibition stand, and 15.6 how to manage the complex process.

4 It is no use having even the best of exhibits if no one comes to it. Section 15.5 deals with how to get them there.

5 At the end of the day results are what it is about – 15.8 suggests how best to measure them.

6 The special case of travelling exhibitions and road shows is the subject of 15.9.

References

1 *What's New in Marketing* (1989), September, p.32.
2 Data from Exhibition Surveys' 'Exhibition Value Analysis', a part-syndicated study undertaken annually.

16 Sponsorship

16.1 Sponsorship, patronage or charity?

What are the differences? How do they differ from advertising? Sponsorship is the provision of financial or material support by a company for some independent activity (usually related to sport or the arts) not usually directly linked to the company's normal business but support from which the sponsoring company would hope to benefit. Sponsorship is usually undertaken to encourage more favourable attitudes towards the sponsoring company or its products within a relevant target audience, such as consumers, trade customers, employees or the community in which it operates. Sponsorship is essentially a business deal whose purpose is to work to the mutual advantage of both sponsor and sponsored. This should be clearly appreciated by both parties right from the start of their relationship.

That some business people do not have a clear understanding of this was exemplified some years ago by a company that reckoned it spent a lot on sponsorship, but achieved only small results. The company was using sponsorship in fact as an umbrella term to cover activities as varied as donations to charity, community relations, personnel relations, gifts from the chairman, and even support for an employee's racing car.

A clear understanding of what sponsorship is and what it is not must be followed by an equally clear statement, or marketing brief, on the role sponsorship is supposed to perform for the company concerned. From this, it is possible to assess the type of sponsorship that should be considered. In deciding between sponsoring sport or the arts, it is important that the differences between the two are fully understood.

In sport it is likely that a fairly immediate return can be demonstrated, particularly if the sponsors' name is televised by being displayed on the periphery of the sports arena, on clothing, on a vehicle (motor sports) or as the title of the event, e.g. the Whitbread Burleigh Horse Trials.

In the arts, on the other hand, sponsorship may have nothing directly to do with the sale of a product or service. Rather, sponsorship may be concerned with the long-term establishment of a company's reputation or image. In some cases the need may not be to establish but to change an image; or it may be to build an image with a certain segment of the market, e.g. youth, which provides tomorrow's potential customers. For example, Lloyds Bank directs its sponsorship activity at the teenage market, and at the same time seeks to embody an educational element.

Sponsorship is not patronage, which may be defined as financial or material contributions made by a company without the expectation of return in the form of publicity. It is undertaken altruistically by the organization in its role of 'good corporate citizen', whereas sponsorship, whatever form it takes, has the fundamental purpose of contributing, directly or indirectly, towards the commercial success of the sponsor's business.

Sponsorship is not advertising either. Although some forms of sponsorship may share goals similar to advertising – increasing product/brand awareness, for example – and spend money to achieve favourable publicity, there are fundamental differences between the two activities. This should be borne in mind when allocating responsibilities and budgets, and also when establishing criteria for considering, planning, executing and evaluating a sponsorship programme.

Advertising's main function is the direct promotion of a company or its products in space or air-time bought for that specific purpose. But in sponsorship the company's name *could be incidental* to the main activity, playing a supportive role to the event or individual being sponsored. Sponsorship works largely through *indirect* communication. On the one hand, this means that it can appear as less overtly commercial, and, on the other, it means that impact and memorability are likely to be considerably less in the short term unless reinforced by repeated sponsorship of regular events or series of events, e.g. the John Player Cup, the Barclay's League, or backed up by other forms of publicity (memorabilia, merchandise, tee-shirts, etc.) – something to be borne in mind when setting objectives.

Sport has always been a natural area for sponsorship, because it appeals to all classes and both sexes. It has a mass audience and is therefore of particular interest to companies marketing consumer goods. Moreover, in the early days, sports sponsorship was inexpensive. Gillette bought in to what became known as the Gillette Cup (cricket) for £6,500. But when NatWest took it on in 1981, it had to pay £250,000. Sport, as many companies are finding, now demands high budgets, and is becoming less cost-effective.

When cricket was sponsored in the early 1960s, the compelling attraction was that the game had not been sponsored since the 1850s, when Spiers and Pond supported the first tour of an English side to Australia. Today sports sponsorship is common, and companies need to think long and hard before committing themselves to it.

However, year-round arts sponsorship can cost considerably less than the production of a 30-second TV commercial. With arts sponsorship, too, uniqueness is still to be found, though the situation is changing. It is becoming very much a case of 'first come, first served', and there are the other benefits of repetition and longevity of association not always available in sport.

However, arts sponsorship is not without its problems. For example, a company's sponsorship of an orchestra, which could cost, over a considerable period, £900,000 (as du Maurier's sponsorship of an orchestra did some while ago), raises a number of issues. What would happen to the orchestra if the company withdrew sponsorship? If the orchestra had become too dependent, very bad publicity would result from the removal of sponsorship. Certainly the company would need to justify such high levels of expenditure to management, to shareholders, and to the company's own employees.

Another danger to all heavy sponsors is that, once committed to the practice of sponsorship, there is a temptation to become miniature impresarios, spending disproportionate amounts of company time and money in pursuit of activities that are enjoyable but often ineffective. It is often better to leave the management to sponsorship specialists, who are experienced in both marketing and the arts and invariably have low overheads.

But how do you decide whether to go into a sponsorship event in the first place? The first necessity is to have a clear view of the reasons for undertaking sponsorship, and to prepare a written brief. Then it is possible to move to the stage of selecting the sponsorship to meet the brief. Sadly, too many companies drift into sponsorship, lured by luscious offerings from needy arts organizations without being clear about the reasons for doing so, or about what they want from the activity.

Consider the following criteria, against which different activities that could be sponsored can be evaluated before making a commitment:

- Does the activity match the company's stated sponsorship brief?
- Is the sponsorship unique? If not, can it be differentiated from the rest?
- Is the activity relevant to the sponsoring company? In the eyes of the public and media the marriage between sponsor and sponsored should be suitable. (White Horse Whisky sponsoring the Girl Guides Marching Band would not be appropriate.)
- Does the activity have repeat or build-up value? This may be achieved as a tournament goes through early rounds leading to a final, by an orchestra playing a series of concerts, or, to an extent, by advance publicity.

- Can the sponsorship be cost-effective? The answer is, to some extent, determined by the clarity of the objective stated in the initial brief. It may be measured by the number of media mentions it achieves, or by orders booked as a direct result of the event.
- Can the activity be exploited? The sponsorship in itself may not provide great news content, but there are ways of ensuring additional mileage. For example, BP supported the London Mozart Players, which led to a series of concerts for children. For these, the company produced explanatory booklets and teaching notes, all helping its image.

Having arrived at the point where a policy decision has been taken to enter sponsorship, a brief established for its fulfilment, and prospective recipients of sponsorship assessed for likely effectiveness, the company must next ensure the best return from the activity. There are eight areas in which sponsorship can be made to work for a company, not all of them concerned exclusively with marketing:

1 Personal relations benefit from offering employees and their families the opportunity to attend the events, either free or at a reduced cost. Cow & Gate regularly sponsored four seats at the Theatre Royal, Bath. Each pair of tickets was raffled free every week for both the Friday and Saturday evening performances. Winners were each asked to donate £2 to charity.
2 The image of the company held by consumers can be improved by sponsorship and the demonstration of enlightened corporate social responsibility.
3 Many a profitable sale or contract has been initiated through contact with customers or suppliers at a sponsored activity.
4 Government relations can be fostered through the judicious use of sponsorship in which VIPs are interested.
5 Participation of local or regional plants, offices or branches in sponsorship activities contributes to good community relations. (For example, Rhône Poulenc sponsored the Dagenham Wildlife Park, which borders their production site.)
6 Relations with the media can obviously be developed to the benefit of both sponsor and sponsored organization.
7 The knowledge and experience of management under training can be broadened.
8 Sponsorship can be aggressively exploited to *sell*!

16.2 Sports sponsorship

In general the high-interest, big-money sports with heavy media coverage, which can attract vast audiences via TV, attract the heaviest sponsorship. Motor-racing, horse-racing, tennis, golf, cricket, soccer, athletics, equestrian events, gymnastics, darts, and snooker are among the most heavily televised sports. Naturally the cost of sponsorship at this level is extremely high although, evaluated directly in terms of message exposure, it may compare favourably with paid-for air-time.

Many more opportunities for sponsorship entail a more modest level of expenditure in the 'grass roots' areas – among the participant, non-professional, youth and minority sports. Almost every type of sporting activity today affords the opportunity for sponsorship of some kind, and enterprise, ingenuity and enthusiasm can often make a modest budget go a very long way. Many companies have achieved remarkable results by shrewd support of a 'growth' sport.

16.2.1   The size of the industry

Information published by *Datastream* (Figure 16.1) shows the boom in sponsorship that occurred through the 1980s, not only in the amount of money being committed to sponsorship, but also in terms of the increase in the number of organizations turning to sponsorship for their publicity (and other) purposes.

Over £158m was spent on direct sponsorship of all sports in the UK in 1987, compared to £50m in 1981. Close to £200m more was spent in 1987 by those sponsors on marketing and promoting their efforts, through advertising, hospitality at sponsored events and so forth. It was estimated in 1987 that the grand total was more than £1 in every £10 spent by British companies on television and press advertising. Sponsorship has become big business. Over 2000 companies are actively engaged in sponsorship, and just the top ten sports-sponsorship deals signed in the period June to September 1988 accounted for nearly £15 million worth of sponsorship:

Philip Morris	4m	World Cup golf
ADT	£2m	London Marathon
Foster's	£2m	Name deal with the Oval (cricket)
NEC	£1.6m	Davis Cup tennis
Philip Morris	£1.5m	US Entry to America's Cup

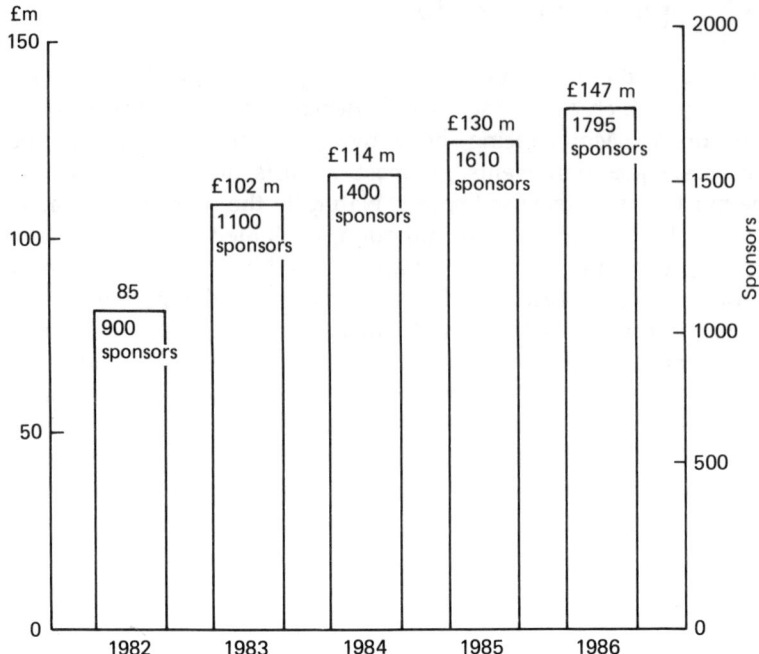

Figure 16.1 *The growth in sponsorship through the 1980s. Source: Datastream*

Budweiser	£1m	Top 20 League American football
Pringle	£1m	Nick Faldo (golf)
Pilkington	£750,000	Rugby Union Cup Competition
Chambers & Cook (Haulage)	£500,000	Two power boats in World Grand Prix
Hi Tec	£500,000	British Open (squash)
	£14,85m	

The future, however, looks a little uncertain. The growth rate is levelling out. While there were increases in sports sponsorship of around 125 per cent from 1981 to 1984, and around 50 per cent from 1984 to 1987, there was a drop of about 10 per cent in 1988. The Sports Council estimated up-front sponsorship to be around £200m. This levelling out does not mean that sponsorship's power is waning; it appears that budgets are getting bigger from individual sponsors, but the smaller investor is finding it more difficult to make an impact in the major areas as the larger corporations protect and exploit their investment.

The problem seems to be that the supply of sports events, particularly televised events, is now drying up. There are therefore two kinds of opportunities for new sponsors. One is waiting to fill 'dead men's shoes' (when sponsors 'such as Tennent's lager withdraw from major snooker deals); the other is to create something new and innovative that may attract TV coverage – see, for example, the illustration of what £175,000 might buy (Section 16.2.4). Another alternative that many companies are now considering is arts sponsorship (see Section 16.7).

With the changes in rules for sponsorship following the 1990 Broadcasting Act, much sponsorship money was poured into this area with apparently excellent results for the sponsors. *Marketing Week* reported on 12 June 1992 that Sony's sponsorship of the ITV rugby coverage was so successful that most viewers thought it was the main sponsor of the actual event. The magazine also reported that Sega, the video games company, was planning to sponsor ITV's football coverage with opening and closing sequences in the form of a video game 'menu'.

At the same time BSkyB, the satellite broadcasting company, was planning to get a £50m contribution from sponsors to the £304m it paid for the 5-year contract for Premier League coverage.

On 11 June 1993 the *Evening Standard* suggested that: 'Total spending (on sponsorship) is expected to reach £350m this year.'

16.2.2   The European picture

'Sponsorship allows brands to improve their image with greater impact than some traditional advertising,' commented Professor S. Picquet, of France's Academie Commerciale Internationale. 'And for products that are either banned from television, such as cigarettes, or simply cannot get enough commercial air-time because of rising media costs, sport is a "backdoor" route into the living rooms of Europe.' At the same time, sports sponsorship helps satisfy the growing hunger for cash among the sports associations themselves, as more and more people take up new sports and governments tighten their belts and withdraw public funds for support. Sports federations everywhere have loosened their restrictions on sponsorship, thus opening the way across Europe for aggressive marketers.

For example, in 1984, the French spent FF900 million on sport-related marketing, an estimated 3 per cent of the country's media spend. Companies in Italy increased their investment 200 per cent to hit 600 million lire. In Germany, where motor sport attracts the most sponsorship, advertisers spent more than DM221 million on sport. European marketers are exploiting sports sponsorship in a big way, for both national and international campaigns. But most activity, in terms of money spent, occurs at the regional and national level. Only a few sports, like football and, increasingly, tennis, have true international appeal, and national sponsorship can ensure that money is invested in ways that have maximum impact in a particular country.

Huge sums can be spent at the national level. Cirio, a tomato paste producer, agreed to pay 13 billion lire for its association with the Naples Series A (First Division) football squad and its star player, Diego (Hand-of-God) Maradona. National sponsorship can also be more modest, like Dunlop's £50,000 commitment to improve facilities for British table-tennis players. National sponsorship can be worked into hard-hitting sales promotions to solve unique marketing problems. The Olympia sock company in France needed to overcome the confusion over brand names with the German typewriter maker. Olympia pumped FF6m into the glamorous Paris–Dakar car rally, backing the investment with 13,000 T-shirts distributed to spectators, and a major print campaign.

Sports sponsorship in Europe is used selectively to target particular consumer groups or buyers of services. Alitalia, the Italian airline, sponsors golf tournaments in Italy to reach its upmarket prospects. Similarly the Italian firm Jaegermeister sponsors canoeing to reach young men. The vital youth market is addressed by Credit Lyonnais (the French Bank) by sponsoring such dynamic, trendy sports as windsurfing. In 1984 a British Airways executive, after playing a friendly game of badminton, hit on the idea of the sport's obvious association with the flight service the company was promoting: the result was a £40,000 sponsorship agreement for the European badminton finals, called the British Airways Super Shuttle European Airways Championships.

Another trend has been towards sponsoring individual sports stars. Puma, the West German sportswear company, is reported to have paid the 1986 Wimbledon tennis champion, Boris Becker, £15.5m for a 6-year contract. ICI Fibres sponsored Nigel Mansell as an individual: not only did he wear the ICI logo, but guests of ICI also got the thrill of meeting him at Grand Prix events. ICI also sponsored Martin Bell, the English skier, as an individual. The 1986 winner of the British Open golf tournament, Australian Greg Norman, landed more than £10m worth of sponsorship contracts running over a 3-year period after that success. They included £1m to promote Swan and Castlemaine XXXX lagers, £2m from a Japanese hotel and leisure group, and £7m from Hertz, McDonald's, Spalding, Reebok, Qantas and others.

16.2.3   Pitfalls of sports sponsorship

Sports sponsorship is not always a bed of roses. 'Ambush marketing' is a grave concern for major sponsors, and is the sponsorship equivalent of advertising knocking copy.

For example, the Olympic Games depends primarily on sponsorship money, and the sponsorship rights fees can be considerable. For this reason, companies like Seagram have used 'back-door' routes to associate themselves with the event: Seagram created a sponsorship programme entitled 'Send the families', through which it underwrote the expenses of sending 550 relatives of US Olympic team members to Seoul in 1988, but did not pay a fee to the International Olympic Committee. As well as achieving enormous media coverage, Seagram linked the scheme to a major sales-promotion programme. The success and cost-effectiveness of the programme and those like it, such as Fuji's attempt to counteract and blur Kodak's official Olympic status, have caused waves of anxiety through the industry.

One of the objectives of sports sponsorship is to generate awareness among a target group. This is naturally the planned by-product of getting the sponsored sport covered by the media, particularly TV. However, the television companies' reluctance to recognize sponsors has caused some bad feeling.

In 1988 there was the culmination of a 3-year battle between Mars and the BBC over sponsorship of the London Marathon. The BBC agreed to accept the title as the Mars London Marathon, and the sweets company was satisfied that it was not pouring £50,000 down the drain. This outcome brought hope to many companies which feel harshly treated by TV stations regarding sponsorship. For every Mars that comes out on top, there are hundreds of sponsors that never get the same recognition, despite their massive investment.

Television coverage of sponsored events is a murky area; it is a mix of fear, anger, big money, wheeler-dealing, politics and a fair amount of confusion. The problem at its most basic, however, is the gulf between sponsors wanting value for money and TV companies hiding behind outdated guidelines and unworkable legislation.

One other obvious pitfall can arise from the sponsorship of teams with a star player, or the sponsorship of the individual themselves, when that player falls from grace, is injured, or goes off form, and stops winning. Naturally enough, contracts may have an appropriate 'let-out' clause to stem the tide of money. Sadly, however, if a good relationship between the company or product has been built up in the minds of the target market with the team or player, the association can continue damaging the hard-fought image.

16.2.4 *What does £175,000 buy?*

What can a company waiting to break into new markets via sports sponsorship get for its money? Suppose we consider a fictitious plastic bandage company called 'Plast-Aid'. This is what one consultant – International Management Group – suggests.

Let us imagine this background brief: the brand is well-established in Germany but now wants to expand into the rest of Europe. The company plans to create a pan-European name inside 2 years, and has earmarked £175,000 for the sponsorship effort.

IMG proposes a 'goodwill' approach for the make-believe company, positioning the brand as an advocate of bicycling safely. Cycling fits in with the family-oriented, good-health association of plastic bandages, and targets the products and users – young married women and their children. IMG's programme comprises:

1 A tie-in with national cycling federations to create 'fun clubs'. Membership will require proof of purchase, and will bring other benefits for Plast-Aid. One is to boost its image generally by including brand-name exposure on club printed material. Another is to provide tactical sales programmes.
2 Sponsorship of a BMX (bicycle motocross) racing team in each country. IMG would coordinate negotiations with bicycle manufacturers and sports federations. Competitive events would attract coverage in the press and on TV.
3 Creation of an international 'all star' team, drawn from each national team, to compete in major competitions. The brand name will feature on uniforms, equipment, etc. Children will be invited to join a 'Plast-Aid BMX support team', and BMX team members will make personal appearances at, for example, retail outlets. The BMX team concept could also form the basis of a trade-incentive scheme.
4 IMG says it encourages its clients to set up trade promotions and point-of-sale tie-ins, all of which would require an additional budget.

From this example we can see not only what one would get for around £175,000 but also how sponsorship ties in with other below-the-line publicity techniques, including on-pack sales promotions, sales literature, clubs, press and public relations, point of sale, and incentive programmes. Each of the areas could be extended and exploited to the full, depending on the available resources.

16.3 Tenuous links between smoking and sport

Tobacco, together with drink, were the first two industries to take up sports sponsorship seriously. They are now a major force, together representing over 12.5 per cent of the total business sponsorship of sport. The tobacco industry's interest goes back well before legislation against TV advertising came into force. Many would argue that even if legislation had not come in, it would still be a major force in sport today. Many of the tobacco-sponsored events are more than a decade old, some even older, and are major events in the British sporting calendar.

There are many who feel that the voluntary agreement on sponsorship between the tobacco companies and the government worked well through the mid-1980s, the key area of sensitivity being the television exposure that the tobacco sponsors receive for their sports events. Note, Martina Navratilova was ordered off court for her tennis shirt endorsement of Kim Cigarettes at Wimbledon in 1983. Tobacco-marketers have since adopted more passive sponsorship techniques. In 1986 Sportscan produced a 5-year comparison showing that tobacco-sponsored sport had only increased marginally, as part of total sports viewing (Table 16.1). Increases from 1984 to 1985 were due to a new golf event, the Dunhill British Masters (20 hours), and the three snooker events sponsored by Embassy, Rothmans, and Benson & Hedges.

However, many organizations, such as Ash (Action on Smoking and Health), the Health Education Council, the British Medical Association, and to some extent also the government, have been agitating for a reduction of the influence that promotions linking cigarette smoking

Table 16.1 *Tobacco-sponsored events on television*

	Total televised sport (hours)	Tobacco-sponsored events (hours)	% of total
1981	1830	253	13.8
1982	2102	280	13.3
1983	2331	303	13.0
1984	2356*	329	14.0
1985	2463	377	15.3

* Excludes 202 hours of Olympics and Winter Olympics.

and the drama and prestige of success in sport can have on people, particularly young people between the ages of 16 and 19. The Census Office's Social Surveys division found that the number of people who take up serious smoking after reaching 20 is virtually negligible, so these youngsters make up the majority of the next generation of dedicated smokers.

Currently, health experts and anti-smoking lobbyists see cigarette advertising, sponsorship of sports events, and peer-group pressure as the main influences on teenagers. While various sports ministers have been dedicated to limiting the influence tobacco companies have over attracting young new smokers, the problem is that they have only limited power. Their main weapon, the Sports Council, has certainly added its own condemnation, and is committed to ending cigarette-company sponsorship outright. But it has little power over the sports that benefit most: snooker, cricket, bowls and darts. Changes will only gradually be implemented and only slowly take effect.

Meanwhile research shows that children as young as six nowadays can accurately identify cigarette brands with the sporting events they promote. Norway, recognizing this, has extended its own advertising ban to embrace everything that could conceivably conjure up the image of a king-size filter, or low-tar menthol – the colour of a cigarette pack, anything decorated with its logo, and any product, however remote from nicotine, that carries its name. Even the Marlboro chevron, without the brand name, is banned. Even so, the Norwegians have succeeded only in halting the growth of the habit; 36 per cent of all adults continue to smoke – around the same proportion in Britain – so addictive is the drug.

16.4 And drink . . .

The active anti-tobacco sponsorship groups have been joined by the anti-drink sponsorship lobbyist, following Daley Thompson's much-publicized action against the £2m offered by Guinness, as the main sponsors of the Thirteenth Commonwealth Games in 1986. Yet drinks-industry sponsorship of sport is the greatest of any industry's in the depth and range of its activities, reflecting the enormous number of brands and breweries spread across the country. One in ten of the major sponsors of sport is a drinks company – representing 160 different brands or brewers with activities in thirty-three different sports.

Despite Daley Thompson's comments, Guinness spent £600,000 on sports sponsorship, excluding its back-up publicity material in 1987. Its Bell's whisky brand received a new marketing drive with £50,000 spent on ski sponsorship. The British ski team sponsorship was offered in response to the British Ski Federation's desperate appeal for funding, and was bolted on to Guinness's sponsorship of the Alpine World Championships at Crans, Montana.

Whitbread's sport sponsorship portfolio has been built up over more than 35 years, and demonstrates the corporation's belief that the benefits can only be measured in the longer term. Whitbread sponsors major events in the lawn-tennis, steeplechasing, rugby league, and equestrian calendars. Under the Heineken name it invested over £250,000 a year in ice hockey's British National League. It even undertook to organize the Whitbread Round the World Race, a yacht event that cost it each year over £2.5m, took 3 years to set up, and lasted 8 months.

However, drink sponsorship is not all good cheer. Canada's Molson Breweries, sole official sponsor in the brewery category of ice hockey, a national sport in Canada, was dismayed to find two other major Canadian breweries 'ambushing' its sponsorship and linking themselves to ice hockey – but there was little it could do.

16.5 Financial players in the sponsorship game

One beneficiary of a sporting body refusing tobacco-company sponsorship was Refuge Assurance. In 1986, when the Sunday Cricket League ended the 17-year backing from John Player, Refuge Assurance put £2.5m behind the league, renaming it the Refuge Assurance Cup.

A survey by Sportscan revealed that spends in the insurance sector on sports sponsorship went from £2.3m in 1984 to £5.4m in 1985 and £8.1m in 1986. Banks and finance companies had an even more dramatic jump in their expenditure: a mere £305,000 in 1984, which shot up to £6m in 1985 before dropping to £5.3m in 1986. Even though these figures contain an element of forward spending, with some contracts running through to the 1990s, the actual totals are likely to be higher still because many firms do not divulge their promotional spends, for competitive reasons. The net is likely to widen as other professional/financial organizations, such as solicitors and accountants, enter the market. In 1987 the Sports Council's sports sponsorship advisory service began to see interest from this group as its regulations changed.

While sponsorship is relatively new to this sector, the larger institutions are making commitments of significant sums of money: Cornhill put £2m behind its 3-year contract to sponsor the cricket test matches, and the National Westminster Bank devoted £2m to a 5-year sponsorship of the NatWest Cup. As the spends from the financial sector mount, with little indication, at least in the insurance area, that a peak has been reached in sports sponsorship spending, there is likely to be more movement from advertising agencies as they struggle to come to grips with the publicity medium, probably with the creation of specialized sponsorship divisions.

16.6   Never mind the width – feel the quality

The opposite, 'Never mind the quality – feel the width', might have been the title of a TV sit-com but it is no maxim for TV sports sponsors; they could do well to note the *quality* of the viewing figures, rather than the *width* of coverage. While 1989 TV viewing figures for sports programmes showed that, as in 1988, snooker continued to have the largest audience share, new methods of analysis indicated that tennis, soccer and boxing could claim to offer a better return for sponsors. AGB Sports Watch can offer sponsors methods to compare the size and quality of the audiences for each sport.

Snooker's apparently impressive performance is put in doubt by the fact that it enjoyed more TV *coverage* than any other sport over the 2-year period. Obviously, total air-time needs to be taken into account when considering viewers' most popular sports rather than those most popular with TV schedulers. But if one takes the percentage of all sports viewers over a given period of time watching a particular sport, divided by the percentage of air-time that sport received over the same period, we have an index or conversion reading.

For example, in the 6 months from January to June 1989 boxing only attracted 3.4 per cent of all sports viewers, compared to snooker's 21.9 per cent over the same period. However, boxing was only on TV for 1 per cent of the time, and 3.4 per cent divided by 1 per cent gives a conversion factor of 340. On the other hand, snooker was on TV 13.6 per cent of the time, its conversion factor being 161.

This conversion technique can also be applied to defined social categories of audience, such as age, sex or class, giving sponsors a snapshot of how well individual sports target certain sections of the population. To see how successfully sports reach the (so-called) desirable AB adult grouping, for instance, the number of AB adult viewers for each sport is divided by total minutage. Using this system, boxing scores highest with 270, and both golf and tennis perform better *vis-a-vis* the other sports on the AB adult conversion index than they do against the general population. Cricket fares less well, with only 78 – lagging behind all sports (including ice-skating and bowls) except for horse-racing, which records only 36.

AGB has, however, developed an improved technique to quantify the impact of sport on a given social group. Called the sports-viewing index, it paints a different picture. Whereas the conversion index shows in absolute terms how many AB adults a sport delivers per time devoted to it, the SVI takes into account the fact that the chosen target group (for our example, AB adults) makes up a certain percentage of a sports audience and calculates how much better or worse each performs against the average. A score of 100 therefore shows that a sport is on a par with all sports in delivering an audience (in this case ABs), while a score of more than 100 indicates greater appeal than all sports to an audience. Figure 16.2 confirms one's preconceptions. Indices such as these lend a much needed professionalism to sponsorship.

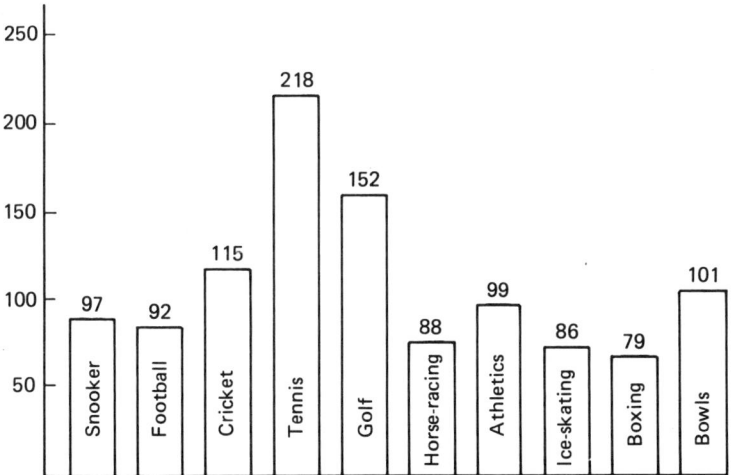

Figure 16.2 *Sports-viewing index: AB adults January–June 1989. Source: AGB Sportswatch/BARB*

16.7 Sponsorship of the arts

While sport, with its enormous following and heavy media coverage, continues to attract by far the largest share of sponsorship expenditure, sponsorship of the arts showed the most dramatic rate of growth in the early 1980s. Economic recession, accompanied by cutbacks in grants and escalating running costs, led arts organizations to become more receptive to the idea of commercial sponsorship. There is still a wide variety of choice, in the nature of activities seeking sponsorship, in the kind of sponsorship available, and in the degree of financial help possible.

Opera, ballet, music and arts festivals, jazz and rock concerts, theatre, cultural exhibitions, film festivals, literary awards, and beauty contests are among the activities that have attracted sponsored support, and the list continues to grow. New sponsorship areas include feature films and television programmes, and even the school classroom has been considered.

The size of the UK arts-sponsorship market grew rapidly from the modest £600,000 of 1976[1] to £15m in 1984,[2] £20m in 1986,[3] £25m in 1987, and £30m in 1988.[4] As in sports sponsorship, there is evidence that arts sponsorship levelled off slightly as the high interest rates of late 1989 and onwards took their toll on British businesses.

The arts have continued to lag seriously behind sports in their ability to attract sponsorship, despite continuing government pressure on arts bodies to be more proactive in gaining support. However, the Arts Council set up a sponsor-seeking unit and its chances of success looked good. There is considered to be plenty of room in the 'upmarket' end of arts events for sponsors who prefer to be associated with brandy and cigars rather than beer and fags. Further, sponsorship consultants, advertising agencies and programme producers are all gearing up for the possibilities of a revolution in TV sponsorship. The future looks rosy.

By way of comparing the sizes of sports and arts sponsorship markets, listed below are the major arts-sponsorship deals agreed in the period January to March 1989 (compare this with list of sports sponsorships):

Brother International	£0.5m	Hallé Orchestra
British Airways	£0.25m	Art/London and Art/Los Angeles contemporay arts affairs
Banci Bilbao Viscaya Spansi	£150,000	National Gallery Exhibition of eighteenth-century Spanish paintings
Digital	£130,000	Digital Dance Awards
Bailey's Original Irish Cream	£100,000	Bailey's Summerstage concert series

Eurotunnel/TML/		
Shepway	£100,000	Menuhin International Violin competition
Sainsburys	£50,000+	National Youth Theatre visit to Moscow
BP	£30,000	International singing competition (Peter Pears Award Trust)
	£1.31m	

A 1991 Mintel report estimated that arts sponsorship in the UK was worth £35m in 1990, representing 6% growth on the 1989 figure. A 1992 report, however, suggested that it was less than £30m. It seems that in this, as in other below-the-line categories, exact and reliable figures are hard to come by. As the 1991 Mintel report itself said 'Lack of accurate statistical data characterises the sponsorship industry and the arts are not an exception.' It went on to say that private sector funding of the arts has shown 'a marked increase during the past decade. Over the same period government funding has declined, in some cases as music, by as much as 25%.'

16.7.1   Governmental support

Sponsorship, which until the end of the 1980s usually meant a branded competition here, a name on a brochure there and hospitality tents all over the place, changed substantially in the 1990s as the government positively supported it. In October 1989 the Department of Trade and Industry announced that it was looking to recruit scores of sponsors to help fund the British pavilion at the Expo 92 World Fair in Seville, finally confirming the government's seriousness about sponsorship.

Wherever public budgets have been pruned – health, education, the social services – there are new opportunities for sponsors. One could argue that one of the reasons why sport and the arts have come to dominate sponsorship is because they have consistently failed to make ends meet as a result of insufficient government support. Traditionally government departments have not been able to seek outside assistance, but the introduction of legislation explicitly encouraging district health authorities and local education authorities to bolster their income by private means has changed the climate. Wherever a shortfall in public image is felt, the government's answer, it seems, is to call on business to make up the difference, and very often that means sponsorship.

The Royal Philharmonic Orchestra was just one arts organization seeking support from industry as the Conservative government revised its policy and approach. However, a scheme introduced by that Government in 1984 to encourage business to take an active financial interest is proving helpful. The Business Sponsorship Incentive Scheme (BSIS), allocated £1m each year by the government, pays awards to arts bodies that have already received other sponsorship. Initially, first-time sponsors providing £7500 or more could get their cash matched by a one-third grant from IBIS. Grants ranged from £2500 to £25,000. The scheme generated £2.5m during its first 6 months of operation. In March 1985 the bottom figure for qualification was lowered to £3000 to bring in smaller businesses. Also a pound-for-pound matching grant was introduced for first-time sponsors giving £1000 or more.

This was politically contentious, but it offered unprecedented opportunities for imaginative companies and their advisers to provide schemes that were sensitive to social need. This resulted in newspaper headlines, unimaginable in the late 1970s: 'Firms urged to help poor pupils attend Prep schools' in the *Daily Telegraph*,[5] and 'School sells pupils' names in quest for sponsorship' in the *Sunday Times*.[6]

But the government's policy had been taking effect much earlier than 1989. Back in 1986 the major state-funded museums and art galleries joined the free-enterprise society. In February 1986 the then Minister for Arts announced that the monies they made on entrepreneurial initiatives such as shops, restaurants, and exhibitions could be kept. In the past the cash earned from such activities had been deducted from the following year's annual grant. Furthermore, the government agreed to continue to pay their current level of subsidy, plus marginally more for inflation, for an additional 3 years to help schemes become established.

One obvious form of income is sponsorship from companies or individuals, and in the 1986 Budget there were tax concessions to encourage even more generosity from friends of museums. Sometimes corporate aid is on a monumental scale, like the Turner gallery raised alongside the Tate, thanks to the Clore Foundation, or the extension for the National Gallery (NG) made possible through a £20m gift from the Sainsbury family. The NG also gained an extra exhibition space with £1.5m from the Sunley Foundation.

The Victoria & Albert (V & A) has also been successful in drawing in commercial sponsors. In 1986 it announced that Trust House Forte was providing the finance for a refurbished medieval treasures gallery. Toshiba sponsored the new Japanese gallery, and Pirelli paid for the new garden, which opened in 1987. In total the V & A has received £1m from sponsorship, and it would have been quite unable to improve its displays without such aid.

16.7.2   Music[7]

A 1986 survey carried out by *Marketing Through Music* showed that 88 per cent of 20-to 24-year-olds and 78 per cent of men and women aged 25 to 29 actively followed music, whereas less than 20 per cent were interested in sport. The survey also showed that, even though the use of music in marketing programmes grew by around 75 per cent in 1985, only £14m was spent on music sponsorship, compared with the £130m up-front spent on sport.

Music sponsorship is not as overt as sports sponsorship; there is a more discreet association, one often used for direct promotional reasons, e.g. turning concert-goers into customers. This is especially true of 'pop' music. Further, music-associated advertising or promotion can establish a favourable awareness among a brand's target audience because of the inherent dramatic and emotional power of the music.

A product can also achieve an image rub-off – and greater kudos – by being associated with artists who are admired or emulated by the target market. For example, in order to gain greater street credibility, Boots' own-label cosmetics brand, '17', sponsored a UK tour by 'King' in 1986. As part of the sponsorship deal, the group appeared in advertisements for '17' in the teenage press, while money-off vouchers for '17' products were placed on seats at every 'King' concert venue.

However, music is not only suitable for targeting teenagers. According to the British Phonographic Industry, more than 50 per cent of all LPs and cassettes are bought by the over-25s, who account for 70 per cent of the total UK population. Virtually any sub-group of consumers can be accessed through music, and music sponsorship can be both specific and discreet – without alienating a brand's existing customers. For example, music could be used if a drinks brand wanted to position itself as a stylish drink for 18- to 24-year-olds without upsetting older existing customers – each sector could be approached separately. Music sponsorship has more to do therefore, with 'psychographics', not just demographics. Music fans might even be from the same age and social group, but the sort of person who goes to a Cliff Richard concert is different from someone who goes to watch Madonna.

The range of opportunities available to music sponsors is now wider than ever, as recording artists adopt a more open-minded and business-like approach to commercial tie-ups. For example, the sponsor's brand name can appear:

1   On the stage.
2   On the tour programme.
3   On tour merchandise.
4   At the concert venues.
5   Using exterior posters and displays.
6   On all press and poster advertising for the store.
7   On the sides of tour trucks.
8   On concert tickets.
9   On front-of-venue advertising, pre-event.
10 On packing for singles, LPs, cassettes, and CDs.
11 As products are featured in the group's music videos.

In addition, music sponsorship provides many PR opportunities for the sponsor, including access to the best seats at the group's concerts, attendance of the artist at client receptions, and editorial coverage resulting from the sponsorship deal. It may also be possible for the artist/sponsor link to be made even closer through direct endorsement by the artist. In fact, the number of commercial uses to which the marriage of music and a brand can be applied is limited only by both parties' creativity and imagination, and their willingness to understand each other's needs.

Despite the growing sophistication of music sponsorship, some potentially successful tie-ups have fallen through because of a clash between the short lead-times involved in mounting artists' tours and record releases and the long-term planning required for many companies' marketing budgets. Both sides need to understand each other's problems, and they must also ensure that the parameters of sponsorship activity are clearly understood from the outset. Above all, the basic rule must be: what's in it for the artist must equal what's in it for the sponsor.

In 1985 the Royal Philharmonic Orchestra faced a £70,000 cut in grants, which, when compared with its £2.2m annual turnover, might not seem much; but with each rehearsal costing £2000 and even full houses at the Royal Festival Hall generally resulting in a loss, every penny counted. Sponsorship money was crucial, just as it is in many other areas of the arts. The RPO was one of the pioneers of sponsorship and was able to attract substantial funds from businesses. Its glossy brochures explained the reciprocal benefits of sponsorship and of what goes on behind the scenes. The efforts of the orchestra to reach beyond the elite and to widen its appeal were underlined, with explanations of how young and old were bussed-in to special performances and of how orchestra members undertook school visits while on exhausting national tours.

At the end of 1984 the RPO had a 1-week residency in the North East of England – the first such extended regional residency for any national orchestra – and worked morning, noon and night in schools and theatres throughout the area. Local sponsorship raised £11,250 towards the £60,000 cost, and this brought in an extra £3750 from BSIS. The £15,000 total made the tour possible. One of the local sponsors, Marchon Works in Whitehaven, part of the international chemical company Allbright and Wilson, accepted that modest local sponsorship would not help their international image. However, this type of sponsorship helped to spread the name of the company among the local community and to develop goodwill.

16.7.3 Books

'Books are bullets in the battle for the minds of men': Franklin D. Roosevelt's epigram perfectly sums up the reason why books in every shape and form have a distinct place in the publicity mix for many products. One of the most recurrent areas where books have a place is in 'product education'. How often, for example, can a salesman find the time, or an advertising campaign find customers sufficiently attentive, to explain complex products and services adequately. Table 16.2 shows examples of the way books can act to underpin advertising campaigns and other marketing efforts, both above- and below-the-line, and all of them are linked to product education.

Besides 'product education', education', several other categories may be influenced. For example:

(a) 'Consumer loyalty' – *The Shooting Field* for Holland & Holland.
(b) 'Customer response motivation' – *Everybody's Historic London* for Sun Life, and *Collecting Original Prints* for Christies Contemporary Arts.
(c) 'Off-pack premiums' – *Easy does it Cookbook* for Bachelors.
(d) 'Industrial goodwill' – *Emergency Indonesia* for Ultramar.
(e) 'Fund raising' – *Seston* for the Army Benevolent Fund.

Less direct-marketing oriented and more PR-oriented are the varying forms of company histories and books that show past and present excellence, for use as gifts, educational publications for school projects (*The Story of Chocolate* for Cadbury), and to help trade on a long-established quality image. Examples include *Broadwood by Appointment* for Broadwood Pianos, *Birth of a Legend – The Spitfire* for Rolls-Royce

Table 16.2 *Companies' book titles and their effects on product education*

Company	Book title	Effects
Solid Fuel Advisory Service	*The English Fireplace*	To inspire architects to include fireplaces in every home.
Manpower Ltd	*How to survive the Office of the Future*	To educate the bosses and the secretaries that Manpower cares about and has tackled new technology.
Peter Dominic	*Everybody's Wine Guide* *Practical Cocktails*	Reflects knowledge and expertise of staff and shows range of drinks stocked in off-licence chain.
Hennessy & Cie	*Cognac Country*	To establish the beauty of the region and link it to the quality of the product.
European Ferries	*French Entree 1–5*	To help ferry-users to get more from their break, thus promoting brand loyalty.

and British Aerospace, and *Eyes Right* for the 200-year-old opticians Dolland and Aitchison.

Finally, there is the category of the bestseller, with no special relevance to the company product. The *Guinness Book of Records* must be the best example.

Books have a long life and a penetration way beyond their sales figures, through library and other lending practices. The companies who sponsor them can often help expose them to those not in the book-buying habit without the expenditure of overmuch management time – in fact books have developed a definite place as a cost-effective support to the major campaigns.

So how can one identify their cost-effectiveness? The average cost of a book would be in the £1500 bracket, depending on such things as length, number of pictures, number of copies and so forth. This is not a negligible sum, but the results can be rewarding. The book can sell to a company's customers as well as the book trade, completely covering the costs; it can command column yards of press reviews; and it can be used as a gift – appreciated because of its cover price. It can also become a standard work over a number of reprints and new editions; it can sell overseas editions, earning the company royalties or even heralding overseas expansion; and it can sell into mass paperback, book club or newspaper serialization. Moreover, it can be adopted as a classroom text or put in a technical college reference library; it can prove the simplest and cheapest method of answering customer queries; and it can feature as part of an above-the-line campaign. It can even become a profit centre if used to redeem direct-response offers.

All these potential benefits can certainly add up to cost-effectiveness, but only if the uses for the book are carefully thought through before commitment. *The Oxo Book of Meat Cookery*, produced in the late 1960s was brilliantly conceived and produced, and destined to become a bestseller in the bookshops. However, this particular success did not *breed* success for companies that copied the idea, and as its successors piled up in warehouses around the country, the whole bubble seemed to burst. Today some companies still nurse wounded memories of pulping, remaindering or even quietly incinerating unwanted stock.

One veterinary company produced a *Scour Notebook*, designed to help veterinary surgeons encourage former clients to keep accurate stock records, and notes of medicine usage, as well as detail how the company's range of products fitted into modern farm management systems. Thoroughly researched in content, over £18,000 was invested in thousands of copies of the *Scour Notebook*. The company could not give them away: it was too long-winded and no veterinary surgeon had the time to spend on the book with each and every farmer client. More straightforward methods of recording medicines used were already supplied by industry and governmental bodies. The company could salvage nothing from the book – even the paper could not be used for recycling because the book was in half a dozen coloured sections. The caution now exercised by these and other more sceptical companies is more than justified.

Well over 55,000 new books are published in the UK every year. The bookshops are filled up to the gunwales with new books – cats of the world, dogs of the world, wine guides and cookbooks on every dish under the sun. The non-fiction bestsellers we all wish to be associated with are indeed elusive, and a responsible publisher will not only enthuse over the prospects of a well-conceived project but will cast doubts on the majority that are not. That is why it is important for the publishing/marketing organization to be publishers first and PR or marketing men a very long second.

While it is not easy to write, edit, design, print, and bind a book, it is even harder to conceive a package that will serve the company's long or short-term marketing aims and be sought after in the shops against all the competition. That is the art of getting consumers actually to pay to receive the company's message. The premium or sponsored book is a growing trend among companies looking for a marketing tool that combines longevity, effectiveness and economy.

16.7.4   Cinema

Using the movies to advertise goods is almost as old as cinema itself. It was common enough, even in the 1930s or 1940s to thank airline or car companies in the credits for travel or free props; and, unofficially, props managers, when dispatched to find a car, would take backhanders from local dealers. Then came along the idea of 'product placements', where manufacturers paid handsomely for the privilege of getting their product into films. It is cheaper than television advertising; and during the life of a big budget movie it reaches more people and it creates a public image without the public realizing the fact. The agencies who set up such product placements make a good margin, and the film-makers find their budget pressures are eased.

Specialist agencies receive scripts from the studios long before shooting starts. The scripts are vetted for 'placement opportunities', and the agencies produce a newsletter outlining new productions and the sort of props that might be required. Clients can pay a basic £50,000 a year and are guaranteed placements in, say, six movies. The bigger the movie, the greater the competition, and the higher the bidding. For anything by Spielberg, companies will tend to deal with the studio direct, cutting out the agencies. But there are now so many placements that there is something for everyone in every big movie.

Back to the Future (1) had no fewer than thirty-seven product placements, including Toyota, JVC, Camcorders and Pepsi-Cola. But the greatest product placement coup of all was in *ET*. When the small boy lured the cuddly alien from his hideout, he used a trail of sweets. These were Peeces Reeces; thanks to the film, sales instantly shot up by 85 per cent. Another sweet – said to be 'M 'n 'Ms', the American equivalent of Smarties – had originally been specified in the script, but it was changed to accommodate the highest bidder. The placement of Peeces Reeces was so successful that everybody in the business now claims credit, and nobody is now sure who closed the deal.

The biggest known placement was the $5m put into *Santa Claus* by McDonald's hamburgers. Yet the average placement costs relatively little, e.g. a product that just happens to be lying on a table may be the cheapest level of exposure, but every additional degree of emphasis costs more. A line of dialogue such as 'Gee, these widgets are great!' is the ultimate.

Many feel that product placement in the USA has been given a bad name by scatter-gun tactics, which pay no attention to the precise placing of a product. This is where the true value of placements lie; with ordinary advertising one can only say so much, yet with placement one can hint at what kind of product it is far more effectively. For example, in car advertising one may be trying to create a character driving the car that the intended target market can associate with. But placement of a car in Tom Cruise's hands (provided it is not abused) can say so much more about the kind of car driven by this kind of man.

Peter Finch, a director of the agency, Ayer Barker, has come out fiercely against the whole idea. Writing in *Campaign*, advertising's trade magazine, he said: 'It represents a fundamental blurring of the distinction between advertising and editorial that compromises one of the basic strengths of our business. Advertising is founded on an essential honesty: we always acknowledge we're making a sale.'[8] Finch wants agencies to make clear that they 'will not compromise the integrity of the product even if film-makers can be tempted to compromise theirs'. The implication is that placement comes perilously close to subliminal advertising.

The placement people do not see it that way. Their readiness to discuss the industry as a serious respectable business reflects a certainty that the shadow of the back-lot, car dealer backhander has long since gone. Film sponsorship, where one puts a Slazenger tennis racket in the hands of say, Richard Gere, at the cost of £100,000, is probably better than paying some temperamental tennis star millions, only for him to be banned from the next tournament for throwing his Slazenger into the crowd!

16.7.5 Television

In the mid-1980s, as the marketing men began to consider product placements on television, and as advertising executives in the UK began to worry about the ethics of the idea, the independent television companies realized they could not fund the rising costs of programme production, and neither could the media owners. This led the Independent Broadcasting Authority (IBA) and the BBC to rethink the regulations governing television.

The BBC, financed by the television licence, is slow to alter the situation as far as sponsorship is concerned. One casualty was the Leeds Piano Competition, sponsored by drinks company John Harvey and Son since 1978. The contest, held every 3 years, got coverage on Radio 3 and also on BBC TV. When Harveys promised long-term sponsorship if the company's name could be incorporated in the title, the organizers were delighted, but the BBC flatly refused to play ball. For an investment of around £8500 in 1987 in the competition, and a considerable contribution to social events around it, paid in kind, Harveys felt hard done by, as all the BBC was prepared to do was to make the occasional mention of the company name – and not a logo in sight!

The chief obstacle is the 1981 Broadcasting Act, which limits programme sponsorship 'to factual portrayals of material or events which have an existence independent of television coverage', and categorically prohibits anything that impinges upon the editorial control and integrity of the broadcaster. The result was a great disappointment for the supporters of programme sponsorship. All that has really been allowed in the past is part-funding of off-the-shelf programmes in return for measly end credits. In a sense the value of the sponsorship property goes beyond the programme itself and covers the surrounding promotional activity to which it leads. But, even here, the IBA, which interprets and upholds the 1981 Broadcasting Act for independent television, has exercised its statutory powers to limit many of the opportunities, e.g. cross promotional references in advertising.

However, early in 1989, the IBA softened its interpretations of the regulations, allowing sponsorship of instructional programmes, weather reports, and arts review programmes. Companies have also been supplying programme packages of their own in certain categories, such as Yorkshire Television Enterprises' *Go-Getters* – The *Anchor Challenge*, and Granada's *Pets and People*, a morning series sponsored by Pedigree Petfoods.

Further relaxation of the regulations governing ITV, Channel 4, and BSkyB (satellite) means that since January 1991 sponsorship of television programes has become possible. The 1990 Broadcasting Act is confidently expected to open the door much wider than before. Whether that will be an immediate bonanza for the television contractors remains uncertain. While some of them have made it clear that there are enough firm enquiries from companies interested in sponsorship to enable them to pick and choose among the contenders, they are also indicating that they are not going to be rushed. Careful assessment is the order of the day.

Since January 1991, the sponsoring of transmission of programmes on ITV stations, as well as radio and satellite channels, has become subject to new regulations. The BBC does not, at present, accept sponsorship.

The rules concentrate on keeping unacceptable sponsors away, and creating a balance between acknowledging a sponsor's contribution while ensuring that the programme does not become an advertising medium in itself.

Sponsorship offers the chance of increasing name awareness, and the benefits of association with programme matter; either of relevance to the product (though not directly of commercial benefit) or to enhance consumer perception in a more abstract sense. Any or all of these take place in the environment of the programme, not the advertising break.

Including regional sponsors, Mintel believes sponsorship is now running (at May 1992) at a level approaching £20m Autumn to Autumn, and radio adds another £5–N £8m depending on definition used. An explosion to some £250m at current prices is widely forecast by the year 2002, following the French example which is, however, in many respects different.

New research shows a very large consumer awareness of programme sponsors: 48% of Beamish, 33% of Legal & General, 32% of Powergen and 31% of Barclaycard. Several achieving lower mentions overall nonetheless had high mentions in potential target groups, in particular among ABs.

While Britain may not have full television sponsorship, it is the leading market for home videos. More than 60 per cent of UK homes possess a video-cassette recorder (VCR) and the signs are that video publishing is beginning to thrive in this country. According to one report the rental market for prerecorded video cassettes was worth as much as £478m in 1988.[9] More interesting to a potential sponsor perhaps, the sales market for cassettes was expected to reach £250m by 1990. A large proportion of the sales comes from videos retailing for less than £10; and the report highlights the potential of video for defraying the cost of programmes such as children's drama, notoriously expensive to make relative to the returns that could be expected from television advertising during programme screening.

But for liberal rules on programme sponsorship, which allow for extended opening and closing sequences, ample product placement and cross-promotion through advertising and other elements of the communications mix, it is necessary to turn to Italy and France. In Italy the practice has flourished since the early 1980s, and programme sponsorship now stands at roughly 10 per cent of annual advertising investment. In France programme sponsorship did not really begin until deregulation in April 1987. However, the opportunity was quickly seized and an estimated £60m was spent on programme sponsorship during 1988. French sponsors have been able to create most effective branding for themselves in the title sequences, as well as just-before and just-after commercial breaks, and these are priced at a 15–20 per cent premium over usual commercial air time rates.

However, back in the UK, according to Malcolm Wall, sales director of Granada Television, and author of the ITV submission on sponsorship in response to the Government White Paper on broadcasting, programme sponsorship may amount to no more than 2 per cent of annual advertising revenues within the present ITV franchises, but could achieve a 15 per cent shove by the year 2000. That of course will depend greatly on the broadcasting regulations.

16.7.6 Sponsorship in the classroom

The Education Reform Act encourages individual education establishments to seek extra income from whatever sources they deem appropriate. Garth Hill School in Berkshire actually raised more than £4.5m in 6 years from such activities, and Windsor Boys School in the same county is offering the names of all pupils who go on to higher education to companies that give financial backing. It is no longer unusual to hear local education authority administrators refer to pupils' parents as 'customers'.

This sort of thing has been going on for years in the 'private' sector. One public school, Langley School, Loddon, in Norfolk, has since the 1960s regularly opened its gates to the prestigious Langley Park over two weekends in the spring to run the so-called 'Daffodil Sundays'. Parents, families and friends all took part in inviting the public to look round the spacious house and grounds, home of the Beauchamp family for centuries until the school took it over in the 1950s. Funds raised from gate monies, guided history tours, as well as the usual refreshments, were ploughed back in to supply school equipment, the schools' virtual only other income coming from fees and donations.

The government's change of heart, which has allowed companies access to pupils - a prime (and impressionable) market, is changing the whole approach in the state-run schools and colleges. The 500,000 students who took GCSE exams with the Southern Examining Board, or an A-Level with the Associated Examining Board in the summer of 1988, will have received a results card stamped with the Barclays Bank eagle and a form inviting them to send off for financial advice from the bank.

The Department of Education and Science is inviting schools to take part in a trial whereby decorating and cleaning firms sponsor schools in return for a promise to keep them free of graffiti. Sponsored books and educational aids are now commonplace in classrooms throughout the UK.

American Express became the first sponsor of a GCSE after it launched its Travel and Tourism course. The company developed the course, which was taught in 160 schools in 1989, from scratch after successfully sponsoring courses in economics in New York. It now runs the programme in conjunction with Trust House Forte, Crest Hotels, the British Tourism Authority and Harry Goodman's International Leisure Group. Naturally Amex is careful to keep the company's involvement at arm's length, as it would totally undermine the credibility of the course if it was seen to be pushing its own sectional interests. Amex hopes that the brighter pupils will be tempted to look at travel and tourism as a career, and that it will generally improve standards in the industry. The course is being seen as a model for the future and has aroused international interest.

One area that could prove very fertile for sponsors is school trips. Under new legislation, schools are no longer allowed to levy mandatory charges on parents for trips to places much a museums and zoos. This gives companies the opportunity to pay for the visits themselves – hiring transport and supplying packed lunches – in return for perhaps some subtle branding on lunch-boxes.

At present the only guidelines that exist were produced in 1988 by a National Consumer Council working party made up of representatives from business, consumers, teachers and LEAs. The NCC drew up twelve guidelines, prohibiting sales messages, use of merchandising slogans, demonstrations that imply that a particular product is superior to others, and sampling.

One possible way to avoid the potential hazards is to introduce employers into schools by more subtle means, as Lloyds Bank is now doing with its Young Theatre Challenge and Fashion Challenge. The promise of performing at the Royal National Theatre or being flown to Paris for the Paris fashion shows has been irresistible – more than 1000 schools asked for entry forms to the Fashion Challenge within 2 weeks of it opening at the beginning of the Autumn Term in 1989. At each local heat a local Lloyds Branch manager gave a short speech and presented awards.

Until recently much of the money put into all types of sponsorship has been given in an unstructured manner, with little research into its effectiveness. In the future sponsorship beyond sport will be seen as a useful alternative to sales promotion, advertising, or PR, and ideal in certain circumstances. The problem may turn out to be not to encourage businesses to support the sponsored events, but to persuade such organizations that they are not being exploited for commercial purposes but that profit – and pleasure – may result.

16.8   Summary

1   A clear distinction must be made between sponsorship, patronage and charity.
2   Expenditure on sponsorship should provide a clearly defined return to the provider as well as to the receiver of the sponsorship funds.

3   A clear and specific brief must precede any sponsorship activity and results must be carefully monitored to ensure a good return on the investment.
4   There is a wide range of choice for sponsors of sports and the arts. Deciding on a suitable event calls for careful selection and good timing.

References

1   *Marketing* (1985), 19 September.
2   *Ibid.*
3   *Financial Times* (1986).
4   *Marketing* (1988), December.
5   *Marketing* (1989), 28 September.
6   *Marketing* (1989), 24 September.
7   Extra information from *Marketing Week* (1986), 18 September.
8   If you suspect 'dishonesty' in advertising, the Advertising Standards Authority would like to hear from you.
9   *What's New in Marketing* (1985), August.

Index